What people are saying abou

ANATOMY OF
EMBODIED EDUCATION

Anatomy of Embodied Education: Creating Pathways to Brain-Mind Evolution is an artful piece of work that condenses the past 70 years of literature from the fields of neuroscience, learning, psychology and human wellbeing. This is a resource that integrates centuries of bright minds, a collage of perspectives and rich discussion leading to optimizing human potential. The authors have unpacked the imperative beyond the growth of a healthy, functioning brain toward developing an inquisitive, creative and intelligent mind.

This accumulation of comprehensive knowledge interwoven with keen perspectives engages the reader in an in-depth discussion of a path to access human potentials across many levels. The journey begins with simple brain-body physiology, articulating the essentials of healthy development through early and ongoing extension of the brain-mind that drives purposeful thought and character. Comprehensive as any work on the brain as it relates to "mind," the focus encompasses a span from individual achievement to species potential. The gestalt of this work eclipses an amassing of scientific knowledge, applying such to living life well, as one learns and lives in accordance with nature's agenda.

Burns and Brown have done a spectacular reflection of the essence of the body/brain and the mind/spirit of human potential. They have left no stone unturned in the pursuit of human growth and possibility.

> – Robert K Greenleaf, EdD, President, Greenleaf Learning,
> Former public education teacher, principal, superintendent and faculty
> development coordinator, University System of New Hampshire

In this treasure of a book, Burns and Brown weave a tapestry from the collective threads of their lineage traditions, experience and wisdom as veteran educators in human development and consciousness. The reader is invited on a learning adventure integrating theory, philosophy, and offering practical tools grounded in biology and contemporary relational neuroscience. The eclectic array of chapters tickle the reader's curiosity and orient us toward a future where learning is accessible to and inclusive of diverse learning styles. As illuminated here, mindful, embodied education offers pathways that foster deep intelligence and consciousness rooted in the senses, the earth and the inherent values of Goodness, Truth and Beauty.

> – Kate Cook, MA, LPCC, TEP
> Director of the Applied Interpersonal Neurobiology Certificate
> Program Southwestern College, Santa Fe, New Mexico, U.S.A

Anatomy of Embodied Education: Creating Pathways to Brain-Mind Evolution is a well done and courageous book dedicated to propelling us into creative thinking on how to develop optimally functioning mind-body consciousness through our lifetimes, beginning in childhood. Burns and Brown skillfully weave classical and current neuroscience theories that allow the reader flexibility to reimagine our minds in new ways. It is a special joy to elevate cosmic consciousness of the numinous in education.

> – Ernest Rossi PhD and Kathryn Lane Rossi PhD
> Psychotherapists, authors, editors, *The Collected Works of Milton H. Erickson, MD* (16 Volumes)

In their new book *Anatomy of Embodied Education: Creating Pathways to Brain-Mind Evolution*, Burns and Brown draw our attention to the process of exploring human potential as an evolutionary trend that leads us towards a more positive future. Through a thoughtful analysis of neuroscientific research, coupled with the authors' mindful and highly engaging insights, the reader is challenged to rethink the narrow, utilitarian paradigm of education that many of our schools have adopted for too long. Any parent, educator or education leader who seeks to better understand the nature and importance of lifelong learning should read this book.

> – Peter Bateman, PhD, Executive Director,
> African International School Association

This is a landmark exploration of the fundamental constituents of human wholeness - neuroscience, wisdom traditions and common sense - that each of us as educators and parents must understand and integrate in order to nurture 'the human birthright of developmental wholeness, healthy wellbeing and integrated intelligence.'

A timely book as the disruptions of the COVID 19 pandemic provide the opportunity to envision anew the intentions of education and co-create adaptive educational approaches, platforms and praxis that are relevant, engaging, equitable, and meaningful and integrate brain, body, heart and spirit to foster whole children, whole youth, whole adults and whole communities.

Practical, applicable, and inspirational, this hopeful book provides powerful information and guidance for aligning educational and parenting practices to nurture and authentically educate individuals and collectives to be compassionate, creative and accountable to self, to one another and to our planet.

> – Amy McConnell Franklin, PhD, Author of *Choose to Change: A Practical Guide for Fostering Emotional Intelligence in the Classroom*

Just a glance at the Table of Contents leaves one astounded at the breadth and depth of this profound treatise for a revolution in human intelligence. The authors succeed in the challenging endeavor to move from the theoretical to the practical, with information that is timely, accessible and easy to immediately put into practice for teachers, counselors and parents. This book is a beautiful invitation to the adventure of lifelong learning. The final chapter, which summarizes the integration of body, mind and heart intelligence, is a must read for anyone interested in translating the latest brain science into creating a better world for future generations.

– Victor la Cerva, MD, Board certified Pediatrician,
   Author, *Letters to a Young Man in Search of Himself*

Anatomy of Embodied Education is a complex, multilayered and multileveled, holistic synthesis of scientific, pedagogical, practical, spiritual and intuitive approach to education, based upon centuries of human experience, traditional wisdom and basic common sense. Dedicated to personal, educational and societal development and common wellbeing, the book includes wholesome strategies, routines and environmental enrichments. It is a clear, comprehensive, well organised manual, meant as a guide to support individuals, parents, teachers, policy developers and, hopefully, leaders in impacting the development and nurture of (every)one's learning, progress and wellbeing.

– Irena Steblaj, Director,
   Danila Kumar International School, Ljubljana, Slovenia

ANATOMY OF EMBODIED EDUCATION

CREATING PATHWAYS TO BRAIN-MIND EVOLUTION

by

E. TIMOTHY BURNS

JIM BROWN, PhD

PSYCHOSYNTHESIS PRESS

MOUNT SHASTA, CA

PSYCHOSYNTHESIS PRESS

Exploring the Deeper Possibilities of Human Life

ANATOMY OF EMBODIED EDUCATION

CREATING PATHWAYS TO BRAIN-MIND EVOLUTION

Published by Psychosynthesis Press
psychosynthesispress.com

ISBN-13: 978-0-9913196-2-6

First Psychosynthesis Press edition • November 2021

To our children:
Gregory, Cassidy, Cea, Ashley, and Megan,
of whom we are immensely proud;

our grandchildren:
Benjamin, Summer, Stella, Avery, Emerson, Ayla and Ryan,
in whom we take great delight;

and their children's children's children,
into the seventh generation… and beyond.

Preface

A culmination of our combined century-plus of learning, teaching and writing about topics near and dear to our minds and hearts, this book represents our contribution to a bright and shining future for all forms of life on this deeply imperilled planet. As best of friends and intellectual companions for nearly half-century, we have shared a common and abiding interest in a vexing human predicament: that of having seemingly limitless potential while exhibiting and enjoying so little of it. To that end, we have endeavoured to clarify that predicament while plumbing the depths of human potential and how that might best be achieved—sooner rather than later, given the social and environmental conditions in which we find ourselves.

Credit must be given straightaway to scientists, artists, thinkers, writers and teachers whose commitment to the search for goodness, beauty and truth have contributed enormously to the worldview expressed in this book. If we have accomplished anything truly worthwhile—and we very much think we have—it is to have made a meaningful and eminently approachable synthesis of their combined exertions to clarify and improve the human and planetary condition.

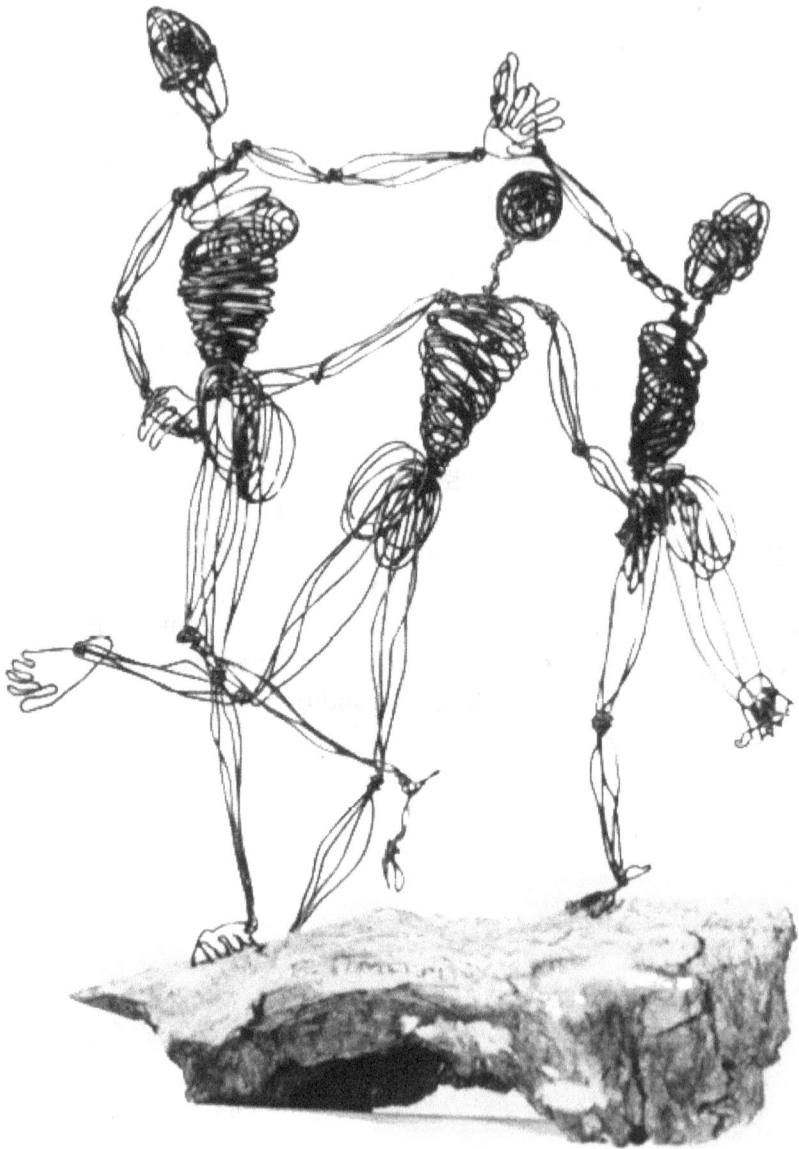

Embodiment
Sculpture by Tim Burns, 1970.

Table of Contents

Introduction

When we began writing this book our intention was to offer a humane, science–based work suggesting pathways by which education could become more effective in preparing our offspring to adapt happily and successfully to life on a planet that is in dire peril. The primary peril facing humanity at that time was catastrophic climate change (and the cultural/economic biases that led to it). The scientific consensus was that global heating was rapidly reaching a crisis point that would vastly disrupt the viability of creatures on this planet (humans definitely included).

Of course, no one knew exactly when that time would come, but there was a general sense that it would not be *immediately*. We authors felt that there would be time for our culture to develop and refine, via refurbished education, requisite capabilities that would help humanity deflect or minimize catastrophic change, and create a just and equitable society. We hoped this book would be a useful tool in that endeavor.

Then, a short time before the book was to go to press, the COVID-19 epidemic began and rapidly became a global pandemic. Very suddenly, we no longer have lead-time. What we do have is an immediate planet-wide infectious peril in addition to the deferred climatic one we had intended to prepare for.

COVID-19 is clearly lethal to many, and perhaps hundreds of thousands of people will succumb to this pandemic before it runs its course—especially among impoverished and oppressed groups. But the virus is not predicted to decimate the population. What is being predicted is that this pandemic and its accumulated effects will challenge and possibly elevate the consciousness of a significant number of humans who survive it, along with their collective cultures and economies.

This book is dedicated to the renewal and advancement of civilization beyond the COVID-19 pandemic. We still hope, for example, that the book's contents will have a positive influence on healing the constricted brain-mind functioning that led to catastrophic climate disruption and wide-spread systemic racism and oppression. We are aiming for broad-based evolution of human intelligence as defined and discussed extensively in the following pages.

On further reflection, given the scope and immediacy of our planetary crises, let's call what we are aiming for *revolution* of human intelligence. The radical changes in living conditions and social patterns forced on humanity by the pandemic may harbor an unprecedented opportunity to dismantle unworkable institutions bolstered by flawed assumptions, and create in their place nature-friendly, humane, truly adaptive responses to challenges currently sweeping over the planet. That would constitute true human intelligence as we understand it. And to accomplish that quickly, while this opportunity is at hand, would be revolutionary!

So, quickly, let us begin ...

Every human on earth comes equipped with a brain, which grows and develops into each person's unique version of the most complex three pounds of matter in the known universe. The care and feeding of this organic birthright, this miraculous work-in-progress, is enormously important to the quality of its owner's life. Yet how many of us have more than the most rudimentary knowledge about this precious gift? How many of us ever think or wonder about it—its structure, its function, how to tend to it for optimum use?

One can argue about whether such knowledge is really important for most people. It is true that humans have stumbled along for eons without giving their brains much thought. Yet there is little doubt that, for a growing number of us, knowledge and understanding of the human brain (and mind) is of paramount importance. Most certainly, professional educators are among that growing population.

And so are the increasing number of people—nonprofessionals—who, at some point in their lives wake up to a sense of needing to reach deeper into who they are and who they can become. Parents who feel a strong drive to parent purposefully and intelligently—these parents have a sharp sense of that need. It is primarily for the benefit of their children that the need exists. Such parents feel responsible to know as much about nurturing their children as they possibly can. And knowing about healthy brain development, about optimal nutrition, environment, and interaction, can support that level of nurturance.

Yet in no way are the benefits of that knowledge confined to optimal child-rearing; parents can certainly apply such knowledge to nurturing themselves as well as their children. Keep this emphatically in mind: the implications of this book's contents for living a more fulfilled life extend *beyond* the formative years of childhood and adolescence. As will be seen in the culminating chapters, the entire human life span constitutes an arc of development that can be enriched by understanding the discoveries and principles described in these pages.

This book, based on an exhaustive survey of neuroscience discoveries (both classical and current), is written for those who have a professional or personal need (most likely both!) to understand more about the human brain. Readers who are inclined to devote significant time and focus toward gaining that understanding will find a rewarding array of material to satisfy their need. The information conveyed by the book is technical, carefully organized and well-documented, yet presented in a way that the authors hope is engaging even for the nonprofessional reader. And because of the inclusive, inviting tone that the authors have deliberately adopted (occasionally addressing readers directly, for instance), combined with the wide array of neuroscientific information presented, readers who prefer to browse casually are likely to find nuggets of information that significantly advance their understanding.

Ultimately, the information leads to some philosophical conclusions about the relationship between brain and mind, the nature of intelligence as it applies to the learning process, and the implications of all of this not only for *optimal parenting and teaching*, but also for *optimal living beyond parenthood and school*. The scope of these conclusions may come as a surprise to some readers, for we intend nothing less than to promote a radical re-visioning of the narrow, utilitarian paradigm of education so prevalent in the western world over the past hundred years or so.

Part of our re-visioning includes this understanding: *learning that fosters true intelligence is a lifelong project*. Our intent here is to model a coherent, comprehensive set of principles, informed by neuroscientific research, that facilitate and enliven that lifelong project.

The main component of our model is a comprehensive understanding of the embodied human brain (the importance of the descriptor "embodied" will be made evident in the early chapters). The most basic topological features of this brain are introduced in Chapter 1, along with a fundamental neural vocabulary that will build steadily throughout the book.

Following that are chapters detailing theory and research about brain maturation and development from infancy onward. The developmental pathways laid out in Chapters 2 and 3, are foundational to our thesis: educational practices must take these pathways into account in order to maximize learners' potential for contributing to a world that truly sustains us all.

Chapter 4 carries the exploration of brain development to a deeper level as it explores the types and functions of individual nerve cells, with special emphasis on neurons—their complex structure, their electrochemical nature, how they grow and group themselves into networks, how they communicate among themselves and thereby generate macro-levels of brain activity such as thoughts, feelings and perceptions.

Issues pertaining to brain hygiene are presented in Chapter 5, specifically those related to the non-negotiable need for sufficient physical exercise plus sufficient and well-timed sleep. We explore the responsibility of schools to take these needs into account—to support students' healthy brain development by adapting school schedules and classroom activities to the students' needs rather than expecting students to adapt to policies that are based on a host of other factors. (Obviously, challenging the tendency of mainstream school policy to reverse priorities in this way is a persistent theme of this book.)

Next we explore how the fields of genetics, and its recent offshoot epigenetics, inevitably tie into the potentials and unfolding of the learning process. Then comes a chapter about the importance of environmental enrichment for optimal brain development, followed by a chapter on stress—what it is and how it affects the brain and the learning process. Implications for each of these topics concerning educational policy and classroom practice will become increasingly clear to readers concerned about these matters.

Chapter 9 deals with the phenomenon of rhythmic cycles within the embodied brain, and emphasizes how important it is for educators to know about these cycles as they go about designing and conducting optimal learning environments. Chapter 10 extends the exploration of rhythmic cycles, focusing on electromagnetic fluctuations known as brainwaves, and how brainwave patterns relate to cognition, states of consciousness, stages of development and ultimately to the learning process.

Chapters 11 and 12 present mind-boggling information about the extended brain, explicating the notion of "embodied brain" at a level that may be brand new, and quite startling, for many readers. These chapters bring us to the verge of a grand synthesis of the rich store of information presented in the book thus far.

The synthesis begins in Chapter 13, in which we summarize and integrate a rich amalgam of discoveries by several highly regarded systems thinkers/neuro-philosophers who have contributed greatly to our understanding of the relationships among brain, mind and the pivotal issue of attention, key to both brain plasticity and to learning. Such a synthesis is of central importance in grasping the significance of the array of neuroscientific information presented in this book, specifically as that information pertains to the project of human education. Much of the information is brought forward in this chapter and discussed extensively in light of its implications for educational practice and policy.

The integrative summary woven into the fabric of Chapter 13 prepares the reader for the penultimate chapter that follows it. In Chapter 14 we present extensive material supporting adoption by schools of an array of methods known collectively as "mindfulness" practices. Included in this material is a thorough review of research spanning several decades that details the rationale and evidence forming a solid foundation for applying a range of methods promoting brain/mind/body integration for human well-being in general. These methods, research has shown, can substantially aid the overall mission of education: to develop students' adaptive intelligence.

Finally, in Chapter 15, five "core concepts" are presented and explored thoroughly—concepts that tie together the primary themes undergirding this entire book. The culmination of that exploration is an overarching framework that ties together the "big picture" of human learning, development and potential to the practical, day-to-day loving exertions of classroom teachers.

For the convenience of teachers and parents who are beset with time challenges (one of the stressors acknowledged in Chapter 8), we have sprinkled passages throughout the final chapter that guide the reader's attention to earlier parts of the book in which the subject matter preceding each of these passages is discussed and documented more extensively. *Our aim in doing this is to give readers the option to skip immediately to the final chapter, read and absorb it, and use the references to prior chapters as a directory to earlier material of particular interest to each reader.*

This feature also enables the option of skimming quickly through the text (rather than skipping it altogether), perhaps slowing down to absorb content that is particularly intriguing, with the comfortable assurance that the final chapter contains guidance about returning to intriguing content missed in the initial read-through.

Chapter 1

Introduction to the Human Brain

"If you look at the anatomy, the structure, the function, there's nothing in the universe that's more beautiful, that's more complex, than the human brain."

– Keith Black

"There is no scientific study more vital to man than the study of his own brain. Our entire view of the universe depends on it."

– Francis H.C. Crick

When we, as learners, parents and educators, gain a basic understanding of how the brain develops and functions, we stand a much better chance of fostering developmental balance, intelligence, and wholeness in children, young people and students of all ages. The primary aim of this book is to examine what it means to grow and learn in a complete and balanced manner. Growth and learning comprise processes that permeate our entire being. Understanding these processes more fully has obvious implications for the quality of the lives we lead.

Let us emphasize from the outset that all the capacities we enjoy— our abilities to perceive, think, feel, sense, create, hope, dream and imagine—are reflected by myriad electrochemical interactions within our brains. We relate, communicate, learn, love, maintain health, recover from illness, and bounce back from adversity because of processes controlled by or conducted within our brains.

Let us also understand that these functions, taken completely for granted by us as adults, are nowhere near fully formed at birth. The brain can conduct its amazing feats only when it becomes sufficiently organized and integrated. This takes time—years—and, equally as important, requires timing in the application of requisite stimulation, along with plenty of practice.

Learning and intelligence arise and unfold together interactively as the brain, body and emotions grow and mature together. We posit that these three aspects—the brain, the body, and the heart—are equally important to learning. This assertion underlies most of what this book contains, and we urge the reader to think in these terms from now on. When you see the word brain, know that it refers to the embodied brain, not merely to the cerebrum inside the skull.

In Chapter 11 and elsewhere, we will explore this triadic concept more fully.

In this first chapter, our intent is to present fundamental information about the first third of the triad, the organ interchangeably known as the brain, the cerebrum or the central nervous system. We will look at the anatomical organization of this miraculously complex organ, keeping in mind that when the slowly maturing, genetically timed and environmentally triggered integration and coordination of biological functions is supported and encouraged in learners, they develop in a way that is balanced and fulfilling.

As with each chapter, our aim and purpose is to present information that will directly inform our proposed model of, and approach towards, learning and teaching, which we present in the final chapters. But we think it is important that throughout this journey we allow ourselves to enjoy being immersed in information, knowledge, science and research.

> Our aim and purpose is to present information that will directly inform our proposed model of, and approach towards, learning and teaching.

Let's begin with an overview of the main geographic features encountered as we look at the brain as a whole, from the outside. We will introduce some of the key anatomical areas and terms that will be used throughout this book. In later chapters, we will look at childhood and adolescent development with a view toward understanding the critical elements necessary for integrated development (elements that include the need for an enriched environment, a field of neuroscience developed over decades of fascinating discoveries).

Later on, we will examine the interplay between body and brain states that both reflect and affect learning, including sleep, dreaming, downtime, reverie, activity, and more. From time to time we will discuss how this information can be applied every day to improve classroom instruction, student learning and overall well-being. But first we must describe some basic anatomical features of the central nervous system— that part of the embodied brain encased in one's skull (which we hereafter shorten to "the brain" in the interest of brevity).

The average adult human brain weighs about three pounds, three times the weight of a newborn's brain. Removed from the skull, it looks a bit like a large pinkish-gray walnut. The pink hue is due to the enormous vascular system that supplies the brain's blood-born oxygen and nutrients. (Even though it accounts for only two percent of the body's weight, the brain contains about 20 percent of the body's blood supply.) The gray color derives from the neurons on the surface of the brain.

The Cerebral Hemispheres

The Latin word cerebrum is just another term for "brain." It is the newest (evolutionarily) and largest part of the brain as a whole, situated around and over the brainstem. The outer surface of the cerebrum is referred to as the cortex (Latin for "bark"). This is where functions that comprise thinking, such as perception, imagination, planning, judgment, and decision-making, occur. The cerebrum divides down the middle lengthwise into two halves called the cerebral hemispheres (see Figure 1).

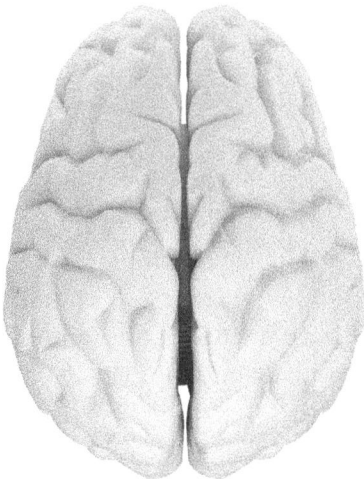

Figure 1. Hemispheres of the Brain.
Image by Maksymilian Rose.

While each side of the brain tends toward the specialized areas of operation, the specialization is not exclusive. Both hemispheres participate to some extent in all functions.

Each side of the cerebral cortex is divided into four lobes by various sulci and gyri. The sulci, or fissures, are the "valleys" and the gyri are the "hills" that appear on the surface of the brain. The folding of the cerebral cortex produced by these valleys and hills increases the amount of cerebral cortex that can fit in the skull. Unfolded, the cerebral cortex would be a thin sheet of tissue about the thickness of a small coin, covering just over 300 square inches—the size of a large pizza or full page of newspaper. Imagine the multitude of folds necessary to insert that tissue into a bony enclosure about the size of half a bowling ball! In general, we all have the same patterns of gyri and sulci on the cerebral cortex, but of course no two brains are exactly alike.

The Features of the Brain

The cortex is anatomically divided into lobes that—almost as much as hemisphericity and furrowed enfoldment—are among the most discernible features on the surface of the brain.

While neither the brainstem nor the cerebellum is considered a lobe of the brain, both are clearly discernible features regarded from the outside and as a whole. For that reason, they are included in our survey of the brain's main geographic features. Each of these features has its own function, described very briefly as follows:

Brainstem

The brainstem is located at the juncture of the cerebrum and the spinal column. It consists of the midbrain, medulla oblongata, and the pons. Within these structures are networks that control alertness and arousal, breathing, blood pressure, digestion, heart rate, and a number of other autonomic functions. (We will describe and discuss the "autonomic nervous system" in detail later, especially in Chapter 8).

Lateral View of the Brain

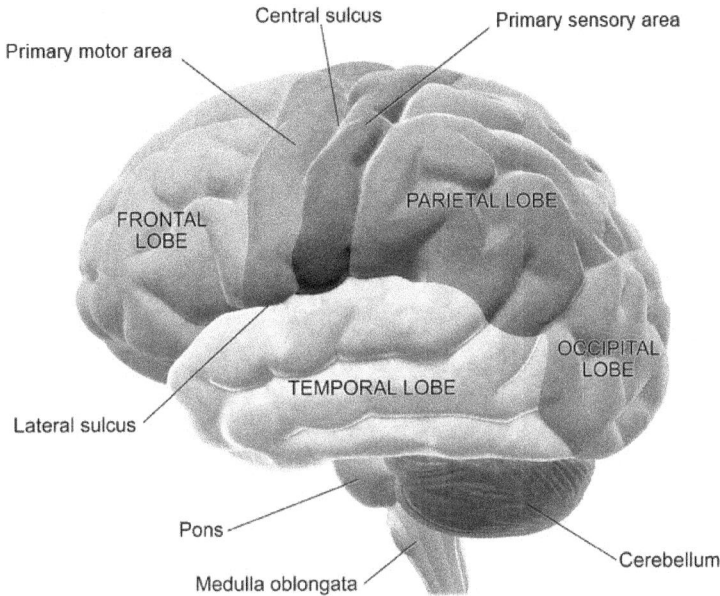

Figure 2. Lobes of the Brain.
Image by Bruce Blaus.

Cerebellum

Latin for "little brain," this is the portion of the brain, located at its base toward the back, that helps facilitate balance and muscle coordination. In addition, neuroscientists have recently shown that this ancient and primitive area of the brain plays a key role in activating and modulating the most recently evolved portion of the brain, the frontal lobes.

Now, let's look at the lobes themselves (keeping in mind that there are two of each, one in each hemisphere):

Occipital Lobes

Found at the back of the brain behind the parietal lobe and temporal lobes, the occipitals entail many aspects of vision.

Temporal Lobes

Situated along the lower edges of the brain on both sides, these lobes contain the primary auditory cortex, which is important for interpreting sounds and language. The hippocampus, in the limbic system below the cortex, is adjacent to the temporal lobe, making this region of the brain essential to the formation of memories (see Figure 3).

Parietal Lobes

The parietals are located in the topmost, posterior region of the brain. Within these lobes, sensory stimuli related to touch, pressure, temperature and pain are processed, giving rise to perceptual experience of these senses.

Frontal Lobes

Occupying a position just behind the forehead and comprising about one-third of the entire volume of the brain, these lobes are chiefly concerned with reasoning, planning, aspects of speech, control of emotions and problem-solving, as well as such purposeful acts as judgment and creativity.

Even more importantly, if this area fails to develop or is severely damaged, functions such as empathy, compassion, conscience, and all attempts at abstract thought are doomed to fail.

Across the very back of the frontal lobes, just in front of the central sulcus, lies the motor cortex. It is a narrow, bilateral band of cortical tissue that controls body movements.

Below the Cortex

Using Figure 3 as a visual aid, let's look at just a few of the key features of the brain beneath the cerebral cortex, restricting ourselves for the most part to those that most play a role in thinking, learning and memory.

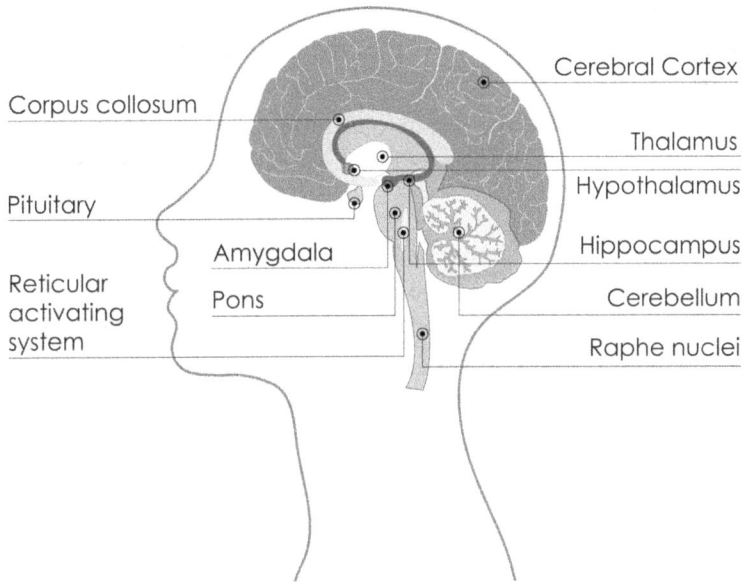

Figure 3. Beneath The Cerebral Cortex.
Image by Maja Petrović/Inspired By Learning.

Hypothalamus

Often referred to as the "brain of the brain," the hypothalamus is a pea-sized structure containing nerve connections that relay messages to the pituitary gland, which controls the endocrine system. It also plays a significant role in learning, specifically the formation of long-term memories.

Pineal Gland

In some mammals, the pineal gland controls responses to darkness and light. Although its exact function in humans is not yet clear, it appears to have some role in sexual maturation.

Thalamus

Situated above the hypothalamus, the thalamus serves as a relay station for almost all sensory information that travels to and from the cortex, except for the sense of smell. It also plays a role in pain sensation, attention and alertness.

Pituitary Gland

Extending downward from the hypothalamus, and under its supervision, the pituitary gland synthesizes and deploys most of the hormones by which the brain communicates with major glands throughout the body. The pituitary has been called the "master gland of the brain."

Having now surveyed some of the basic geography and anatomy of the learning brain, we have set the stage for understanding its physical growth and maturation. In our view, one of the best approaches to these themes is a theory of the brain that encompasses both evolutionary and lifetime development: Paul MacLean's theory of the triune brain, to which we now turn in Chapter 2.

Chapter 2

The Triune Brain Revisited

"An interest in the brain requires no justification other than a curiosity to know why we are here, what we are doing here, and where we are going."

– Paul D. MacLean, MD

More Timely and Relevant Than Ever

We begin our survey of brain maturation and development, from birth through adolescence, by acquainting ourselves with a fascinating model of brain evolution. Its genesis is a decades-old research project—one of the largest ever undertaken in the brain sciences—headed by the late Dr. Paul MacLean who, from 1971 to 1985, served as Chief of the Laboratory of Brain Evolution and Behavior, National Institutes of Mental Health. The research focused on the comparative neuro-behavior of animals in semi-natural conditions. It was MacLean's seminal discovery that the human brain is tripartite—or what he called The Triune Brain (see Figure 4). He held the view that the human brain evolved as three interconnected "biological computers," each imbued with its own special intelligence, subjectivity, memory, and sense of time and space.

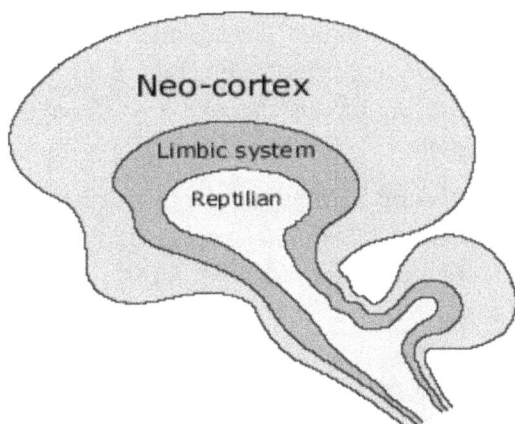

Figure 4. The Triune Brain. Image by Tim Burns.

Intelligence, Briefly Noted

Having broached the topic of human intelligence above, this is a good place to set forth, if not a definition, at least a working description of how this term applies to our narrative. Later we will take a much closer look at this important construct, making a distinction between intelligence and intellect among other things, since it is so central to the main theme of this book.

As a starting point then, let us say that intelligence is the capacity to respond to new situations, adapt to changing conditions, and learn from experience. As stated above, we will be looking more closely at this construct as we go along.

> As a starting point, let us say that intelligence is the capacity to respond to new situations, adapt to changing conditions, and learn from experience.

The fields of evolutionary biology and neuroscience have, in recent decades, shown much of the research upon which MacLean formulated his model of the Triune Brain to be inadequate and sometimes mistaken. This is not surprising given the development of increasingly refined technologies for parsing the finer details of neurons. However, it would in our view be a mistake to overlook the broader directions of understanding human development and potential towards which MacLean was pointing in his seminal investigations. In short, the notion of a triune brain is not at all irrelevant. On the contrary, some of the central insights are timeless and possibly unsurpassed, especially when viewed as an undergirding element in a broad framework for understanding the "upward movement" and spiral maturation of the brain and childhood development. Moreover, MacLean's insights on the fundamental elements of healthy mammalian brain development, covered at the end of this chapter, are—to our way of thinking—simply without equal.

This conclusion is supported by a timely and provocative book titled *The Evolutionary Neuroethology of Paul MacLean: Convergences and Frontiers*, its editors, Gerald Cory and Russell Gardner (2002), take aim at dismissive critics of MacLean's broad-based views of the human brain and assert the accuracy of MacLean's discoveries and conclusions. They write, "Through impressive mental gymnastics and a profound mind-blindness, MacLean's critics presume holistic approaches offer little; yet their approaches fail to envision how different levels of organization exist in nature" (p. xiii). They continue: "Some recently have claimed that MacLean's limbic-emotional brain concept misleads and is therefore of no use to modern neuroscience. Such a conclusion speaks more loudly about human arrogance than thoughtful neuroscience" (pp. xiii-xiv). They go on to emphasize that insightful inquiry in neuroscience and learning must focus on big, system-wide concerns, in addition to giving attention to fine details.

In any case, it is always helpful to be reminded that, quoting the statistician, George Box (1987), "Essentially, all models are wrong, but some are useful" (p. 424). MacLean's model, we are confident you will agree, is highly useful!

The Triune Brain

Because of its elegant and broad revelations, the Triune Brain theory also provides a marvellous entry point into what scientists refer to as the most complex matter and system in the known universe: our three pounds of brain.

1. A lower sensory-motor brain, or what he sometimes referred to as the reptilian brain;

2. A mid-brain limbic system (from the Latin limbus, meaning "border," or "ring-like"), also referred to by MacLean as the "paleomammalian" (ancient mammal) brain; and

3. A forebrain with its neocortex, or what he called the "neomammalian" brain.

A detailed discussion of each of these levels is given below.

1. The Lower Sensory-Motor Brain

According to MacLean's view, each of the three brains operates both independently of and interdependently upon the others. The most evolutionarily ancient of the three brains—the lower sensory-motor or reptilian brain—is located in the hindmost and bottom area of our skull (see Figure 5). It consists of the brainstem—the point at which the large human brain merges downwards with the spinal cord, allowing an ongoing neural conversation with the entire body—and the cerebellum (literally, "little brain," from Latin), the cauliflower-like appendage at the very back and bottom of the brain.

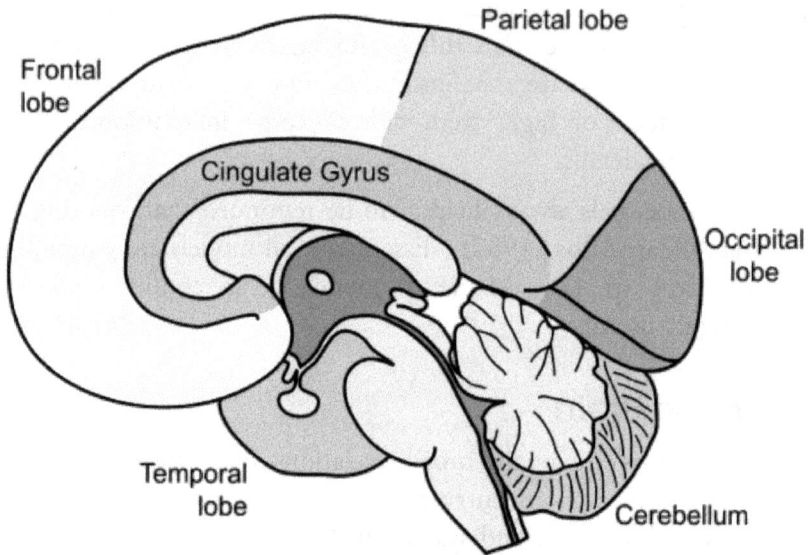

Figure 5. Brainstem and Cerebellum.
Image by NEUROtiker.

The sensory-motor component of the central nervous system is the most "hard-wired" area of the brain, meaning that its functions are the most species-driven or genetically determined. These functions operate precisely in the same way that they do in a lizard, a snake, or would have in an ancient dinosaur: instinctively or, when it comes to behavior, reflexively. Some of these functions include the survival mechanisms of hunger and thirst, body temperature, locomotion, reproductive drive, respiration, heart rate, breathing, fight/flight/freeze, and a whole host of other subtle and not-so-subtle bodily functions that, as humans, we never have to think about.

The fact that no thought or conscious direction of these functions is required does not mean, however, that there is a lack of intelligence. On the contrary, there is a vast intelligence at work here, but its nature is reflexive; it is predetermined, automatic, and is probably best when left alone. The wisdom of these many interacting and complex biological systems is innate, self-regulating, and largely beyond our conscious control. In fact, if our thinking (and often scheming and manipulative) brain gets excessively involved it can clearly lead to problems—for example, dieting to the point of self-harm, dictated by a social fashion for appearing thin.

On the other hand this autonomic nervous system can be, potentially, brought much more under our conscious control (as a result of, for example, biofeedback training or meditative practice), leading to greatly improved health and enhanced levels of human performance. Beyond the survival needs of the (human) organism, the main functions of the sensory-motor brain are, as the name suggests, to facilitate the smooth and integrated process of the senses and the myriad physical movements of the body. In its essence, this is the body brain.

> The autonomic nervous system can be, potentially, much more under our conscious control (as a result of, for example, biofeedback training or meditative practice), leading to greatly improved health and enhanced levels of human performance.

2. The Mid-Brain Limbic System

Lying over and surrounding the brainstem, and below the cortex, is the ring-like structure of the limbic system (sometimes called limbic brain). This complex circuitry (see Figure 6) has evolved to any extent only in mammals, reptiles having few if any of the anatomical regions usually associated with it. Few scientists agree about which exact anatomical features comprise this system, although for our purposes that debate matters less than the general knowledge about the functions of this fascinating region of the brain.

The Limbic System

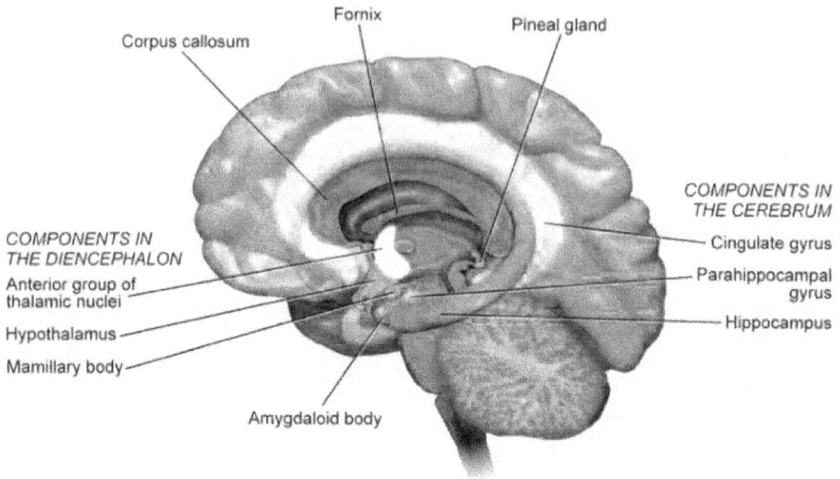

Fornix

Pineal gland

Corpus callosum

COMPONENTS IN THE CEREBRUM

COMPONENTS IN THE DIENCEPHALON

Cingulate gyrus

Anterior group of thalamic nuclei

Parahippocampal gyrus

Hypothalamus

Hippocampus

Mamillary body

Amygdaloid body

Figure 6. The Limbic System.
Image by Bruce Blaus.

This system, wired into all paleomammalian species (dogs, cats, rats, etc.), results in a clear and distinct evolutionary advantage over reptiles, as it affords something altogether missing in reptiles: an emotional life. Consider that, compared to reptiles, mammals display a remarkable range of emotions, from the more primitive survival-oriented ones like fear, anger, jealousy, and feelings related to territoriality, to those associated with maternal attachment and social bonding. In humans, these softer emotions provide the foundation for all higher learning, for only with attachment and bonding (aspects of what we humans think of as love) can the much more extended lengths of time needed for mammalian learning be accomplished.

> Only with attachment and bonding (aspects of what we humans think of as love) can the much more extended lengths of time needed for mammalian learning be accomplished.

This "something extra" that bonds mammals emotionally with their young, not only motivates greater protection but also prolongs the time mammalian parent and offspring spend together for the sake of survival and even, in humans, what could be termed 'thrival'. This increases the opportunity for basic levels of learning such as imitation, feedback and trial-and-error. Consider what an evolutionary advance this is over reptiles that apparently do not dote on their offspring—nor do their offspring rely on their parents' teachings for their own survival.

As Joseph Pearce (1992, 2002) points out, all mammals learn through modeling, vocal and visual communication, feedback, practice and repetition, unlike reptiles whose behavior is instinctually limited—determined by a lower level stimulus-response, reactive learning. It has been aptly stated that emotions are the basic currency of human exchange. This point captures an essential element of human learning, for there is always a relational and emotional component to it. Beyond the fact that emotions associated with bonding and protection are what make mammalian learning possible to begin with, human learning and intelligence invariably occurs and unfolds in a social context. That is why some commentators refer to the limbic system as the 'social-emotional brain', or the 'relational brain'. To sum up paleomammalian learning (again, think dogs, cats, rats), we note that it is qualitatively different compared to reptiles. Whereas reptilian intelligence is reflexive—what we might call stimulus-responsive and almost entirely genetically determined and derived—ancient mammal learning is stored as memory, leading to the intelligence of hindsight. Thus mammals, rather than being strictly subject to predetermined and stimulus-response reptilian-style intelligence, can learn, adapt, remember, and act accordingly.

> However we label or describe it, human learning suffers when we forget or neglect the primacy of relationship.

3. The Forebrain or Neocortex

The third of the triune brains, the cerebral cortex (also referred to as the neocortex) plus other structures surrounding the limbic system constitutes what MacLean designated the neomammalian brain. Larger than the other two parts combined, it is this component of the brain that most relates 'higher mammals' (such as primates) to humans, while at the same time distinguishing humans from all other animals. This most recently evolved feature of the brain is not only responsible for perceiving and interpreting information sent by the five senses and initiating directed action such as walking or talking, it makes possible all higher forms of learning: planning, problem-solving, analysis, evaluation, creativity and empathy to mention some of the most important. Many neuroscientists believe that the neocortex is linked to self-awareness and consciousness as well.

Although most mammals, even small animals such as rats, possess the important surface layer required for thought, called the neocortex, it is largest and most highly developed in the human brain. The distinction between humans and other mammals is most notable in the amount of surface area contained within it; much larger in humans compared to other animals (see Figure 7). The surface area of our adult brain, if all its folds and fissures were smoothed out, would be even more extensive than the 17-pound brain of a whale.

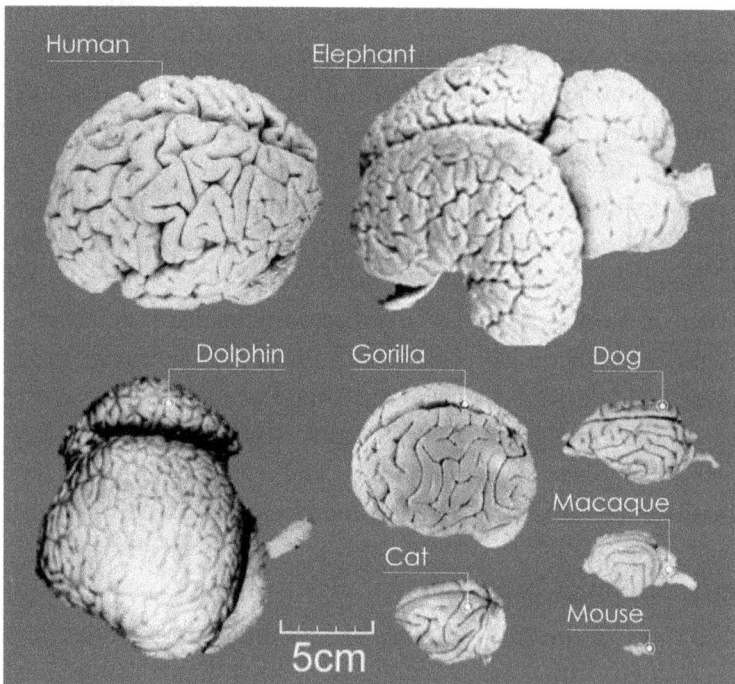

Figure 7. Comparable Cerebral Cortices.
Image by Miguelferig.

The cerebrum's outermost layer, called cerebral cortex, consists entirely of 'gray matter' as the layers of neuronal bodies that comprise the cortex are often called (later we will cover the two types of brain matter, gray and white, in considerable depth). To fit within the confines of the skull, the neocortex folds into itself to such an extent that two-thirds of the cortex is hidden in the depths and crevices. This highly convoluted and deeply fissured and grooved surface gives the surface a walnut-like appearance (which is worth mentioning, given that walnuts contain Omega-3 essential fatty acid, a crucial nutrient for healthy brain functioning!). The neocortex varies between three to five millimeters in thickness (roughly that of thin orange rind), depending on the location. More highly used processing centers such as those involving vision have a correspondingly greater thickness. The main difference between humans and other mammals lies in both the amount of neocortical surface area and, more importantly, the amount found in the frontal lobes and prefrontal cortex, which makes up roughly one-third of the cortical area in humans. As the surface area increases, so too does the total number of neurons and possible operations that a brain can perform.

So, whereas the intelligence of the sensory-motor/reptilian brain is reflexive and instinctual, and the mid-brain/paleomammalian brain one of hindsight, the large neocortex that humans and other primates have allows for a different type of intelligence: foresight. Defined literally, this means "the ability to view forward." It gives our species the amazing capacity to foresee the consequences of our behavior and to plan accordingly. How much ability other primates have to "foresee" is a much debated topic these days. Scientists are making more discoveries about primate behavior—problem solving, tool making, planning, and even language—that are forcing a greatly needed revision of long-held notions about non-human intelligence.

Furthermore, humans enjoy yet another remarkable ability that, arguably, seems absent in any other species: insight, the ability to look within and reflect upon the very act of knowing oneself. This ability varies considerably among individuals of course, although the potential, as in any field of intelligence, is always there.

There is no guarantee whatever that a given individual, group, or even society will develop this innate and decidedly important capacity, which is cause for deep concern. Individually and collectively, we live during an unprecedented period of global interconnectedness and planetary crisis, a time of both tremendous danger and amazing opportunity. The challenges we face—accelerating environmental degradation, alarming disappearance of species, potentially catastrophic global warming, growing economic and social chaos—can be successfully addressed only when enough of us develop the requisite level of intelligence.

Albert Einstein is reputed to have said, "The problems that exist in the world today cannot be solved by the level of thinking that created them." Although this quote cannot be precisely sourced, it serves as a succinct and memorable paraphrase of the concluding statement in the paragraph above.

FIRST BRAIN	SECOND BRAIN	THIRD BRAIN
Brain Stem Reflexive/Instinctual	**Limbic** Hindsight	**Cerebral Cortex** Foresight/Insight
Self-Preservation	Memory and Emotion	Thought and Language
• Approach/avoid • Vital functions monitored • Fight/flight/freeze	• Emotions related to protection and pleasure • Social bonding	• Problem-solving • Judgment, empathy • Self-awareness

Table 1. Intelligence and the Three Brains.
Image by Tim Burns.

Keys to Successful Brain Development

MacLean (1985) made it clear that the successful maturation of the mammalian brain depended on an interacting triad of developmental imperatives, what he termed the family triad of needs (see Figure 8). These are nurture, feedback and play. Building on MacLean's seminal formulation of mammalian development, Pearce (2002) has this to say: "As with all mammals, our human nature rests on these three interdependent requirements, without which we could not long survive as a species" (p.99).

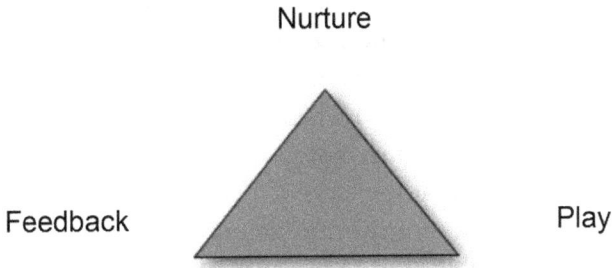

Nurture

Feedback   Play

Figure 8. Foundation for Mammalian Intelligence.
Image by Tim Burns and Jim Brown.

Nurture

All mammals require nurture (also known as bonding and attachment) to survive and thrive. Without appropriate touch and stimulation, a high percentage of mammals, including humans, will simply fail to develop normally or in some cases to survive. This was tragically brought to the attention of the world when, shortly after the collapse of the Soviet Union in the 1980s, the Western world press gained admittance into the once dictatorial country of Romania. To the great shock of journalists and subsequent horror of the world, the horrific conditions of the state-controlled orphanages brought to light the plight of thousands of young children (those who had not simply died) who showed terrible signs of neglect: ill health, weakened constitution, and massive developmental delay. Some subsequently died and most were, to some degree, mentally undeveloped, and the reason was this: most infants had languished unattended and untouched in their cribs day after day, except for diaper changes and feeding by bottles propped up in a way that made it possible to receive nourishment. The lack of touch, nursing, and human interaction took its inevitable toll, as their brains and bodies simply failed to develop properly.

Feedback

As a condition necessary to their survival, adult mammals successfully communicate with their young using vocalizations and visual recognition. MacLean focused on this audio-vocal communication for maintaining maternal-offspring contact, which has reached its most advanced and intricate level in humans. As our brains have evolved the ability to communicate with vocalized language, the very sound of the human voice—the so-called phonemes, or discreet sounds (such as the sound of the vowels, A-E-I-O-U) which number over one hundred—is essential even to the developing movements of a fetus. Scientists have discovered, for example, that the fetus of a non-vocal or mute expectant mother, prevented from hearing the sounds of the mother's voice, will be delayed in its ability to move until after the time of its birth (Condon et al, 1974). Studies in the 1970s revealed that there is a direct correspondence between a particular sound made by the mother's voice and the development of a specific muscle group in the fetus. Specifically, from the seventh month of pregnancy and continuing into the neonatal period, investigators measured a precise pattern of muscle movement in response to the mother's voice. We may conclude that, both before and after birth, humans respond to specific phonemes with a specific muscle response.

These studies demonstrate that sensory connection with the environment is essential to the development of the embodied human brain. Such connection includes much more than vocal and visual channels. We are multi-sensory beings in need of many complex forms of feedback interaction with our environment, including sounds, sight, touch, smell, taste, movement, balance, posture, sensitivity to temperature (warmth and cold), well-being, aliveness, and sense of the other.

Clearly, babies and young children need sensory flow into the brain to initiate the stimulation and integration of all its areas. This fact will lead us into interesting territory later on, as we look into the studies on brain enrichment and at the effects of increasing numbers of children raised in what Richard Louv (2008) calls the "electro-media bubble" (p. 148). It is alarmingly clear that youth spend about half their waking hours interacting with screen-based media. That is to say, they are engaged about half their time in various forms of two-dimensional, virtual reality.

As media entertainment and, more generally, screen-time has grown to replace the rich and multi-sensory environments of the natural, social, and cultural (including the arts) world, the feedback loops so critical to balance and whole-brain development have been increasingly (and ominously) reduced down to just auditory and visual. Think of television, computers, and increasingly smart phones: they use only two senses. Risky for adults and even moreso for children.

<u>**Play**</u>

The third part of the three-legged stool of balanced and supported development of the mammal brain is play. MacLean considered play an activity crucial to human development both at the individual level and, evolutionarily, at the species level. And how delightful it is that all mammals play and depend upon it for their survival! There is a growing body of research and literature on play and its effects on human development, and we will certainly explore it more fully in a subsequent chapter.

For now, suffice it to say that without play—a condition found, fortunately, in only the most dire and unusual circumstances of animal and human existence—the brain simply cannot develop normally.

The Great Model Imperative

As foundational as is the family triad, Pearce (1992, 2002) emphasizes one other element, without which human development and potential cannot unfold, an element which, in effect, enfolds the family triad: what he calls the model imperative. Pearce (2002): "The family triad includes by default nature's imperative that a model be given for all aspects of development" (p. 100). "Nature's imperative, then, and her over-arching developmental rule, which has enormous consequences, is that no intelligence or ability will unfold until or unless given the appropriate model environment. Mind and environment give rise to each other through the new-born brain only if the environment is there" (1992, p. 20).

Equipped with what we see as an elegant and straightforward brain-based framework for human development, we begin in the next chapter to explore the course of human intelligence as it unfolds according to what Pearce (1992) calls "nature's agenda for development" (p. 14).

Chapter 3

Brain Maturation and Development

"The ancient philosophers and poets remarked about the way spirals appear in thousands of places in visible nature, wherever life seeks the most efficient way to both conserve and propel matter or energy."

– Harold Kent Straughn

"Consistent with the views of Piaget, Steiner, Montessori, scientists now use a 'spiral staircase' metaphor for different periods of development."

– Jane Healy

The previous chapter introduced a theory of how the human brain evolved over eons of time, then moved into a discussion about healthy development in the brain as it is now constituted. It will become obvious as this book proceeds that healthy brain development is a primary theme of the book. The current chapter delves into more detail about how human brains grow and develop.

The physical maturation of a brain expresses itself not unlike many organisms in the natural world. Consider that many species of flowers and trees, an untold number of shell fish species, various fruits and vegetables, galaxies such as our own Milky Way, and even DNA all uncoil as spirals (see Figure 9); air currents up to and including tornadoes and hurricanes move as spirals; and water drains from sinks and bathtubs in a spiral, just like the blood that flows in our veins. In fact, the spiral shape is one of the most ubiquitous in the universe. From galaxies to DNA, vegetables to seashells, much of life owes its existence to the mathematically perfect spiral.

Figure 9. A Universe of Spirals.
See figure references (pp. 373-376) for image credits.

Now, without simplifying things too terribly, consider that the brain develops as follows: bottom to top, inside to outside, side to side, and back to front. We'll use Figures 9 and 10 as points of reference for this description of the arc of development.

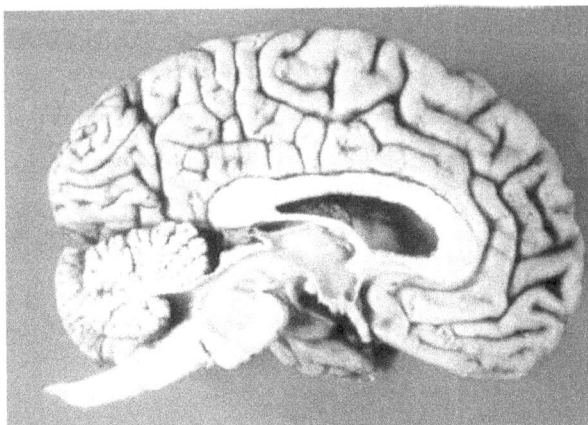

Figure 10. Human Brain Cross-Section.
Image by John A Beal, PhD.

Rise and Fall of the Biogenetic Law

Tim recalls hearing the phrase "ontogeny recapitulates phylogeny" in a college biology course, and being mightily impressed by its obvious erudition. The concept itself—attributed to Ernst Haeckel and known as the "biogenetic law" (Barnes, 2014)—is a simple one: members of a given species across the developmental lifespan re-enact the entire evolutionary sequence of the entire species. For example, a human fetus spends some of its earliest days with what appear to be the gills of a fish, then develops a reptilian-like tail, and sometime later is completely covered with hair (resembling paleo-mammalian life forms). These apparent evolutionary vestiges disappear prior to birth (although the rare baby is born still covered in that vestigial fur coat, known as lanugo, which it quickly sheds).

Although the so-called biogenetic law has been largely rejected in modern developmental biology, it illustrates an important feature of scientific advancement: the power of imagination to create novel hypotheses, followed by rigorous research to test them leading to equally creative refinements in the hypotheses. That is the case with Haeckel's idea about ontogeny recapitulating phylogeny.

This dynamic of refining a previous theory of fetal development has led, for instance, to the arguable hypothesis that when the fetal journey is complete and the world is blessed with another baby, we can be assured that that baby—even if it is born full-term at nine months—is actually premature. This perspective arises from the notion that when our human progenitors became principally upright, the female birth canal became modified to accommodate the newfound ability, resulting in babies who had to be born smaller, thus earlier, than in previous evolutionary times.

In any case, while most of the brain's construction has occurred within the womb, the long journey of brain maturation has only just begun at the time of birth.

...while most of the brain's construction has occurred within the womb, the long journey of brain maturation has only just begun at the time of birth.

Bottom to Top

Once the architecture of the fetal brain is complete, or largely so (the frontal lobes of the brain continue building their neural scaffolding through approximately the first two years of life), the wiring together of the neurons begins in earnest. What neuroscientists mean by "wiring" is that the neurons establish numerous, strong connections with one another, a process that is genetically driven but increasingly dependent upon environmental factors once birth occurs. The term wiring also incorporates the maturational process known as myelination, wherein the wiring becomes insulated in order to more quickly and efficiently conduct electrical impulses.

Thus, while somewhat over-generalized, it remains true that the bottom-most, hindmost areas of the brain must mature first. These areas consist of the brainstem and the cerebellum, which together comprise the sensory-motor apparatus of the ancient brain. It takes anywhere from about eighteen to twenty-four months for the wiring to establish itself sufficiently for an infant to gain basic control over the functions of that area. We as adults witness this in babies as the slow, arduous, but apparently delight-filled attempts at, and final mastery over, bodily control: beginning with moving the limbs of the body, then rolling over, sitting up, crawling, standing, walking, talking, bowel and bladder control, to mention the most important milestones.

This eighteen to twenty-four month timeframe was referred to by the Swiss child development expert Jean Piaget as the Sensory-Motor period. It was one of several critical stages he identified as he studied the subtleties in the progression of childhood cognitive development.

In placing Piaget's findings alongside other developmental experts (see Figure 51, page 326), matching their stages of development with the major milestone stages of brain maturation, birth through adolescence and beyond, what emerges from this comparison is a widely agreed-upon correlation between behavioral milestones and the major stages of brain development. This correlation is examined in great detail in this book's Chapter 15; it constitutes a conceptual and organizing principle for the material presented throughout the book.

We acknowledge that nearly all these developmental experts worked within the dominant "Western" culture, so some of their conclusions might not apply to all humans. Moreover, some cultures may do a better job at supporting optimal brain-mind development than the dominant culture currently does.

The following sections summarize these major developmental stages. The title of each one suggests spatial dimensions as an aid for visualizing the dynamic growth processes described in that particular section.

Inside to Outside

As we have discussed, the overall direction and momentum of brain maturation moves from the deepest, hindmost, and inner areas outward and upward. Once the bottom and hindmost areas of the brain have sufficiently matured, the mid-brain (limbic system) develops more robustly. Piaget put the

> ...the overall direction and momentum of brain maturation moves from the deepest, hindmost, and inner areas outward and upward.

timeframe for this at roughly ages eighteen to twenty-four months to about six or seven years, the stage he named Pre-operational. This is a somewhat intangible term until one recognizes that his major interests converged in the direction of cognitive development during childhood— that is, how the child's thinking process matures over the course of the years between birth and adulthood. While not a subject of this book, the brilliant experiments he designed and conducted revealed the way in which, from one stage to the next, a developing human perceives and mentally processes the world.

The Pre-operational stage of development recapitulates the epic journey of the paleo-mammalian brain structure, which is pre-eminently a social-emotional one. It is during this stage that the child is absorbed in imagination, fantasy, and play. This consumes much if not most of the child's time and energy, and well it should; the ability to imagine and play are perhaps the major determinants of how the structures of the high-brain develop, and to a large extent how creative, integrative, and satisfying a life might be.

The description Piaget used to describe this period of development is so much more revealing than the term "Pre-operations", for he offered that this was the stage of "the dreaming child." As we shall see later, he could not possibly have been more accurate, for the main brain wave frequency that predominates during these formative years of imagination and play precisely correlates with the trancelike dream state.

Side to Side

As illustrated in Figure 11 below, the two hemispheres of a human cerebrum generally serve different functions. The explanation for this division of functioning, and for how it came about, is a subject of much exploration and debate. It is a fascinating topic, and for readers drawn to delve into it we recommend *The Master and his Emissary: The Divided Brain and the Making of the Western World* by Iain McGilchrist. It is the deepest, most comprehensive treatment of the topic that we have discovered in a single volume.

Yet even to attempt to summarize relevant parts of McGilchrist's masterpiece is beyond the scope of our book. Instead, we will draw upon an earlier authority who has been researching the development of hemispheric distinctions since the 1970s, Robert Ornstein. From his work we know that the two cerebral hemispheres develop at different rates from birth through early childhood (thus the heading of this section, "Side to Side"). And thanks to his book, *The Right Mind: Making Sense of the Hemispheres*, we also have a succinct and plausible explanation for how that fact determines the differences in function between the left and right hemispheres. That explanation will be summarized here, and its considerable implications for educational and parenting practices will be explored.

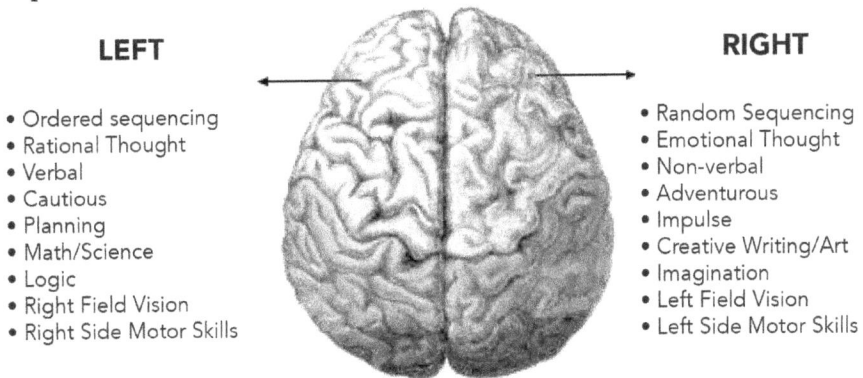

LEFT

- Ordered sequencing
- Rational Thought
- Verbal
- Cautious
- Planning
- Math/Science
- Logic
- Right Field Vision
- Right Side Motor Skills

RIGHT

- Random Sequencing
- Emotional Thought
- Non-verbal
- Adventurous
- Impulse
- Creative Writing/Art
- Imagination
- Left Field Vision
- Left Side Motor Skills

Figure 11. Hemispheric Functions of the Brain.
Image from Gutenberg Encyclopedia.

Ornstein (1998) tells us, "...the right hemisphere, particularly the frontal area, matures earlier, its functions develop earlier..." (p. 150). On the other side, "there is a delay in the left hemisphere's development near...the area of the brain that is most involved with language. The neurons' complexity of interconnections with other neurons also develops later in the left hemisphere than in the right" (p. 150). He terms these differences in timing "growth asymmetries" (p. 150), and suggests that they underlie the asymmetries of function that develop later on.

How so? Here is an example:

> The right hemisphere matures and becomes responsive to the effects of the outside world at the time in the infant's life when spatial abilities, such as finding the mother and control of the large limb movements are getting wired up. These are obviously necessary for survival. And the left hemisphere begins to become more and more mature and comes on-line... when the baby is exposed to spoken language and learning the more refined movements of infancy. (p.150)

In other words, the differential maturation of each hemisphere coincides with different levels of development in the brain overall. Thus, the right hemisphere becomes functionally tied to spatial abilities and large movements, whereas the left hemisphere becomes tied to language and more refined movements.

The march of hemispheric asymmetry, both structural and functional, proceeds as each sensory system matures, little by little. The right hemisphere tends to process the broader, more general aspects of the sensory world (e,g, visual shapes, vocal tones, emotional nuances), while the left hemisphere specializes in more complex information such as the fine details of the visual world, accurate sensorimotor feedback, and precise muscle movements (e.g. writing, performing surgery).

That, in a nutshell, is Ornstein's view of how the two cerebral hemispheres grow to govern the distinct yet complementary sets of functional characteristics shown in Figure 11. In developing this view he ultimately emphasizes the complementary aspects rather than the distinctions between hemispheric functioning. He acknowledges that:

> The two sides handle the world differently, one focusing on the small elements of a worldview and linking them tightly

together so they can be acted upon, produced, reproduced, like a formula. The other links together the large strokes of a life's portrait, where we are, where the parts fit, the context of our life. (p. 162)

It is also true that

...during the period from 3 to 6 years, both frontal and occipital areas of the left hemisphere develop more rapidly than corresponding areas of the right hemisphere. This is the period that is also critical for the acquisition of grammar for which the left hemisphere is usually dominant. (p. 155)

It is interesting to consider the developmental phenomenon noted above in light of the fact that the period from 3 to 6 years is precisely the time when most English-speaking children are entering school systems– the same time that the left hemispheres of their brains are reaching maturity. School curricula and classroom practice in the U.S. and U.K. are geared largely to left hemisphere activities, which seems developmentally appropriate. But let us not forget the need for "nurture" emphasized near the end of the previous chapter, because the right hemisphere also continues to develop during this period.

Keep in mind that mammalian learning most often occurs in an interactive social context and this makes emotional resonance and attunement, the key elements in nurture, critically important. Researchers such as Seigel (2011, 2012), Porges (2011), Schore(2003), and others make it abundantly clear that social-emotional processes are right-brain contingent. This means that the earlier maturing, emotionally resonant, right hemisphere—featuring direct, unmediated neural connections to the limbic area of the brain (the left hemisphere is mediated through the right)—must be well attended to in order to gain access to the special functions of the left hemisphere (including linear and analytic thought processes, reasoning capacities, and so forth), functions clearly emphasized by educational systems world-wide. Therefore, it only makes sense to take

> ...mammalian learning most often occurs in an interactive social context and this makes emotional resonance and attunement, the key elements in nurture, critically important.

the time and make the effort first, foremost and often to establish and maintain warm teacher-student and student-student relationships. In sum, when it comes to mammalian learning, relational attunement and resonance is everything.

Our impression is that school systems, at least in the U.S. where we authors live, too often overlook the ongoing need to establish and maintain relationships while also forgetting (if they were ever aware) that both hemispheres of the brains of their students need to be cultivated in a balanced manner. Ornstein addresses this head-on when he says about schools referred to here that "…there is far too little effort [toward] connecting what is learned to the experience of the learner–that is putting the information in relevant context" (p. 171). In this statement he has bluntly criticized mainstream education as ignoring the needs of fully half of its pupils' growing brains.

He becomes even more blunt: "We're trained for drills and learning things without connecting them to the world…. Given the amount of information taught without context we don't need a special right-brain learning program, but simply to put the large picture first in front of the student" (pp.171-172). In saying this, Ornstein is not advocating a de-emphasis on left-brain learning; he is advocating, emphatically, an equal emphasis on cultivating the properties and functions unique to the right hemisphere.

Everyone who is concerned about the healthy development of the human brain needs to understand the importance of equal emphasis on the cerebral hemispheres, second only to the primary need for social connectedness. Each hemisphere has unique functional characteristics, and the brain as a whole requires full interaction between both (which, you may recall is enabled by the corpus callosum). The robust integration of the two hemispheres is paramount. This enables the efficient interplay of their respective functions, operating together in service to problem-solving, creativity, and effective responsiveness to novel situations and challenges, in the context of community.

Integration in concert with differentiation is a vitally important phenomenon applicable to all levels of human existence. We will explore it more fully in Chapter 13 and 14. For now, we resume our spatially-oriented description of the brain's development.

Back to Front

As the brain slowly grows in maturity, it is in general to the posterior or rear portion of the outer layers of the cerebral cortex that the energies of development proceed. The back of the cortex is the region specializing in the organization and integration of the sensory world (see Figure 2). Vision, especially, is processed in the rearmost part of the brain, the occipital lobes, whereas hearing is processed in the temporal lobes, located along both sides of the brain and—along their posterior edges— adjacent to the occipital lobes.

Just in front of the occipitals, the parietal lobes—along with the somatosensory cortex—simultaneously integrate all sensory signals received from other areas of the brain, including vision, hearing, touch, locomotion, proprioception, taste, pain, heat and memory. Finally, motor planning occurs mainly in a strip known as the primary motor cortex located just in front of the somatosensory cortex and behind the frontal lobes.

It is during the span of childhood years from around age six or seven to approximately eleven or twelve (the onset of puberty) that the posterior portion of the cortex goes through an intense stage of neural integration and maturation. Accordingly, Piaget recognized the need for an education that stressed equal measures of "hand, head, and heart," calling this period Concrete Operations, for mental operations at this time are much rooted in what the child has learned through direct sensory perception. It is critical that children throughout these years build up structures of knowledge about their environment through all their senses, forming an extensive experience-base that will in time come to undergird the next stage of development: the triumph of understanding the sensory world. Clearly, the optimal way by which a child can gain these structures of knowledge is through close contact and interaction with the natural, social and cultural realms.

Clearly, the optimal way by which a child can gain these structures of knowledge is through close contact and interaction with the natural, social and cultural realms.

Then, with the onset of puberty, the hormones that initiate both physical and sexual changes in the developing body—most especially testosterone, of which males produce a great deal and females a lesser amount of a similar hormone—also bring the frontal lobes of the brain more fully into use (Dahl & Forbes, 2010). Gradually, throughout adolescence, the remarkable powers of the frontal lobes and prefrontal cortex begin to make their appearance, stabilizing over time, and the "adult becoming" (the literal meaning of the word "adolescent") shifts into yet another mode of apprehending and interacting with the inner and outer. For it is during this stage that the keen powers of insight and foresight become more manifest.

Piaget referred to this remarkable period as Formal Operations, having demonstrated that the emergent mental processes being carried out were more in the realm of abstraction, with theorizing and hypothesizing, as well as analysis, synthesis, evaluation becoming more evident (see Table 2). In addition, other critically important capacities become possible during this period: empathy, reflection, consequential thinking, impulse control, and conscience formation, to name some of the most important.

• Envision the future • Dream big dreams • Set goals • Make plans • Detect problems • Solve problems	• Manage emotions • Control impulses • Consider consequences • Learn from mistakes • Conscience formation • Empathy and compassion

Table 2. Functions of the Mature Frontal Lobes. Image by Tim Burns and Jim Brown.

The stages described in the last few sections could justifiably be called Nature's Plan for development: the stable and balanced unfolding of intelligence in a genetically primed and sequenced process, one that is intimately coupled with and

> The stages described in the last few sections could justifiably be called Nature's Plan for development.

dependent upon the kind and quality of environment that either supports or suppresses the flowering of innate human potential.

Conclusion

We began this chapter with an overview of the main geographic features of the brain as a whole and from the outside, while continuing to introduce some of the key anatomical areas and terms. From there we looked at childhood and adolescent development by observing how the brain matures bottom to top, inside to outside, side to side, and back to front. This sets the stage for an in-depth examination of the micro-brain structure upon which the drama of human learning and development is written: the neuron.

Chapter 4

The Brain Up Close

"Essentially, all expressions of human nature ever produced, from a caveman's paintings to Mozart's symphonies and Einstein's view of the universe, emerge from the same source: the relentless dynamic toil of large populations of interconnected neurons."

– Miguel Nicolelis, PhD

"Your brain is built of cells called neurons and glia — hundreds of billions of them. Each one of these cells is as complicated as a city."

– David Eagleman, PhD

Introduction

Chapter 1 surveyed the major anatomical features of the human brain–from the cerebral cortex with its hemispheric structure and the bilateral lobes of the cortex, down through the subcortical structures (hypothalamus, pituitary gland, and other vitally important components).

Chapter 2 began situating the brain's anatomical functions in an evolutionary and developmental context, introducing MacLean's theory about the brain's triune (i.e., three-in-one) nature, augmented by an initial discussion of intelligence and how to nurture it.

Chapter 3 continued the developmental theme, relating the growth of the brain to the developmental stages observed and reported by Piaget.

This current chapter looks more deeply into developmental issues by examining the neural substrates of growth, maturation and development of what might be called "the learning brain," emphasizing key points central to the themes of the book. For the most part, these points revolve around "neuroplasticity," an exciting feature of the human brain only recently discovered. That the brain—unlike any other organ of the body—can change both its structural and functional organization through experience is without a doubt one of the most significant scientific discoveries in the past century.

This amazing capacity emerges from the three-way interactions among genome, environment, and perception. In this chapter we focus mostly on the genomic-environmental, or "nature and nurture" relationship. In following chapters we touch on aspects of the perceptual element.

Evidence for the brain's plasticity begins at the embryonic/fetal and neonatal stages of development, during which neurons go through the processes of proliferation, aggregation, migration, connection, competition, and elimination. The dynamics of plasticity continue to impact learning and human potential through the life-long processes of neurogenesis, synaptogenesis, arborization and pruning, apoptosis (cell death), and myelination.

Survey of the Brain and Its Interior

Perhaps the most striking features of the brain are the intensely folded topography (see Figure 12) and the color. While the ridges (gyri) and valleys (sulci) are the most obvious geographic feature, the pinkish-gray hue results from two factors.

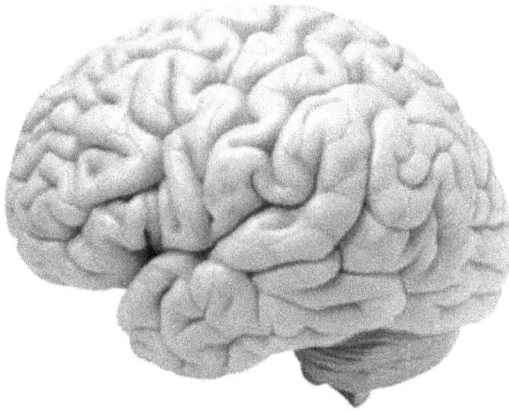

Figure 12. Human Brain.
Image by _DJ_.

The pinkish color is related to the dense vascular system that carries approximately 20 percent of the body's entire volume of blood (although the brain itself weighs in at only two percent of the body's mass); and the gray is the coloration of the neurons with their unmyelinated axons (we'll cover myelination shortly) that constitute the outermost surface of the brain (see Figure 13).

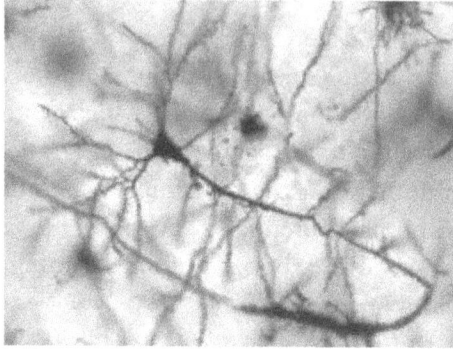

Figure 13. Neuron.
Image by MethoxyRoxy.

The following short but comprehensive survey of the interior of the brain is organized by these sub themes:

a) Gray matter: "Cells That Think"
b) Development and Organization of the Cortex
c) Anatomy of a Neuron
d) Stages and Processes in Neurodevelopment and Learning
e) Brain Plasticity: Shape-Shifting Through Experience
f) A Closer Look at Neurogenesis: Born Again Brain Cells
g) Gray (Neuronal) and White (Glial) Brain Matter
h) Learning and Myelination: Practice, Repetition, Variation.

Gray Matter: "Cells that Think"

The human brain is composed of no less than one trillion nerve cells, ten percent or roughly 100 billion of which are the neurons. The vast majority of these cells, about ninety percent, are neuroglia, or simply glia (Latin for "glue"). Neurons—of which there are several different types—constitute what is known as gray matter, and form the basic units of the cerebral cortex (the outermost layer of the brain), serving as the network for communication throughout the brain. They process incoming sensory information and can be thought of, in the aggregate, as "cells that think."

While some glial cells contribute to neuronal communications in ways that have only recently become known, it is primarily the neurons, arrayed in their stunningly vast networks, that allow thinking and many other brain/body functions to occur. This is because each neuron is connected to thousands upon thousands of other neurons; some scientists estimate 10,000 and possibly as many as 50,000 of these connections are formed, on average. Let's look at these numbers from a perspective familiar to everyone: if we multiply our 100 billion neurons (roughly equal to about half the number of stars in the Milky Way galaxy) by the 10,000 connections formed by each of them, we reach the staggering number one-thousand trillion, or a quadrillion. Now consider that our galaxy, the Milky Way, has an estimated 300-400 billion stars, and that it would take 10,000 galaxies of that size to have the number of stars equal to the number of neural connections in the brain! It is this degree of intricate multiplicity that has earned the brain the sobriquet of "the most complex three pounds of matter in the known universe."

Networks of neurons comprise both the sensory input systems and motor output systems that underlie our actions and movements, as well as the planning, decision-making, and emotional control systems in the frontal lobes. Gray matter constitutes the outermost layer—the cortex—of the cerebrum, and forms the gyri and sulci that give the cortex its undulating appearance. Spread out, the cortex would be a little larger than the size of an opened newspaper (about 2.5 square feet), and it is the thickness of a thin orange rind.

Underlying the gray matter of the cortex is the brain's so-called white matter (see Figure 14), to which we shall turn our attention later in this chapter.

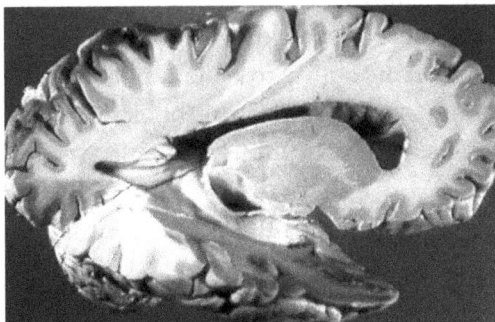

Figure 14.
Gray and White Matter.
Image by John A Beal, PhD.

Development and Organization of the Cortex

Beginning with fetal development, the organization of neurons into a fully functional cortex goes through some six formative stages (see Figure 15).

According to Marion Diamond (1999), the first three stages occur principally during fetal development, while the fourth, fifth, and sixth stages occur both during fetal development and into the earliest days, weeks, months and years of postnatal life. Whereas the first three stages of organization are mostly genetically controlled, the last three are much more affected by environmental interaction—a theme to which we shall return.

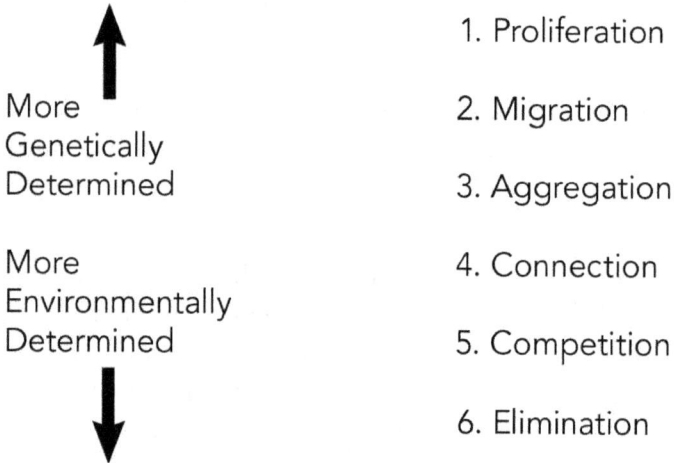

More Genetically Determined

More Environmentally Determined

1. Proliferation

2. Migration

3. Aggregation

4. Connection

5. Competition

6. Elimination

Figure 15. Stages of Neural Organization.
Image by Tim Burns and Jim Brown.

Research by neuroscientists continues to demonstrate that the brain organizes and reorganizes itself throughout the life span through a number of processes, known collectively as neuroplasticity, which account for the brain's ability to remain pliable and adaptive. Neuroplasticity is a phenomenon crucial to this book's central theme, and will be discussed extensively as we go along.

The cortex comprises six layers of neurons that are highly interconnected, the layering of which can be seen in Figure 16. The three images on display in this figure—each one using a different staining technique—depict the work of Santiago Ramon y Cajal, often referred to as the "father of neuroscience" after winning the 1906 Nobel Prize for Physiology or Medicine, awarded for establishing the neuron, or nerve cell, as the basic unit of the nervous system.

Even a casual glance at the images captures the layering effect, each of which has its own predetermined functions. The deepest layers, four through six, act as the sensory input and motor output processing areas of the brain. The fourth layer receives incoming signals from the sensory systems found in the peripheral nervous system, and the fifth and sixth layers govern outgoing motor activities. Together, according to Diamond, the deeper three layers account for over sixty percent of the brain's cortical thickness. The top three layers carry out the mental processes of the brain and constitute about forty percent of the thickness of the cortex.

The bottom layers, sensory-motor in function, mature before the outermost, exemplifying an important characteristic of the maturation of the brain which we addressed in an earlier chapter: the bottom-to-top aspect of the "spiral of development."

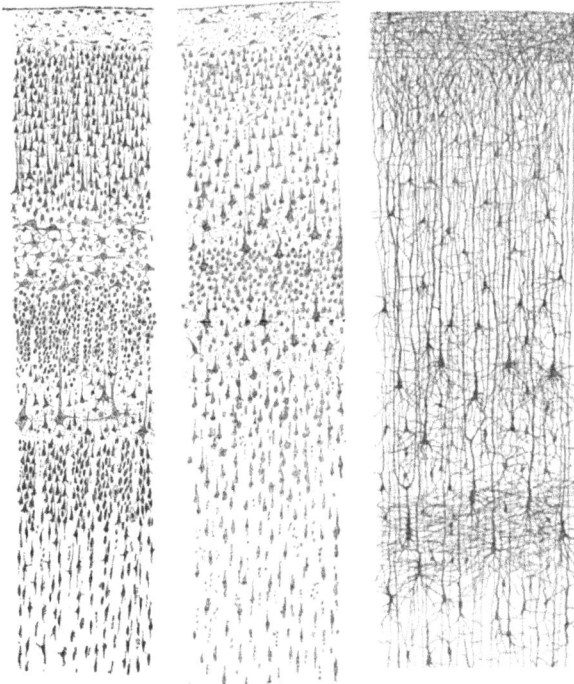

Figure 16. Cortex: Six Cell-Layers Thick.
Image by Looie496.

Anatomy of a Neuron

Neurons, are the most basic functional units of the brain. There are several types, resulting in a variety of shapes and sizes. Of the various types, the one associated most with thinking is the so-called pyramidal cell, named after its tell-tale shape. Most often when the word "neuron" is used, this is the one to which we refer. Without these neurons, thinking (and all other forms of intelligence) would not be possible. Each neuron, no matter its variation, consists of a soma or cell body, an axon, and the dendrites (see Figure 17).

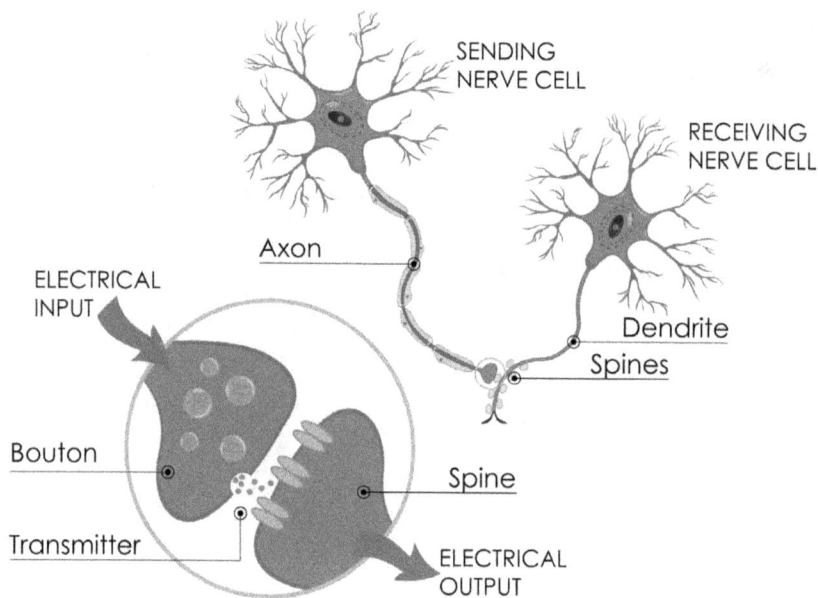

Figure 17. Anatomy of a Neuron.
Image by Maja Petrović/Inspired By Learning.

Dendrites (Latin for "branch") are the root-like appendages that extend from the body of each neuron. They receive electrochemical signals from other neurons and generate, as stated earlier, at least 10,000 connections with other neurons (some neuroscientists claim it's more like 50,000, and at least one (Lowrey, 1998), puts the number as high as 600,000). Whereas the dendrites bring signals from other neurons to the soma, or cell body, axons send or carry information away from the soma to other cells. In general, there is only one axon fiber extending from the soma of a neuron that, like the dendrites, branches out at the end to connect with many other cells.

The small gap between the axon of one neuron and the dendritic spine of another (the site of electrochemical information exchange to be described later) is known as the synapse. While not labeled as such, this gap can be seen in the enlarged lower left of Figure 17; it is the space between a "bouton" and a "spine" across which chemical messenger molecules known as "transmitters" move from one neuron to the next.

The main difference between axons and dendrites (beyond the fact that one carries electrical impulses away from and the other toward the soma) appears on their surfaces. Dendrites have no insulating myelin sheath and contain many spines, making it possible for other cells to "dock" or connect. In axons, spines are lacking altogether and there is typically only one axon for each cell. A further difference is that the branching of axons occurs well away from the cell body, whereas with dendrites the branching can be near or far.

The basic operation of a single neuron is fantastically complex—much moreso than even a very sophisticated computer—when all of its electrochemical processes (the understanding of which is still unfolding) are considered. Even so, the overall result of this complex operation is fairly straightforward: either the neuron fires (transmits a signal) or it does not; and if it does it can fire faster or slower. When enough firing occurs, processes that are well beyond the capability of any one cell are initiated. When considering the immeasurably complex operations even within one neuron of the brain, then multiplying those by trillions of simultaneous firings and quadrillions of possible combinations, and one begins to see how the brain is vastly more complex than even the most powerful computer designed and made by humans. Thus, while we might be able to get away with comparing a single neuron to the corresponding component of a computer—since each one, like chips in a computer, either fires or does not—a more fitting analogy for the entire brain would be a complex ecosystem such as that of a jungle, wherein new species of flora and fauna continually emerge. The

...a more fitting analogy for the entire brain would be a complex ecosystem such as that of a jungle, wherein new species of flora and fauna continually emerge.

brain's myriad operations give rise to wild, novel diversity through processes known collectively as emergence—a theme we take up in a later chapter—an understanding of which is crucial to a full appreciation of human development and potential.

Stages and Processes in Neurodevelopment and Learning

Thus, the developing brain becomes a functional organ through some six formative stages: proliferation, aggregation, migration, connection, competition, and elimination. These stages involve five critical processes that altogether add not just to the functionality (or lack thereof) of the maturing brain, but to its ongoing ability to learn and remain plastic as well. Over the last century, but most especially so in the past decade or two, our understanding of these processes has fostered something of a revolution not only in the brain sciences but also our views and practices related to education, health, aging and, more broadly speaking, human potential. Let's take a more detailed look at these processes, as they will undergird most of the assumptions about learning, well-being and human potential upon which this book is based.

Process 1: Neurogenesis and Synaptogenesis

What Diamond (1999) referred to as proliferation, is the original spawning of neurons within the first few weeks of embryonic life. Most proliferation, or neurogenesis, occurs during the second and third trimester of fetal development. Although the number of new cells being created falls off precipitously once birth takes place, research over the past few decades supports the possibility that neurogenesis continues for the entire life span. This finding, if confirmed, would qualify as the most exciting neuroscience discovery in the past century.

The importance of this revolutionary discovery cannot be overemphasized, in part because of the long-standing (but likely erroneous) view that we are born with all the neurons we will have for a lifetime, and that we lose neurons every day of our lives, the result of which is an inevitable and irrecoverable loss of brain matter and therefore mental power. While the latter assertion is partly true, the former—that we are born with all the neurons we shall enjoy for a lifetime—seems not to be the case. As a consequence of this recent finding, a long-held tenet in scientific circles finally has begun to loosen its grip.

This assumption-turned-tenet came about and has held sway for so long as a result, in part, of the pronouncements made by that early pioneer in the study of the brain, physician-turned-neuroscientist, Ramón y Cajal, who, in 1928, famously stated that, "In adult centers the nerve paths are something fixed, ended, immutable. Everything may die, nothing may be regenerated" (Ramón y Cajal, 1959, p. 750).

"Everything may die, nothing may be regenerated." This conclusion, widely held by Ramón y Cajal's contemporaries, was the conventionally held view of the brain by both the scientific and lay communities for nearly a century. Over the past few decades, however, the pessimistic notion that intelligence is fixed at birth, that human potential is circumscribed by our genetic endowment, and that as we age the brain is inexorably heading towards decrepitude, has been challenged by a body of research that has aroused hope for a better outcome.

We shall return to the engaging and important story of neurogenesis later in this chapter.

Synaptogenesis is a phenomenon intimately related to neurogenesis. Perry (2002) calls the synapse "the most experience-sensitive feature of the neuron" (p. 84). Through a very complex exchange involving the conversion of electrical impulses into chemical message carriers (the neurotransmitters, neurohormones, and neuromodulators), of which there are a hundred or so types, the trillions of synaptic junctures grow, shape themselves, strengthen or weaken through usage. The forming and modulating of these junctures between neurons constitutes synaptogenesis. The process refines and sculpts the brain throughout one's lifetime, involving the interaction of genes, perceptions, and environment. Chapter 7 contains a detailed discussion of this interactive phenomenon.

Process 2: Migration and Differentiation

Once the cells—around a trillion glial and about 200 billion neuronal (the latter culling down to half that number by the time of birth)—come into existence, they must find their way to a functional location somewhere in the brain, a complex process that is "guided" by glial cells and a variety of chemical markers (e.g., cellular adhesion molecules and nerve growth factor). Thus, neurons cluster, sort, move and settle into a location in the brain that will be their final "resting" place (Perry, 2002).

Each newly migrated and localized neuron has a highly specialized function, the designated term for which is "differentiation." In the end, there may be 50 or more different types of neurons in the brain, each doing a different kind of task (Schwartz, 2002, p.104). A cortical cell, for example, will take on a different form and have a different function than a cerebellar cell. This can be seen in the variety of different types—and therefore differing shapes and functions—of neurons and, for that matter, glial cells (see Figures 18 and 19).

BASIC NEURON TYPES

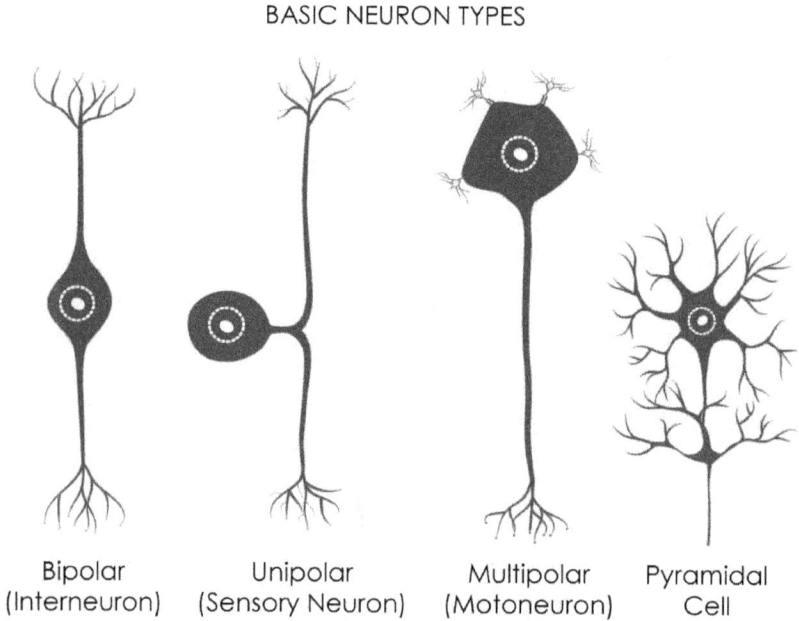

| Bipolar (Interneuron) | Unipolar (Sensory Neuron) | Multipolar (Motoneuron) | Pyramidal Cell |

Figure 18. Neuron Types.
Image by Maja Petrović/Inspired By Learning.

As can be seen in Figure 18, neurons differ in form and size. In addition, neurons use any of over eighty different neurotransmitters, from serotonin to dopamine, GABA to acetylcholine. Moreover—and this is central to our thesis of how important environment is to unleashing human potential—as Perry points out:

...neurons are specialized to change in response to chemical signals. Therefore, any experience or event that alters neurochemical or micro-environmental signals during development can change the ways in which certain neurons differentiate, thereby altering the functional capacity of the neural networks in which these neurons reside. (Perry, 2002, p.83)

GLIAL TYPES

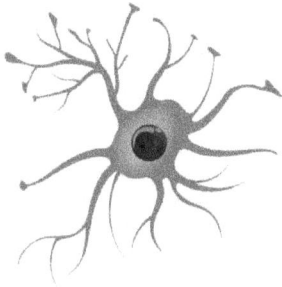

Fibrous astrocyte   Oligodendrocytes

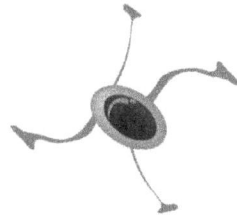

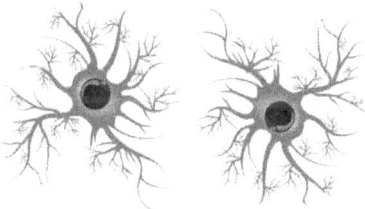

Protoplasmic astrocyte Microglial cell

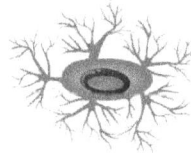

Figure 19. Glial Types.
Image by Maja Petrović/Inspired By Learning.

Process 3: Apoptosis

During fetal development the brain's supply of neurons numbers approximately 200 billion. Many of these neurons—eventually about half—will not be utilized in many areas of the brain, and will be unceremoniously discarded prior to birth. This process is known as apoptosis, or "cell death." This fetal oversupply speaks to the incredible flexibility and adaptability of the human central nervous system and in a practical sense prepares each human baby with the potential to readily adapt to the environmental, social, and cultural circumstances into which she is born. The process combines genetic, perceptual, and environmental determinants, and is a crucial component of the brain's plasticity. It is a simple proposition for the brain: "use it or lose it," and cell death plays a key role.

Process 4: Arborization and Pruning

Like a tree, the neurons in the brain continually branch out and make new connections with myriad other cells and, like a fruitful and productive tree, needs to undergo constant pruning as well. The density of any branch, or dendrite is determined by how much and how often inter-neuronal signaling activity takes place. This phenomenon, perhaps more than any other, is exceedingly "activity-dependent," meaning that when there is a great deal of neural activity linked to environmental stimulation (or internal processing of same) the brain is stimulated to arborize. Stated simply, more dendritic activity takes place.

On the other hand, because various areas of the developing brain have a great surplus of neurons, the brain eliminates those that are unable to "wire-in" to the emerging neural networks. Diamond (1999) refers to this process as competition, which also relies on what could be thought of as activity-dependence. Again, "Use it or lose it" proves to be much a part of Nature's Plan for the organization of the brain. According to at least one estimate (Eliot, 2000, p.32), an amazingly large number of synapses—about 20 billion—are pruned each day during childhood and the onset of adolescence.

This process of continual branching and pruning—the entire dance of genetic and environmental interaction in fact—can be summed up as follows: genes are wholly in control of the timing and order (or sequence) in which the various regions of the brain come on line, while experience in a given environment determines the strength and development of various brain circuits. As Schwartz says, "The basic principle is this: genetic signals play a large role in the initial structuring of the brain. The ultimate shape of the brain, however, is the outcome of an ongoing active process that occurs where lived experience meets both the inner and outer environment" (Schwartz and Begley 2002, p.117).

More needs to be said about pruning, the elimination of weak or unused connections between cells for the sake of greater efficiency. Engaged practice and repetition determine which connections are strengthened, and consequently which ones will ultimately be pruned, since those most often made active are the ones that survive. Neuroscientists are convinced that, because of the enormous complexity and staggering number of neural connections, an important design function is to eliminate unnecessary or unused synapses, analogous to the way a sculptor removes material to reveal the sculpted form.

For example, Richard Haier of the University of California at Irvine has shown that the brain becomes more efficient through synaptic pruning. From birth until about five years of age the number of synaptic connections in the brain steadily increases. Following that, from five to twenty years of age, a huge number of these connections wither away. During this process, Haier says, the brain is weeding out unnecessary synaptic connections. The importance of this cannot be overstated, because should this necessary process of pruning fail, the brain would have too many connections attempting to perform the same task, and the result would be loss of efficiency. Haier (1992, p.117) continues: "On a PET scan, such a person would have a higher than normal metabolic rate, as these brains try to use the whole brain to solve problems you don't need the whole brain for." Interestingly and contrary to what one might expect, excellence or mastery, in any field of endeavor has been shown to reduce the amount of metabolic activity in the corresponding areas of the brain when compared to amateurs or non-experts.

The pruning process makes complete sense when we consider that a six year-old has perhaps five times more neural connections than does a typical adult. Nature deems it important that a child has a vast potential for adaptation to any circumstance—thus all the connections—while at the same time requiring improved brain efficiency. Again, the rule for the brain appears to be the same as for muscles: "use it or lose it."

Figure 20 shows the process of dendritic growth and pruning over time. Note the very small number of connections in the brain of the newborn compared to those of the three-month old baby—the result of a gray-matter growth spurt. By age twenty-four months, a veritable forest of branches has appeared. Clearly there are greater possibilities in store for the two-year-old; the potential is virtually unlimited. By age six, however, the branches have undergone a remarkable thinning, even though there are still considerably more connections than adults have. The important result of this difference is a much more efficient brain.

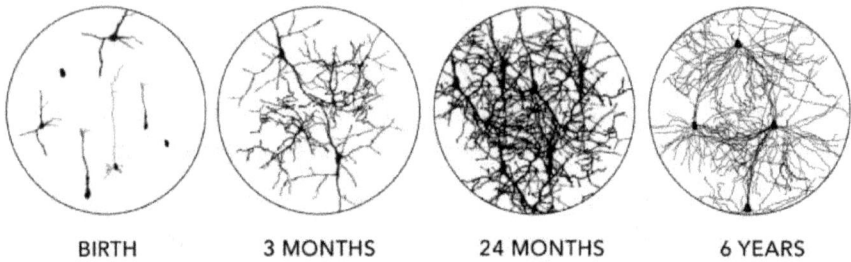

BIRTH   3 MONTHS   24 MONTHS   6 YEARS

Figure 20. Dendritic Growth and Pruning.
Image by Maja Petrović/Inspired By Learning.

The fact that a two-year-old has twice the number of synaptic connections as an adult means that it will be possible for a given child to adapt to any environment, culture, or language on earth. Once that adaption begins, however, other possibilities gradually begin to diminish. A child can learn this language or that language, perhaps even three or four of them, reasonably well; but he or she cannot learn all languages everywhere. Over time and with on-going pruning, the balance between limitless potential and adaptive learning and development shifts. Nature is not just interested in promise; it requires efficiency, and rewards capacities that serve performance.

It is worth pausing here to reflect on the implications for educational practice of the statement just made. Nature (the nature of brain development) dictates that every learning experience guides the learner into a more narrow field of possibilities for future learning, and away from a wider field of what might otherwise be learned. This implies a great responsibility on the part of educators and parents to choose wisely what lessons are taught, how they are taught, and in what context. We are not merely imparting information or training skills, we are changing the neural structure of our students' brains.

The view that a singular period of overproduction of gray matter during the first 18 months of life, followed by a steady lifelong decline (as unused circuitry is discarded), has been a long-held tenet of neuroscience. In the late 1990s, however, the National Institute of Mental Health's Dr. Jay Giedd and his colleagues discovered a second wave of overproduction of gray matter just before puberty (Giedd et al, 1999), followed by a second bout of "use-it-or-lose-it" pruning during the teen years. This discovery and others like it have stimulated discussion about "growth spurts" in the brain, comparable to the visible tendency of bodily growth and development to accelerate during critical periods of youngsters' lives.

Process 5: Myelination

To complete this section's listing of major processes in learning and development, we will briefly mention myelination. In early stages of brain development, myelin sheaths begin to surround the axons that conduct electrochemical signals from one neuron to the next. Myelin functions as insulating material for the axons that enables a more rapid, efficient and effective, transmission of electrochemical impulses. We will say more about this crucial facet of brain development and ongoing plasticity later in the chapter.

As Perry (2002, p. 85) makes clear, the functionality of the brain depends on the timing and patterning of these key neuro-developmental processes as they unfold in a subtle, intricate dance between the genome and environmental cues. (Later we will discuss the crucial role of individual perception as a player in the dance.) Any disruption of this unfolding can have a deleterious and long-term effect. Perry underscores the point that "while the structural organization and functional capabilities of the mature brain can change throughout life, the majority of the key stages of neurodevelopment take place in childhood" (Perry, 2002, p. 86).

Thus, while the good news is that it is possible to change the brain after early childhood, no one can deny that it would be much better to get it right then rather than to remediate problems down the road. The 'wait and remediate' option is a dicey enterprise fraught with challenges, as we have found both in education and in society as a whole.

Brain Plasticity: Shape-Shifting Through Experience

Let us now turn to a recent discovery in the brain sciences, one with the most astonishing implications for understanding human learning, health, recovery from injury, and creative potential: neuroplasticity.

Certainly, one of the most important and exciting discoveries in the history of brain science, neuroplasticity refers to the fact that a person's neurons engage throughout the life span in the rearrangement and reorganization of their networks in response to sensory stimulation and new experience (or lack thereof). That the brain does so we now recognize as the bedrock basis of learning and human intelligence—an idea, as we have seen, completely at odds with the assumptions of brain science throughout much of the past century.

One way by which the brain demonstrates plasticity is through "reassigning" neurons to do jobs other than that for which they were originally intended. For example, an individual born congenitally blind is very likely to develop a heightened sense of hearing and touch as the region of the brain devoted to vision (the occipital cortex) is taken over by the adjacent areas ordinarily serving the senses of touch and hearing (the somatosensory and temporal areas, respectively).

In fact, many different kinds of change occur in the brain, including changes not just to neurons but to the glia and vascular cells as well—and not just in the brains of children but also in adults' brains. While it is true that these changes can and do occur throughout the span of life for young and old alike, it is equally true that the degree to which the brain is and remains plastic is very much tied to the so-called "windows of opportunity".

Neuroplasticity is the general term for all structural adaptation in the brain and is thus the key element in our earlier description of human intelligence as "the capacity to respond to new situations, adapt to changing conditions, and learn from experience." We now know that

> Neuroplasticity is the general term for all structural adaptation in the brain and is thus the key element in our earlier description of human intelligence as "the capacity to respond to new situations, adapt to changing conditions, and learn from experience."

neuroplasticity is a primary characteristic of the brain, second only to the brain's principal function as the main regulatory organ of physical survival.

This adaptive phenomenon occurs in a number of ways as we have seen, including the change that takes place in the neuron itself as the synaptic cleft becomes physically strengthened and altered through use, and/or by an actual increase in the number of connections between cells (synaptogenesis). It was the Canadian neuropsychologist, Donald Hebb, who inspired the phrase, "neurons that fire together, wire together" (Shatz, 1992), which poetically captures an essential and basic operation of the brain. As neurons repeatedly fire, the synapses grow stronger and more permanent. Thus is learning encoded.

Now that we grasp the plastic nature of the brain, it turns out to be so widespread that we can consider it the norm rather than something extraordinary. There are three basic conditions under which it occurs: (a) when the brain, fetal through adult, is developing normally; (b) as a compensatory mechanism following injury to the central nervous system; (c) as a regularly occurring response by any individual to the particular environment with which the individual repeatedly interacts. Whereas the first condition is principally genetically derived, the latter two are more environmentally determined, since they both reflect the fundamental capacity of the brain to change with new learning.

Whatever the conditions under which it happens, there is no longer any debate about whether synaptic alterations or dendritic increases occur with continuing use. It follows that the richer the environment and the more interactions with it, the more connections form and the stronger they become.

On the other hand, the opposite of branching and strengthening can and does occur, even in normal development. We will return to this topic when we examine the impact of impoverished environments—those that offer little in the way of healthy nutrition or those lacking in novelty, supportive interaction, or challenge.

A Closer Look at Neurogenesis: Born-Again Brain Cells

Within the general study of neuroplasticity, one of the most exciting recent neuroscience discoveries is neurogenesis: the brain's ability to generate new neurons after it is well past its formative stages. Originally discovered in the mid-twentieth century, it took a few more decades of improvement in imaging techniques to finally convince skeptics that this thoroughly world-altering view of the brain was indeed a fact: the brain produces new neurons. But how?

The answer lies in the nature of so-called progenitor cells, long known to exist throughout the body but discounted as a possibility for the brain. Conventional wisdom had held to the view for over a hundred years that the brain, while losing neurons every day, was incapable of producing new ones. This began to change when scientists discovered in the early 1960s the existence of what are known as neural stem cells.

Stem cells have the unique capacity for endless self-replication, and the ones in the brain are no exception. Once they replicate, these non-specialized cells then become specialized as either neurons or glial cells. The story of the scientific proof of neurogenesis is an interesting one. To prove their existence, scientists had to develop a way to highlight and distinguish between pre-existing and new neurons. By the 1960s a way had been discovered to distinguish old from newly formed neurons, one that involved the use of radioactive stain injected into the bloodstream, where it is then taken into the brain of a live subject and subsequently absorbed into the DNA of neural stem cells—and only stem cells—as they divide and differentiate. For whereas undifferentiated stem cells absorb the stain as they divide (which then shows up in the images), the differentiated or specialized neurons are incapable of absorbing the stain. This procedure enabled scientists to see an image such as that shown in Figure 21. However, and much to the dismay of these early pioneers, their finding about the presence of new neurons was dismissed out of hand as unacceptable, so violently did it clash with the reigning mindset of the day (Begley, 2007, pp. 52-56).

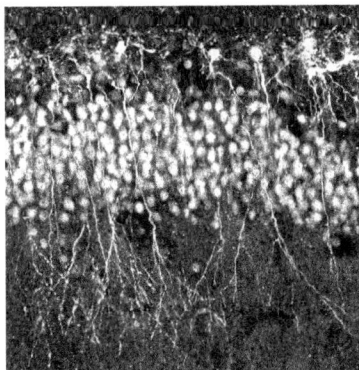

Figure 21. Neurogenesis: Stained Newly Created Neurons.
Image by Jason Snyder.

Neurogenesis was originally found to occur in the olfactory bulb (responsible for processing the sense of smell), but it has since been shown in numerous studies that the hippocampus—the area in the limbic system responsible for turning sensory information into memories—also replaces its neurons in an active manner, although at a much slower rate than during fetal development or immediately after birth. As it turns out, over the course of a lifetime, all the neurons in our hippocampus are replaced perhaps two to three times over. This is exceedingly good news for obvious reasons related to learning as well as the potential for the treatment and perhaps even prevention of Alzheimer's disease, which destroys existing cells in the hippocampus. As we shall learn in Chapter 7, there are at least two demonstrable ways to increase the number of new neurons produced each day in the hippocampus (plus a few more awaiting possible "proof").

Researchers have discovered that other sites within the brain contain neural stem cells as well. These areas include the striatum (involved in processing movement) the septum (involved in processing emotions), and the spinal cord. The cerebral cortex, where thoughts are processed, has also been shown to contain neural stem cells. Beginning with research conducted on adult macaques (monkeys that have brain structures similar to that of humans), these cells have been discovered in three cortical areas: the prefrontal, temporal, and parietal, all of which are important to cognitive functioning. This is exciting news, with exciting implications related to lifelong learning.

To temper this initial good news, it is important to note, as Doidge (2017) reports, that except for the olfactory bulb and hippocampus—areas of demonstrable replication and production of new cells—neural stem cells have so far proven to be inactive and dormant in cortical areas of the brain. Scientists are currently exploring ways to actively recruit and engage these cells. Moreover, while the evidence is clear that the promulgation of new cells most certainly plays an important role in lifelong learning, there is another angle to the emerging story. According to at least one report, "Recent studies indicate that an excess of adult neurogenesis can be as detrimental as a deficit. In some cases, the clinical relevance of increasing neurogenesis may need to be reconsidered" (Scharfman and Hen, 2007, p. 337). The authors go on to point out that in at least one instance – that of epilepsy – neurogenesis may create more problems than it resolves because of the fact that in animal studies it can lead to "inappropriate migration, differentiation, and integration of many of these new neurons." Despite this disclaimer and word of caution, the general sense in the scientific community remains wedded to the view that the discovery of neurogenesis has fundamentally and positively altered our view of the human brain and human potential.

The techniques for studying neurogenesis continue to improve. For example, a new method of identifying the presence of new neurons has recently become available. In 2007, the journal Science reported that investigators from Stony Brook University Medical Center, had discovered a way to image a particular bio-marker that would indicate the presence of neural stem cells in a living human brain (Maletic-Savatic et al, 2007). This discovery now permits researchers to monitor neurogenesis in both a noninvasive and nontoxic way for the first time ever. Originally used in studying the brains of rats, a radioactive dye can be used to highlight newly replicated cells. Researchers are fairly confident that this new technique will allow for the diagnosis and treatment of multiple sclerosis, Parkinson's disease, depression, and other disorders of the central nervous system where neurogenesis becomes disrupted. But perhaps equally important, this technology may allow various aspects of learning and development to be monitored in real time—an intriguing possibility indeed.

It should be noted that, following the research cited above, another study has been reported that contradicts the evidence for life-long neurogenesis in humans. A report issued by University of California–San Francisco (ScienceDaily, March 7, 2018) describes the findings of a team led by scientists associated with Arturo Alvarez-Buylla, "a leading expert in brain development who over the past 30 years has played a key role in convincing the scientific establishment that new neurons are born throughout life in animals such as songbirds and rodents."

In the report, Alvarez-Buylla says about the study: "We find that if neurogenesis occurs in the adult hippocampus in humans, it is an extremely rare phenomenon, raising questions about its contribution to brain repair or normal brain function."

We do not expect the controversy over neurogenesis to be solved rapidly, given that Alvarez-Buylla has already been engaged in research about it for three decades. We do expect a great deal more research to follow before anything resembling a consensus about the issue is adopted.

Even if lifelong neurogenesis in humans is disconfirmed, the research on synaptogenesis, and neuroplasticity in general, remains on solid ground. Beyond the medical implications of these findings on plasticity, pruning, and cell promulgation, it is equally exciting to consider the implications for the education and wellbeing of children. While education remains an inherently conservative societal institution, the accelerating pace of worldview-changing neuroscientific discovery will soon force us (we can only hope), to let go of outdated notions of human development and learning, while simultaneously embracing the emerging redefinitions of human potential.

Gray (Neuronal) and White (Glial) Brain Matter

While it has been known for some time that a vast overproduction of gray matter occurs during the first 18 months of life—followed by a steady decline as the unused neurons are eliminated—the late 1990's caused a completely new understanding of the process. As stated earlier, Giedd and colleagues at the U.S. National Institutes of Mental Health discovered a second wave of overproduction of gray matter just before puberty, followed by a second bout of "use-it-or-lose-it" pruning during adolescence (Giedd et al, 1999). Not surprisingly, their research found that the first areas to mature are those with the most basic functions, such as processing senses and movement. Regions involved in spatial orientation and language (parietal lobes) mature next, while the frontal lobes, responsible for more advanced functions such as reasoning, mature last. In effect, what happens during pruning is that the gray matter overproduction begins to thin, from back to front, and is simultaneously replaced by white matter (the nature and function of which we take up next). Figure 22 shows the progressive thinning of gray matter from age five through twenty. We see that even at age twenty the back of the brain has achieved a greater thinning than that of the front, indicating that full frontal development has yet to be reached; the frontal lobes remain immature even at that age.

We see that even at age twenty the back of the brain has achieved a greater thinning than that of the front, indicating that full frontal development has yet to be reached; the frontal lobes remain immature even at that age.

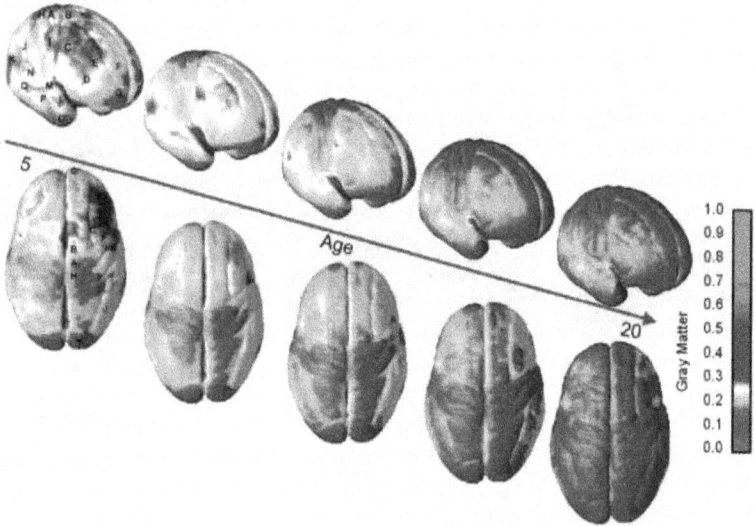

Figure 22. Gray Matter Thinning Age 5-20.
Image by Giedd et al.

As stated earlier, there are two types of brain matter: gray, which consists of densely packed neurons, and white. White matter's special properties add an important dimension to what the brain is designed (after its most basic function of looking after survival needs) to do: learn.

Whereas neurons specialize in processing information, white matter ensures that the neural networks are well connected and are capable of moving information efficiently and rapidly from one area of the brain to another. White matter derives its coloration from the myelin sheath that coats the axons (see Figure 23), and that consists primarily of fatty protein substance of which 80% is lipids.

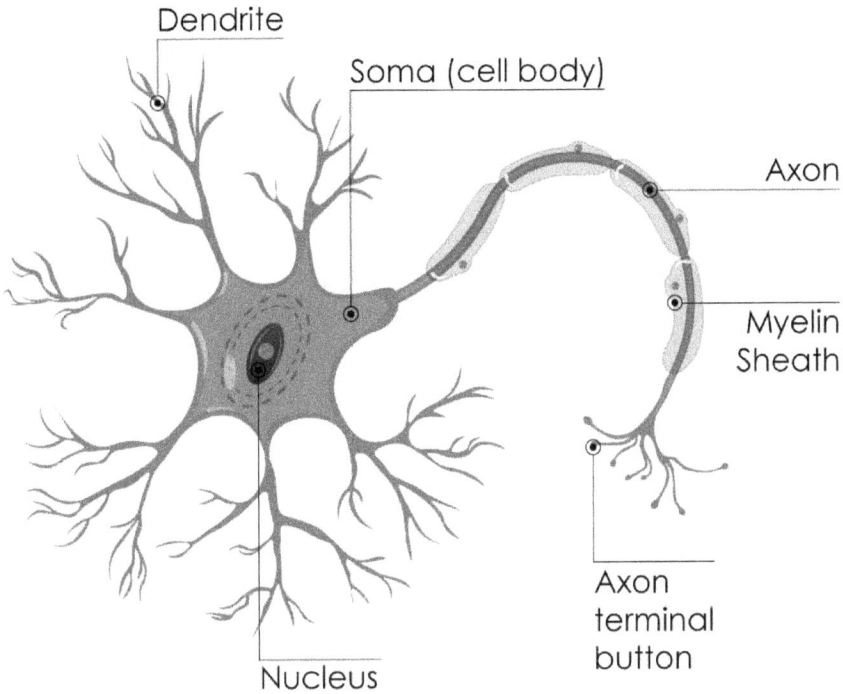

Figure 23. Neuron with Myelin Sheath.
Image by Maja Petrović/Inspired By Learning.

Both jobs, processing information and connecting the information with other areas of the brain, are crucial operations. Together they take well over two decades to fully mature. This gradual buildup of the insulating sheath of myelin permits the flow of electrical impulses to move more rapidly and efficiently. Thus, in unmyelinated fibers (those that conduct pain or temperature signals, for example), conduction velocity along the axon is approximately one-half to two meters per second (about as fast as one can walk or jog); velocity in the most thoroughly myelinated axons, however, can be as much as 70–120 meters per second (about race car speed), although the diameter of the axon can greatly affect this speed (Susuki, 2010). This 100-to-300-fold increase in conduction speed leaves no question about the adaptive role of myelin in neural functioning.

It is worth mentioning that a principle ingredient in myelin is omega-3 essential fatty acid, a dietary lack of which can have long-term consequences for the growing brain. Since omega-3 is available only in fresh, non-processed foods such as cold-water fish, cold-pressed oils, nuts, seeds and leafy green vegetables, a child born into an impoverished environment, possibly lacking the dietary substrate of sufficiently healthy fats (and perhaps very likely subsisting on processed foods, the processing of which destroys the fragile omega-3 fatty acid), is decidedly at risk for shortage of this crucial nutrient. The result can be a permanently compromised brain.

Another circumstance in which the brain can be compromised occurs when a child experiences extreme isolation and neglect. In this case the lack or wrong kind of stimulation can result in a paucity of myelinated neural networks, something that can be difficult, if not impossible, to remedy. On the other hand, a child born into a sufficiency of nourishment and nurture is allowed the opportunity to develop optimally.

Where does the all-important insulating myelin come from? Glia, a word that originates from antiquity, meaning "glue" (in Latin). Early anatomists observed, obviously without benefit of microscopes, a white glue-like substance underneath the gray strata of the cortex. They deduced that this gluey looking substance served to hold the brain together and provide support for the neurons.

But we now know, glial cells (a micrographic photo of which is seen in Figure 24) do far more than act as a passive paste. Two types of glial cells known as oligodendrocytes (found in the central nervous system) and Schwann cells (their counterpart in the peripheral nervous system) secrete myelin along the axons.

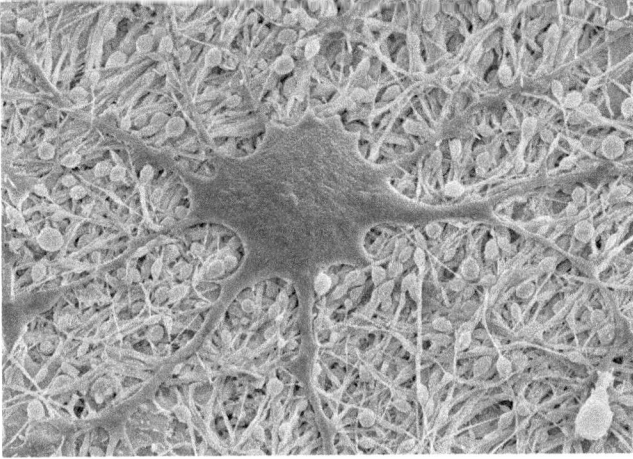

Figure 24. Glial Cells Surround the Larger Neuron.
Image by Thomas Deerinck and Mark Ellisman.

The myelin forms a sheath around the axons that is interrupted every millimeter or so by a node—a brief space with no myelin. It is this combination of insulating myelin sheaths interrupted by nodes that enables such rapid conduction compared to non-myelinated axons. Figure 25, depicts a glial cell, shown with fibers wrapped around bundled axons. The glia depicted here is an oligodendrocytes, which serves neurons in the brain (central nervous system). Their counterparts in the peripheral nervous system, Schwann cells, serve only one axon each.

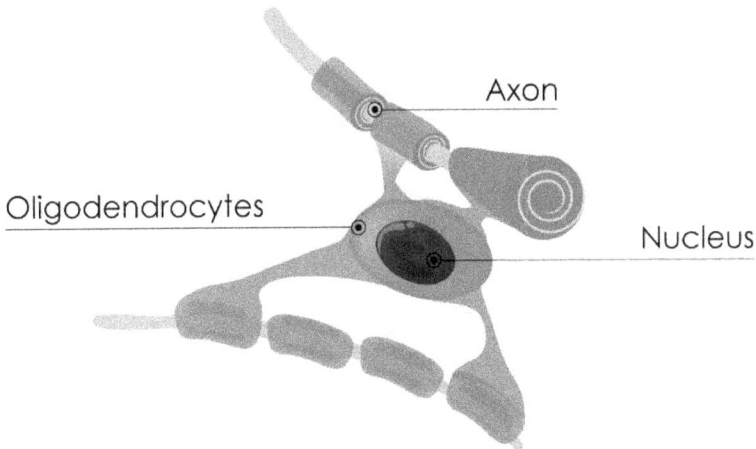

Figure 25. Glial Cell forming Myelin Sheath.
Image by Maja Petrović/Inspired By Learning.

Eventually, as the cross-section of the axon and myelin reveals in Figure 25 and the two images comprising Figure 26, the sheath begins to thicken, taking on the appearance of something akin to growth rings in a tree. At some point, further myelination is no longer needed as the axonal fiber (or, within the brain, an axon pathway consisting of thousands of fibers) has become fully functional. Babies, as we discussed earlier, are born with a certain degree of well myelinated fibers specifically involving such rudimentary responses as breathing, eye movement, and the reflexive behavior of suckling, along with certain gross motor movements such as arm waving, are all myelinated at birth. The degree is strictly a matter of genetics; a baby is effectively pre-myelinated for these abilities at birth. Beyond these basic capabilities, however, all else is determined by a gene-environment interaction.

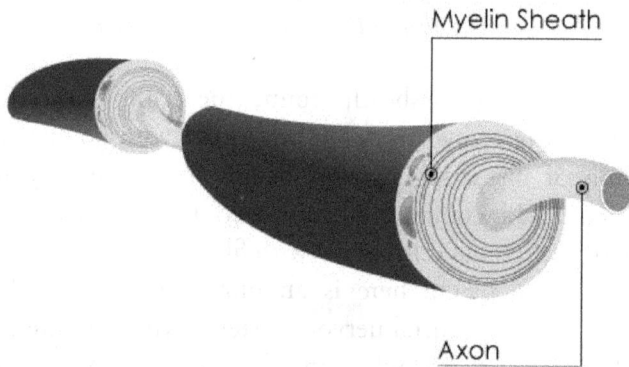

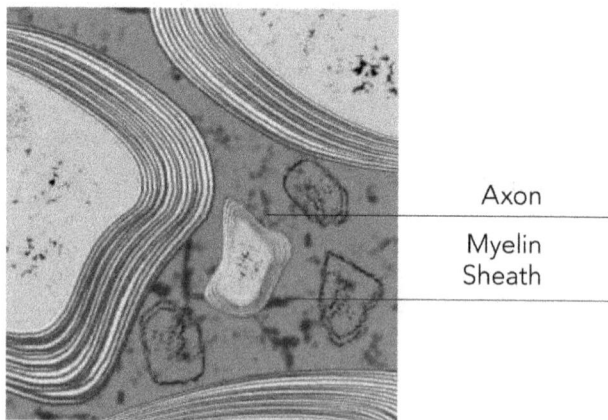

Figures 26/26b. Cross-sections, Axon and Myelin Sheath.
Images byMaja Petrović/Inspired By Learning.

Learning and Myelination:
Practice, Repetition, Variation

How does this gene-environment interaction proceed? While the details are immensely and impressively complex, the overall picture is fairly straightforward. Basically, those areas of the nervous system that are called into play by repeated usage are the ones that get myelinated. In its most straightforward and simplified formulation, this means practice, repetition, and variation, ingredients essential to all learning.

Consider any learned skill, riding a bicycle for example as most of us can recall the experience reasonably well. As children, we observed someone riding a bike, perhaps on numerous occasions. This is what Pearce called "the model imperative" (Pearce, 1992, p.20). Once the model appears and demonstrates the possibility of something new—given that the individual is sufficiently motivated to learn it—the next step is practice and repetition. As each practice session adds to the strengthening of the neural synapses—a process directly related to the formation of memories—and myelination of the axon pathways in the central and peripheral nervous systems gets well underway, we develop better and better balance and riding skills until—voila!—we become "masters of the craft." This pattern of modeling, practice, repetition, and variation is endlessly played out in the myriad of learnings that occur across a lifespan.

There is another highly important dimension to this business of insulating the axon pathways, one that is also related to the mechanism of pruning: only those axons lacking myelin are eliminated. The myelin sheaths protect their axons from being dissolved during routine pruning operations within the brain. This natural point/counterpoint—myelination or pruning—is one of the fundamental undergirding processes that determine whether a child's potential will either be become reality or remain a promise unfulfilled.

Summary and Conclusion

This chapter has examined in detail the structure and function of the brain's component cells (neurons and neuroglia), how they develop, interact, and link together in patterns, and how the cells and their patterns either thrive or fade away as the brain learns and grows. We saw how crucial the relationship of neurons and glial cells is to the fate of the vast network of neural connections.

We have seen how the brain manifests plasticity both early and late in life, and introduced the relative roles of genetic endowment and life experience (nature and nurture) in the brain's unfolding. In following chapters we will look much more closely at some of the life conditions that affect the embodied brain's health and development.

Chapter 5

The Real Brain Basics: Exercise and Sleep

"Learning, thought, creativity, and intelligence are not processes of the brain alone, but of the whole body."

– Carla Hannaford, PhD

"The students may be in school, but their brains are at home on their pillows."

– Mary Carskadon, PhD

When it comes to improving the function of the brain—not to mention improving mood, energy levels, and overall health—there simply is no substitute for proper diet, adequate hydration, vigorous exercise and sufficient sleep, the real brain basics. Neglecting any one of these can have negative consequences for the complex and energy intensive operations of the brain. Unfortunately, neglect in all four areas has become commonplace for far too many, the consequences of which run a gamut from irritability and exhaustion to devastatingly poor health. For our purposes we have chosen to omit diet and hydration from the text of this book, directing our focus instead to the topics of exercise and sleep as they are so integral to the discussion of brain plasticity and in particular neurogenesis.

The Importance of Exercise

Three Forms of Exercise

Getting the right kind of exercise in the right amount can create a banquet of benefits for each of us. There are three basic forms of exercise: strength or resistance training, stretching or flexibility enhancement, and cardiovascular or endurance exercise. Each type has obvious benefits, and a combination of the three provides synergistic enhancement for body, brain and spirit. It is left to the interested reader to learn more about (or, better yet, engage in) the first two forms of exercise. Our principal interest here is in improved brain function, and of the three it is the cardiovascular form of exercise that provides truly unique and, as well perhaps even surprising, benefits.

Benefits of Cardiovascular Exercise

By engaging in regular cardio-exercise we:

- Bring oxygen rich blood to the brain
- Elevate serotonin for balanced moods
- Increase endorphin levels for positive mood
- Improve mental clarity
- Raise brain-derived neurotrophic factor (BDNF)
- Stimulate neurogenesis

In addition, maintaining an elevated heart rate during cardiovascular exercise also acts to:

- Reduce stress
- Relieve depression and anxiety
- Improve cardiovascular health

Let's briefly survey the myriad benefits of cardiovascular exercise and then look at a reasonable formula for ensuring maximal benefits.

When it comes to oxygen, the brain is a real hog. At about two percent of our body weight, the brain easily consumes no less than 20 percent of the available blood supply. The brain is a unique organ in many ways, one being its very limited capacity to store energy. This means that to function normally it requires regular and often high amounts of glucose, blood, and oxygen, the basic mix of ingredients that optimizes brain performance.

Raising the heart-rate increases the supply of blood, and therefore oxygen, in all tissues of the body, including the brain. This enables the cells of the brain to acquire sufficient "fire" to burn the principal fuel which is glucose. This means we have greater energy, mental clarity, and—coincidentally—improved mood. The best, quickest way to get the heart-rate elevated is through exercise.

Both serotonin and endorphin levels are raised through exercise, resulting in balanced moods and an enhanced overall sense of well-being. The neurotransmitter serotonin helps to relay messages from one area of the brain to another, acting as something of a "volume control" in the nervous system. Neuroscientists refer to this function as modulation, and as such serotonin is thought to be a master control neurotransmitter—one that affects, directly or indirectly, mood, sexual desire and function, appetite, sleep, memory and learning, temperature regulation, and some social behavior.

Exercise also stimulates the release of endorphins, the body's natural painkillers, which work exactly like morphine does (both substances attach to the same neural receptors). The word endorphin is a contraction of the words endogenous and morphine. It refers to a class of molecules originating within the central nervous system and the pituitary gland, which all serve in some way to modulate neural activity, thereby affecting human experience. The effects of raising serotonin and endorphin levels are straightforward: we think more clearly, feel better, and experience a sense of enhanced wellness.

In addition, exercise sets off molecular and cellular cascades that support and maintain brain plasticity, neurogenesis, and neuronal resistance to injury and damage. In particular, exercise elevates the production of an ingredient essential to neurogenesis: brain derived neurotrophic factor, or BDNF (Cotman and Berchfold, 2002). When BDNF is sufficiently high, new neurons get created; when too low we get fewer cells. No wonder that BDNF is sometimes referred to as "Miracle-grow for the brain."

Significantly, these effects occur in the hippocampus, a brain region central to learning and memory, and BDNF availability appears to be crucial for these mechanisms. Exercise recruits experience-dependent plasticity mechanisms that prepare the brain to encode meaningful information from the environment. By combining exercise with an enriched learning environment, as we shall see in subsequent chapters, many more new neurons are apparently produced. By inducing BDNF and

Scientific studies are now strengthening the premise that exercise can benefit brain function, which is encouraging news for us all—and news that schools should most certainly use!

other molecules, exercise strengthens neuronal structure and facilitates synaptic transmission, thus priming activated cells for encoding.

The clinical literature has recognized for years that exercise affects overall health and brain function.

Suggested Formula for Cardiovascular Exercise

While not strictly scientific, the formula shown in Figure 27 provides a reasonable framework for the proper amount, intensity and duration of exercise, and is one that is commonly adhered to by those wishing to either "get in shape," or maintain a basic level of fitness. Most fitness centers have charts that depict these recommendations, or a close approximation, as well.

CARDIO-WORKOUT Heart Rate Framework

Formula: 220 beats per minute (BPM)

              ·   (minus) your age

              =

          x .65 =   Your minimum BPM

          x .85 =   Your maximum BPM.

Target range = _____ to _____ BPM   (which is 65% to 85% of your maximum)

Frequency: 5 to 6 times a week.

Duration: 40 to 50 minutes each workout

Figure 27. Cardiovascular Fitness Recommendations.
Image by Tim Burns and Jim Brown.

About the Recommendations

Perhaps something more needs to be said about the fact that there is such a wide range in frequency and duration in the above formulation. The U.S. Department of Health and Human Services has an excellent publication that describes recommendations for achieving and maintaining both basic and higher-level fitness (U.S. Department of Health and Human Services, 2008). In addition, the Centers for Disease Control and Prevention has a similar set of recommendations. In both sets of recommendations—based on a careful review of salient research and the recommendations of recognized experts—attention is paid to the fact that fitness exists on a continuum that reflects the needs, desires, and demands placed upon individuals seeking to improve their health. Because of this, the CDC, for example, offers a guideline that offers minimum through moderate levels of involvement. Thus, at a minimum, the recommendation is to partake in at least two and one-half hours (150 minutes) of exercise each week.

The World Health Organization, or WHO, makes similar recommendations to those above as the following document entitled, "Physical Activity Strategy for the WHO European Region, 2016-2025," makes clear. "WHO recommends that adults, including older people, undertake at least 150 minutes of moderate-intensity aerobic physical activity each week. The existing recommendations emphasize the health benefits of moderate-intensity activities and that the recommended levels can be accumulated in relatively short bouts of activity at a time." (World Health Organization, 30 July 2015, p. 5). It goes on to say that, "Children and young people should accumulate at least 60 minutes of moderate-to vigorous-intensity physical activity every day. A higher level of physical activity is likely to provide additional health benefits both for adults and for children" (pp. 5-6).

Sleep and All the Rest

Sleep plays a critical role in overall health and a very special role in learning. While much of the reason sleep is even needed remains something of a scientific mystery, clearly sleep plays a critical role in both early brain development and in later brain change as well.

Professor Matthew Walker, director of the Center for Human Sleep Science at the University of California, Berkeley has stated that sleep deprivation affects "every aspect of our biology" and is widespread in modern society (Walker, 2017). He considers it a modern epidemic that is implicated in a wide range of common health problems.

Sleep and Overall Brain Health

Scientists recently discovered a previously overlooked, yet critical, function of sleep and its role in maintaining brain health. According to a National Institutes of Health (NIH) study involving mice (Xie et al, 2013) researchers discovered that sleep may literally clear the mind, suggesting an altogether unexpected role for sleep in promoting health. The study is the first to show that the space between brain cells may actually expand during sleep, allowing the brain to flush out toxins that build up during waking hours.

In the study, scientists reported that—along with its well-known role in consolidating and storing memories—sleep may be also be the period when the brain cleanses itself of toxic molecules. The results, published in *Science*, show that during sleep the so-called glymphatic system (essentially a plumbing system) opens, letting cerebral spinal fluid—a clear liquid surrounding the brain and spinal cord—flow more rapidly through the brain. In the process, the fluid carries away such toxic waste as beta-amyloid, the protein associated with Alzheimer's Disease. Apparently sleep is just the thing needed to routinely clean out the brain.

Sleep and Learning

The growth and strengthening of synaptic connections occurs in the deepest, quietest periods of sleep, rendering the cortical changes that occur as a result of our experiences during episodes of learning into something we can return to and reliably call upon in the future (Yasmin, 2011). In other words, our memory system.

It is impossible to overstate the importance of adequate sleep when it comes to the consolidation of learning.

It has been shown that the degree of neuroplasticity in the brain depends in part on the quantity and quality of sleep, especially the amount of dreamless, deep sleep (Mednick and Ehrman, 2006). As Susanne Deikelmann (2011), a sleep and memory researcher at the University of Leubeck in Germany points out, short-term memory transfer and strengthening, from short-term in the hippocampus to long-term retention in the neocortex, takes place during slow-wave sleep. This is known for certain when it comes to the early, developing brain and it is highly likely that the same need is present throughout one's life span.

By examining more closely the various stages of sleep we can learn a great deal about some of the important ingredients of learning itself.

Two Types of Sleep

Neurophysiological research shows that sleep is composed of distinct stages of neural activity within the brain. In general, experts describe two types of sleep: desynchronized (dream, or D-sleep) and what is referred to as synchronized (slow-wave, or S-sleep). Just to complicate things a bit more, the former is also known as REM-sleep, which stands for Rapid Eye Movement, a characteristic of humans and other mammals discovered decades ago when scientists found a correspondence between the rapid back-and-forth movement of the eyes (while asleep) and the dream state (Mednick and Ehrman, 2006). Slow-wave sleep is also known as Non-REM (NREM) sleep, consisting of some three or four—depending on the researcher—discreet stages (see Figure 28). All these terms appear to be used fairly interchangeably at the current stage of sleep research.

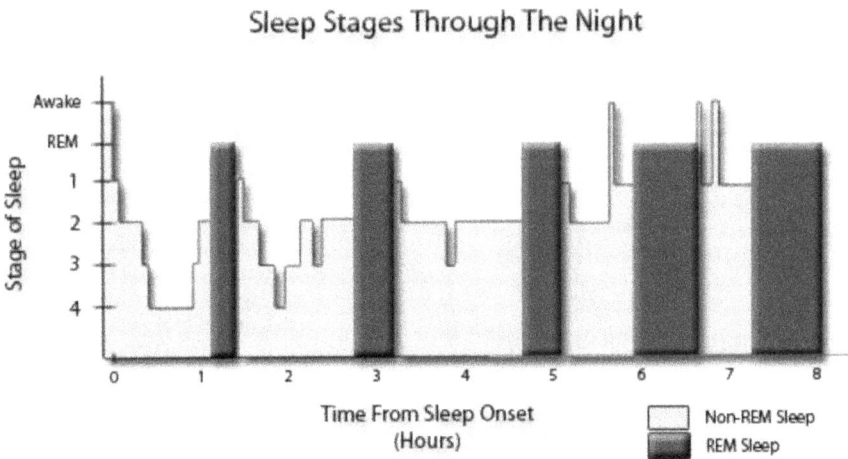

Figure 28. Stages of Sleep.
Image by I, RazerM.

Stages of Sleep and Brainwaves

Slow-wave or Non-REM accounts for approximately 75% of total sleep time, and is generally broken into four distinct phases or stages during which time brain activity as well as heart rate, respiration, and body physiology undergo important changes. At each successive stage of sleep, brain waves become progressively slower until the deepest stage of sleep is reached. Then the pattern reverses itself and sleep becomes progressively lighter until REM occurs once more.

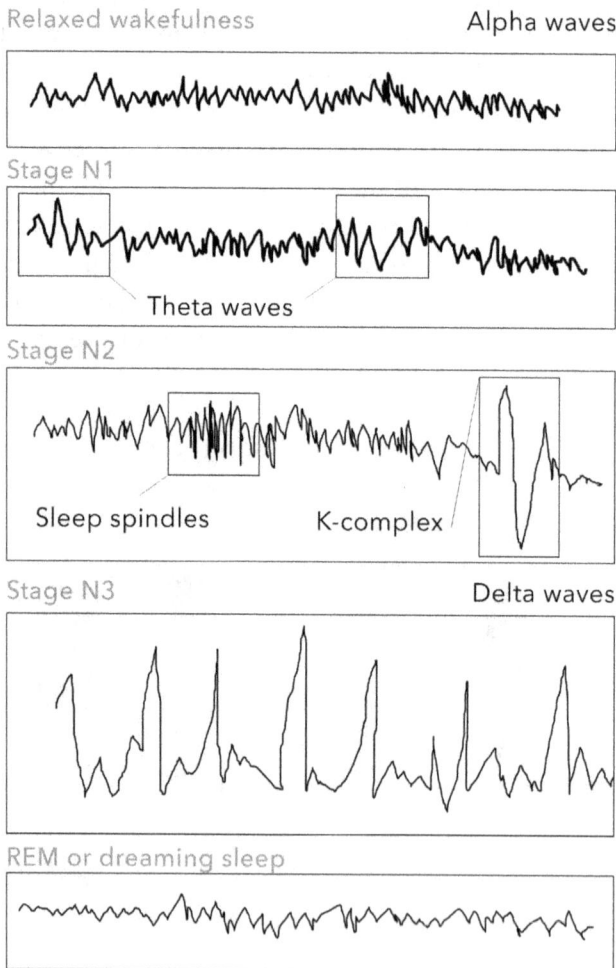

Relaxed wakefulness   Alpha waves

Stage N1

Theta waves

Stage N2

Sleep spindles   K-complex

Stage N3   Delta waves

REM or dreaming sleep

Figure 29. Electrical Signatures and Stages of Sleep.
Image by Maja Petrović/Inspired By Learning.

While sleep researchers don't always agree on the number of stages of sleep or what exactly to call them, one thing is clear: each stage of sleep has its own signature brainwave frequency (see Figure 29) and unique contribution to health, learning, and well-being. For just this reason, renowned sleep researcher, Sara Mednick, refers to these sleep stages collectively as a veritable "banquet."

Let's briefly tour each stage, using Dr. Mednick's work as a reliable guide—keeping in mind the entire cycle takes from 90 to 120 minutes, or one ultradian cycle (a topic which we will examine thoroughly in Chapter 9).

Stage One: Transitional Sleep

Often referred to as the transitional stage, the first stage of what is sometimes referred to as non-REM sleep, is precisely that: a transition from relaxed wakeful consciousness, accompanied by increased levels of sleepiness (what sleep researchers call the "sleep pressure wave") as we drift into a light stage of sleep-induced unconsciousness. This stage is hallmarked by a significant increase in alpha brain waves, with accompanying spikes of the slower theta wave, about which we will have much more to say later. For now, suffice it to say that the term "brain waves" refers to various rhythmic neuroelectric fluctuations that can be measured in the cortex and presented as EEG (short for electroencephalographic) traces. These fluctuations occur over a range of frequencies from nearly zero to about 70 Hz (cycles per second), which have been identified and increasingly well understood by science over the past 100 years or so.

Stage Two: Recharge and Replenish

More than 50% of the sleep cycle is spent in Stage Two. Evidently this stage is exceedingly important for recharging the brain, replenishing the body, and encoding specific types of memory. From a brain wave perspective, alpha waves (8-12 Hz), which increased and predominated during the transition stage, now subside and the slower, more powerful theta waves (4-7 Hz) pick up notably. As theta waves increase we experience an increase in dreamlike imagery, though it may not be the stage of REM dreaming as such. At the same time, the heart rate slows and body temperature decreases.

The benefits of Stage Two sleep are numerous. Primarily due to the rest and recuperation of key organs of the brain, including the thalamus (the relay system for all incoming raw sensations into the brain), the brainstem, prefrontal cortex (seat of the highest thinking processes), and the cingulate cortex (which helps with new learning), we awaken feeling more alert and refreshed when Stage Two sleep is plentiful.

In addition, new motor learning is encoded, important because nearly everything we learn has a motor component to it. A glance back at Figure 29 shows two of the signature phenomena of Stage Two: spindles and the K-complex. Spindles, quite numerous during Stage Two, are 12-14 Hz oscillations related to the strengthening of synaptic pathways in the motor learning networks of the brain. This is reminiscent of the famous neuroscience dictum, "Brain cells that fire together, wire together." In essence, more durable bonds are formed during this process of "welding together" neural circuits (a useful analogy for a spindle can be likened to a welder's torch fusing together two disparate pieces of metal). This business of wiring together is known as Long-Term Potentiation or LTP, both caused by and resulting in the kind of high-intensity neural firing that results in strengthened neural networks and thus new learning.

The "K-complexes" are large-amplitude EEG spikes emanating from the cortex. Appearing once every one to two minutes and lasting about a second, they are associated with a descent into slower wave activity, the hallmark of a shift into a deeper stage of sleep. Beyond that, apparently not much is known about their presence or function.

Along with new motor learning a second form of learning is also encoded during Stage Two. Known as implicit learning (also referred to as non-declarative learning) it can be thought of as that which requires no conscious effort on our part; it is acquired by a passive process of merely being exposed to information. In other words, it is unconsciously acquired learning. In addition, once something is learned passively we can recall it with no effort. Early childhood language acquisition falls into this category; it is learned without conscious effort.

Explicit learning (also referred to as declarative learning), on the other hand, is characterized by a focused, active process of seeking out the structure of any information and attempting to consciously learn and remember it. Using the example of language learning, this might entail learning a second language later in life.

Some learning theorists argue that as much as ninety percent of what we learn during the normal course of life is learned implicitly, not explicitly. They cite activities such as language learning, bicycle riding, and other complex activities, as examples of implicit learning.

These are activities that people can do automatically and well, yet are unable to explain how they do it.

It is worth noting, as Sara Mednick points out, that it isn't the simple learning tasks that necessarily require sleep to encode; rather, it is the more complex learning that necessitates sleep in order to be coded into memory.

...it isn't the simple learning tasks that necessarily require sleep to encode; rather, it is the more complex learning that necessitates sleep in order to be coded into memory.

Stage Three: Slow Wave Sleep

Stage Three, also referred to as Slow Wave Sleep, or Synchronized Sleep, is hallmarked by high amplitude (strong signals), low frequency brain waves. This means more theta (4-7 Hz) and delta (0.5-4 Hz) waves have appeared as a deeper stage of sleep is entered. All manner of important health-and learning-related phenomena occur during this stage.

For instance, cortisol levels drop to zero, meaning that the catabolic breaking down of tissues and/or foodstuff is occurring. Parasympathetic activity increases in the autonomic nervous system (below the cortex), which translates to a cessation of the stress response, and the maintenance of nervous system balance and health.

At the same time, the pituitary gland is producing human growth hormone to promote muscle and bone growth, tissue repair, protein synthesis, and metabolism of fats and carbohydrates, which helps to slim the body (it's true: weight loss while you sleep!). Overall, the body and mind are restored while decreasing stress, anxiety and the possibility of illness.

As for its role in learning, Stage Three sleep makes at least two important contributions. The first is that explicit learning is encoded. Again, explicit learning refers to those things that we are consciously attempting to acquire through attention, practice, repetition, and application. From an educational perspective, most of what is taught is school falls into this category.

The second contribution has to do with unlearning. It is thought that because we accumulate—knowingly or not—so much information and learning in a given day, the information acquired can clog the neural communication network, making it difficult to form new pathways. Fortunately, the brain has a remedy that is applied during this stage of sleep: Long-Term Depression or LTD, which dismantles responses to memories supposedly no longer necessary (not called upon), by uncoupling the neural connections upon which they are based.

Evidently, the brain regards unlearning as important as learning—not such a bad thing when we stop to consider what a burden it would be to never forget anything. There is actually a medical condition that describes this

> ...the brain regards unlearning as important as learning

malady as hyperthymestic syndrome, from the Greek thymuses, for remembering, and hyper, meaning well above normal. It describes those individuals who suffer from this baffling condition. They are apparently quite prone to depression. In any case, our learning and knowledge base, cleared of "deadwood" as it were, grows stronger and larger during Stage Three. Thus, deep sleep and learning go together in a fundamental and biological way.

Stage Four: Mostly Mysterious

While not shown on Figure 29, above, Stage Four is the deepest stage of sleep and the stage about which the least is known. Beyond the fact that production of human growth hormone continues during this stage of sleep (in itself quite important for physical growth in children and tissue repair in adults), this deepest stage of sleep largely remains a mystery to scientists. What is known is that physiological processes continue to slow, while short, fast brainwaves almost completely disappear.

After the sleeping brain rebounds from Stage Four into Stage Two for several minutes, REM (Rapid Eye Movement) sleep kicks in. And what an important stage this is!

REM Sleep and Dreaming

Approximately ninety minutes after the onset of sleep, brainwaves begin to desynchronize: an electroencephalograph would register a fast activity pattern quite similar to, although not identical with, the waking state. Accordingly, this stage of sleep is variously known as paradoxical sleep, active sleep, or desynchronized sleep.

It is marked by rapid movement of the sleeper's eyes, a discovery scientists connected with dreaming many years ago.

This period, better known as REM (Rapid Eye Movement) sleep, occurs regularly every 90-120 minutes in humans. And although the activity of the brain looks surprisingly similar to the EEG of a person in a state of wakefulness, it is in fact difficult to awaken sleepers in REM sleep, indicating that it is still a stage of deep sleep. The first REM period usually lasts five to ten minutes and the last one sometimes more than thirty.

Mednick points out that dreaming is necessary to consolidate and encode the most complex forms of learning, those that go beyond mere knowledge and fact acquisition into the realm of problem solving, synthesis, evaluation, application and the like. Clearly, dreaming plays a critical role in lifelong learning.

Further Aspects of Sleep

Stages Three and Four, sometimes referred to together as "delta sleep," dominate the slow-wave periods in the first one-third of the nightly sleep cycle, yet are often completely absent during the later part of the cycle, usually the early morning hours. This may relate to the observation that for most people, the best, most "productive" sleep occurs before the hour of midnight (by going to bed somewhat earlier at night we may feel more rested and alert the following day). Increasing progressively until it completely dominates the slow-wave period toward the end of the night, Stage Two sleep acts as a prelude to increased REM sleep and dreaming.

In other words, deep sleep cycles are increasingly replaced by shallower, quicker brain wave activity as the night progresses.

Both deep sleep and dream time are crucial to overall well-being. Research continues to reveal the effects of each on physical and mental health. Because human growth hormone is secreted during the deepest stage of sleep, one can only wonder what price we are paying in terms of health for the sleep deprivation which, according to recent surveys, is suffered by an increasing number of American adults and youths (see Figure 30).

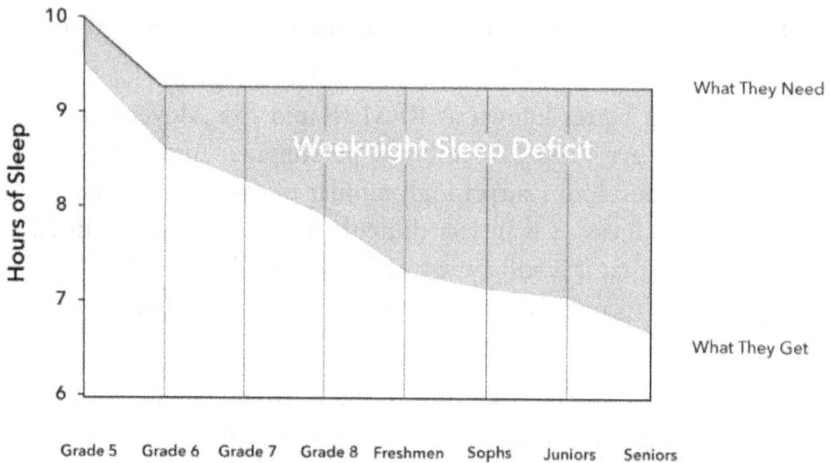

Figure 30. Sleep Requirements By Student Grade Level.
Image by Po Bronson & Ashley Merryman.

It isn't just American students either. Studies that compare childhood and adolescent sleep patterns in various parts of the world show a similar pattern of reduced hours. For example, a study by Judith Owens (2014) showed similar patterns of decreased sleep durations with increasing age among adolescents. In it we learn that, for example, in Northern Taiwan, Germany and India the average sleep duration dropped to below 8 hours for high school-aged students. Indeed, the graphic above appears to be indicative of world-wide trends.

Dreaming too is essential for well-being, for it fulfils a myriad of functions. While every animal sleeps—even flies enter a sleep-like state— only mammals are thought to have dreams. So important is dreaming that its deprivation can cause any mammalian species, which of course includes humans, to show signs of mental instability and perhaps even madness. Apparently, dreaming serves the critical function of integrating and helping to assimilate our daily experiences, most especially those with significant emotions that accompany our experiences.

In addition, dreaming appears to be absolutely necessary for learning, a special class of genes being made active in order to consolidate the recent learning as memory, while at the same time enhancing problem solving and creativity. As Rossi (2002) states, referring to two classes of genes, "Dreaming is viewed as a creative process integrating behavioral state-related gene expression with activity-dependent gene expression, and neurogenesis" (p.153). In our next chapter we further explore recent discoveries that tie together gene expression, learning, and human potential.

Chapter 6

Gene Expression, Learning, and Human Potential

"For the growing brain of a young child, the social world supplies the most important experiences influencing the expression of genes, which determines how neurons connect to one another."

– Daniel Siegel, MD

"Genes can be active or inactive, and...everything we do affects the activity of our genes....For example, genes activate the exploratory network in a child's brain, and the more enriched the child's environment, the more genes turn on, and the more the child explores."

– John J. Ratey, MD

How we understand and approach the "nature versus nurture debate" has quite a significant affect upon our worldview and expectations concerning childhood development and human potential. The debate about which holds greater sway—nature, meaning genetics, or nurture, meaning environment—has a long and interesting history. Over the decades new discoveries and opinions have pushed the pendulum back and forth. Recently the debate seems to have quieted as more scientists and lay persons alike have come to understand that both are necessary, for in truth neither works without the other. Rather than an either-or debate, it is now recognized as a both-and conversation, an ongoing dialogue between genes and environment. Every aspect of life depends upon genes and genetic expression, and genes—as it turns out—are highly responsive to the environment.

> Every aspect of life depends upon genes and genetic expression, and genes—as it turns out—are highly responsive to the environment.

New discoveries within the field of genetics offer fresh insight into the degree to which intelligence and learning are predetermined versus open-ended and changeable. The fact that the Human Genome Project revealed far fewer than the anticipated 100,000-plus (an anticipated 30,000 regulatory and over 70,000 protein-coding structural) genes came as a completely unexpected blow to those holding forth the position that human attributes (not just anatomical, but emotional and behavioral as well) were tightly controlled by genetics. Fully two-thirds of the anticipated genes necessary to uphold such a worldview simply failed to show up; they did not exist! As molecular biologist Bruce Lipton (2005) points out, the fact that the Human Genome Project "failed" to confirm this widely held expectation suggests how fundamentally flawed is the basic underlying assumption of genetic determinism as the key mechanism undergirding all life. The failure of that view, says Lipton, means that we can no longer attribute the characteristics of life expression—especially in humans, with our large brains—solely to any genetic programming.

Clearly, genetics plays an important role in all of development, and few experts would disagree with the assertion that early development is an intricate dance between nature and nurture. However, researchers are also producing new evidence that in the early years nurture, the environment, leads that dance. Moreover, and even more significantly, it is our perception or interpretation of the events comprising our lives that initiates much of the genomic expression. Thus, the latest scientific discoveries, including brain plasticity, neural pruning, and neurogenesis, have cast aside the old assumptions of genetic determinism conclusively, relegating it to the junk heap of formerly acceptable scientific dogma.

> It is our perception or interpretation of the events comprising our lives that initiates much of the genomic expression.

This is exciting news for educators and parents, and brings with it a host of new questions: just how responsive and amenable are our genes to changes in the environment? Does the environment in which a child is raised or a student educated make a difference for which genes are expressed and which are not? And how can we, as a society, use this knowledge to help our children respond intelligently, harmoniously, and creatively to the daunting challenges that lie ahead of them?

In this chapter, we delve more deeply into the forces working to shape the developing brain, with an eye towards how best to support the emergence of innate potential. We begin with a basic overview of genetics, then move into the realm of gene expression and the recently discovered mechanisms determining which genes are expressed and which are not, and why: the emerging field of epigenomics.

Genes: The Book of Life

Let's begin with the basic building block of the body, the cell; each human comprises around 100 trillion of them. Each cell works in cooperation with all the others to support our every thought, desire, and movement. Inside every cell (see Figure 31) is a nucleus where 23 pairs of chromosomes, threadlike structures that carry genetic information, are found.

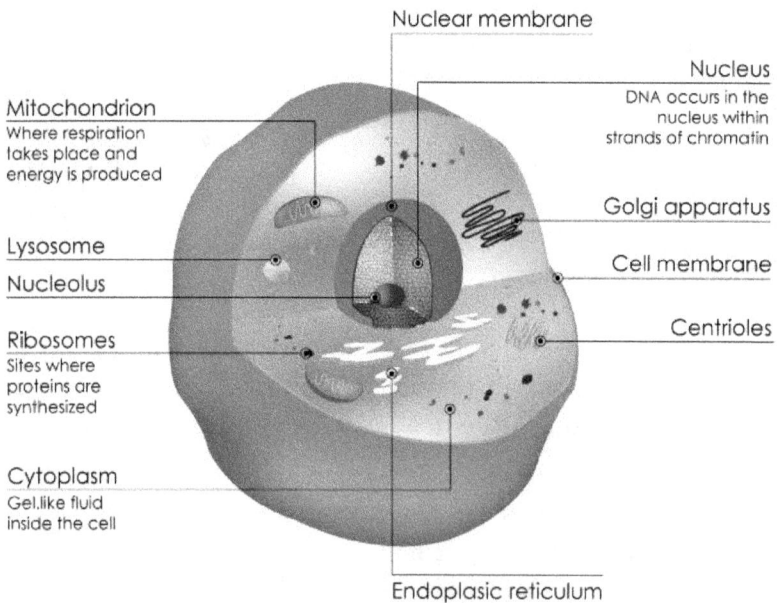

Figure 31 Human Cell.
Image by Maja Petrović/Inspired By Learning.

Tucked within each of the 46 chromosomes is the double helix of DNA, or deoxyribonucleic acid (see Figure 32).

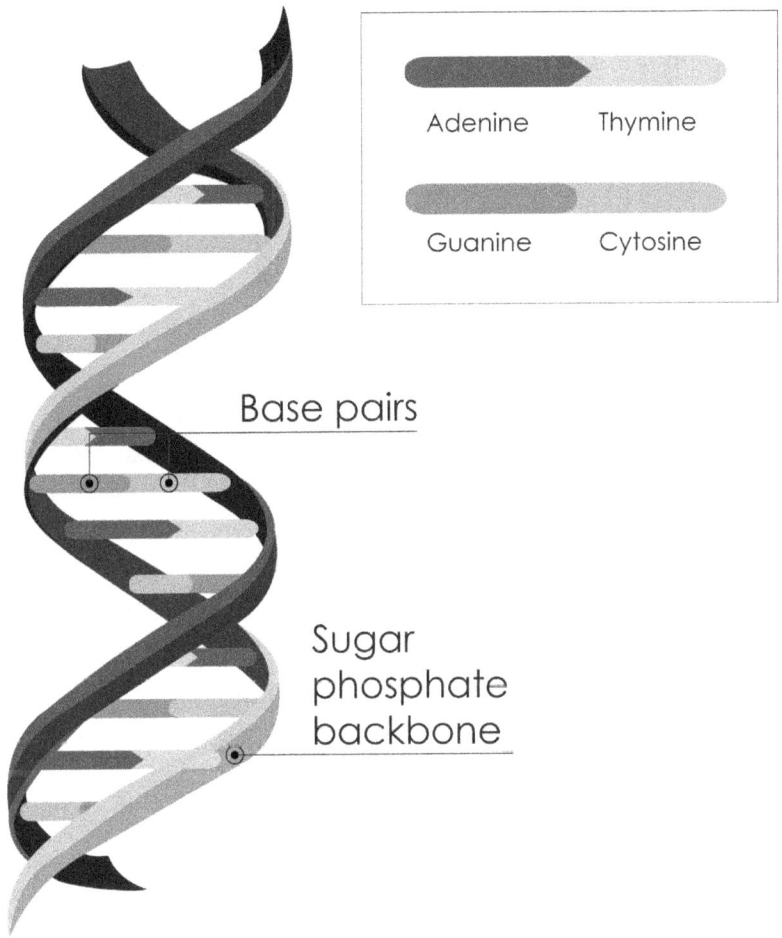

Adenine   Thymine

Guanine   Cytosine

Base pairs

Sugar phosphate backbone

Figure 32. DNA, or deoxyribonucleic acid.
Image by Maja Petrović/Inspired By Learning.

DNA is the self-replicating material and main constituent of chromosomes, the sole carrier of genetic information. Half of each pair of chromosomes is inherited from each parent, i.e. 23 chromosomes from the sperm and 23 from the egg. This double helix is so tightly coiled that if stretched out, it would reach a length of six feet!

Every strand of cellular DNA carries a copy of the entire human genome, containing all the information necessary to construct an entire human being. At present, the function of as little as three percent of our DNA is well understood. This three percent constitutes our genes. The remaining 97% has, until recently, been believed to be useless garbage, commonly called "junk DNA" by molecular biologists (Harris, 2005). However, increasing evidence points to the fact that this DNA is not junk at all, but instead has various regulatory roles other than just a transcription (duplicating) or coding one (Smith, 2005, Barry, 2007). Thus, whereas the first phase of the Human Genome Project successfully catalogued genes and their molecular structure; attention is now turning to the second, much more difficult, phase of determining their various mechanisms and regulatory functions.

The conventional view of DNA was that it does nothing more than serve as a repository of instructions, or codes, that are copied into a molecule of RNA, or ribonucleic acid. RNA, acting as a template, then delivers the DNA's genetic information to the cytoplasm, or living material of a cell where amino acids are manufactured. Amino acids in turn join to make proteins, the essential component of all organs and chemical activities of the body.

But contemporary geneticists are telling us that the environment— the nurture pole of the nature versus nurture dichotomy—is now known to directly influence the way in which genes are transcribed or made active. We will return to this point later in the chapter in the discussion about epigenomics.

Genes: Structural and Functional

Genes function in a myriad of ways, playing a role in virtually every facet and moment of our lives. Beyond determining physical traits, they are responsible for dozens of life-sustaining tasks including hormone regulation, cell replacement, immune system operation, and metabolic activity. They also play a critical role in sleep, dreams, wakefulness, consciousness, stress, learning, remembering, moods and perception. Moreover, we now know that approximately half of our genes depend upon environmental stimulation for activation. An entire branch of science called 'functional genomics' has undertaken the task of exploring how networks of genes are turned on and off In response to signals from all parts of the body, as well as the outer environment.

Ernest Rossi, one of the most accessible writer-scientists on the topic of gene expression, states that, "The popular but over-simplistic idea of genetic determinism is incomplete: it needs to be amended to include the complementary concept that human experience and behavior can modulate gene expression" (Rossi, p. 2003). He goes even further in saying that,

> Learning to do something new initiates cascades of… genomic processes that are termed activity-dependent gene expression. This special class of genes generates the proteins and growth factors that signal stem cells in the brain to differentiate into newly functioning neurons with new connections between them. (2002, p. 482)

In other words, learning something new initiates genetic processes and leads to new neurons. New neurons, in turn, can support enhanced learning. Interestingly, the opposite process seems to occur with depressive states: depression is known to slow the production of new neurons which in turn can dampen enthusiasm (the opposite affect from depression) for new learning.

Learning something new initiates genetic processes and leads to new neurons.

The human brain, as we have learned, seems capable of generating new brain cells throughout the life cycle; exercise and an enriched learning environment can increase the number of new neurons. What Rossi adds to these extraordinary discoveries is the fact that novelty (defined as new experiences associated with the generation and reconstruction of memory, learning, and behavior) can activate gene expression and lead to new neurons as well.

Novelty, as we shall see in the next chapter on enrichment, is a necessary component of all higher learning. Thus, Rossi adds a third factor known to play a role in neurogenesis, while linking them all to gene expression. This additional finding means that human experience, as in the case of learning, is inextricably bound to the underlying biological process of gene expression, and has resulted in a rather dramatic shift in the balance of the nature-nurture conversation even more towards the nurture, or environment side.

Key Discoveries from Genomics

To help orient us to the emerging knowledge on gene expression let us familiarize ourselves with the entire range of gene classes, focusing on three that undergird the emerging worldview of enhanced human possibility. Table 3 and the following discussion are from Rossi's groundbreaking book, *The Psychobiology of Gene Expression*.

TIME FRAMES IN THE ACTIVATION, FUNCTIONS and DOMAINS OF GENE EXPRESSION			
Gene expression	**Approximate Time**	**Major Function**	**Research Domain**
Evolution	Eons	Origins	Darwin
Inheritance	Generations	Replication	Mendel
Development	A lifetime	Growth	Embryology
Housekeeping	Daily	Metabolism	Functional genomics
Clock genes	Circadian	Synchronization	Chronobiology
Late activated	4 – 8 hours	Immune system	Immunology
Intermediate and early active	1 – 2 hours	Environmental responses	Psychoneuro-immunology
Behavioral state-related	Hours	Wake, sleep, dream, mood	Psychology
Activity-dependent	Minutes to hours	Memory, learning	Neuroscience
Immediate early	Seconds to minutes	Arousal, stress (and relaxation)	Psychobiology

Table 3. Domains of Gene Expression.
Image by Rossi.

Scanning down this list of gene types, one realizes that genes operate within timeframes ranging from generations (i.e., Mendelian heritability) and even eons (i.e., Darwinian evolution) all the way down to hours, minutes and even seconds. Most of us have at least a passing knowledge that genes are involved in human evolution, and that they control the inheritance of traits. We might even know that genes are involved in physical growth and development from conception onwards across the lifespan.

These tasks are structural in nature: the job of the first three classes of genes (those found at the top of the list) is largely to provide instructions for building physical features – i.e. bones, organs, eye, hair color, and so forth. They also influence personality traits and dispositions. Thus, the structural aspect of the genome is more deterministic; this is far less the case when it comes to the functional side of the equation. Take for example the following three gene types: the so-called behavioral state-related, activity-dependent, and immediate-early genes.

Behavioral State-Related Gene Expression

Different states of behavior and consciousness—waking, sleeping, dreaming, emotions, motivation, and stress—are all associated with varying patterns of behavioral state-related gene expression. This gene type fundamentally links psychological and biological processes. As neuroscientist Jeffrey Schwartz and acclaimed science writer Sharon Begley convincingly demonstrate, the brain remodels itself throughout life, in response to both passively experienced factors such as enriched environments, and also to active changes in the ways we behave, pay attention, and think (Schwartz & Begley, 2002). This means that behavioral state-related gene expression can be modulated though experiences designed to orchestrate learning, health, performance, and healing.

> The brain remodels itself throughout life in response to both passively experienced factors such as enriched environments, and also to active changes in the ways we behave, pay attention, and think.

Activity-Dependent Gene Expression

As Rossi (2002, 2003) points out, learning to do something new initiates cascades of molecular-genetic processes called activity-dependent gene expression. These cascades in turn generate the proteins and growth factors that signal stem cells living in the brain to differentiate into functioning neurons with new connections between them.

In addition, stem cells that live in tissues throughout the body receive signals that enable them to replace injured cells with healthy ones. It is important to note that this process begins within minutes or hours of learning something new!

Immediate Early Gene Expression

Genes classified as "immediate early" can respond within minutes to inner (psychological), and outer (social cues and significant life events) experiences in an adaptive manner. Rossi (2002, 2003) describes these genes as the newly discovered mediators between nature and nurture. They, like all genes, receive signals to initiate and code for the formation of proteins, which then carry out the adaptive functions within cells.

This discovery has generated one of medicine's newest fields, psychoneuroimmunology (PNI), the study of how perceptions and beliefs directly and indirectly affect the development and function of the nervous and immune systems. Setting aside for now the importance of PNI to this discussion, let's round out our exploration of gene expression by looking at an emerging field of study in genomics; one that is rapidly altering our understanding of how, exactly, nature and nurture interact and ultimately influence human adaptation, health, and wellbeing.

The Epigenome: Where Nature and Nurture Meet

It should be clear by now that the genetic activity and structure of an organism changes by way of interaction with its environment. The older dogma that genes change very little—except in the case of mutation (usually assumed to be randomly caused and rarely beneficial)—has given way to a view of genes as much more influenced by environmental stimulation than we had once believed. Subsequent to the discovery of DNA in the 1950s, geneticists turned their attention to how differences in its sequence could be tied to health and disease. Over time it became increasingly clear that a direct link between specific genes and specific biological processes related to disease (or health) were not—with very rare exceptions—going to be found. This is true in part because multiple genes are typically involved in a given biological process, which contributes to the complexity by which the ensuing mechanisms of gene expression take place. As reported by the developmental neurobiologists,

Isabelle Mansuy and Safa Mohanna (2011), "Discovering that such complexity is at play led researchers to acknowledge that the genome on its own is likely not sufficient to sustain all biological functions, and that another level of regulation is contributing" (p. 2). Enter epigenomics.

The term epigenome derives from the Greek word epi, which literally means "above" the genome. According to Laura Elnitski, chief investigator with the National Human Genome Research Institute, U.S. National Institutes of Health, "The epigenome consists of chemical compounds that modify, or mark, the genome in a way that tells it what to do, where to do it, and when to do it. Different cells have different epigenetic marks. These epigenetic marks, which are not part of the DNA itself, can be passed on from cell to cell as cells divide, and from one generation to the next." The latter discovery—the heritability factor—is redefining the field of genomics, for it has succeeded in undermining many of the earlier claims and assumptions surrounding genetic determinism, while gaining the attention of scientists (ranging from geneticists to developmental biologists), psychologists and (we can only hope) educational policy makers.

Unlike the DNA sequence, which is fixed and static, epigenetic processes are dynamic and changeable. In essence, the epigenome consists of various enzymes that modulate gene activity along two axes: by turning genes on or off and, when made active, by augmenting or diminishing their function. While the myriad biochemical mechanisms are well beyond the scope of this book, the known outcome of these complex processes is highly supportive of a central thesis addressed within it: Facilitation of optimal learning environments is the key to making active the innate intelligences of all children, not just the lucky (by dint of birth and socioeconomic status) few.

Clearly, environmental factors such as life style, stress levels, diet, toxins and drugs exert a strong influence—both positively and negatively—on the epigenome. So, whereas negative environmental factors such as traumatic events and severe chronic stress in early life can have a powerful and even lifelong effect on every aspect of health —a possible, even likely, result being heritable transmission (Mansuy & Mohanna, 2011)—positive factors such as environmental enrichment, exercise, strong interpersonal relationships (ranging from family and friends to teachers and therapists) can beneficially "mark" the DNA and boost positive outcomes for health, again, with a possible, even likely, heritable result.

In other words, epigenetically induced changes in DNA can and do remain stable across generations unless, that is, the environment changes and induces—for better or for worse—change once again. This point is brought home by the authors of the paper under consideration when they (along with many others) found in their animal studies that,

> Early stress can persistently alter the epigenome in multiple tissues and cells, and that the alterations occurring in germ cells can be maintained and passed on to subsequent generations... The correlation among early childhood experience, behavioral symptoms, and epigenetic alterations demonstrated in rodent models has also been observed in humans. (p. 6)

Coming right to the point, Mansuy and Mohanna (2011) assert that, "Early childhood experiences can influence the brain for a lifetime, but exposure to detrimental stimuli even earlier—particularly in the womb and shortly after birth—can also increase susceptibility to diseases" (p.6).

Yet the changes caused by environmental factors do not end in childhood. As the authors point out, experiences during adulthood can also profoundly modify the epigenome, an effect that has been shown in several studies of identical twins (who are, of course, born with precisely the same genome, yet who can vary significantly in their susceptibility to disease as the decades of life continue). Perhaps most provocatively, the authors assert that, "Epigenetics can change with or without environmental influence" (p. 7). While they fail to elaborate, the statement opens the door to a yet unanswered, but crucial question: What other kinds of influences might alter, for better or for worse, our individual DNA, our genome? Is it possible, for example, that an organism's perception of the environment, apart from all other factors, can initiate epigenetic alterations? If so, what about an organism whose brain is so highly evolved that the very act of perceiving—a thoroughly studied aspect of human psychology—is powerfully shaped by interpretation, conditioned bias and worldview? [1] [2]

The Role of Perception in Gene Expression

According to cellular biologist Bruce H. Lipton (2005), recent research demonstrates that a primary mechanism for the way by which environment causes genes to alter is indeed the organism's perception of the environment. Lipton makes an important distinction between lower and higher animals. Both perceive the environment, but whereas lower animals have little if any room for interpreting experience, higher organisms have a "learning bias" that exists between the environment and the organism. In other words, between the outer world and oneself are the acts of perception and interpretation, which entail taking in, making sense of, and ultimately finding meaning in one's environment. In humans, the pattern detection function of the lower brain combines with meaning-making drive of the higher brain, the result of which becomes a learning bias, belief system, or worldview.

This bias or worldview is typically very subjective; one who interprets or believes that the environment is hostile, even if it is not, will react

---

1   Quotes pertaining to the definition can be found at https://www.genome.gov/ Glossary/index. cfm?id-529

2   Op cit. Mansuy and Mohanna. A historical perspective on the issue of heritability is fascinating. As the authors of this paper point out, "although the concept of epigenetics has had a revival in the past decade, it was first discovered in the 18th century. About 50 years before Charles Darwin published his famous book *On the Origin of Species*, French naturalist Jean-Baptiste Lamarck was the first to propose that surrounding conditions can modify characteristics acquired during a person's lifetime, and those characteristics can be passed on to the offspring. According to Lamarck's theory—which his contemporaries largely overlooked and even criticized—a person's make-up can change within a generation depending on environmental factors. As it turns out, this postulate forms the basis of the underlying principles of epigenetics and provides a conceptual framework for the question of how the environment impacts an organism and its offspring. Because this concept is so fundamental to the understanding of biological functions, some scientists proposed that Lamarckian principles be integrated into evolutionary theory. This remains a disputed issue, however." I (TB) find this to be utterly fascinating since, in my first college science classes in the early 1960s, I recall one teacher openly ridiculing Lamarck and castigating anyone so stupid as to believe in his assertions. How things do change!

stressfully. Given that belief, genetic expression—always dynamically interactive—will alter to accommodate the resulting perception, producing changes in the brain chemistry and body physiology designed to facilitate adaptation to the surmised hostility in the environment.

This finding has enormous implications. In our media-saturated day and age, our perceptions are overly affected if not overwhelmed by media input—what Richard Louv (1991) refers to as life inside the electro-media bubble—a powerful force that impacts upon and shapes our perceptions at least as much, if not more, than the worlds of social interaction and nature.

Children's brains, being the most vulnerable to impression, are particularly affected by the increasing amount of "screen time." Why? Because our system of education, parents and peers—in a word, culture— inevitably shapes our take on reality. The well-being of any offspring, be it human or other mammal, is therefore related to how it interprets the environment and this interpretation, according to Lipton, has a greater effect on biophysical processes than the actual environment itself.

Gene Expression and Creativity

Here, then, is some of what is known about the nature/nurture/ gene expression interplay related to the development of the brain:

- Our genetic endowment combines with experience to determine the degree to which we can tap our innate potential as adults.
- Environment modifies genetic expressions—both for better and for worse—through the mechanism of epigenetic process.
- Experiences in childhood influence brain growth through a process called gene transcription, which affects how genes are rendered active.
- Interaction with the environment can produce adaptive or maladaptive changes in gene expression.
- Positive experiences (nurturing) can make active genes that synthesize new proteins and that, in turn, can strengthen healthy neural connections, promote learning, and prompt a healthy immune response.

- Negative experiences (threat) can induce a cascade of chemical and hormonal changes in the brain that impede the development and integration of various brain systems as well as undermine health in both the short and long terms.
- Attentional systems within the central nervous system mediate changes in the brain, for better or worse: that which we pay most attention to has the greatest influence on our personal beliefs or worldview.

In summary, it is the scientifically demonstrable triad of novelty, cardiovascular exercise, as discussed in Chapter 5, and environmental enrichment (at the very least) that prompts activity-dependent gene expression to reconstruct the physical brain and the way it works.

Closely associated with novelty is creativity; hallmarked by a highly motivated state of consciousness, creative activity can turn on and focus gene expression, protein synthesis, neurotransmitters, and neurogenesis. Therefore, finding outlets for creative expression should be a high priority in our daily work of building a better brain.

This principle is especially important when considering the developing brains of children and teens. Within mere minutes of engaging in novelty associated with a positive sense of curiosity and wonder (typified by any creative, inventive act involving the hands, heart, and head), activity-dependent gene expression occurs. And this, perhaps, is the ultimate benefit of what the new biology teaches us: that we have the power to recreate our very beings at a cellular level.

Chapter 7

The Brain and Environmental Enrichment

"Overstimulation does not lead to continued brain development."

– Marian Diamond, PhD

"A lengthening of childhood, as society increases in complexity, is essential to progress. Lack of poise, self-control, power of concentration, purposefulness, and inability to adjust socially are the most striking evidences of one-sided development."

– Marietta Johnson

Setting the Stage: The Early Studies

Several times in our journey thus far, we have touched upon the notion of environmental enrichment. We take up that thread now and weave it into the tapestry of our overarching theme: achieving a clearer understanding of elements within the course of childhood development that either impede or support the balanced unfolding of innate human potential. What exactly is environmental enrichment, why is it so important to understand, and how does it relate to childhood brain development and adult brain plasticity?

As we have seen, prior to 1960 the brain was considered by scientists to be completely incapable of change beyond the earliest years of life. Moreover, the brain was assumed to be completely beholden to genetic control. A corollary belief also dominated conventional wisdom of the day: that intelligence was fixed by genetic control and had nothing whatever to do with the environment (a belief that has subsequently been stood completely on its head). This made sense, given the prevailing assumptions, since intelligence was thought to be derived from the immutable brain.

In the 1940s a Canadian neuropsychologist, Donald Hebb, had undertaken research on rats to better understand what, if any, changes might be possible when environmental conditions are different. Hebb famously took some of his experimental rats home from the McGill University lab at which he worked. He took note of the fact that the rats who had been handled and played with by Hebb's children—and evidently left to explore the house on their own—ended up being noticeably more curious and far more likely to engage in exploration than their counterparts left behind in their sterile lab cages. The take-home rats were considered by Hebb to have been raised in "enriched environments." Hebb, however, did not study this curiosity further, and it was left to scientists like Marian Diamond and Mark Rosenzweig at the University of California in the 1950s to pick up the trail.

Independently of one another, both of these scientists set out to explore what Hebb had inadvertently happened upon: that the mammalian brain is capable of change in response to the environment. Their findings clearly demonstrated that when compared to rats raised in impoverished environments—in which playmates and playthings were lacking—the rats raised in enriched environments had both heavier brains and thicker cortices in certain regions of the brain.

The Overthrow of Old Dogma

Later, William Greenough at the University of Illinois showed why this could occur in the brain. In the 1970s, Greenough (Hirsh-Pasek & Golinkoff, 2003) was able to demonstrate that the enriched rats had a measurably higher ratio of synapse-to-neuron, resulting in a greatly enhanced ability to run mazes effectively and efficiently. In other words, the enriched rats were smarter. Figure 33 illustrates findings from a 2003 study of rat brains. New neurons show up as black dots. The marked differences in the quantity of new neurons in populations raised in different environments are obvious. The control group, raised in non-experimental circumstances, clearly showed the presence of new hippocampal neurons. However, the quantity was significantly less than in the brains of rats raised in environments capable of providing both enriched experiences and routine cardiovascular exercise. Moreover, and perhaps even more importantly, because the rats were kept isolated, with no means of being stimulated by novelty, feedback and challenge, those scant new neurons that were produced predictively failed to "wire-in" since they were not being utilized for new learning.

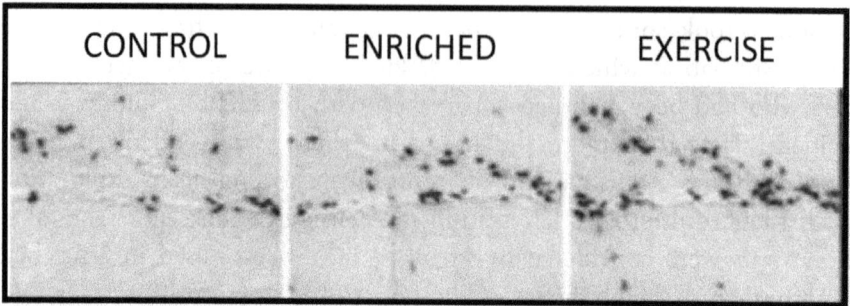

CONTROL	ENRICHED	EXERCISE

Figure 33. Hippocampal Neurogenesis: Three Environments.
Image by U.S. National Library of Medicine.

Marian Diamond (Diamond & Hopson,1999) was among those who were able to demonstrate empirically what happens at the level of branching or synaptogenesis, with her groundbreaking discovery that the number of branches emanating from a given neuron change considerably depending on whether or not a rat is raised in an impoverished or an enriched environment. Turning to Figure 34, two things are notable in the illustration. One, along the various branches of the dendrites can be seen tiny spines that comprise what amount to "docking stations" for the axon terminals (an enlarged view of which is illustrated in Figure 35). Two, notice the branch in Figure 34 with the numbers, 1-6 (in the middle and to the right of the neuron). This is meant to illustrate the results of an enriched environment on the growth of dendritic branching, for it was Diamond's seminal discovery that rats raised in stimulation-poor environments had only the genetically pre-programmed first through third branches; only those rats raised with the basic mix of factors related to enrichment (to be delineated below) had the higher order branches, numbers four through six.

Why is this difference so important?

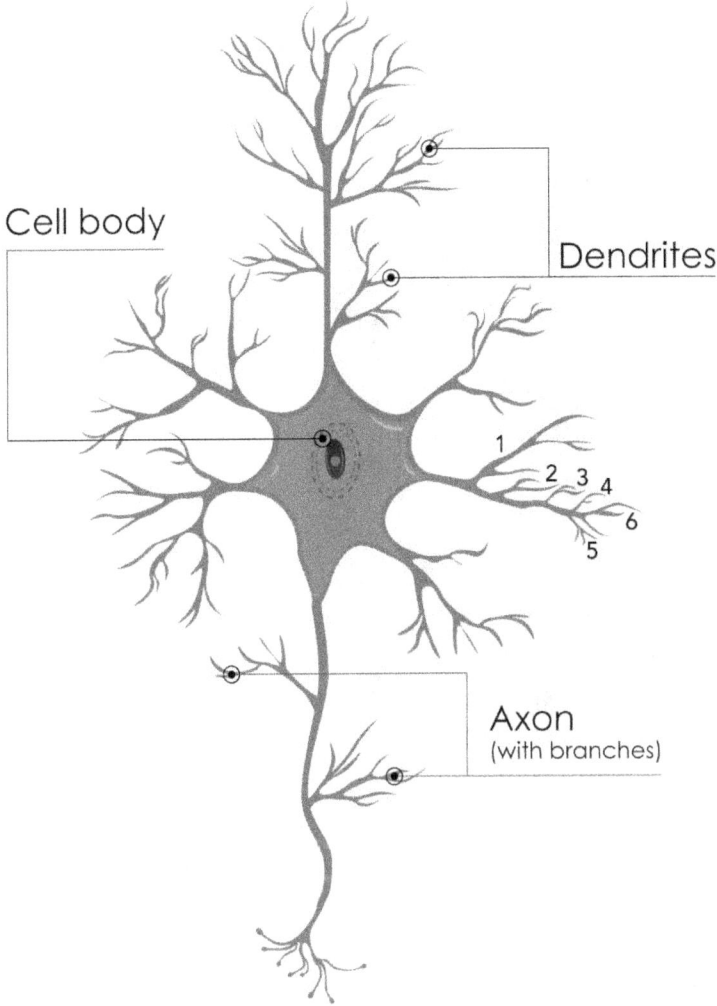

Cell body

Dendrites

1
2 3 4
6
5

Axon
(with branches)

Figure 34. Dendritic Branching.
Image by Maja Petrović/Inspired By Learning.

Remember that on any individual neuron there are numerous dendritic branches, each of which further branches and branches again. Also keep in mind that the total number of connections that each individual neuron is capable of can number in the tens of thousands. What happens when, due to impoverishment, a rat has access to but a few branches? Well, the trials showed that they were consistently far less adaptive and smart than their counterparts who had enjoyed the enriched environments.

Upon closer microscopic inspection the difference in environments seems to make its own case. Figure 35, shows in clear detail the difference.

Standard   Enriched

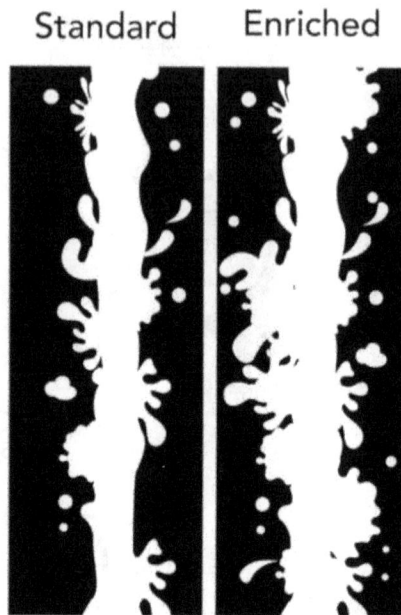

Figure 35. Standard Versus Enriched Dendritic Spines.
Image by Maja Petrović/Inspired By Learning.

When the "standard" environment is compared to the "enriched" it is obvious that there is an apparent difference in the number of spines and therefore possible connections that can be made in the brain. While it is always prudent to resist the temptation to extrapolate from rats to humans, it is still possible to speculate in a general sort of way. It is not a great stretch to say that humans either suffer or benefit from the differences related to an impoverished environment on the one hand and enriched on the other.

Citing ongoing research on enrichment with direct implications for humans, Diamond refers to research on the measurable differences in a crucial area of the brain related to language development in both college-educated and high school-educated individuals, demonstrating that dendrites grow in response to environmental stimulation (Diamond, 2001).

Dendrites grow in response to environmental stimulation

Research such as this on humans has both confirmed and extended the finding that in the area of the cortex responsible for understanding speech (Wernicke's Area), higher levels of education resulted in more fourth, fifth, and sixth-order branching of the dendritic trees. Not surprisingly it appears that by learning and using more words and complex ideas, more complex growing and branching of dendrites occurs in the corresponding areas of the brain.

This particular finding also set the stage for a complete upending of that other long-held dogma of psychology: that the intelligence quotient, better known as I.Q., was a genetically predetermined and quite fixed entity. In fact, I.Q. has been conclusively shown to be directly related to language acquisition, which stems directly from how much language exposure a child has before a certain age, perhaps as young as three years of age (Hirsh-Pasek & Golinkoff, 2003).

Interestingly, some of the rats from the impoverished environments (one rat in a cage, no playmates and no playthings) were placed by one of Diamond's graduate students—still in the cage—into the enriched environment of the more fortunate peers. In other words these poor fellows could only watch from the cage the interesting things going on, not participate in the stimulating activities. Not only did the caged rats get absolutely no neural benefits, they lost ground neurally speaking. Evidently benefitting the brain is not achieved as a spectator sport; nature demands active involvement to improve the brain. In the intervening decades, an intense and heated debate about the effects of screen-time on the growing brain can trace its genesis to this kind of early finding.

Linking Enrichment to Plasticity and Neurogenesis

The demonstrable fact that environmental enrichment is capable of modifying the structure of the brain launched the quest to prove what every knowledgeable scientist now holds to be axiomatic: the mammalian brain—and most especially that of humans—is plastic by nature. As Diamond and Hopson (1999) put it, "The message is clear: Although the brain possesses a relatively constant macro-structural organization, the ever-changing cerebral cortex, with its complex micro-architecture of unknown potential, is powerfully shaped by experiences before birth, during youth and, in fact, throughout life" (p. 2). This also means, however, that the opposite is true. Diamond concluded: "The brain's outer layer can grow if a person or animal lives in stimulating surroundings, but the zone can shrink if the environment is dull or unchallenging."

It was the neuroscientist Fred "Rusty" Gage who deserves credit for what is perhaps the most significant discovery about what we have come to call enrichment: that rats raised in environments most like those of the natural world show an increase in the number of new neurons (Begley, 2007). Equally as important, the survival rate of the new neurons grown by these rats was unexpectedly higher. This is important, for getting new neurons, as we showed in Chapter 4, isn't enough; the new neurons must wire in to be of any use. Gage's work demonstrated that the new neuronal formation and survival rate was about 15 percent higher in the hippocampus, the area of the brain involved in learning and memory, when rats are engaged in enriching opportunities, as compared to control rats whose possibilities for learning were nearly completely curtailed. Moreover, Gage later demonstrated that it wasn't just in young mice that neurogenesis occurred, but in the brains of old mice as well. It turns out that stimulation at any age counts!

Research such as that described above confronts us with vital questions about the design and development of the brain: what exactly (and to what extent) are we, as a species, genetically preprogrammed or predetermined for (the constancy factor); and what are we not preprogrammed for (the changeability or malleability factor)? The answer, from a neuroscience perspective, lies in two highly interrelated processes that have evolved to ensure both adaptability and constancy in the species.

Experience-Expectant Versus Experience-Dependent Process

As we have seen, from the time that the brain begins to form, three months into gestation, it is genetically primed to establish connections or synapses. If the synapses are not formed and strengthened at the proper time, the potential to connect eventually withers away and the neurons are unceremoniously pruned and eliminated. How does this shift from genetic to environmental predominance come about? Scientists have a good idea as well as a clear explanation.

Our species has evolved with an "expectation" that the brain will receive the required stimulation at the requisite time to bring a given brain function into play—referred to as *experience-expectant process*. Experience-expectant process holds true for basic physiological functions, especially hearing. Even language—far from being a "basic" physiologic function—is subject to the same requirement of experience expectancy.

A number of well documented cases have been reported of children raised in situations of extreme isolation, either in the wild (so-called feral children) or through malicious intent. These cases illustrate the nature of capacities that are genetically primed but environmentally triggered. Let's look at two cases concerning language development. In his 1976 book, *The Wild Boy of Aveyron*, Harlan Lane (1976) tells the story of Victor, a boy found in the woods of rural France in 1800. Victor was 12 or 13 at the time of his capture, and was cared for by Jean-Marc Itard, who wanted to teach Victor to speak and socialize normally. Itard was able to do much to help Victor, but Victor never learned to speak, although he was capable of mastering a few simple phrases. Cases like this have been taken to support the existence of a critical period during which a child must receive exposure to language in order to develop full-blown linguistic abilities.

Another oft-cited case in the critical period hypotheses—perhaps the most famous case of childhood isolation—is that of "Genie" (Persell, 1990). This girl was discovered at age 13, having been locked in a dark closet for most of her life. Genie had little exposure to language or any outside stimulation during her isolated childhood. When she was rescued, Genie was undernourished, and had no language or social skills. Though she improved in many areas with the help of researchers, her difficulties with language persisted. Genie was able to learn many words, and even developed the ability to communicate with those around her. However, she never mastered syntax, and would constantly confuse word order, tense, etc. Thus, while some rudimentary elements of language learning are possible after puberty, full language learning appears not to be.

Does the notion of experience expectancy and criticality apply to other areas of development as well? The evidence that it might apply remains less clear-cut than the cases cited above would suggest. What is better supported by contemporary science is the related construct of "experience-dependent process."

Recall the previously discussed findings by William Greenough regarding the effects of impoverished versus enriched environments on rats—and their differing influence on aspects of brain development. His findings prompted him to propose a distinction between two types of information storage in the brain, both induced by the environment. In so doing, he made clearer how experience-expectant and experience-dependent processes work in tandem, as complementary processes.

As Greenough formulates it, experience-expectant information storage (the more genetically determined kind) involves aspects of the environment that are common to all members of a species and is achieved by pruning neural connections, whereas experience-dependent information is unique to each individual and is stored by growing new connections. Thus, a dual process is at work, both sculpting (again, think of Michelangelo removing marble in the process of revealing a sculpture of David) and building (think of a sculpture built up using clay), a complementary dyad of information storage processes that are most dynamic throughout childhood and adolescence.

The development of vision, hearing, and language are examples of biologically based perceptual and learning mechanisms that are beholden to the rule of experience-expectant process; all other learning is governed by experience dependent process. In other words, the vast majority of what we learn across a lifespan is the result of, and dependent upon, interactions taking place within a specific environment. Children in a Spanish speaking environment, for example, learn Spanish, not German; those raised in environments in which people around them read a great deal tend to be better than average readers; and those exposed to the arts early in life tend to be more creative and expressive.

Experience-dependent process was one of several discoveries that shifted the balance in the nature-versus-nurture debate more toward the nurture, or environment, side of things. While it held considerable sway for generations, the view that some children can be expected, based solely on inborn traits, to become able learners and productive workers while others were destined to dimmer futures, is no longer tenable. The assertion that experience and education, while helpful, simply could not be expected to overcome nature's preset genetic limitations is now thoroughly discredited.

The assertion that experience and education, while helpful, simply could not be expected to overcome nature's preset genetic limitations is now thoroughly discredited.

Learning, Enrichment, and Neural Enhancement

From a neuroscientific perspective, the past half-century has proven that new learning involves gene expression leading to the formation of both new synaptic connections and new neural networks. As such, an enriched environment adds the following to neurons:

- Larger cell bodies
- Greater dendritic branching
- Enhanced glial production
- Increased quantity of synapses
- Multiple contact areas (the spines)
- Increased neurogenesis at multiple brain sites.

This is all very good news indeed. However, there is a cautionary tale yet to be told. The caution stems, in part, from the less well-known discovery by Rosenweig that rats left in nature have the best, most amazing brains of all (Hirsh-Pasek and Golinkoff, 2003). Left to their own inclinations and predilections, in combination with the naturally stimulating worlds of nature and rat society, their brains consistently helped them to perform even better than those of the rats raised in so-called enriched (albeit laboratory) environments. What do we make of this, beyond the obvious conclusion that the combined worlds of nature and society offer up the best possible way of organizing a better brain?

Well, for one thing, a few million years of surviving and thriving in the natural and sociocultural worlds—while passing along the adaptive genetics—has proven to be a peerless way to successfully raise generation after generation (tens of thousands of generations in fact) of human beings. And, as the old expression has it, it's not a good idea to mess with Mother Nature!

Yet here is the real point: The human brain builds itself; it is what the so-called "new" biology calls a self-organizing system. That is, the brain, in its marvelous complexity, is evolutionarily designed to adapt to virtually any circumstance—natural, social, cultural—in which it is likely to find itself. And whereas experience-expectant process requires both early life stimulation and interaction to fulfill the species-wide expectations, experience-dependent process operates at another level entirely. The experiences upon which the latter process depends are spread out over a lifetime and are entirely individualized. No two individual brains are alike, each perceives, interprets, responds according to its predilections and dictates. In effect, experience-dependent process is the way by which the brain self-organizes and builds itself in interaction with the environment.

The best news is this: other than a safe and nurturing environment and the innate curiosity with which every child comes fully equipped, nothing special is required to set this self-organizing process in motion.

The best news is this: other than a safe and nurturing environment and the innate curiosity with which every child comes fully equipped, nothing special is required to set this self-organizing process in motion. Combine novelty and curiosity with the experience-dependent nature of nearly everything we learn across a lifetime, from language to reading, to playing a musical instrument, to checkers, dance, writing, learning mathematics, balancing a checkbook, making love, riding a bike, driving a car, then add a measure of challenge, plus a healthy portion of feedback and—voila!—we have the formula for enriched learning. It sure isn't anything fancy or mysterious; after all, as a species we've been succeeding at this for a good while.

So, there it is, in summary form. The enrichment research revealed over half a century ago that four conditions were nonnegotiable, and they are: the absence of threat (some stress, as we shall see, however, is fine) and the presence of novelty, challenge and feedback. Since that time other criteria have been added and we will get to that momentarily.

The Nature of Threat

Before going further, it would be best to clarify the meaning of threat in a more nuanced way. The mammalian brain comes marvelously equipped to sense and respond to danger and, apart from obvious threats such as predatory animals that would have played a crucial role in the evolution of the human brain, there are two categories of emergent danger that can threaten the proper development of the human brain. One is the absence of the kind of stimulation required to initiate experience-expectant process. This is an obvious problem for those unfortunate enough to suffer it. Fortunately, the brain is fairly resilient; it's almost as if we have to work fairly consistently and hard, and to go out of our way to thwart human development. Not that this doesn't ever happen, but at least in theory it's preventable.

The other kind of danger—in some ways under-appreciated for all its potential for actual harm—is too much stimulation. This could well have been what Marian Diamond (1999) had in mind when she famously said, "The typical American child does not grow up in an enriched environment" (p. 5). She is referring to the fact that healthy childhood development is under growing threat from technological incursion. Nor is this the case for American children only; increasingly this could be said of childhood throughout the developing world, given that children spend entirely too much time deprived of the gene-priming worlds of nature and culture, and entirely too much time enveloped in the potentially gene-altering surrogate of so-called "virtual reality."

As one of the world's foremost experts on brain development, Diamond correctly diagnosed the problem inherent in exposing children's brains to such a restricted reality. Warning that as technology enters that might focus children in narrow channels, it is of utmost importance to keep in mind the need to develop what she called whole-brain factions. We are, she emphasized, multi-sensory and as such we require an integrated brain that can ready us to handle the problems of this complex world; this, rather than narrow focused learning which results from overuse of powerful and alluring screen technologies.

Diamond's admonition three decades ago seems prescient when considering the explosive scope and scale of current screen-time usage among children today. As Aric Sigman, PhD, psychologist and Fellow of the British Royal Society of Medicine more recently states, "Too much screen time too soon is the very thing impeding the development of the abilities that parents are so eager to foster through the tablets. The ability to focus, to concentrate, to lend attention, to sense other people's attitudes and communicate with them, to build a large vocabulary—all those abilities are harmed."[3]

The Overly Stimulated Brain

Returning to the issue of over-stimulation as a threat to healthy, balanced development, recent findings have added a new element of concern in the ongoing debate about screen technologies and the developing brain: whether or not overuse of electronic media can be considered an addiction. The argument that these powerful technologies can induce an addiction derives from two well developed sources of knowledge: the function of dopamine in the brain and the defining characteristics of addiction.

A major player in our primary motivation and reward system the multifaceted neurotransmitter, dopamine, triggers feelings of pleasure—nature's way of ensuring that any behavior supportive of survival will be repeated. Thus, dopamine is released in goal-oriented, primary pursuits such as eating, eliminating, mating, and even moving; but it isn't limited to primary pursuits. Functioning as a powerful stimulant and following the internal mandate of the brain to pursue survival-oriented rewards, when dopamine gets activated a behavioral blueprint gets inscribed into the neural networks, making that particular behavior more likely to occur in the future. Thus, whenever a screen is swiped or an internet link clicked, an immediate dopamine-driven sense of gratification takes place. And, as we have discovered, in the vulnerable developing brain such immediate gratification can easily prevail over vital real-world, natural connections and social interactions.

While the growing and heated debate will likely not be settled anytime soon, one thing is known for certain: each time a computer is clicked or a screen swiped, the neurotransmitter dopamine is released. That this less than natural process continues to involve more and more of our daily lives is inarguable. And it is getting harder to argue against findings that bring attention to myriad consequences ranging from media addiction to so-called "digital dementia," a term coined by Manfred

---

3 Quoted in *Psychology Today*, April 17, 2016. https://www.psychologytoday.com/us/blog/behind-online-behavior/201604/what-screen-time-can-really-do-kids-brains

Spitzer, MD, PhD, medical director, Psychiatric University Hospital, Ulm, Germany, and editor-in-chief of the journal, *Trends in Neuroscience and Education.*

Spitzer (2012), author of *Digital Dementia: What We and Our Children are Doing to our Minds,*[4] puts forth a number of compelling arguments based on various lines of research that suggest troubling alterations in neural development in young children extensively exposed to electronic media; children whose average screen-time diet, including at school, approximates an astonishing seven hours daily.

Directly addressing the issue of over-stimulation, Spitzer was among the first to make the connection between the effects of blue-light technologies (television, computer, iPad and iPhone screens) and excessive cortisol levels. This hormone, recall, when chronically elevated has been shown to be toxic to newly forming and existing neurons, as a result of which gray matter shrinkage in both the cortex and the hippocampus have been observed.

The Addiction-Prone Brain

The concern that electronic media can foster an addiction, strictly speaking, depends upon how one defines an addiction. At one time limited to descriptions of physical dependence on mood-altering chemicals such as alcohol, opiates and so forth, medical science and in particular the field of addictology have made significant strides in describing the three main alterations in nervous system function that define the classic signs of an addiction: increase in tolerance, withdrawal, and physical craving. These signs, as most everyone has come to understand, have everything to do with altered levels of dopamine, for drugs release the dopamine stored in the nervous system, which in turn triggers the mood change.

As other forms of chemical use became more mainstream—namely marijuana and psychedelics in the nineteen-sixties—the definition of what constitutes addiction required modification, principally because use of these substances do not show any of the three classic signs. Yet in

---

4   While not yet translated into English, there are many references to the book's contents. See for example, *Psychology Today* online, https://www.psychologytoday.com/us/blog/behind-online-behavior/201604/what-screen-time-can-really-do-kids-brains.

spite of that fact it is clear that some individuals become dependent upon them in a way that is clearly interfering with their wellbeing and health; but the dependence is psychological, not physical.

Thus, by the nineteen-seventies addictologists had expended the model to include three primary characteristics of psychological (also, thought of as behavioral) dependence: loss of control, compulsion or obsession, and continued use in spite of harm to oneself or others. By the Eighties, as advances in neuroscience, behavioral science, addiction treatment and imaging technologies were brought to bear on the study of addiction, a compelling argument was made that not only were mood altering chemicals addictive but also certain behaviors, gambling for example. And while one could debate whether or not food, exercise, pornography, or even moods could be "addictive," at least a standard now exists by which such a determination can be made.

So, is there such a thing as addiction to electronic media? Decidedly, yes, if we measure the behavior against all six criteria (but most especially the latter three): i) needing more and more stimulation to get the same level of desired mood alteration (increase in tolerance), ii) withdrawal as the store of dopamine in the nervous system becomes exhausted, iii) physically craving the sensations that once resulted from more and more hits of dopamine on the reward center, iv) Loss of control, v) compulsion or obsession, and vi) continued use in spite of harm to oneself or others pretty much speak for themselves.

This much is known with certainty: without conscious efforts to curtail them, the trends toward excessive electronic media exposure at earlier and earlier ages, along with pressures to accelerate and hurry childhood, will continue to be a principle threat to childhood health and wellbeing.

Easy Does It: Slowing Down to the Speed of Life

Putting this over-stimulating, even pushy, rushed childhood phenomenon into the framework of windows of opportunity, Kathy Hirsh-Pasek and Roberta Michnick Golinkoff (2003), in the cleverly titled (and well researched, fabulously written) book, *Einstein Never Used Flash Cards,* comment that, "Fortunately most experience-dependent behaviors have a very wide window of opportunity for their development.

That is, you needn't learn them in the first 3 years or even in the first 5 years of life. Even in those cases where there may be an optimal window of opportunity for learning, the window extends well beyond early childhood" (p. 29). Thus, there really is no hurry.

Providing us with a poignant perspective on this issue of the hurried childhood, Marietta Johnson (Johnson, 1996)—whom we quote in the chapter epigraph—wrote in *Organic Education: Teaching Without Failure* that, "A lengthening of childhood, as society increases in complexity, is essential to [developmental] progress. Lack of poise, self-control, power of concentration, purposefulness, and inability to adjust socially are the most striking evidences of one-sided development" (pp. 29-30). Astonishingly, Johnson wrote this statement in 1904, over 100 years ago! In the opening decade of the twentieth century she thought children were being pushed too quickly through childhood. What, we wonder, would this most childhood-sensitive educator have to say about societal conditions in the opening decades of the twenty-first century?

To clinch their argument about the necessity of slowing down, as opposed to rushing, childhood, Hirsh-Pasek and Golinkoff (2003) go on to report on a phenomenon known as neurological "crowding," a thoroughly compelling discovery. Crowding occurs when information has to compete for synaptic connections in the brain—connections that, in earliest childhood, are still under the control of experience-expectant process. Quoting the neuroscientist, Peter Huttenlocher, the authors say: "One has to consider the possibility that very ambitious early enrichment and teaching programs may lead to crowding effects and to an early decrease in the size and number of brain regions that are largely unspecified and that may be necessary for creativity in the adolescent and adult" (p. 29). This finding certainly dovetails with the concerns held by Marietta Johnson a century ago about one-sided development. It is not too much of a stretch to view the act of forcing unspecified brain regions to commit too early as being an unwitting push towards one-sided development.

Interestingly, as the authors point out, Albert Einstein was a lackluster student, thought to be rather dull by at least one teacher. Did this apparent dullness perhaps allow his brain/mind to remain open-ended for an extended time? While we will never know, it's also worth noting that Einstein was remarkably slow to begin speech (nor, per

Hirsh-Pasek and Golinkoff, did he use flash-cards in the service of his later genius!).

So, a little advice straight from a huge amount of research: put away the Baby Einstein DVD's (or whatever the latest-and greatest baby brain "hot-house" fad may be), resist buying single-purpose toys, and think twice before including your toddler in that group of approximately 25% of all two year-olds with a television set in their bedrooms, unfortunately a most effective way to start the young and highly plastic brain on a course exactly opposite to that of enrichment! Here's a better idea: love your children and students unconditionally, set reasonable age-appropriate limits on their behaviors, talk with them lots, and by all means play with them.

The Enrichment Findings

To summarize a great deal of research, perhaps the best, most sensible way to think of enrichment would include several intuitively sound and well-established factors.

Threat-Free Environment

Threats—if excessive and prolonged—pose a real learning problem for the mammalian brain. Granted we have brains that are wonderfully hard-wired for fight or flight. Unfortunately, no new learning is really possible when coping with threat. This is because the forebrain ceases to operate effectively as the powerful mechanisms hard-wired into the hindbrain—and there when we need them for survival—take over. Importantly, a distinction needs to be made between stress (some of which, called eustress, aids learning) and threat (called distress, which causes the brain to "gate down" into survival mode, blocking new learning). The chapter following this one will go into more detail about these factors and their vital impact on the learning process.

We do well with children to provide an environment and an atmosphere free of undue pressure and stress but not without an element of pleasurable intensity. In fact, creative tension fits the bill perfectly. So does cognitive dissonance, the kind of open-ended search for sense and meaning at which the human brain is so adept. When positive emotional support is added, learning comes alive.

Novelty

A balance needs to be struck between the innate pattern-detection nature of the human brain (that seems to thrive on a bit of disorder and chaos) and the safety and security needs of the survival-oriented hindbrain which requires a certain orderliness and predictability in order to engage the higher brain centers. By providing stimulation in an atmosphere that promotes enjoyment, exploration, hands-on activities, and movement, we create an ideal learning environment.

Challenge

A serious but not always recognized issue confronting educators today, in a contemporary environment that can sometimes seem almost hostile to actual education, is finding the appropriate level of challenge for each child. Too little challenge and boredom can quickly set in; too much and a child becomes discouraged. This may serve as one of the great obstacles to deep learning, given the constraints of publicly supported education as we know it. For it takes a great deal of time and skill for teachers to effectively gauge the level of challenge needed to bring out the best in each child in any topic area. Nevertheless, nature seems to take this requirement for maximum brain development far more seriously than do we, her offspring.

The Russian psychologist and much-admired educational theorist, Lev Vygotsky (1896–1934), in fact, worked out an elegant conceptual framework known as the zone of proximal development which is completely consonant with the notion of recognizing and working with the challenge level of individual students. Described as the difference between what learners can do without help and what they are currently unable to do, the concept has proved very helpful in developing age-appropriate and ability-appropriate teaching curricula and strategies.

Feedback

The brain cannot self-organize in the absence of stimulation, nor can learning transpire without feedback. Again, learning a language provides a perfect example. Whereas any child can learn a limited amount of vocabulary from, say, television, language—including syntax, grammar, tense, and a hundred other nuances of usage—cannot be learned via this medium. Why? Television provides no feedback. When encouraged to explore with all their senses (though not necessarily all at once), and allowed social interaction for most activities, children become steeped in multiple systems of feedback. As noted above, feedback is essential to learning. Sadly, schools often find themselves in the untenable position of utilizing only one (questionable) means for validating and determining feedback about learning: tests, and more tests.

Quiet time or downtime, it needs to be mentioned, is also an essential aspect of feedback. Entering into quiet mode allows the brain time for the all-important task of reflecting and connecting current with past learning. This is a form of internal feedback within the multiple neural systems of brain and body. The myriad benefits of downtime will become clearer in the upcoming chapter on brain biorhythms.

Skills Practice

An important ingredient in the enrichment recipe, skills practice is fundamental to every aspect of the enterprise of learning. Practice, repetition over time, and variation are the core elements in all learning that extends beyond the lowest levels of rote memory. When the development of a range of skills—mental, physical, aesthetic, social, emotional, and spiritual—is promoted and supported, the potential of children is enriched.

Problem-Solving

The human brain is, after taking care of survival-oriented needs, nothing if not an instrument of learning. As such, it thrives on pattern-detection and problem-solving. Given this marvelously equipped organ, it can be highly brain-antagonistic to promote learning that is excessively convergent and formulaic. Any teaching derived from a pre-formulated curriculum runs the risk of herding children towards "the right answer," at the expense of a more effective individualized, divergent, and open-ended search.

Physical Activity

Physical movement is a nonnegotiable condition of enriched learning. A great deal of research has recently been devoted to the role of exercise and learning new movements, and the role they play in synaptogenesis and neurogenesis. In Chapter 15 of this book we go into considerable depth, including specific movement recommendations, for this exceedingly important component of brain organization and learning.

Conclusion

Perhaps the best, most simple way to characterize an enriched learning environment is: one that provides a broad array of ways to engage learning. If we think of our many senses, appropriately stimulated through a wide range of activities, as the various threads of a tapestry— the warp, if you will—then the weft would be the natural rhythms of the body and brain as they continue to integrate the learning. Typified by high levels of focused attention interspersed with episodic "downtime," an enriched learning environment is one that synchronizes with basic biological functions supportive of the learning brain—a topic to be explored in Chapter 9. However, before turning to the importance of synchronized biological functions that work on behalf of enhanced learning, we need to more closely examine a potential major impediment to learning and development: noxious stress.

Chapter 8

This is Your Brain on Stress

Since the 1930s when the late Hans Selye began his work, a vast amount of research has shown beyond doubt the corrosive effects of chronic stress on physiological health. The medical and social sciences have been integrating and using this information for a long time. But it is only for the last decade or so that researchers have turned their attention to aspects of chronic, severe stress that should be of intense interest to parents and professional educators—its adverse effects on the brain, and therefore on learning.

Selye is widely regarded as the progenitor of research and theory about the nature of stress and its impact on humans. He was a medical professor at two universities in Montreal and a prolific author (he published well over 1,000 research papers and seven popular books on stress). Selye (1978) originated concepts still prevalent today, most notably the "general adaptation syndrome" or G.A.S. (p. xv), and the distinction between "distress" (p. xvi) and "eustress" (p. 74). Thanks to him, we now understand quite well the role of distress in producing and prolonging human dysfunction, both physiological and psychological.

Selye's work, and the body of knowledge subsequently broadened by others following his lead, is relevant to our account of factors affecting brain development and learning. Recall that in Chapter 7, in discussing the importance of an enriched environment for promoting learning and brain growth in childhood, we touched on the topic of eliminating threat as a necessary precursor to engaging the higher, learning brain. This is because the presence of threat, real or imagined, engages the hindbrain survival mechanisms dedicated to "fight or flight," while simultaneously disengaging the forebrain (the blood literally perfusing out of this area of the brain as the body's blood supply rushes to the limbs in preparation for survival-oriented action).

We also introduced novelty and challenge as crucial components of an enriched learning environment. There we suggested that either too much or too little challenge can harm rather than help development, and that the appropriate level and type of challenge differs with each individual. For instance, extroverts and introverts require quite different learning environments to function optimally. As Susan Cain puts it:

> A third to a half of the population are introverts ... one out of every two or three people you know ... extroverts really crave large amounts of stimulation, whereas introverts feel at their most alive and their most switched-on and their most capable when they're in quieter, more low-key environments. (Cain, 2012)

In this chapter we will explore these topics further, aided by the excellent conceptual tools provided by Dr. Selye and his successors.

Let's begin with the broadest possible characterization of stress. According to Selye (1956), stress is "the nonspecific response of the body to any demand" (p. 63) from the environment for change or adaptation. From this we can conclude that stress is an inescapable fact of life: all organisms must adapt and change, more or less constantly. What makes stress such an important topic is not its existence (which is ubiquitous) but its level of intensity and its potential consequences.

Common notions of stress emphasize its dark side—a level of stress that brings harmful consequences—and often confuse stress (defined above as the response of an organism) with stressor (the demand for change made by the organism's environment). For purposes of our discussion, we must make the distinction between stress and stressor clear. We must also clarify the dual nature of stress. Selye distinguished "eustress" (good stress) from "distress" (bad stress), and we will do the same.

Eustress: Positive and Beneficial Stress

Toward the end of Chapter 7 we summarized several factors comprising "enrichment" beneficial to brain development, including novelty, challenge, feedback, skills practice, problem-solving, and physical activity. Every one of these factors fits the criterion of an environmental stressor calling for change/adaptation in the human brain—which, by definition, is a "stress response". The point we wish to make here is that the set of responses occurring within the context of enrichment constitutes eustress. These responses are, in moderation, essential fodder for the developing brain.

Given the relationship between stress and performance, the challenge for anyone wishing to provide an optimal environment for brain development—whether parent or educator—is to modulate environmental stressors so that the child or student experiences enough stimulation (e.g., novelty, challenge, feedback, activity) to support engagement, but not so much (e.g., anything experienced as a threat to safety or wellbeing) that it impedes learning.

Distress: Harmful and Debilitating Stress

What happens in the latter case, when eustress shades over into distress? This can call forth an adaptive response, illustrating the capability, the evolutionary advantage, given to us in the form of the alarm phase of Selye's general adaptation syndrome. A vivid example is an actual experience Jim had many years ago:

> My wife Molly and I are visiting friends on a warm, sunny morning, enjoying a relaxed conversation in their living room. We are seated on their couch, where we are able to keep an eye on our two-year-old son who is just outside the open front door, sitting on a porch step playing happily with a toy car.
>
> Seemingly at the same instant, both Molly and I notice a pack of dogs running down a side street directly toward our little boy. Without a word we both spring from the couch and through the front door, onto the porch. My wife sweeps our son into her arms and turns to shield him with her body, while I rush toward the street, scoop up some rocks near the curb, and begin throwing them at the oncoming pack. The dogs immediately turn and scatter, ending the threat.
>
> Trembling from the adrenaline rush, we take our boy into the house and close the door. Until this point, not a word has been spoken. The entire incident has lasted no more than twenty seconds.

In that span of twenty seconds, a complex of perceptual, psychological, emotional, physiological and behavioral changes that took eons to evolve flew into the present moment like an arrow, enabling exactly the response it was designed to enable. A sharply defined environmental stressor elicited a precise, sharply executed action—and then it was over. No thought, no strategizing, just giving over to instinctual preservation of offspring; that is the alarm phase in action.

So far, so good; the stress response worked perfectly in this example. Once the threat was resolved, the parents were able to pace around, comfort their child, talk the situation over with their horrified friends, and gradually "come down from" the peaks of adrenaline, noradrenaline and cortisol ("stress hormones" secreted by the adrenal glands) that had instantly roused them to fight-or-flight mode.

Yet it is easy to imagine scenarios—because they happen so commonly—that start with the alarm response (exemplified by the event just described), but do not stop with that. That sort of scenario sets the stage for the troublesome second phase (resistance), and potentially lethal third phase (exhaustion) of the general adaptation syndrome described by Selye (1956).

The General Adaptation Syndrome

The stressors that propel their victims beyond the initial phase, the alarm response, are almost invariably "psychosocial" stressors. Taken all together, they comprise what we referred to in Chapter 7 as "Threat." Woven as they are into the fabric of modern life, such stressors are very difficult to avoid. The complexities and challenges most adults face every day—keeping to a tight schedule, getting to and from work in congested traffic, managing often precarious finances, coping with interpersonal conflict, fulfilling a myriad of duties and expectations, attempting to keep up with information overload (especially that presented, with escalating shrillness, on television and other, ubiquitous, screen technologies)—can feel unending and overwhelming. Some of these, such as interpersonal conflict and time pressures, also plague the

> The stressors that propel their victims beyond the initial phase, the alarm response, are almost invariably "psychosocial" stressors

lives of still-developing young people. In addition, our youth face their age-specific version of status fears and overstimulation, plus the tragically malignant and growing threat of bullying. And for an increasing percentage of children and youth, there is the constant threat of abuse and neglect in the family and community.

But the most ghastly threat hanging over our young people in the U.S.A. that we authors can imagine is the cascading risk of being randomly gunned down at school by deeply troubled people armed with military-style weapons. Within the week just prior to this writing, seventeen more people lost their lives to the grotesque gun violence afflicting our nation.

These modern stressors feel unending, and often crushing. Unless skillful means are found to interrupt them, they tend to dominate most waking hours for most people in our ramped-up western culture. And remember the progression: every stressor interpreted as a threat, whether it is a foreclosure notice, a home invasion, being bullied, or even just turning in an assignment late, elicits an emergency response (intense physical/emotional activation via release of stress hormones into the bloodstream, combined with direct action on the body by the sympathetic branch of the autonomic nervous system). Then, if the threat subsides, the hormones are reabsorbed, the autonomic nervous system regains balance between its sympathetic (activating) and parasympathetic (maintaining everyday functions) branches, whereupon body and feelings calm down. This process is known technically as homeostasis (see Figure 36, next page).

But if the threat does not subside, or another one comes along before body and feelings re-normalize, the autonomic nervous system keeps pumping out stress hormones. Homeostasis goes out the window and the victim gets pulled into the next phase of the general adaptation syndrome, which Selye (1956) identified as the stage of resistance.

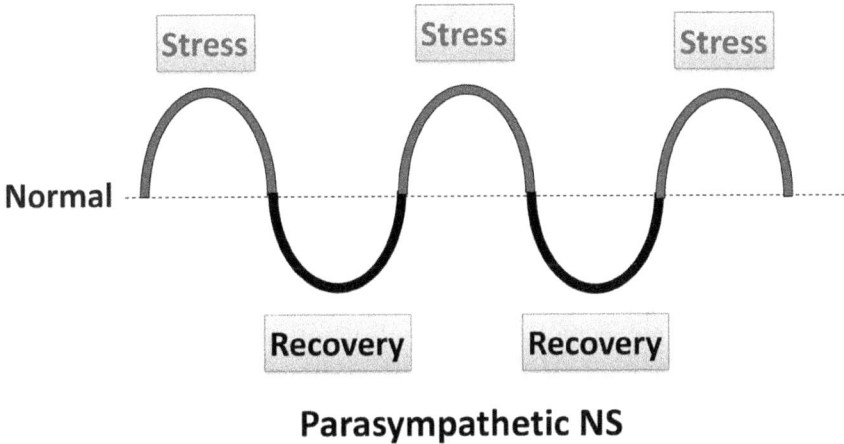

HOMEOSTASIS

Sympathetic NS

Stress   Stress   Stress

Normal

Recovery   Recovery

Parasympathetic NS

Figure 36 Homeostasis.
Image by Tim Burns.

Before describing the resistance stage of the syndrome, we must reiterate the distinction between the kind of stressor that would propel a person into that stage and the kind that would promote zest in life and joy in learning. The first kind leads to distress, whereas the second kind or level of stressor leads to eustress. Obviously, it would be beneficial to learn how to neutralize the first and cultivate the second. To do that, we need to understand the differences between them.

We have already suggested, with the examples above, one very obvious difference: a stressor that leads to distress is one that is perceived as a threat to wellbeing, whereas one that leads to "eustress" is perceived not as a threat, but as something that arouses interest, curiosity, excitement, active engagement. Both kinds elicit the release of stress hormones, but they have completely different meanings for the person experiencing them. As neuroscientist Richard F. Thompson puts it: "The extent to which situations are stressful is determined by how the individual understands, interprets, sees, and feels about a situation" (Thompson,

2000, p. 210). It is the difference in perceived meaning that determines the difference in outcome—that is, whether the individual recovers quickly, responds positively, or proceeds into the resistance phase.

Thompson continues: "The key aspects are uncertainty and control; the less knowledge the individual has about a potentially harmful situation, the less control he or she feels can be exerted, the more stressful the situation is." He describes several studies of hormonal and behavioral responses to stressful situations, by humans as well as animals, that support this assertion. He then concludes: "This research on stress implies that successful strategies for coping involve predictability, understanding, knowledge, and a sense of control."

The issue of perceived control as a determinant separating eustress from distress links to a similar point discussed in Chapter 6 in the context of epigenetics. There we referred to the conclusion reached by cellular biologist Bruce Lipton that an organism's perception of the environment is the mediating factor between the environment and gene expression or alteration. Lipton (see Chapter 6) also maintained that only animals high up on the ladder of evolution are capable of using this perception to good effect—such as by responding reflectively rather than reflexively.

So, whether we are considering stress mitigation or gene expression, the individual's perception of the environment is of paramount importance. The implications of this well-documented conclusion for child-rearing and education are enormous, as you can imagine. We will discuss this further toward the end of the chapter. For now, though, we resume describing what happens in the resistance stage of the general adaptation syndrome, when the stress just goes on and on.

From Homeostasis to Allostasis: Physical Breakdown and Impaired Learning

That the brain undergoes gradual but profound alterations under the continuous influence of high levels of stress hormones is no longer in dispute. One such area is the hypothalamus, the so-called "brain of the brain." This pea-sized organ acts as the major regulatory organ for the entire body, controlling the release of hormones, for example, via the pituitary gland. In the Seventies, scientists established conclusively that under conditions of chronic distress the hypothalamus becomes increasingly sensitized—a phenomenon sometimes referred to as "kindling," (Goddard & Douglas, 1976, p. 18), a kind of neurological hypersensitivity to excessive arousal. In such cases, the individual grows hyperalert and unconsciously primed for fight, flight, or freeze. In other words, a new set-point response has emerged making it far more likely that the individual will subsequently react—or, more likely, overreact—with a stress response than would previously have been the case. Thus, a "new normal" has been established. This process of adaptation, re-adaptation, and eventual maladaptation is a function of allostasis, wherein the body no longer returns to a homeostatic normalcy; instead, it proceeds in a maladaptive direction (see Figure 37, below). This procession is known as allostatic load, a term used to describe the cumulative effects of high, chronic stress leading to eventual physiological breakdown and unwitting self-destruction.

That the brain undergoes gradual but profound alterations under the continuous influence of high levels of stress hormones is no longer in dispute.

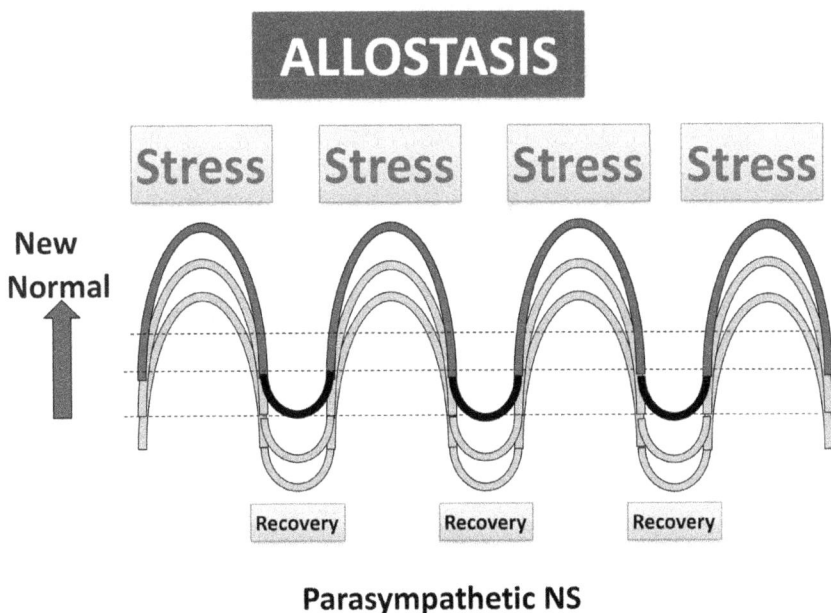

Figure 37 Allostasis.
Image by Tim Burns.

With the onset of allostatic load, our ability to attune ourselves to novelty, challenge, and feedback—the very essence of learning—becomes severely undermined. As that part of the brain central to the consolidation of new learning into memory, the hippocampus (part of the limbic system) operates optimally under normal conditions of homeostasis, the nature of which features periods of focused concentration followed by periods of recovery, even reverie as we shall see. But under conditions of chronic stress (i.e., during the resistance phase of the general adaptation syndrome), something altogether different occurs. Under these conditions the brain strives to adapt, but the results are pathological rather than restorative. In this case, the hippocampus can actually shrink, losing gray-matter mass, as a result of the toxic effects on both new and established neurons of the high levels of stress hormones.

> With the onset of allostatic load, our ability to attune ourselves to novelty, challenge, and feedback— the very essence of learning— becomes severely undermined.

In an article that exhaustively surveys research on the effects of stress on the brain, two European scholars give a detailed description of that difference (note that the "glucocorticoids" referred to below include cortisol, a stress hormone introduced earlier):

> Given that the hippocampus was originally found to be a main target of glucocorticoids and to be responsive to stress, much work on the neurobiological impact of stress has focused on this brain region. The idea behind that is … structural and molecular alterations induced by chronic stress in this brain area will account for the impairing effects of stress in hippocampus-dependent memory tasks … (Sandi and Pinelo-Nava, 2007, no page number.)

Following these statements is a long list of specific types and sites of chronic stress damage within the hippocampus, documented by various researchers. But the damage is not limited to the hippocampus, as vital as that structure is in memory formation; the authors also cite studies documenting comparable damage to the prefrontal cortex resulting from chronic stress. Considering the behavioral outcomes evident from the 167 studies cited in their review, the authors conclude that high stress levels "tend to facilitate Pavlovian conditioning … while being deleterious for spatial/explicit information processing."

Let's draw that out a bit. Chronic high stress facilitates Pavlovian conditioning—the most primitive form of learning—but impedes information processing that enables learning at a higher level. Not only does distress impede that information processing in the present, it causes structural damage that compromises future information processing. Granted, this conclusion is based on animal studies, but it is no great leap to apply it to human learning; the brain structures and neurochemistry are similar enough in form to justify that.

If we, as guardians and champions of optimal child development, accept this conclusion, we must take the next step: we must understand that it is our responsibility to craft the learning environment so that it provides stimulation and support for young brains eager to learn, while simultaneously canceling out stressors that sabotage the learning brain. Let us aim toward an ideal educational system that eliminates threat/distress and its counter-educational consequences, while simultaneously facilitating an optimal learning state in students that could be termed "flow."

As the science exclusively focused upon the role of natural rhythms in human learning, performance and health maintenance, chronobiology has much to teach us about optimizing our capacity to enter into flow states. It is to that fascinating branch of life science that we now turn.

Chapter 9

Chronobiology and the Rhythms of Life

"Giants of Circadian Biology Win Nobel Prize: The award in Physiology or Medicine goes to chronobiologists."

– Headline announcement on The Scientist Daily, 2017

"I cannot emphasize enough how important the circadian rhythm is for prevention of chronic diseases, and for long term benefits toward healthspan and eventually lifespan."

– Zheng Chen

"Timing is everything."

– Duke Ellington

Physiological States and Life Rhythms

Biological processes that greatly influence learning throughout human development encompass underlying physiological states and their relationship to the innate and ever-changing rhythms and fluctuations of the brain, rhythms that govern how, when, what, and even whether we are able to learn. These states, which include wakeful alertness, sleep, dream-time, stress, and much more, play a crucial role in all learning. They affect learning by influencing and regulating levels of alertness, mental functioning, and performance.

These states are affected by many variables: how much rest we've had, what foods we have eaten, the amount and quality of water we consume, our hormone balance at any given time, how stressed or relaxed we feel, the amount of movement and exercise we engage in, our emotional states, and even our breathing and posture. These rhythmic physiological states are linked to equally rhythmic cycles governing brain function. This rhythmic interplay between bodily states and brain function is fundamental not only to learning but to a range of other factors associated with health and well-being, as we shall see. By better understanding the importance of these fascinating brain rhythms—mining the knowledge that has been acquired over the last half century for nuggets that can add to our wealth of understanding—we can be assured of more engaged, less stressful learning, as well as healthier overall development.

By better understanding the importance of these fascinating brain rhythms— mining the knowledge that has been acquired over the last half century for nuggets that can add to our wealth of understanding—we can be assured of more engaged, less stressful learning, as well as healthier overall development.

Nature's Rhythms

Everything in nature operates according to recurring patterns; no living thing is exempt. The annual planetary journey around the sun, the four seasons, the 28-day lunar cycle, tidal ebb and flow are obvious examples of naturally occurring rhythms. Nearly all organisms, from bacteria to plants, animals, and humans have internal, "biological clocks" that help maintain these natural rhythms.

The notion of biological clocks—internal mechanisms that can generate cycles of behaviors even without environmental cues—has been around for decades. That these biological clocks are independent of environmental cues was proven by the earliest studies (typically involved placing plants, animals, even humans in caves for weeks or months) where there was no possible way of knowing the time of day. Despite not being able to orient directly to the day-night cycle, human subjects kept a circadian rhythm that was constant within about an hour of the 24-hour diurnal/nocturnal period.

Today, the existence of biological clocks is not only a widely held and accepted scientific tenet but has recently taken on rather unexpected prominence. In 2017 the Nobel Prize for medicine was awarded to three American scientists for their work on discoveries of molecular mechanisms controlling the circadian rhythm. Publicizing the event, the Nobel Foundation announced that, "With exquisite precision, our inner clock adapts our physiology to the dramatically different phases of the day. The clock regulates critical functions such as behavior, hormone levels, sleep, body temperature and metabolism."[5]

The branch of science that concerns itself with these rhythms is known as chronobiology (Kreitzman and Foster, 2004), the study of the relationship between rhythms, cycles, or periods, and biological processes. Chronobiology encompasses all research areas focusing on a wide spectrum of biological timing, from high frequency cycles such as gene-switching and hormone secretion that occur in distinct pulses throughout the day, to daily cycles of activity and rest, to various monthly and annual cycles. Not surprisingly, the ongoing discoveries about the timing of virtually all biological processes dovetails perfectly with the findings on gene expression covered in Chapter 6.

It is perhaps helpful, as we go along, to think of these psychobiological rhythms as nesting, one within the other. Nested within the larger seasonal rhythms, for example, are the lunar fluctuations; within the monthly cycles are the daily or circadian cycles; within the circadian are the ultradian, and so forth—all the way down to the extremely rapid gene cycles. Keep in mind that it works both ways: the larger tempos affect the smaller and the smaller affect the larger. Life, it appears, is infatuated with rhythm.

Chronobiology: When Timing is Everything

From plants to fruit flies to humans, it seems all of life is beholden to the pulse of nature. Bears hibernate, caribou and wildebeest migrate, fish spawn, and honeybees gather nectar—all on genetically prescribed rhythms. Even when isolated from sunlight in dark caves, plants open and close their leaves on a 24-hour cycle, meaning, as scientists concluded early on, that the source of this fluctuation must lie within the plant itself. In 1985 scientists finally discovered a genetic source for this type of naturally occurring rhythm, and thus was launched the quest to catalogue and better understand the role of these "biological clocks," or "clock genes" (Rossi, 1991).

---

5   As reported on National Public Radio (NPR), Nobel Prize In Medicine Is Awarded To Three Americans For Work On Circadian Rhythm, October 2, 2017. https://www.npr.org/sections/thetwo-way/2017/10/02/554993385/nobel-prize-in-medicine-is-awarded-to-3-americans-for-work-on-circadian-rhythm

The underlying structures that constitute the "clock" differ from one species to another. In mammals, including humans, biological tempos are regulated by the brain's hypothalamus (the structure in the mid-brain region that regulates, among other things, hormone levels), which means they play a key role in overall health, emotional well-being, and behavior. In some insects this clock is located within the structure of the eye, whereas in birds the clock is located in the pineal gland, an even smaller structure that responds to alterations in light. Since these clocks are usually linked to some form of light-sensing cell (called a photoreceptor) sunlight plays a key role in synchronizing the clock to the 24-hour day. Light serves to turn on genes that affect patterns of sleep, alertness, body temperature, hormone levels, blood pressure and so forth. Most of us know from direct experience how disruptions of these biological rhythms can interfere with mood, energy levels, attitude, learning, sleep and health. In fact, one of the "hard-earned lessons" nearly all of us are struggling with these days is how disruptive to all these ingredients of well-being is the amount of radiant light (as opposed to natural light) we ingest daily through screen technologies.

Studies have found that the internal clock consists of an array of genes (and the protein products they encode) that regulate various physiological processes throughout the body (Vitaterna et al, 2001). Beginning in the 1980s, the discovery of specific genes related to the underlying mechanism of so-called "gene clocks" (sometimes referred to as "molecular clocks") has resulted in a growing list of genes known to regulate functions of the brain, heart, liver and other tissues of the body, as well as many common everyday psychobiological states such as waking, sleeping and dreaming. Moreover, as Ernest Rossi points out (Rossi, 1991, p. 15), our mental abilities, emotional tone, blood chemistry, physical strength, eye-hand coordination, and resistance to disease all vary according to the time of day. Scientists have also ascertained that the endocrine and immune systems, including the genes that control them, are also governed by biological clocks.

Infradian, Circadian, and Ultradian Cycles

The science of chronobiology has come a long way since its official establishment as a field of investigation in 1960, at national meeting of biologists in Cold Springs Harbor, New York. As a biologically-based interdisciplinary field of investigation, it interacts with medical and other areas of research such as jet-lag sleep disorders, endocrinology, geriatrics, sports medicine, space medicine, as well as the biological basis of learning. Three biological cycles around which a great deal of research has taken place are covered below.

Infradian Cycles

One of the cycles most studied by chronobiologists includes the so-called infradian rhythms, referring to those cycles—such as menstruation or the tidal rhythms that follow the lunar cycle—that are longer than 24 hours. While these examples are lunar, or monthly, there are others that of course follow the four seasons. Seasonal Affective Disorder (SAD), for instance, which affects about ten percent of the population is just that: seasonal. Biologists who study rhythms that are approximately one year in duration—reproductive cycles and hibernation are examples—call them circannual, meaning approximately of a years' duration.

These regularly recurring patterns are typically referred to in the science literature as oscillations, and they are found throughout the natural world. El Niño, for example—the famous seasonal weather-generating pattern emanating from alterations in the overall temperature of the southern Pacific Ocean—is actually referred to in scientific literature as the Southern El Niño Oscillation Effect. Both the body and brain are highly subject to the influences of these seasonal oscillations, even though we may be only dimly aware of the effect that they are having. We will have more to say about oscillations and their role in development, awareness, attention, learning and health as we go along.

Circadian Cycles

Circadian cycles or rhythms, from the Latin, *circa*, meaning "about" or "approximately" and *dies*, meaning "day," last approximately 24 hours. Most biological rhythms are synchronized, or entrained, to the circadian cycle which itself consists of a diurnal, or daytime, phase and a nocturnal, or nighttime, phase. Lasting less than 24 hours are the ultradian rhythms, which are processes that most often cycle in periods from 90 to 120 minutes. It is the circadian and ultradian rhythms that we will be considering in some detail below, although it is important to note that other rhythms are at work as well. For example, cellular rhythms—which control such processes as cell division, oxygen release, genetic activity, and hormone secretion—operate on genetically established cycles that can be measured in seconds or even fractions of seconds.

Returning to circadian rhythms, one of their most outstanding properties is the absolute pervasiveness throughout nature. It has been shown, for example, that the rhythms of unicellular organisms such as algae are much the same as rhythms of highly complex mammals. Another property is that these rhythms appear to be generated, and to a large extent controlled, at the cellular level. It appears that a timekeeping mechanism of genetic origin underlies circadian cycles.

Despite the pervasiveness of biological and behavioral rhythms in humans, most of us remain fundamentally ignorant of their importance. However, there is a great deal of scientific interest in the properties of these rhythms, since they play a key role in virtually every aspect human health, performance, learning, and disease. Consequently, fields such as science, medicine, and sports now recognize the ever-increasing role that circadian rhythms play in physical and mental health, and performance.

> Despite the pervasiveness of biological and behavioral rhythms in humans, most of us remain fundamentally ignorant of their importance.

Commenting on the pervasive, and at times unexpected, nature of circadian rhythms, Judith Willis points out the following (Willis,,1990, p. 18-21):

- The duration of sleep is related more closely to body temperature rhythms than to how long the person has been awake. In experiments, even after being awake more than 20 hours, people free of time cues slept twice as long after going to bed when their temperature was at its highest (in early evening) than when it was at its lowest (in the early morning).
- The senses of hearing, taste and smell are more acute at certain times of day. Studies show sensory acuity is highest at 3 a.m., falls off rapidly to a low at 6 a.m., then rises to another peak

between 5 and 7 p.m. (This cycle is related to the hormone cycle: when steroid hormones are released, sensory acuity falls.)

- Women go into labor most often between 1:30 and 2:30 a.m. and least frequently about midday. Moreover, births between 2 and 4 p.m. are associated with increased probability of complications in both the baby and the mother.
- In one study, eating one meal a day of 2,000 calories resulted in a weight loss when eaten as breakfast, but produced a weight gain as supper.
- Heart attacks are twice as likely to occur between 8 and 10 a.m. as between either 4 and 6 a.m. or 6 and 8 p.m.

Ultradian Cycles

In his marvelous book, *The 20 Minute Break: Using the New Science of Ultradian Rhythms*, Ernest Rossi (1991) discusses how numerous and pervasive are the 90-to-120-minute ultradian cycles. As Rossi says, "These ultradian rhythms [affect] performance across an extremely wide range of mental and physical tasks: cognition, attention, concentration, learning, short-term memory, creativity, eye-hand coordination, athletic ability, reflexes, and energy level" (Rossi, 1991, p. 10).

The following figure reveals the pervasive nature and myriad functions that fall under the influence of these all-important and life-sustaining rhythms.

As they pertain specifically to the brain and to learning, there are at least two ways in which ultradian rhythms have a subtle, but profound, effect. One has to do with the patterned rise and fall of energy levels, as measured by the rise and fall of "brain waves." The other effect has to do with the rhythm of alternating cerebral dominance, the subtle shift of energy and activity from one hemisphere, or side, of the brain to the other—right to left and left to right. Before detailing those two rhythms, let's look at how they fall within the larger circadian tempo.

ULTRADIAN RYHTHMS
Modulated Mind-Body Activities

MIND

Right-left brain dominance
Attention
Concentration
Learning
Memory
Sensations
Perceptions
Emotions
Dreaming
Fantasy
Imagination
Creativity

BODY

Left-right nasal dominance
Autonomic nervous system
Gene-cell metabolism
Endocrine system
Immune system
Breast-feeding
Hunger and sex
Digestion
Work and sports
Stress response
Psychosomatic response
Cellular metabolism

Figure 38. Mind-Body Activities Modulated by Ultradian Rhythms. Image by Rossi.

Brain Biorhythms, Human Learning and Performance

The study from which the ensuing exploration comes, dating back to the mid-70s (described in Austin, 1998), provides a good example of how interlocking cycles can affect such critical aspects of learning as attention, awareness, and perception. One of the graphics taken from the study (see Figure 39), depicts how the rise and fall of physiological states occur within the diurnal and nocturnal alterations of the circadian cycle.

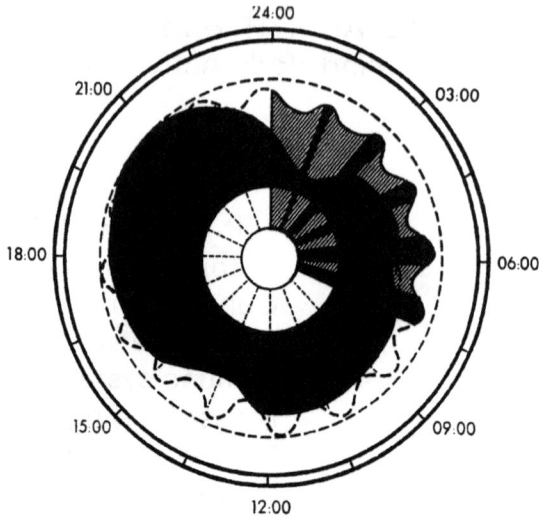

Figure 39. Biorhythmic Variation in the Circadian Cycle.
Image by James Austin.

Let's get oriented to the graphic. By use of a 24-hour clock (the 24 at the top of the graph is midnight and the 12 at the bottom, noon) the circadian rhythm is clearly revealed. The superimposition of the black, irregular shaped, donut-like shape plots (in the aggregate) the timing of high and low periods for the research subjects in the realms of mental alertness, consciousness, and performance. The thick areas denote periods of high or optimal performance and the thin portions the low. The time just after midnight is the lowest ebb, as one would expect.

Note that these capacities increase in the direction of optimal slowly, throughout the day, not reaching maximum until sometime during the evening hours for the average person. This has to do with several interrelated body and mind factors, among which are included an overall rise in body temperature and certain hormones as the day goes on. These capacities then decline rather steeply upon falling asleep.

This "rising tide" of alertness and performance is as natural as the rise and fall of the ocean tides. Everyone—in fact every species—experiences this and lives according to its dictates. It is biologically based and has a very direct effect on the cycle of learning. Let's look at a couple of examples of how learning and well-being for children and teens (adults as well) are affected by these biological rhythms: school-start times and downtime.

Circadian Rhythms, Children and Teenagers

In an article entitled, "When School Schedules Collide with Biological Clocks," chronobiologist Timothy H. Monk, the parent of a teenage son, reflects on the significance of a commonly observed circadian shift that takes place with the onset and progression of adolescence. While anecdotal, any parent (or teacher) of a teen can certainly relate.

> For many of my son's friends, the difference in daily habits, from the noon wakening and late bedtimes of summer vacation to the 6 a.m. waking of the high school day, represented a change in schedule equivalent in magnitude to that of a flight from New York to Berlin. In the short term this meant that like millions of their peers, these kids were experiencing the adverse symptoms of "jet lag" for the first week or two of school. These symptoms include sleep disruptions at night, and irritability, inattentiveness, and drowsiness during the day—hardly a recipe for a productive start to the school year! Sadly, though, biological changes to a young person's sleep and biological clock make these temporal adjustments even more difficult to accommodate and are likely to make them last for much longer than the first few weeks after a vacation.' (Monk, 1994, p. 36)

Monk goes on to describe how few high school students are able to accommodate their sleep schedules to early start times, resulting in a buildup in sleep loss during the school week and low levels of alertness during the school day, particularly in high schools with very early start times, while at the other end of the school day their brains are only just beginning to wake up and become truly receptive to learning.

Ironically, Monk points out, the opposite situation exists for elementary school students who start the school day later even though their alertness levels are highest in the morning. "Would it not make more sense," Monk asks, "to switch the schedules around, having the elementary school students start earlier in the day and high school students later in the day? There would be no extra stress on bus schedules since the change represents just a switch. The parents of elementary school students would have fewer morning baby-sitting problems and, most importantly, our high school students would not be in the position of being half asleep for much of their school day, and at their most alert when school is over. Of course, there are benefits and drawbacks to any change in schedule. At the moment, though, we are not even debating the issue but are content to do things the way they always have been done" (p. 136).

Science-based ideas such as this have led some school districts to start the school day later in the morning at the high-school level, sometimes coupled with offering classes into the late afternoon and evening—wise choices when it comes to adolescence for more than one reason.

The Teen Night-Owl Syndrome: Blame It on Hormones ... and Blue Light!

Perhaps the best-known research on the topic of later start times is that of Kyla Wahlstrom and her research team at the Center for Applied Research and Educational Improvement (CAREI), (Wahlstrom, 2002). Based on their study—ongoing since 1996—regarding the impact of later start times on educational achievement in two different Minneapolis, U.S.A school districts, other districts have decided to shift as well. To date, no fewer than three dozen school districts across the country now begin the school day later, with many reporting a significant reduction in school dropout rates, less depression, and students earning higher grades, according to the CAREI report.

According to Wahlstrom, medical researchers found this cycle is tied to the maturation of the endocrine system: "From the onset of puberty until late teen years," she reports, "the brain chemical melatonin, which is responsible for sleepiness, is secreted from approximately 11 p.m. until approximately 8 a.m., nine hours later. This secretion is based on human circadian rhythms and is rather fixed. In other words, typical youth are not able to fall asleep much before 11 p.m. and their brains will remain in sleep mode until about 8 a.m., regardless of what time they go to bed" (cited in Paul, 2006, p. 9A).

Further complicating the circadian shift affecting teen sleep patterns (staying awake later, thus sleeping later into the day, owing to the hormonal changes taking place) is the ubiquity of screen technologies in the lives of teens.[6] There are a number of issues related to the growing concern about poor sleep hygiene among teens. As stated succinctly in the Harvard Medical School, Health Publishing bulletin, "Blue wavelengths—which are beneficial during daylight hours because they boost attention, reaction times, and mood—seem to be the most disruptive at night."[7] The reason for this is straightforward: looking into a radiant light source skewed towards the blue end of the color spectrum (as are all screen devices) has a stimulating effect: It requires higher than normal levels of catecholamines (epinephrine, norepinephrine, dopamine) to extract information out of radiant light than does natural, reflected light— reading the print on page of a book, for example.[8] The over-stimulation of course makes it more difficult to fall asleep in a timely manner.

At the same time that blue light is causing excitatory response in the brain it slows the production of melatonin. As reported in the journal, *Chronobiology International* (1992), "The best-known acute suppressor of nocturnal melatonin is light exposure…; of the visible wavelengths, those in the blue range seem most effective in suppressing melatonin production,"[9] How much suppression? As reported in the book, *The Best American Science and Nature Writing* (2015), "Researchers at Rensselaer Polytechnic Institute showed that two hours of exposure to a bright tablet screen at night reduced melatonin levels by about 22 percent" (p. 52). Thus, combined with the naturally occurring hormone-driven teen

---

6   Of the numerous studies reporting on increased screen-time and its role in sleep deprivation is one reported by the American Academy of Pediatrics, saying that: "In the study of more than 2,000 fourth and seventh graders 54 percent said they slept near a smartphone. Kids who slept in the same room as a cell-phone, smartphone or iPod touch—what they call 'small screens'—got almost 21 minutes fewer sleep than those who didn't. They also went to bed, on average, 37 minutes later than those without phones in their rooms." Source: Pediatrics. "Sleep Duration, Restfulness, and Screens in the Sleep Environment" Jennifer Falbe et al, January 2015.

7   Source: https://www.health.harvard.edu/staying-healthy/blue-light-has-a-dark-side.

8   The difference between the demands placed upon the nervous system is easily explained by the fact that, as a species, we have not evolved to extract information from a radiant light source which, prior to the advent of screen technologies, was only encountered by gazing into a campfire (or perhaps the sun, which immediately proved to be a big mistake).

9   Quote taken from the abstract appearing at https://www.ncbi.nlm.nih.gov/pubmed/1423740.

"night-owl" syndrome, the factor of melatonin suppression can result in a cascade of learning and health problems.

The need for additional sleep during adolescence in order to accommodate the important physical changes and the growth-spurt that they are undergoing is well known. Human growth hormone, essential for the healthy growth of the body and repair of tissues, is secreted and used by the body during the deepest stages of sleep. The fact that blue light technologies have been shown to be so disruptive to sleep for teens also means, of course, that children and we adults are likewise affected. Hopefully this knowledge will help all of us to make wiser decisions concerning the technologies known to interfere with circadian rhythms.

Insofar as understanding the innate ebb and flow of brain activity remains unrecognized and underutilized it can make learning, and thus the job of teaching, much more difficult and frustrating than necessary. The more we know about the natural functions of the brain, the more brain compatible—and conversely, the less brain antagonistic—the whole enterprise becomes.

> The more we know about the natural functions of the brain, the more brain compatible—and conversely, the less brain antagonistic—the whole enterprise becomes.

In Chapter 5, for example, the crucial role of sleep in the consolidation of learning was discussed. Other applications of the cyclical nature of learning apply as well, another example of which is the under-recognized and under-utilized role of "downtime."

Downtime: A Missing—and Exceedingly Important—Key

Reporting on an intriguing study initiated in the 1970s by Burton White, at Harvard University's Child Development Center (White, 1995), the late Joseph Pearce[10] describes an unexpected yet telling finding

---

10 Joseph Pearce shared this nugget at a talk attended by TB in the late 1980's. Author of some of the best, most articulate and provocative books available on childhood development and human potential, Pearce has had a marked influence on the thinking of thousands of individuals, myself (TB) most definitely included. See the bibliography for a listing of his insightful books.

by researchers. The ongoing, decades-long study under consideration had as its focus children who, according to Pearce, were considered to be gifted, well-adjusted and happy (apparently a very small percentage of the population). The study was designed in part to find out why these children were able to learn with such enthusiasm, ease, flexibility and adaptability. The team soon discovered that the children shared an unusual trait (for which they evidently tended to be notorious among their teachers): a tendency to "space out" more than usual. That is, they periodically entered a trancelike state, staring blankly into space, off in their own world, so to speak.

As it turns out, this "space out," or "trance" time, is a well-known and very common occurrence for each one of us, every day—several times a day in fact. What hasn't always been known—and what has most certainly not been especially appreciated in our schools or society—is that this unusual state of mind is an essential component in not only the learning cycle, but good health as well. Commonly referred to as "downtime," it is a function of the brain and body that is innately, inextricably and genetically bound to learning, the development of intelligence, health, and creativity. Let's find out why.

Returning to the fanlike area of the graph (Figure 39) we note the scalloped appearance along the outer edge of the fan-like shape. It depicts the regular 90-120 minute fluctuations of energy levels in the brain as they rise and fall throughout the sleep cycle and, importantly, beyond. Present throughout the sleep-cycle this ultradian fluctuation continues to exert its subtle yet powerful effect throughout the day, determining our level of wakefulness and alertness (or, conversely, drowsiness), and more.

Obvious to almost everyone, the brain (and body) goes through high and low energy phases throughout the day. Sometimes we feel alive, alert, and awake; focus and attentiveness come easily. We feel productive in our attempts to accomplish tasks. Later in the tempo of 90 to 120 minutes we feel less so as we head, inexorably, into the "downtime" part of the cycle. Setting aside for now the discussion about brainwave alterations during the cycle (detailed in the upcoming chapter), let us focus on the connection between downtime and learning, development, and well-being.

The Role of Downtime in Learning and Memory

It is during downtime that the brain processes information, a necessary component in the initiation of new neural connections (recall those immediate early and activity-dependent genes) following periods of focused attention and activity. Too much "uptime," featuring attention given over to incoming information, hinders the brain in transferring that information to the association areas of the anterior cerebral cortex in a way that permits sufficient replay and processing. At a minimum, this can lead to a subsequent loss of memory consolidation. A number of studies conducted on rats have led scientists to take seriously the essential need for downtime in all mammalian species, us included. For example, in a typical yet telling experiment with downtime as the variable in learning, researchers Mattias Karlson and Loren Frank (2009) describe how rats, when allowed to rest after completing an unfamiliar maze (and thus given time for processing) appear to replay the experience of navigating the maze. When attempting the same maze later, the rats navigate through it more quickly. On the other hand, when rats are allowed no downtime and immediately faced with a new maze challenge, placed in the same maze they are unable to navigate it any faster than happened the first time. Clearly, the mammalian brain requires downtime in order to process and consolidate new learning.

> It is during downtime that the brain processes information, a necessary component in the initiation of new neural connections (recall those immediate early and activity-dependent genes) following periods of focused attention and activity.

One reason for this is that, as we strain to keep our energy and attention levels high, we put stress on the adrenal glands and their production of, among other things, cortisol. Too much stress interferes with the consolidation of memories and can also lead to adrenal exhaustion, possibly one of the most common, yet unrecognized, sources of ill health in our society.[11] This, of course, is consonant with the findings

---

11 For a thorough explication of the dynamics resulting in adrenal exhaustion (and the possibility for recovery from same), see Schwarzbein, The *Schwarzbein Principle, II*, Deerfield Beach, FL: Health Communications, Inc. 2002.

on the effects of screen technologies detailed by Manfred Spitzer, MD, PhD (see Chapter 7).

There is another factor involved here that is well addressed by downtime. Working memory (primarily associated with the hippocampus) is anatomically located in the temporal (side) lobes of the brain, whereas the association area (where linkages are made between the various senses as well as to prior learning) is more toward the rear. In addition, the frontal lobes—engaged whenever "higher learning" (reflection, analysis, synthesis, evaluation) is called for—are involved in anything other than rote learning. Too much sensory overload, not enough appropriate downtime, and the blood remains pooled in the rearmost portion of the brain. When this occurs, the result is a breakdown in the rhythm of learning and memory consolidation.

Downtime and Brain Blood-Flow

Let's look more closely at the issue of brain blood-flow. In the early 1980s scientists using newly developed imaging technology began to notice that, under a high sensory load (in particular, high auditory and visual stimulation), the brains of subjects under study literally "lit up the screen" in the rear or posterior region, as it became engorged with blood (Frackowiak, 1980). To the researchers, there was a clear connection between the sensory stimulation and the images that were being produced.

In Positron Emission Tomography, or PET-scans, and the newer functional Magnetic Resonance Imaging, or fMRI-scans, cerebral blood-flow is tracked quite accurately (the latter technology having the added advantage of being cheaper, simpler and more sensitive than PET-scans, not to mention the fact that PET-scans use radioactive tracers to track the blood-flow).

The presence of more brilliant (often depicted with warmer—yellow, orange, red—hues) colors in a given area of the cortex indicates either high oxygen consumption (oxygen that is, of course, carried by blood) or greater glucose (i.e., brain fuel) consumption in that area of the brain. This translates as greater brain activity relative to other areas of the brain. The advantage of "functional" MRI is that an image of the brain can be captured in real time, while an individual carries out a mental (or emotional, or physical) task. These and other technologies, while far from perfect (leading to cautionary statements from the scientific community regarding their use and interpretation), have done much to forward an understanding of the operations of the brain.

In any case, regarding blood-flow, a salient discovery was this: observed under a low-load (i.e., quiet) sensory environment, blood volume in the brain is shunted forward into the frontal, or anterior, cortex (Ronnberg et al, 1998). Since frontal lobe activation determines the extent to which one is capable of doing all higher mental operations, it is essential that sufficient downtime be provided in reasonable proximity to the new learning. Thus, by creating learning environments that are both spatially harmonious and inviting and temporally aligned with circadian and ultradian cycles of activity and recovery, we create the optimal environmental context for the enhancement of learning—this, before we even commence teaching!

> Since frontal lobe activation determines the extent to which one is capable of doing all higher mental operations, it is essential that sufficient downtime be provided in reasonable proximity to the new learning.

Making Sense and Assigning Meaning

There is a further dimension to downtime and its relationship to learning that needs to be considered; one associated with higher forms of intelligence such as problem-detection and -solving, analysis, synthesis, evaluation, and application. It is directly related to the ultimate mechanisms by which the brain converts working memory into long-term memory (without which recall cannot occur, therefore making whatever learning in which one is engaged useless). A twofold process, it involves, first, the degree to which any new learning makes sense to an individual and, second, whether or not personal meaning or significance can be extrapolated from the experience. Common sense dictates and learning experts would no doubt agree, that making sense and finding meaning are critical, non-negotiable processes related to memory retention (Sousa, D, 2001, p. 46-49).

The business of sense and meaning cannot be understated, because the sad fact is that very little of what gets taught in school is actually learned—that is, retained in long-term memory. Whether it is entirely accurate or not, it is sometimes reported that the amount of information retained by the average student, after twelve years of education, at around two percent, and by the brightest, most academically gifted around four to five percent! One has to wonder how much improvement could be attained by the simple act of proactively providing downtime.

Another important aspect of downtime in forging a sense of meaning comes from the discovery of the so-called default mode network (DMN). Apparently an entirely accidental finding, evidence for its existence occurred when researchers first measured brain activity during periods of undirected mental activity. While not designed to explore these states, that evidence began to accumulate and eventually attract attention due to the specificity of certain brain regions activated during periods of rest and quiet; this, in opposition to areas most active during goal-directed tasks. Confirming the blood-flow studies from decades prior, the increased brain activity during periods of quiet rest is specific to those that include the frontal lobes and prefrontal cortex. Moreover, scientists have recently confirmed that the DMN and alpha brain waves are "coupled." Those reporting the coupling (Jue Mo et al, 2013) state that, "the default mode network, a key system mediating introspective processes… appears to exhibit behavior similar to that of alpha. It is suppressed or deactivated on average when subjects are actively engaged in demanding cognitive tasks (p. 112)." Evidently, when provided the opportunity, we "default" to a state of quiet self-reflection, the brain's innate way of ensuring that from our experiences we will derive sense and acquire meaning.

If the highest intelligences are to be invoked—those related to issues of moral and ethical judgement, empathy, conscience, creative response—even more reflection time appears necessary. One of the signature abilities of the frontal lobes, and in particular the prefrontal cortex, of the brain is self-reflection, without which the highest intelligence capacities appear to be constrained, and without which we are relegated to a life more beholden to instinctive reaction than active reflection. In that case our response to experiences would be primarily under the sway of the perceptual mechanisms, memories, and survival strategies of the posterior lobes and the low-brain.

Arguably, the greatest longing of a human being is to find meaning and purpose in life. This may be why practices involving silence and solitude have been long-standing traditions in the world's great religious and spiritual traditions. Things—especially important things like deep understanding, creative intent, purposeful commitment to moral activity, to name a few—often take time, stillness, and silence to clarify and manifest.[12]

"Fixing-In" Learning

Downtime—the routine and rhythmic tendency towards sensory disengagement during the waking hours—is an essential ingredient in all learning, for it initiates and facilitates the "fixing-in" of new learning into the neural structure of the brain. Switching on the genes related to the formation of new protein structures that become both new dendritic connections and new neurons, begins as a result of the interplay between periods of engaged learning (especially when novelty, challenge, and feedback are present), followed by periods of downtime, as the brain goes through its programmed and predictable state-changes (as reflected in the ultradian increases and decreases of brain waves). Active learning combined with downtime promotes the expression, as we have learned (see Chapter 6), of at least two classes of genes that code for the proteins involved in the creation of new neurons and new connections. Simply stated, without periods of downtime the process of learning cannot take place with anything approaching optimal results.

> Simply stated, without periods of downtime the process of learning cannot take place with anything approaching optimal results.

In its essence, downtime needs to be non-challenging time, since the presence of added stimuli such as challenge, feedback and even novelty competes with the brain's need to strengthen the newly acquired

12 Two books of interest are related to this important theme. One, *Thinking Fast and Slow*, by Daniel Kahneman, recipient of the Nobel Prize in Economic Sciences, was selected by the New York Times Book Review as one of the best books of 2011. The other is *Hare Brain, Tortoise Mind*, by Guy Claxton (2000).

neural fields, thus further encoding the new learning. And, the more complex and novel the information or experience being learned, the more downtime is needed. What Eric Jensen says rings true when he asserts that one could be a great teacher and still have the kids' attention for only 20 or 30 percent of the time! (Jenson, 2000). Acceptance of this simple fact of the physiology of learning and intelligence could revolutionize pedagogical practice, for it implies a firm belief not only in a child's innate capacity to actively seek out areas of engaged interest and learning (the crux of the issue in innate motivation!)—it also means having greater trust in the natural learning rhythms of the child.

Despite a great deal of scientific evidence in support of appropriate downtime, disengagement, relaxation, reverie—it goes by many names—most schools today are excessively, if not exclusively, caught in "uptime" cycles. While all this busyness is certainly well-intended, it can only result in diminished learning potential. Unfortunately, downtime has been given a bad name, since—in our task oriented, increasingly accountability driven work places and schools—it looks like time is being wasted. In the educational system a long-standing belief is that children can only learn while paying close attention; thus, educators have concerned themselves almost exclusively with how to engage attention and keep it engaged. As we have seen, this systemic bias is far from the truth, for both activity and downtime are necessary, with routine doses of reverie thrown into the equation.

Reflecting on the role of downtime in learning, Dawna Markova comments: "We are allowed no time to digest our thoughts, so... we acquire facts and spit them out. There's no time for the brain to go through all that it goes through, this incredible metabolism, to create new patterns...In our culture, we are now so outer-directed that when a child begins to experience their mind going into wonder, we consider it a deficit" (Markova, 1996).[13] Another commentator put it this way: The daydreaming child, or adult, is usually an object of contempt or considered in need of therapy. This certainly rings true. In spite of this unfortunate and all too pervasive attitude, downtime will continue

---

13 The quote comes from an interview on New Dimensions radio. http://www. iamplify.com/store/product_details/New-Dimensions/Dawna-Markova-How-We-Learn/product_id/2278. Her 1996 book, *An Unused Intelligence*, is a full explication of this central idea.

to play an essential role in learning, the development of intelligence, creativity and well-being.

Thus, we have become increasingly influenced by the mistaken belief that downtime (reverie, fantasy, daydream, call it what we will) is somehow wrong or bad for our children. Schools can unwittingly exacerbate the problem by allowing almost no quiet downtime (many have even eliminated rest-time in kindergarten!) during the day. Teachers, many of whom know how important downtime is to learning, will often say that they feel guilty or at the very least uncomfortable about the fact that they are likely to be viewed with suspicion by fellow teachers or administrators if their students don't appear to be busy, active and "on-task" at all times.

Some years ago, a high school science teacher in one of Tim's workshops reported, after hearing the information on the importance of downtime to the learning process, that he'd read about this line of research some years previously. Thinking that it made sense he decided to see what would happen with the students who were in his class immediately following lunch—a group, he said, that was performing very poorly, and about whom he felt concern and frustration because of their seeming incapacity to settle down and focus. Out of curiosity (borne of desperation, he admitted) he announced to the students that henceforth when they came into the classroom the first 5-10 minutes of class would be completely devoted to quiet time. He turned the lights off and permitted no talking, reading, or studying. The only permissible options were to sit quietly or to put one's head down on the desk.

It was amazing to hear his story unfold for a couple of reasons. The first was that he reported seeing an almost immediate improvement in the class once students settled into the new quiet-time routine. He went on to say that in the time remaining for each class period the students accomplished more work, participated more fully, seemed to better comprehend the material, and did better on their work than they had done before the downtime "experiment." The second reason that the story was so poignant was his admission that because of the growing guilt he felt about the amount of downtime ("non-instructional time") they were getting, he became increasingly self-conscious about "what my colleagues might be thinking or saying" and ended up abandoning the practice altogether—this, in spite of the positive results he was achieving.

Interestingly, after sharing this story with the group he vowed to return to the practice of building in at least some routine downtime for his students!

This isn't to say that children (or students) ought not be busy, active and engaged in learning. Of course, that ought to be happening. In fact, it's probably the clearest hallmark of true learning. And everyone would readily agree that it would be great if it were happening more of the time for more learners in school. The point is that the outwardly focused, engaged aspect of learning is just that: one aspect, or one half of the learning cycle. The other aspect reflects the rhythmic, oscillating nature of consciousness; one that involves periodic withdrawal of the senses during which the inner processes of pattern extraction, assimilation, connection and creative reworking of the experience assures that new learning will indeed occur.

Adults, Too, Need Downtime

The omnipresent phenomena of overactivity coupled with lack of downtime is really just a reflection of our society, is it not? Busyness, coupled with hurry, is the order of the day in practically every facet of our lives. We're the "24/7" society. Yet we pay a high price, personally and collectively, since productivity and health both suffer when the brain and body requirement for downtime—also known as "taking a break"— is neglected or ignored. The following graphic (Figure 40) illustrates what is known as the Basic Rest and Activity Cycle (BRAC), the 90-to 120-minute cycle that occurs approximately twelve to sixteen times every day, a crucial element of which is the roughly 20-minute period of rest and recovery. While the graphic reveals the natural rise and fall of activity levels and performance for the now familiar—you guessed it—ultradian cycle, two other rhythmic processes occur which are not shown on the graphic: the body's regulatory systems and the variation in states of mind.

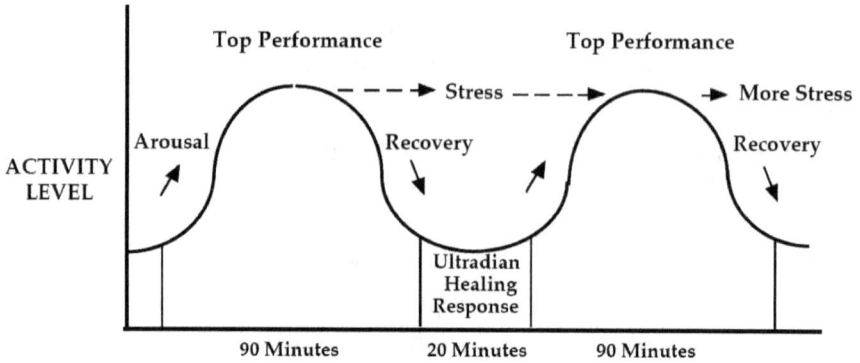

Figure 40. Ultradian Performance.
Image by Rossi.

A glance at the graphic shows what we all experience as true: periods of heightened attentiveness, focused activity, and the peak of performance are most assuredly followed by a trough in which we experience a notable decline. At the same time, and often at the same place in the cycle, a rise and fall in the efficiency of the self-regulating major systems of the mind and body occurs, including the autonomic nervous system (regulating cycles of activity and rest), the endocrine system (regulating hormones and messenger molecules), and the immune system (regulating disease-fighting capability). A regularly recurring period of rest and recovery is crucial to the well-being of these systems, which is presumably why Rossi labeled the graph the "Ultradian Healing Response."

Alternating states of mind also accompany the ultradian cycle. In the same way that we experience regularly recurring periods of dreaming during sleep (these periods appear as black spokes on the scallop-shaped fan, Figure 39), we experience periods of daydream, fantasy, and reverie when we are awake. As the mind shifts to an inner focus and our unconscious is allowed free-reign, as it were, we go through a period during which we are more likely to find the solution to a vexing problem, make connections between past learning and present understanding, and/or accessing creative insight and inspiration.

It is clear to most of us that a hurried, harried work and lifestyle is often at odds with the dictates of this natural rhythm, which is why we have taken the liberty of adding to the graphic the dotted lines with arrows, and the word "stress." For, when we drive ourselves to operate in peak performance mode—in spite of the requirements for rejuvenation that natural rhythms dictate—we unwittingly increase our stress levels and overtax our autonomic nervous system, which in turn can set the stage for disease and eventual illness. Over time, as the high level of stress takes its cumulative toll, we risk losing all that we had hoped to attain: high-level performance, good health, and creative expression.

A final example of how the ultradian cycle bears directly upon learning and well-being can be appreciated by an understanding of the regularly occurring shift between the two sides of the brain.

The Dance of the Hemispheres

Here's a quick experiment to conduct. Cover one of your nostrils with a finger, breath normally, and note the relative airflow entering the other; then compare it to the other nostril when its opposite is covered. Most people will observe a difference: one nostril is more open while the other is more closed or congested. There's a reason for this and it has to do with two interacting and interdependent ultradian rhythms.

Over 50 years ago researchers established the fact that throughout the day (and night) one hemisphere of the brain is generally more active or dominant than the other, in cycles roughly approximating the same 90-to-120-minute (with variations of up to three hours and more, depending on circumstances) ultradian rhythm so familiar to us by now. In addition, for more than a century medical science has known that one of the body's natural rhythms is the blood flow alternation directly affecting the opening of right and left nostril passages (Rossi, 1991). When blood flow is greater in the left nostril, for example, its size and shape are affected, making airflow more difficult because of the engorged tissue and relative congestion. In comparison, the right nostril is less congested, leading to ease of airflow.[14]

Interestingly, this phenomenon is linked to cerebral hemispheric balance in the brain. Keeping in mind that each hemisphere controls the opposite side of the body, the left nostril directly relates to activity (and control) in the right hemisphere, while the right nostril relates to the left cerebral hemisphere. As stated, nasal airflow differences oscillate in a

---

14 There is a wonderful CT-image that clearly shows this phenomenon, found at
https://en.wikipedia.org/wiki/Nasal_cycle#/media/File:Concha_nasalis.gif

rhythm lasting approximately one and a half hours to three hours. The physiology of this phenomenon is pretty straightforward and describable (Shannahoff-Khalsa, 2001). As air flows through the nostril and across the olfactory bulb, neurons relay the sensation to the raphe nuclei located deep in the brainstem. The raphe acts to control the rhythm of hemispheric dominance. Greater electroencephalographic (EEG) amplitudes can be measured in the brain hemisphere that corresponds to the predominating airflow in the opposite nostril (Shannahoff-Khalsa, 1993). The nasal cycle is also known to be tied to and regulated by the sympathetic (think, arousal) and parasympathetic (think, relaxation) branches of the autonomic nervous system (Austin, 1998). Evidently the sympathetic arm of the ANS produces vasoconstriction and decongestion in one nostril, while a simultaneous parasympathetic dominance exists in the other, producing vasodilation and congestion resulting in reduced airflow (Shannahoff-Khalsa, 1991).

Intriguing research exists on the topic of nasal and hemispheric alteration, especially as it relates to human performance (Klein et al, 1986). The data clearly suggest that mental alertness and activity can be brought more into conscious control and enhanced through awareness and synchronization of breathing rhythms. In addition, this cyclical awareness suggests a means by which one can consciously match the type of mental activity one wishes to engage in, with the possibility of enhancing its efficiency. For example, it has been shown that verbal efficiency is greater while breathing primarily through the right nostril (thus activating the left, more verbal, hemisphere), whereas spatial skills were better facilitated during left nostril breathing (right cerebral hemisphere engaged).

...mental alertness and activity can be brought more into conscious control and enhanced through awareness and synchronization of breathing rhythms.

It is worth noting that by intentionally opening the nostril that is more closed (i.e. through forced breathing by plugging the more open nostril and breathing through the more congested one; or lying down on the side opposite to that which one wishes to have more open) one can enact a shift in hemispheres. This can be helpful when one is feeling out-of-sorts, for example, or headachy. By intentionally breathing through the congested nostril, the out-of-sorts or headachy feeling often begins to change—sometimes within minutes. This is due, in part, to the fact that during this cycle of hemispheric shifting there are measurable differences in mood. It has long been known, for example, that the right side of the brain tends toward more of a downbeat or pessimistic affect, while the left side tends to be somewhat more upbeat or optimistic in mood throughout its half of the cycle (Austin,1998).

Since moods surely affect our perceptions and ability to think and learn, it is important not only to be aware of how they relate to brain rhythms, but also to realize that we can exert some control over our mood. Later we will look at the special state that emerges when the hemispheres are in a balanced state, something that happens midway between the alternating cycle of left to right, right to left.

Summary

Let's summarize what we covered on the Nobel-prize worthy topic of chronobiology. We began by putting forward the idea that physiological states—and therefore learning states—are under the direction of innate biological rhythms or cycles. These naturally recurring periods, and particularly circadian and ultradian cycles, have a direct influence on learning, as well as on health and well-being. Three examples of these influences were covered in some detail: the altered circadian pattern that occurs during the teen years, the need for downtime as a central feature of the ultradian cycle, and implications of the rhythmic cycling between right and left hemispheres of the brain.

In the next chapter, we build on the knowledge gained thus far about innate biological rhythms by taking an in-depth look at the various states of mind or consciousness that affect learning and human performance as measured by the ultradian rise and fall of neuro-electrical oscillations known as "brain waves."

Chapter 10

Brainwaves, Mind States, Learning, Performance and Well-Being

"High-frequency electrical activity in the brain...can destabilize the entire mind-body system and contribute to a host of problems, from apprehension to worry, emotional reactivity, impulsivity, and impatience."

– Les Fehmi, PhD

"EEG activity during childhood reveals, at every developmental stage, a predominance of a specific brain wave."

– Bruce Lipton, PhD

Reviewing What We Mean by Brainwaves

As the 100 billion neurons throughout the brain energetically connect with each other to form complex networks, their activity generates rhythmic fluctuations of electrical potential, or voltage, with field effects that can be detected at the surface of the scalp. When captured and traced by the electroencephalograph, or EEG, these rhythmic fluctuations appear as sine waves (see Figure 41, below). Collectively designated "brain waves," they are commonly characterized by frequency (Hertz, or "Hz," which are cycles per second), which can range from below 1 Hz to as many as 100 Hz.

Besides varying in frequency, brainwaves also vary in amplitude, which corresponds to the amount of voltage—energy—generated in the cortex at the site being measured. The voltage is miniscule compared to, say, the voltage of a flashlight battery; it is measured in microvolts (millionths of a volt). That it can be measured at all is a triumph of modern electronic technology. The instrument used for this measurement is called an electroencephalograph, or EEG.

Brain Waves

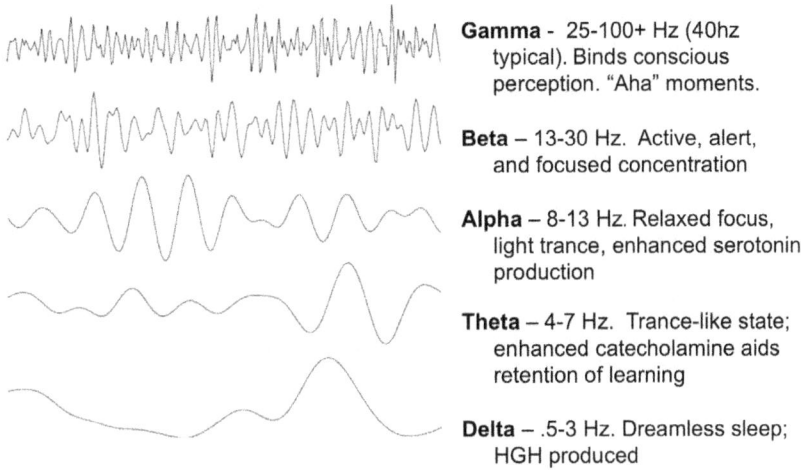

Gamma - 25-100+ Hz (40hz typical). Binds conscious perception. "Aha" moments.

Beta – 13-30 Hz. Active, alert, and focused concentration

Alpha – 8-13 Hz. Relaxed focus, light trance, enhanced serotonin production

Theta – 4-7 Hz. Trance-like state; enhanced catecholamine aids retention of learning

Delta – .5-3 Hz. Dreamless sleep; HGH produced

Figure 41. Brainwave Activity as Shown by EEG.
Image by Tim Burns and Jim Brown.

More than a half-century of research has gone into correlating EEG frequencies with various states and conditions of consciousness. Figure 41, above, summarizes some of this research. It follows the conventional grouping of frequencies into bandwidths named by Greek letters.

The kind of computerized EEG's now in use can provide immediate feedback on the brain's electrical activity according to location, frequency, and amplitude (more sophisticated measures such as coherence and synchrony between or among multiple measuring sites are increasingly available as well). The overall pattern of brain wave activity, called a "state," shows up as a different set of amplitude and frequency signatures. According to the kind of activity an individual is engaged in, one brain wave state may be dominant at any given time, though all brain wave states will remain present at some level. If any of these states are deficient, excessive, or difficult to access, mental performance can suffer and bodily health can eventually fail.

This, then, is the story of brainwaves (also spelled brain waves).

Brainwave Frequencies and Associated States of Mind

Beginning with studies on the sleep state, EEG research has continued over the past half century, resulting in a system of classification of several brainwave states. These states range from low amplitude/high frequency to high amplitude/low frequency electrical signatures. Moreover, early research established the overall pattern of these brain states, which is an oscillation (or movement up and down), throughout the diurnal/nocturnal cycle, on a rhythm of (not surprisingly!) approximately 90-120 minutes, very similar to the hemispheric cycle described in the previous chapter. This oscillation appears as the continuous scallop-like wave around the edges of the 24-hour circadian graph back in Figure 39 (Chapter 9).

The four originally studied and designated states include beta (wakefulness), alpha (daydreaming and relaxed reverie), theta (drowsiness and transition to sleep), delta (deep sleep), and REM (Rapid Eye Movement sleep associated with dreaming). They remain the benchmark states used in contemporary research, although more recent research—and a great deal of interest and excitement—has added additional states such as those designated epsilon, or extremely low frequency, and gamma, extremely high. We'll be looking at each of these states in what follows. Throughout the circadian cycle the brain goes from beta to alpha, theta, and then back "up" through theta, to alpha and beta. At night, we fall into delta, or deep sleep, followed by REM, or dream sleep.

The range of brainwave activity in cortical neurons was originally established at between 0.5 hertz in delta, up to around 30-plus hertz in beta—though there is a lack of agreement on the upper range of beta. Current research involves exploration of frequency ranges much higher than beta. We'll explore each of these brainwave states in more detail, including some of the more recently discovered non-ordinary and intriguing but, because of lack of complete understanding, more controversial brainwave states.

Beta Brainwave State

Moving from the peak of the diurnal activity cycle to the trough, the brain goes through several changes in energy and awareness levels. Beta brainwave (or beta wave, or more simply, beta) predominates when the brainwaves are between roughly 13 and 35 hertz. This state of brain function is associated with externally directed linear thinking, alert mental functioning, and focused problem solving. It is the state that the brain is in when we have our eyes open and are listening and thinking during analytical problem solving, judgment, decision-making, as well as actively processing information from the world around us. In humans accustomed to the normal day and night activity cycle, beta is most prominent during the day. It is not at all a constant state; nor are any of the others. At night low-level beta may occur but only at brief intervals during sleep such as when we awaken briefly, turn over, and fall asleep again. However, if we then begin to think too much the rising tide of beta can keep us awake indefinitely.

Beta has a relatively large range, and consequently has been divided into low, mid, and high ranges. The highest range of beta activity (18 hertz and above) is associated with alert attention. However, it can also relate to agitation, stress and anxiety, and it can also be associated with attentional problems such as Attention Deficit Disorder (ADD) and Attention Deficit Hyperactive Disorder (ADHD), conditions hallmarked by difficulty in focusing, screening or dampening extraneous sensory input, and therefore in concentration. The mid-range (15-18 hertz) relates to normal processes of attention, a time when the brain registers, screens and attends to a variety of sensory inputs, while being an optimal frequency for mental ability, focus and concentration. The low end of beta, like the upper range of alpha, is associated with relaxed focus, an ideal state for periods of distraction-free mental activity and inner focus.

Alpha Brainwave State

Following beta, as the 90-to-120-minute ultradian brain wave cycle continues, a gradual shift into alpha occurs, a state hallmarked by an overall slowing of brainwave frequency. Here the brain operates within the frequency range of about 8 to 13 hertz. Alpha is a common state for the brain and occurs whenever a person is alert but not actively processing information. The brainwaves during this state are strongest over the occipital lobe cortex (back of the head) as well as the frontal cortex, indicating a state of relaxed alertness.

First discovered about one hundred years ago, it took at least 50 years to understand the amazing benefits that accrue from enhanced alpha states, including improved immune response and enhanced mental acuity. By the end of the 1960s biofeedback technology was affording subjects a way to train their own brains in generating increased alpha wave activity. Scientists by that time knew a great deal about alpha and what made it appear and disappear in the brain, for it isn't always present. Alpha, for example, disappears in deep sleep and in such high arousal states as anger and fear. In other words, alpha is highly vulnerable to stress.

Alpha biofeedback training (a topic to which we will return) was first introduced by Joe Kamiya in 1962 (Fehmi and Robbins, 2008, p. 32-33), when he demonstrated that subjects who were required to guess whether or not alpha was present in their EEGs (and were subsequently informed of their accuracy) could, within a few hours, identify with high accuracy when they were producing alpha. He also found that those subjects who were successful in discrimination-training could also produce or suppress alpha activity at will. He later successfully used auditory alpha biofeedback devices which informed subjects of their alpha production through the presence or absence of a tone generated by their own alpha rhythms. The mental states which Kamiya's subjects associated with increased alpha production were reported to be feelings of relaxation, "letting go," and pleasant affect.

By the 1970s feedback training had made its way into mainstream medical and wellness settings, since ongoing research had shown the effectiveness of alpha training in reducing tension, stress, anxiety, and pain. It had also been found to be effective in the treatment of a variety of maladies, including migraine headache, cardiac arrhythmia, chronic fatigue, asthma, and even diabetes (Peper et al, 1979). Clearly, alpha training had proven itself as a viable method to enhance health, overcome certain illnesses, and tap human potential.

The alpha state then is generally experienced as one of relaxed alertness and is a common state for the brain when not actively processing information. When alpha predominates most people feel at ease and calm. Serving as the bridge to deeper states of consciousness—the "portal" between conscious and unconscious experience—alpha has been linked to heightened creativity (creative subjects show more alpha when listening and coming to a solution for creative problems[15]), effortless problem solving, and positive mood tone. Thus, it is an ideal state to be in when learning or performing any task that requires problem solving or creative activity.

It is thought that people of uncommon creative genius are somehow able to remain in this relaxed alpha state during periods of intense work or study. Evidently, these fortunate individuals are able to generate large bursts of alpha wave activity, especially in the left hemisphere of the brain (Robbins, 2000). Less creative people apparently do not produce these bursts when faced with problems, so they are less able to come up with creative ideas and solutions, relying instead on set patterns of reaction.

Bursts of synchronous alpha brain waves also precede peak performance states (Fehmi and Robbins, 2008, p. 116). This state, also referred to as "flow" or "the zone," is one in which our activities and accomplishments seem effortless, engaging, enjoyable and highly efficient. Sports and performance psychologists have taken a keen interest in these special states and they were among the first to turn brainwave research into practical (and at times highly lucrative) application. It is theorized that elite athletes produce large bursts of synchronous alpha in their left hemisphere just before their top performances. Neuropsychologist Les Fehmi associates this phenomenon to a state of superbly balanced attention he terms "Open Focus," which may be the equivalent of "flow." Due, in part, to the intense pressure to perform well and maintain a competitive edge, a unique "high-end" market catering to the needs of elite athletes and performers has emerged over the years.

Alpha training has been found to improve performance in the same way that improving performance through training can lead to increased

---

15 For more on this intriguing aspect of alpha enhancement, see Robbins, *Symphony in the Brain: The Evolution of the New Brainwave Biofeedback.* Atlantic Monthly Press, 2000. This is an excellent resource for parents and teachers alike.

left hemisphere alpha; in other words, it works both ways. Thus, a clear link has been established between optimal performance and enhanced alpha production in the brain, one that holds promise not just in athletics and the performing arts, but in schools, the workplace, and homes of everyday folks. And while any of us could benefit from alpha feedback training, it isn't necessary to go to all the expense involved. Fortunately, one can increase alpha rhythms in a number of ways, such as simply closing one's eyes for a few moments (apparently there is an increase of alpha when looking up with eyes closed) or doing some slow, diaphragmatic breathing. Keep in mind, however, that training the brain to produce more alpha habitually does require learning and engaging in such slow, rhythmic movements as mindfully walking, or the ancient Chinese practices of qi gong or tai chi. Training the brain to reliably produce more synchronous alpha can also be accomplished by developing a meditation practice, practicing a series of Open Focus exercises every day over an extended period,[16] as well as engaging in one of the arts (a topic taken up in Chapter 14).

> ...a clear link has been established between optimal performance and enhanced alpha production in the brain

Theta Brainwave State

Research has long shown that the brain's natural rhythms reveal periods of greater attention followed by periods of low levels of attention. That means the brain is designed for and requires downtime to function properly; further reasons for which are revealed with an understanding of the next stage in the ultradian cycle of brainwaves, theta.

After alpha comes theta, the range between 3 or 4 and 7 hertz. The gradual drift down into theta state is associated with deep relaxation, reverie, day dreaming, the free flow of mental imagery, fantasy, and has been credited with enhanced creativity, sudden insights, and inspiration. In short, theta is a trance-like state. This is also the frequency range

---

16 Although there is a fee involved, we can recommend Femhi's Open Focus resources for at-home or in-classroom practice sessions, available at https://openfocus.com/home/. For background and in addition to the excellent book, the interested reader is also directed to his comprehensive 2003 journal article (see references), a treasure-trove of very readable and highly credible information.

associated with deep meditative states, as some of the earliest research on meditators demonstrated. Deep, or low, theta is characterized by drowsiness and the light sleep that precedes the deepest levels of sleep associated with delta.

Overall, the brain uses this state to release tension and is therefore exceedingly restorative. This is partly because in theta state, brain cells are able to restore their sodium and potassium levels, the electrolytes essential for proper brain functioning. Sodium and potassium levels are involved in osmosis, the chemical exchange process that transports chemicals into and out of brain cells. After an extended period in the beta state, for example, the ratio between potassium and sodium is out of balance. This is the main cause of what is known as "mental fatigue." A brief period in theta (around 10 minutes) can restore the ratio to normal resulting in mental refreshment, emotional balance and decrease in muscle tension. The ability to handle stressful situations is thereby enhanced along with a greater sense of clarity, flow of ideas and a positive mental state. Not surprisingly, we are talking about the biophysical need for routine downtime.

It is a well-known fact that therapeutic hypnosis—with its excellent record of helping people plagued by mental or emotional problems—does its healing wonders when the brain is in theta state. Decades of research has also shown that theta is the state where subliminal suggestion—either from a hypnotherapist or self-induced—works best, for it is in theta that one can eliminate old beliefs, remove blocks, and program in new beliefs. It is very effective for accessing and modifying deep structures like belief systems.

The fact that in theta state one can readily program new beliefs has not missed the attention of those performance and sports psychologists (mentioned earlier) with an interest in peak performance states. They have taken advantage of theta research just as they did with the earlier alpha studies. In the case of theta, a process known as rehearsal has been developed, a term used to describe the use of conscious mental control while in a partly dissociated state, all the while producing or reviewing specific skills and strategies. Typically done during a low-end alpha and high-end theta wave state (known as theta-alpha crossover, as it occurs in the 7 to 10 hertz range), rehearsal can be a powerful way to program the brain to perform in optimal ways. Often, theta and alpha training are combined; with theta the optimal state to rehearse new behaviors or moves, and alpha the best state in which to perform them.

There is another feature of rehearsal during this crossover state that commends itself to use by all of us—rehearsal need not be limited to elite athletes seeking to improve their game and peak performers aspiring to enhanced ability. The context for this feature is a well described temporal- and state-phenomena appearing in both the sleep and consciousness research. Known as hypnogogic and hypnopompic states, these are two periods of heightened susceptibility to suggestion (as the prefix, hypno-, as in hypnosis, implies) that take place in the transition between sleep and being awake. Respectively occurring just prior to entering into a deeper stage of sleep and again upon emerging out of sleep, both are characterized by the trancelike, imagery-laden states of consciousness typical of heightened theta wave activity.

This trancelike state is thought to serve as a bridge between the conscious and the unconscious mind, and as such can be used to great advantage to "program" (or even deprogram) the mind with positive beliefs, cherished goals and the highest aspirations. Like all forms of learning, this requires a period of training and, admittedly, can be a decidedly tricky affair given the almost gravity-like pull and pleasant allure of pending sleep. The mind training entails the maintenance of alert awareness during the 5-to-10-minute theta wave period that precedes deep sleep, during which the mental suggestions occur and/or rehearsal images are produced. This can also be accomplished in the morning, during the hypnopompic phase; just prior to opening one's eyes (part of the recommendation) upon awakening one then uses the same protocol. Again, not so easy but well worth the effort—as the example of Thomas Edison's famous practice of "catnapping" suggests.

With over one thousand registered patents, it seems Edison's prodigious inventiveness and productivity was due in part to his frequent excursions into the realm of his creative unconscious. The story goes that he would periodically retreat to his office, pick up coins near his chair, then sit back comfortably until he found a certain level of relaxed drowsiness, where dreamlike imagery commences. At some point, as he approached the level of sleep, the coins clenched in his fist would be released, fall into a metal pan on the floor, the noise immediately awakening him. He would then write in his notebook the images and possible insights, having learned from experience that these freewheeling reveries often contained clues, if not outright solutions, that could guide his work. Since we all have this innate capability, it awaits only our intention to develop it, combined with effort over time—who knows to where it might lead?

Creative Reverie, "Hemi-Sync" and the Alpha/Theta State

An important facet of the low alpha/high theta frequency range is its relationship to creativity. There is a natural and predictable tendency during each 90-120-minute cycle to enter into a state of relaxed reverie. This typically follows a more active phase of the ultradian rhythm, one in which the focus is outward and our attention is absorbed in the performance of a task. When the time comes to rejuvenate, we become more sensitive and attuned to the inner world, and it is at this time that new and creative ideas begin to attract our attention. This phase of the ultradian cycle—when the window separating waking states of consciousness and the inner, creative mind opens—can be used to play with ideas, gain insight, receive inspiration, or find answers to our most important problems. Joseph Pierce refers to this unique state as one of "recombinant play,"[17] referring to the marvelously playful way in which the brain effortlessly combines and recombines images, ideas and experience an essential ingredient in the process of creativity.

The naturally occurring state of reverie appears to be related to another interesting feature of downtime: inter-hemispheric synchronization. Because the activity of each hemisphere changes in dominance at more-or-less regular ultradian intervals, there exists a phase during which the hemispheres are in a balanced state. It is during this period of time— ten to fifteen minutes or so—that our mental process inclines inward, as the Task Positive Network (TPN) switches off. Recently described as a network of four specific brain regions, active whenever we focus upon or engage with the outside world or attentively perform any task, TPN is accompanied, as we might expected, by an increase in beta-wave frequency in the prefrontal cortex. In contrast, the Default Mode

---

17 A term that has been credited—though we are unable to find a source reference— to Albert Einstein and his own description of the creative thought process.

Network, or DMN (governed by brain regions that work in opposition to the TPN), is thought to be a neutral state of mind, governed by a rise in alpha wave activity. Operating in the background at all times (thus, "by default"), the DMN takes over during periods when focused attention is no longer required and serves as a period of refreshment for body and brain. When the DMN becomes active, we withdraw from the world of the senses and have an opportunity to engage in recombinant play, daydreaming, reverie, and fantasy.

In brief, the TPN switches on whenever our attention is focused and directed. This automatically deactivates the DMN, since they work in opposition to one another. Thus, we are enabled to go between states of outer directed, goal-seeking activity and periods of inner-directed, self-reflection. This is where mindfulness training can be of immense value, as we undertake to train the TPN to pay attention to attention, the result of which enhances of our capacity to better focus on the present moment (a topic to which we return in great detail in Chapter 14).

In an apparent attempt to keep things in balance and prevent overload, the brain periodically switches modes—unfortunately, something we have conditioned ourselves to fight against in our determination to say in-focus and on-task. What we desperately need, however, is balance. Unfortunately, in our hurry-up world much of the time we either ignore or refuse the invitation to enter these wonderfully regenerative and potentially creative downtime moments. All too often this important phase of the brainwave ultradian cycle is dismissed as "mere" daydreaming, so we power up with a cup of coffee or a candy bar. We're too busy (what has been described, not inaccurately, as "hurry-sickness"), pressured or stressed by the constant demands that others, or we ourselves, set. It's easy to lose sight of the fact that if we simply took up the invitation and allowed ourselves the pleasure of a few moments of reverie, we would emerge greatly refreshed and revitalized. Sadly, in today's high-pressure, high-stakes school and workplace environments we are systematically eliminating the gift—and that is exactly what it is—of reverie and downtime.

A potent method for cultivating a state of consciousness called Open Focus (mentioned above in the discussion on alpha brainwaves and previously in Chapter 9) has been developed over the past 40 years by neuropsychologist Les Fehmi (Fehmi and Robbins, 2008). Described in the book, *The Open Focus Brain*, this state gives smooth and equal access to several "attentional styles," each of which is useful for certain circumstances but not, by any means, all. The set of accessible attentional styles includes the one described in the previous paragraph, which Fehmi terms "narrow-objective focus." That is the mode of attention, Fehmi has found in his clinical work, that we Westerners rely on most, all too often excluding the other modes available to us. Open Focus, Fehmi has found, is accompanied by synchronous alpha activity throughout the cerebral cortex—which is why, with his clients, he augments Open Focus practice with neurofeedback, as a way by which to increase synchronous alpha.

In today's high-tech environment, there are some interesting items being produced that purport to induce the brain to enter into alpha, theta, and/or hemispheric synchrony (or "hemi-sync") states by using something called "binaural beats." You can check it out yourself on the internet and try it, but here is the basic approach. A musical score is used or created, often with soft and relaxing nature sounds or ambient tones, and into the music are imbedded tones that operate at slightly different frequencies for each ear (headphones are usually recommended for best effect). Then, for example, if a pure tone of 400 hertz (Hz), or cycles per second, is presented to the right ear and a pure tone of 410 Hz is presented simultaneously to the left ear, what is called an "amplitude modulated standing wave" of 10 Hz (which is the difference between the two tones: 410 minus 400) is experienced as the two waveforms mesh in and out of phase. This binaural beat is not actually heard in the ordinary sense of the word, yet it is perceived by the brain as an auditory binaural beat with a frequency of 10 Hz—which is in the alpha range—and many listeners experience the effects of that: a relaxed yet alert state.

There is another way to bring the brain into hemi-sync mode, and it's been around for a good while. In fact, it's an ancient yogic technique that's been studied here in the West since the 1970s and introduced to the reader earlier. It's called circular or rhythmic breathing and it's very simple. Hold one nostril closed and breathe (normally) through the open nostril, then close the open nostril and breathe out the opposite side. Then breathe in through the previously closed nostril and so forth. Repeat this process for a few minutes and the brain responds by bringing the two hemispheres into a balanced state. We'll have much more to report about the benefits of attentive breathing, to be taken up fully in Chapter 14.

Delta Brainwave State

The lowest frequencies, those between 0.5 and 3 to 4 hertz, are called delta. The more delta appears in the brain, the less awareness there is of the outside world; therefore, it is most present in the deepest stages of sleep. It is the dominant rhythm seen in the infant brain up to about two years of age. The appearance of too much delta when one is awake can severely restrict one's ability to stay attentive and focused. Paradoxically, individuals with Attention Deficit Disorder have been shown to increase delta brain wave activity when attempting to focus, which has the opposite effect of diminishing the ability to attend. On the other hand, peak performers show a clear decrease in delta waves when they focus and attend.

To briefly reiterate what was covered earlier in Chapter 5, delta produces profound levels of stress reduction, which can have a very healing effect on the body. During deep, delta related sleep, human growth hormone is synthesized by the body, which is essential for the growth of the body and is a critical ingredient at work during both childhood and the teenage growth spurts. It is also a key ingredient in maintaining health during the adult years. Since most delta sleep occurs in the first third of the night, those (like teens) who stay up late may not get enough delta sleep and can therefore be more prone to stress, health challenges, and learning difficulties.

Gamma Brainwave State

More recently, a fifth state related to brain wave activity—occurring well above the normal range of beta—has been discovered and researched. These brain wave patterns range in frequency from above 30 to over 100 hertz, a state sometimes referred to as hyper-beta, but more commonly as gamma, which are both the fastest and strongest wave signals produced by the brain.

The first discovery about the function of gamma oscillations dealt with their role in what is called "temporal binding." Immediately following sensory input, gamma waves appear to sweep across the entire brain, apparently to promote binding (also referred to as blending) together of all our senses. Apparently, this has to do with different regions of the brain harmonizing, as neural pathways begin to oscillate at the same frequency in perfectly blended synchrony. This is necessary in order to create a unitary cognitive experience from the rush of incoming information from all sensory areas of the cortex. For example, where the different areas of the visual cortex separately process the color, shape, size, dimension and movement (using five different areas of the occipital cortex) of a seen object, gamma rhythms evidently function to bind them all together into a singular cognitive experience. Thus, it is theorized that gamma provides a way for neurons to correlate and encode information into a coherent perceptual whole. Taking place in bursts taking no more than one-fifth of a second, this happens with such rapidity, smoothness and efficiency that we take no notice of it.

The next discovery established a connection between this instantaneous blending of sensory experience (which takes place, as indicted, below our level of awareness and continuously) and the "Aha!" experience that seems to happen unbidden. This discovery has led some researchers to dub gamma the insight wave. Happening in small, almost unnoticed ways throughout the day as we negotiate and resolve various challenges, from finding our way to a new location while driving, to getting an insight into a personal or work-related dilemma. They also occasionally happen when a solution to a more vexing problem is suddenly revealed or some new, creative insight appears. Combining brain synchrony, heightened perception and high-level information processing these so-called Eureka! moments are experienced as states of elevated consciousness, leaving some of us to wonder if and how it might be possible to live in such a heightened state more of the time.

Now from the research laboratory comes the intriguing news that it might—just might—be possible to stabilize this brain state and thereby experience it more consistently than would normally be the case. Apparently, this can and does happen, at least for some of us. This, according to Richard Davidson, PhD, Co-founder and Director of the Center for Healthy Minds at the University of Wisconsin – Madison, a leading institution for research in contemplative and neuro sciences. Davidson is the author of some 375 scientific and popular articles, mostly on topics related to the effects of meditation on the brain. In a recent book (Goleman and Davidson, 2017), he reports on a completely unexpected finding; one that emerged from a study of the brains of some 21 so-called world-class meditators. The most striking feature relates to how long-term meditation practice appears to actually stabilize gamma waves, resulting in a set of common traits among these experienced meditators, including heightened levels of compassion, presence, peace, resilience and resourcefulness—attributes that apparently differ somewhat according to the specific type of practice undertaken (more on this topic in Chapter 14). According to research at the Laboratory for Affective Neuroscience, for example, significantly more gamma activity occurs in various cortical regions of experienced Tibetan Buddhist meditators while they are engaged in meditation on loving kindness than in comparable regions of meditating control subjects who have received briefer training in that particular form (Lutz et al, 2004).

These particular traits are apparently due to the fact that these meditators function in gamma wave range, all the time. Continually! Unexpected and highly unusual to say the least, yet also promising since the potential to evoke this state and the above qualities is available—in theory at least—to us all. While further confirmation of this amazing discovery needs to take place, it can be added to the growing list of purported beneficial outcomes of undertaking a mindfulness practice (covered in-depth in Chapter 14).

Other Brainwave States

Besides the normally occurring brainwave states covered above, researchers have been charting other unusual and intriguing brain states. For example, the highest frequency range studied to date—around 200 hertz and referred to as lambda—appears to be related to what some refer to as ecstatic states of consciousness. There may also exist a co-occurrence between these extreme high-end frequencies and the super-low frequencies, less than 0.5 Hz and measured as low as one wave every 10 seconds or so, known as epsilon. This state of "blissful stillness" emerges when lambda and epsilon appear together. It is thought that this state can appear during meditative, creative, insightful, and even religious states of consciousness, although much more research is needed to validate this. We can anticipate learning more about these lines of research in the future.

From Theory and Research to Application: Neurofeedback

Brainwave research holds real potential for understanding the mysteries of human consciousness, and to that end decades of research producing thousands of studies have been catalogued. Beyond that, it also offers the promise to alter these states of consciousness, thereby leading to improved learning, enhanced performance, heightened intelligence, and improved health. Neurofeedback, using EEG feedback from the brain to directly enable one to actively alter brain function, has been proven by decades of research to improve brain activity.

Neurofeedback training is really very simple, even though the equipment used is quite sophisticated. In brief, whenever a certain threshold of brainwaves (say, alpha) is detected in the brain, a transducer changes the brainwave information into a signal that is audible (a slight beep or tone) and/or visual (a blinking light or an entire display, perhaps even a computer animation or game), thus giving "feedback" to the subject. This direct feedback provides the immediate cues that assist the subject in recognizing the unique state of mind and/or body associated with a particular frequency range.

Over time the practitioner learns to reproduce the desired state of body and mind without use of the equipment. That is, the brain state that corresponds to the neuronal changes becomes completely accessible without the need for feedback equipment. The truly exciting thing is this: the brain develops new neurons and new neural pathways through this kind of regular feedback practice and repetition. In effect, the brain has done that which it does best: adapt and change to fit the requirements of the environment into which it is situated.

A common objective of neurofeedback is to train the brain to better focus, by altering the patterns of brainwave activity that interfere with concentration. That neurofeedback training can accomplish this permanently is nothing short of miraculous for students and parents alike. One of the common applications whereby concentration can be improved, for example, is to increase beta frequencies, dampen down theta frequencies, or both. This is being done every day with thousands of individuals for diverse problems, including students diagnosed with ADD and ADHD.

It is also clear that alpha brain wave function can be strengthened with neurofeedback, which can lead to improved learning, performance, and enhanced creativity. While currently expensive, due to the equipment involved, expertise required, and the time it takes (usually a minimum of 20 sessions with a trained psychologist), it is highly probable that as the technology improves and costs come down we will see this wonderful technology used within schools to help children gain control and mastery over their own brain states.

Getting the Most from Brain States

Each brain state is related to a different level of consciousness or awareness; no one brain wave is best for all the challenges of life. One researcher used the analogy of driving a car to make this point: We get into trouble if one of the gears on our car goes out, or if we forget to use some of the gears. For example, if we drive our car starting in first gear, and then shift directly into fourth gear (skipping second and third): we will have high gas mileage but huge repair bills. The same is true of our brains. Continuing the analogy, many people often skip their second and third brain gears (alpha and theta), the consequence of which can be low productivity and high medical bills.

This can happen, for example, when we wake up abruptly from a deep sleep (delta), aroused by an alarm clock, followed by stress and anxiety (high beta) about being late or being under time pressure, which is augmented by disturbed and insufficient sleep, plus coffee to force wakefulness (caffeine suppresses theta and alpha, while stimulating beta). Then comes the common experience of stress, pressure, and time urgency (constant beta) at school or work, as portrayed by Figure 40, Chapter 9. By the time the harried, beta-saturated day ends we fall into an exhausted, deep sleep (delta), a direct consequence of having spent too little time slowly unwinding, relaxing, and drowsing in the natural alpha and theta rhythms—the Default Network Mode that we are meant to experience periodically throughout the day.

This scenario—the experience of shifting our brains suddenly and forcefully from delta to beta, and then back to delta, missing altogether the restorative and healing alpha and theta states— commonly happens day after day in our culture. Surely there has to be a better way, and it is up to each of us, as adults, to find it. When it comes to children, however, we have a responsibility to them to ensure that they can enjoy the amazing benefits of each frequency range and its associated state. Moreover, as adults we need to seriously consider the fact that children's brains and bodies grow and mature best within the innate frequency ranges for each state in their development, the final topic in our exploration of brain basics, to which we now turn.

> ...we need to seriously consider the fact that children's brains and bodies grow and mature best within the innate frequency ranges for each state in their development...

Brainwaves States and Stages of Childhood Development

One of the most powerful arguments on behalf of a kinder, gentler, and certainly more child-centered approach to early education comes from the research on brainwave states during each stage of brain development. As the opening epigraph by neurobiologist Bruce Lipton emphasizes: "EEG activity during childhood reveals, at every developmental stage, a predominance of a specific brainwave" (Lipton, 2005, p. 163). The literature is quite clear that there is a patterned sequence of EEG expression tied to specific stages of brain maturation. More specifically, as Barriga-Paulingo et al (2011) point out, there are two features predictive of this developmental sequence. The first is that for theta and alpha rhythms, maturation begins in posterior regions and ends in anterior regions; and, second, with increasing age through childhood, lower frequencies decrease and higher frequencies increase—specifically, a decrease of absolute and relative power in the delta and theta bands and an increase in the alpha and beta bands during brain maturation (p. 144). The opposite, greater power in the lower frequency ranges, is demonstrable at younger ages. They describe this shift from low to high EEG frequencies as a characteristic signature of brain maturation.

Let's recall the stages of brain and childhood development, weaving in the information about brainwave states just covered.

Infancy and Delta Brainwave

Infants spend most of their time asleep, and there is a very important reason for doing so: the body and brain are going through an enormous growth spurt. At birth the brain weighs about one pound; by age two it has doubled in weight (an adult brain weighs about three pounds). At no other time does the rate of growth come anywhere near that taking place in the first two years. Recall that delta is the frequency associated with deep sleep and that human growth hormone is synthesized during that time. It makes sense that infants would necessarily be generating a great deal of the frequency that is associated with growth and sensorimotor integration, and so it is.

Early Childhood and Theta Brainwave

Piaget, as we discussed earlier, called the period from around age one and a half or two until six or seven, Pre-operational. The description he used, which perfectly describes the child at this stage was "the dreaming child." This view of the young child as existing in a world of fantasy, imagination, dreams, and play is highly consonant with the specific frequency domain most predominant during this stage: theta. As we saw, adults experience theta stages periodically throughout the day. They are times during which we tend to "space out," daydream and so forth. It's difficult as adults to imagine being in that state all the time, for we'd probably accomplish very little and achieve next to nothing. Well, this is the world of the child, who lives in a very different frequency domain than we do.

Later Childhood and Alpha Brainwave

From about age six or seven up to the onset of puberty—what Piaget called Concrete Operations—the predominant EEG frequency of the child is alpha. Alpha is strongest in the occipital lobes at the rear of the brain, diminishing towards the frontal lobes of the brain. The state of relaxed alertness accompanying alpha is one that facilitates learning in both children and adults. There is a difference, however, and it is this. The alpha state is the natural abode of children, but as hurried and harried adults we can and do lose contact with it. Overtaxing the Task Positive Netword can become normal, as we forget about activating the Default Mode Network and our stress levels inexorably rise, the allostatic load growing weightier.

It is vitally important to provide environments of safety, security, and enrichment for children, to ensure that they can engage in learning within the resonance of the alpha frequency. Not only is learning enhanced, but positive emotions are much more accessible, discipline problems are greatly reduced and—as an added bonus—the immune system is strengthened due to an overall reduction in stress and anxiety and an increase in serotonin, the master mood regulator.

Teen Years and Beta Brainwave

With the approach of puberty, and the changes initiated by sex hormones, the frequencies of the brainwaves change as well. The predominant EEG frequency with the onset of adolescence is beta, found principally in the frontal lobes. From an evolutionary perspective beta allows us to take in and assess new information quickly, which was certainly necessary for survival. Beta makes active all physiological systems, thereby demanding and using large amounts of physical resources. However, when beta goes into overdrive, and recovery-downtime is missing, it eventually results in physical exhaustion. Think of constantly running through a jungle, not knowing were the next sabretooth tiger is going to come from, but feeling they are all around all the time! Unfortunately, that is the norm for far too many teens, for although tigers are no longer a threat, their nervous systems are constantly being overstimulated and potentially exhausted. Developing a meaningful sense of self requires the essential ingredient, reflection. This can only occur of course in downtime-mode which, for many if not most teens, is an ingredient entirely missing from the mix.

In summary, each stage of childhood and adolescence has been found to have its own natural abode when it comes to the innate unfolding of the powers of the brain. We would do well to better understand these natural phenomena and continue to find creative ways of applying them in our own lives and those of our students. We can do this by finding common ground with those who contribute each day to making our schools a place of refuge for those who need it and providing enriched learning for all who spend time there.

We have now completed our survey of the human brain; its form and function, development and maturation; its largely untapped potential and possibility. In subsequent chapters we focus on two other extraordinary aspects of the human nervous system—referred to in some scientific circles as brains in their own right—the body-brain in Chapter 11 and the heart-brain in Chapter 12. That will be followed in Chapter 13 by an exploration of the origins and development of the human mind. In Chapter 14 we closely examine the concept and scientific studies of mindfulness meditation as a means by which the various aspects of the human nervous system might be significantly enhanced. Finally, in Chapter 15, we pull everything together into a framework, offering suggestions for practical implementation of the ideas put forth in the book.

Chapter 11

The Intelligent Body: Sensing, Intuition, and the Embodied Mind

"If learning isn't in your body, where is it? No learning is really yours until it is in your body."

– Andy Bryner and Dawna Markova

"Our culture…insists that our thinking happens exclusively in the head. And so we are stuck in the cranium, unable to open the door to the body and join its thinking."

– Philip Shepherd

Introduction: Key Scientific Insights Leads the Way to a New Understanding

Up to this point we have been focusing exclusively on the cranial brain, those aspects of it that we think of as the "learning brain:" Its structure, its function, its dynamic maturation and development. Our goal thus far has been to elucidate the wonders of this three-pound universe, carried about within the shelter of the cranium, of which we are all the fortunate bearers and custodians. Before we move away from the brain and take up the all important topic—so far having been scarcely touched upon—of the *mind*, and its inseparable relationship to the brain, there is one more topic we must consider, and consider deeply. For it is fundamental to our pursuit of those elements deemed essential to integral development.

The contents of this chapter stand, we think, as an exciting challenge to conventional thinking about how humans develop, learn, and fulfill their potential. For the fact is that as humans we have not one but three exceedingly sophisticated brains. Thus, our learning and adaptive capabilities—our very intelligence in other words—depends not upon the cranial brain alone but upon the integrated development of all three brains.

Over the past half century, and especially in the last two decades, scientific investigations have made key discoveries about two neural systems other than the cranial brain that play a significant role in learning, the purpose of which, always, is to acquire more appropriate and adaptive behaviors. The most common names applied to these neural systems are simply, the "body brain" and the "heart brain." As will be seen, these neural systems build upon and add significantly to MacLean's earlier formulation of the Triune Brain.

The implications of these research findings afford us a unique opportunity—at a particularly auspicious and critical juncture in our evolutionary journey—to re-examine assumptions which have for far too long served a worldview of human development and destiny that has more than reached its expiry date. Moreover, given that the vicissitudes of our rapidly changing planetary environment will increasingly reverberate in every aspect of human affairs, it is not only critically important but downright urgent that we re-examine those assumptions. The research findings that we are about to explore can provide us with a feeling of optimism and excitement about the possibility that we may yet foster a new worldview of the possible human, out of which might emerge a future very different from the one towards which we appear to be heading.

Meet Our Other Brains

That we have three brains, not just one, is not really news in some scientific circles. Originally well outside the mainstream of conventional scientific research, this idea has slowly been gaining traction. To those scientists who cared to take it seriously and inquire deeply it gradually became clear that the body or "gut" brain (essentially the enteric nervous system)[18] and the heart brain both operate neurologically in ways that share similarities (as well as differences of course) with the cranial brain. Functionally, for example, the body brain appears to operate both

---

18 Also known as intrinsic nervous system, the enteric nervous system is one of the main divisions of the autonomic nervous system and consists of a mesh-like system of neurons that governs the function of the gastrointestinal tract.

interdependently with and independently of the cranial brain, using the sheaths of neurons embedded in the walls of the long tube of the gut, or alimentary canal system, some 29 feet end to end (Hadhazy, 2010). Consisting of some 100 million (perhaps as many as 500 million) neurons (more than either the spinal cord or the peripheral nervous system) it uses more than 30 of the same neurotransmitters that the cranial brain uses in carrying out its electrochemical functions. There is, in effect, "a vast brain-based intelligence at work here."

A long-held assumption holds that the nervous system in the gut was relegated solely to the role of digestion and assimilation (which are most assuredly two of its principle functions). Emeran Mayer, professor of physiology, psychiatry and biobehavioral sciences at the David Geffen School of Medicine at the University of California, Los Angeles, puts it, "The system is way too complicated to have evolved only to make sure things move out of your colon." Mayer points out, for example, how shocked scientists were to learn that about 90 percent of the fibers in the primary visceral nerve, the vagus, carry information from the gut to the brain, and not the other way around. Clearly, the body brain is commanding so much of the attention of the cranial brain for a reason.

Much of the information sent up to the cranium from the viscera has to do with a variety of important visceral functions (digestive, assimilative, eliminative), of course.

At the same time, we know that what we think and how we behave is directly affected by our moods, and *they* (as recent scientific inquiry shows) are very much affected by what is going on in the gut. This has a great deal to do with the bacteria that reside there, according to a spate of recent publications (Robinson, 2013). Moreover, it's hard to dispute the contention that intuition—an important information source and unique intelligence—largely involves our "felt sense" or "gut reaction" to the events in our lives, another role that our body brain fulfills.

The heart brain—to which the next chapter of the book is entirely devoted—although having a very different job to do than the body brain or cranial brain, does share some commonalities with both. Consisting of some 40,000 or so neurons (Armour, 2003)—termed sensory *neurites* in the heart—and dozens of the same neurotransmitters and neurohormones (Young, 2012) used by the cranial brain to conduct its business, it has the capacity to perceive, remember and react to information independent of the cranium. Yet, similar to the body brain, the heart brain of course operates interdependently as well.

The emergent recognition that we have not one but three brains and an accompanying three kinds of intelligence which serve different but interrelated functions is not just compelling, it is worthy of our full attention and our deepest curiosity, for it is freighted with implications concerning optimizing human learning and development.

A Needed Course-Correction for a "Head-Centric" Culture

While perhaps well-intended, the exclusive emphasis on mentation and rationality, while overlooking body and heart intelligences, has resulted in a serious neglect of holistic, balanced development. Such neglect has proven to be fraught with significant self-limiting, troubling and even dangerous consequences. For, without something to put a check on the brain's clever cerebrations, it is highly likely that the human world will continue to go increasingly out of balance, becoming far more obsessed with technology, faster-paced, complex and confounding, and disorienting, all of which will add to the already oppressive burden of isolation, alienation, and distress for increasing numbers of people worldwide. All of these characteristics add up to a world that seems increasingly *soulless.*

This viewpoint was strongly expressed by Gregory Bateson (1972) half a century ago, when he wrote: ' …mere purposive rationality unaided by such phenomena as art, religion, dream, and the like, is necessarily pathogenic and destructive of life…' (p. 146).

Joanna Macy (2013), expanding on Bateson's sentiment some forty years later: "As Bateson explains, our self-reflective purposive consciousness illuminates but a small arc in the currents and loops of knowing that interweave us. It is plausible to conceive of mind as coexistent with these larger circuits, with the entire 'pattern that connects" (p. 152).

Contrast this vision of a soulless and disconnected world with the story told by ancestral, so-called "primitive" peoples throughout recorded history and from cultures around the world, a story that placed the heart at the very center of human affairs. For them, the heart was considered to be central to bodily functions and equivalent to life itself. To them, the heart was equal to the mind—a heart-mind in the widest sense that included feelings, will, intellect and most importantly, the soul, the spirit, something that allows us to touch and feel as one with the cosmos and great mystery that is life.

Obviously without access to knowledge about the neuro-physiologic specifics of the three brains, these ancient peoples and more contemporary, highly regarded scientists and eco-philosophers still grasped the essential point: there is more to the mind than our cranial brains can account for. Disembodied intellect not only fails to serve us all that well, it is downright dangerous. We've been an extremely "head-centric" culture for far too long. That trajectory needs to change, and it stands a better chance of doing so once we get used to the scientifically backed notion of three separate but highly commingled brains whose contribution to balanced human potential can be immense.

Intellect Versus Intelligence: A Distinction Whose Time Has Come

Joseph Chilton Pearce asserts that *intellect is not necessarily intelligence,* that *intellect* seeks to know only "Is it possible?" whereas *intelligence* asks a much more subtle yet much more pivotal question, "Is it appropriate?"[19] To be clear, the type of intellect that Pearce refers to here is the often clever machinations of the brain-mind that can easily sidestep the issue of unforeseen consequences, whereas intelligence encompasses a vastly more subtle inquiry arising always from the heart-brain in consideration of the broader consequences of a particular undertaking. Thus, "Is it possible to…build a more powerful weapon of mass destruction?" or "…clear-cut a forest of old-growth trees faster, more efficiently and economically?" versus, "Is it in the best interest of all concerned that this be built, that this be undertaken?"

---

19 Pearce made this assertion in nearly every publication he proffered over the span
 of some five decades. A wise teacher, tireless investigator and prolific writer,
 he delved into a wide swath of leading-edge scientific research in his quest
 to understand the issue of appropriate human development, synthesizing his
 findings brilliantly. Each of his many important works further embellished and
 extend the basic premise that intellect is not necessarily intelligence. See for
 example, his early work, *The Magical Child Matures.*

Seeing the need for a considerably more balanced approach in attaining what is important in life, scientist and author, Paul Pearsall, comments: "We don't have to and should not give up our quest to learn more about the remarkable brain and our respect for its magnificent powers of reason in order to begin to learn more about the untapped spiritual info-energetic wisdom of the heart…If we are willing to try to combine the best the brain has created, and will create, with the wisdom of the heart's code…we can become much smarter than we have ever been" (1998, p. 17). To this we would add only: And become *even smarter* when we combine these two intelligences with a third, that of the body.

The ability to self-correct the dangerous socio-cultural and environmental trajectory that we appear to be on, and to survive and thrive into the future, depends to an extent perhaps even greater than we can currently imagine, on our ability to foster the highest functioning intelligence in a far greater number of individuals. We believe such intelligence comes about as a result of a balanced and integrated development of all *three brains*, for creativity, flexibility and adaptability depend not upon cognitive processes alone, but on an integrated tripartite intelligence that expresses itself through *keen insight, discernment, positive intent under the influence of well-honed intuition and a vibrant imagination.*

We believe such intelligence comes about as a result of a balanced and integrated development of all three brains, for creativity, flexibility and adaptability depend not upon cognitive processes alone, but on an integrated tripartite intelligence that expresses itself through keen insight, discernment, positive intent under the influence of well-honed intuition and a vibrant imagination.

From Survival to "Thrival": The Creativity, Cooperation and Compassion Imperative

Millions of years of evolution simply cannot be wrong: we are hard-wired and our brain prioritized to carry out functions designed to significantly enhance our chance of living long enough to procreate, the proverbial "bottom-line" for nature's agenda. The so-called reptilian brain, as we have seen, regulates and assists in the operation of myriad bodily functions of which we may remain happily unaware. From respiration and digestion to the imperative of "fight and flight" behaviors (when absolutely required), this fully dedicated part of the cranial hind-brain also regulates the flow of sensory information to the cerebral cortex by way of the reticular activating system. If all is in good working order the brain provides us with a reasonably accurate apprehension of the world around us, as a result of which a situation-appropriate response (i.e., neither over-reacting nor under-reacting) enhances not only survival, but "thrival" as well. The word *thrival* is meant to suggest a felt-sense of overall well-being: our brain-mind, freed from the imperative to be vigilant and on-guard against potential threat, can easily up-shift to modes of thought otherwise unavailable, such as eliciting positive ideation (Einstein's notion of "recombinant play" resonates) or pondering a bright and shining future, while our body enters into a state of dynamic rest.

The cranial brain has, of course, evolved far beyond its essential hardwired, genetically driven survival functions, enabling humans to flexibly and adaptively learn over the course of a lifetime. This capacity for learning is, however, contingent. Recall MacLean's insistence on nurture, feedback, and play, the so-called *family triad*, without which proper brain development (and therefore the ability to flexibly learn) may all too easily become compromised. As well, there appears to be a predictable stage-wise progression undergirding mammalian learning.

Harvard professor, Burton White,[20] described such a progression as universal to all mammals. It begins, he averred, with the *stimulation of a model*, followed by *practice, repetition and variation*, which in turn sets

---

20 This is in reference to Burton White's famous Harvard Preschool Project, which existed from 1965-1978. His brilliant insights culminated in the work, *Raising a Happy, Unspoiled Child* (Fireside, 1995) and the earlier, *The First Three Years of Life* (Fireside, 1985 with revised editions up to 1995).

the stage for what he referred to as *application or generalization*. The latter, while common to a limited extent for all mammals, is so greatly enhanced in humans as to largely set us apart from other species. This heightened ability is undoubtedly related to the fact that the human neocortex comprises roughly 77% of the volume of the brain (Swanson, 1995, p. 473); clearly, most of the human brain is dedicated to higher learning. The neocortex appears to have evolved thus far for one primary purpose: to accommodate new learning and thereby make enhanced adaptation possible.

There appears to be a predictable stage-wise progression undergirding mammalian learning. Harvard professor, Burton White, described such a progression as universal to all mammals. It begins, he averred, with the stimulation of a model, followed by practice, repetition and variation, which in turn sets the stage for what he referred to as application or generalization.

While the basic design-functions of the learning brain are reasonably well understood by cognitive neuroscientists,[21] there is still an urgent need to better understand and appreciate other capabilities of the cranial brain. We refer to capabilities which often remain dormant or underdeveloped for lack of specific model stimulation. Some of the more important yet mostly neglected or ignored capacities that call out for the modeling process described in the paragraph above include *creative imagination*, the impulse toward *collaboration and cooperation* (versus a near-pathological overemphasis on *competition* that still rules our society); and, at the highest reaches of human potential, the cultivation of *wisdom and compassion*. While it is an oversimplification to put it this way, we cannot rely upon the cranial brain alone for the attainment of a maximally fulfilling, purposeful, meaningful, and passionate life. For that we depend upon intuition, the province to a

---

21 The process—from perception, or what we here term apprehension, to insight and intention—has, of course, numerous intermediary steps including, but not limited to, the better known attributes of cognitive intelligence: knowing, understanding, analyzing, synthesizing, generalizing, evaluating (to use Floyd Bloom's well-regarded Taxonomy of Learning Domains).

large extent of our gut feelings, and upon inspiration and insight, the domain, not just metaphorically but literally, of the heart.

> We depend upon intuition, the province to a large extent of our gut feelings, and upon inspiration and insight, the domain, not just metaphorically but literally, of the heart.

In the remainder of this chapter and the next, we turn our attention to intriguing scientific investigations into these other remarkable brains, and in the process shed an altogether different light on the nature of human intelligence.

The Body Brain: Solidly Intelligent, With A Mind of Its Own

We began this chapter with a general discussion of the growing realization that we are in fact three-brained beings, with the body brain and heart brain joining the cranial brain (which, you may recall from Chapter 2, is itself of a triune nature) to comprise a three-fold intelligence. We now go into considerably more detail supporting the assertion that the body has its own brain, with its own intelligence, even a mind of its own; one that operates both independently from and interdependently with the cranial brain. Until now the consensus has been that there is but one brain, located in the cranium or head.

Before moving into this fascinating material, and to help clear up any doubts or uncertainty about this assertion, let's take a moment to address the issue of definition. For while most anyone can provide a reasonably good definition of a brain, this more than likely would not be the case when it comes to defining the more nebulous terms, "intelligence" and "mind."

The brain—using the definition found in the Merriam-Webster dictionary (online version)—is *that portion of the vertebrate central nervous system that: is enclosed in the skull; is composed of neurons; integrates sensory information from inside and outside the body while controlling autonomic functions (such as heartbeat and respiration); coordinates and directs correlated motor responses; coordinates and directs the process of learning.* For its part, the body brain also has neurons, concentrated for specialized functions in the viscera, while contributing to many other functions and organs outside of it as well (the cranial brain most certainly, and respiration for sure, to mention two). Too, it integrates sensory information from inside and outside the body while controlling autonomic functions (such as digestion, assimilation, and elimination); and is more involved in learning than we might think, as will be made clear.

Merriam-Webster defines intelligence as *the ability to learn or understand things or to deal with new or difficult situations*, which is very close to the definition we used at the outset of this book: *the capacity to respond to new situations, adapt to changing conditions, and learn from experience.* The body brain is characterized by each of these elements as well—being responsive, adaptive and fully capable of learning, which constitute the definition of intelligence. In addition (and similar to the cranial brain, though we note that it is not included in our dictionary definition), it is capable of forming its own perceptions, memories, and activities independent of, yet interdependent with, the cranial brain, a crucial point to which we shall return.

And the mind? Again Merriam-Webster: *that element or complex of elements in an individual that feels, perceives, thinks, wills, and especially reasons.* Strictly speaking, thinking and reasoning, in the sense of cogitative processes, is not something that the body brain is capable of, but then again that is not its design-function. Nor do we need a second "thinking brain" since we have one that can (or should) serve that purpose marvelously well. Clearly, however, the body brain does form its own perceptions, as well as create its own memories, based upon what it senses and—let's admit it—can be downright willful as well. When it comes to getting the cranial brain upstairs to pay attention to its needs, the body absolutely has a mind of its own; meaning that it can, of course, willfully get its needs for air, food, water, elimination and movement fulfilled sooner rather than later; even if we deem the timing inconvenient!

Although our culture and especially the educational system, with all the best of intentions, gives primacy to the cranial brain with its vaunted (and certainly important) ability to identify and solve problems, plan for the future, "get the job done," and so forth, the fact is that our culture also recognizes and rewards (often outrageously so) physical performance in the arts and athletics. Most of us find it intrinsically satisfying and fulfilling to not only participate in those areas at various times in our lives, but to be a party to those performances as well. In fact, it can be one of life's more uplifting moments to witness—though we would hardly ever think about it in these terms, much less express it as such—acts of embodied intelligence, acts that combine three distinct yet interrelated intelligences: body, mind (in the cranial brain sense), and heart.

Embodiment, Mastery Learning and the Intelligent Body

Embodied learning is, to us, a compelling term, for it suggests a deep level of physical mastery, displayed in apparent natural ease and often evoking a sense of admiration or perhaps even awe in the viewer. Embodied learning as the sum of disciplined effort often displays an evocative and perhaps charismatic quality, or a compelling congruence and sense of gracefulness as found in such endeavors as performance art, music and athletics. We assume that it is also present—if far less obvious—in mastery of an abstract nature, such as mathematical prowess or philosophical erudition, as we shall see below.

This is an important point: learning is to be found, not just in the head, but in the body. As quoted in the epigraph, Bryner and Markova (1996), experts on physical intelligence and its markedly overlooked status in society, comment, "If learning isn't in your body, where is it?" (p. 7). Making the point about what constitutes excellence in any area, they directly invoke the notion of embodiment: "No learning is really yours until it is in your body (p. 22)." Indeed. Let's develop their assertion, based upon how the nervous system is designed to foster embodiment.

Embodied learning—synonymous with mastery learning—is the result of the process whereby a literal transfer or shift of learning takes place within the neural fields of the brain. Whereas conscious learning is initiated and hopefully sustained in those areas of the "high brain" involved in working memory (physically located on the sides of the frontal lobes), the learning is eventually transferred to the "low brain" or cerebellum (involved in patterned movement and coordination) and other areas of the central nervous system located at the bottom, hindmost portions of the brain. While this is primarily the case with procedural learning—any learning that largely involves a physical component such as riding a bicycle, driving a car, dancing, writing, and so forth—it is also true of learning of a more abstract nature (semantic and mathematical, for example).

Commenting on the issue of neural transfer, John Ratey, MD (2008), puts it this way:

> Brain scans show that when we learn [something new], the prefrontal cortex lights up with activity... Once the circuit has been established the prefrontal cortex goes dark This is how we come to know things and how activities like riding a bike become second nature. Patterns of thinking and movement that are automatic get stored in the basal ganglia, cerebellum, and brain stem—primitive areas that until recently scientists thought only related to movement. (p. 42)

This includes, as stated above, abstract learning such as memorizing multiplication tables: initially the working memory is completely involved in the task, whereas once learned the cerebellum is much more involved.

In her fine book, *Smart Moves: Why Learning is Not All in Your Head*, aimed principally at educators and parents, the public-school teacher-turned-neurophysiologist, Dr. Carla Hannaford, emphasizes the crucial connection between the body-in-motion and physical intelligence as a core component in embodied learning. Hannaford (1995):

> The more closely we consider the elaborate interplay of brain and body, the more clearly one compelling theme emerges: movement is essential to learning. Movement awakens and activates many of our mental capacities. Movement integrates and anchors new information and experience into our neural networks. In short, movement is vital to all the processes by which we embody and express our learning, our understanding and our selves. (p. 96)

Embodied learning, mastery learning: interchangeable terms that are in many ways synonymous with excellence, the pursuit of which is, or ought to be, one of the foremost, purposes of education. Experiencing excellence is a primary means by which we attain satisfaction and happiness in life, on the path to achieving a sense of meaning and significance. Yet by disavowing its critical importance our society has managed to make the achievement of this satisfaction, happiness and meaningfulness much more difficult, and for many a near impossibility.

To a large extent this is due to the thoroughly worn out yet intractable assumptions undergirding child-raising and educational practices. Just as a quick example, take the assumption that high-stakes testing will lead to both enhanced learning and improved academic achievement, when in reality interjecting this kind of stressor only undermines enthusiasm for learning, often accompanied by an unsurprising lack of achievement, while simultaneously wreaking havoc on the morale and wellbeing of students and teachers alike.

Or, take the example of movement (or what is more likely, the lack thereof) as a core component in and necessary condition for learning, without which it is made far more difficult than it need be. It is a scientifically demonstrable fact that children must move to both organize (while in the formative years) and (throughout life) actively engage the brain in order to initiate learning. Yet observe the majority of classrooms today and it is stunningly lacking. But why? Why, if movement plays such a key role in brain development and in the steps leading to mastery learning, are we not fully embracing and applying this knowledge in the field of education.

> It is a scientifically demonstrable fact that children must move to both organize (while in the formative years) and actively engage the brain for learning.

Perhaps a brief foray into what we might think of as "a history of the body," or better yet, "a history of the body-mind" might help clarify one of the more pernicious biases of our culture; a bias that serves a set of assumptions that continue to exact a great cost when it comes to fulfilling the promise of genuine education.

Human History ... With the Body in Mind

In a fascinating *Sun* magazine interview (2013), author and film director, Philip Shepherd[22] offers a fascinating angle on human history, beginning in the Neolithic Age, the theme of which is the human

---

22 Shepherd is the author of *New Self, New World: Recovering Our Senses in the Twenty-First Century*, Berkeley, CA: North Atlantic Books, 2010.

race's inexorable movement away from the body as the main source of sensing and knowing the world, while simultaneously becoming more head-centric over the millennia. According to Shepherd, the shift of emphasis to the cranial brain as sole carrier of human intelligence was accomplished by the time of Plato, around 350 BC. As articulated by Plato in his dialogues, thinking was reckoned as being carried out exclusively by the head. Shepherd states: "In his dialogue *Timaeus* the title character explains that the gods made us by fashioning the soul into a divine sphere, the cranium, and then gave it a vehicle, the body to carry it around. So, the head has the spark of divinity, and the body is a machine. That's been our metaphor ever since" (p. 9).

With this epochal shift the stage was then set for the eventual denouement, as proffered by the seventeenth century French philosopher, Rene Descartes who famously asserted, "I think, therefore I am." The implications of this pronouncement led, in the Western world at least, to the dualistic cleavage of mind from body. Thus, by the seventeenth century, intelligence was assumed to be wholly ensconced within the confines for the cranial brain, completely divorced from the body which was viewed solely as carrier of the mind.

Turning his attention to recent history, Shepherd describes the cultural difficulty of gaining widespread acceptance for the scientific fact that there exists an actual body brain apart from (but decidedly interrelated with) the cerebrum or cranial brain. Remarkably, the body brain, as he points out, was discovered, forgotten and rediscovered on three separate occasions during the twentieth century, most notably in the 1920s when the autonomic nervous system (ANS) was mapped out by Johannis Langley. It is worthwhile recounting these historic shifts in our collective attention to and understanding of where intelligence is "located".

According to Shepherd (p. 9), it was Langley who first described the three divisions of the ANS: the sympathetic, parasympathetic and, very importantly, the enteric nervous systems (embedded in the esophagus, stomach, small intestine, and colon), with its large quantity of neurons or gray matter. The enteric nervous system is synonymous with what we are calling our body brain.

Again, according to Shepherd, even earlier in the century the enteric nervous system, governor of gastrointestinal functions, had been described by the anatomist Byron Robinson, in *The Abdominal and Pelvic Brain*, as an independent brain operating in the gut, apparently leading Robinson to the conclusion that this brain is "the center of life"—a phrase that harkens back to the ancients' view of the body as the seat of our deepest intelligence (p. 9). Unfortunately, as Shepherd points out, the enteric branch of the ANS was widely ignored and medical students subsequently learned only about the other two divisions.

It was left to Dr. Michael Gershon in the 1960s to rediscover the brain in the gut. Gershon, Chairman of the Department of Anatomy and Cell Biology at New York–Presbyterian Hospital/Columbia University Medical Center, is an acknowledged expert in the field of neurogastroenterology, the study of the nervous system in the gut. In his popular book, *The Second Brain* (1998), he details how the brain-in-the-gut functions both independently of and interdependently with the cranial brain, using those 100 million or so neurons and more than 30 neurotransmitters (including serotonin, dopamine, glutamate, norepinephrine, nitric oxide and the enkephalins, one class of the body's natural opiates) to carry out its own electrochemical functions.

Because of its distinctive nature, Gershon asserts, the body brain perceives, decides, responds, and remembers (is capable of forming memories) on its own: sever the main nerve trunk, the vagus, connecting the two brains, and the body brain continues doing its work without any guidance from the cranial brain. It differs from the cranial brain of course in that the enteric system is widely distributed throughout the lining of the gut, unlike the cranial brain which is a concentrated three-pound mass. The body brain, in other words, is less a lump of gray matter and more like a web, often described as a mesh-like system of neurons. Thus, Gershon argues, while they are quite distinct in both form and function, clearly they are both to be considered as brains.

To be clear, as Gershon points out, the body brain does not carry out rational thoughts or make conscious decisions. It does not "help with the great thought processes…religion, philosophy and poetry, [which] is left to the brain in the head" (p. 1). It does, however, play a role—sometimes subtly and sometimes profoundly—in our everyday thought processes and especially in our moods. It is very difficult, for example, to ignore common ways by which the gut brain makes its "needs" known to us (setting aside those digestive and eliminative functions): so-called "butterflies," cramps, loose bowel, tight gut, the proverbial "gut feeling," queasiness, and so forth. Gershon maintains that, while it is true that we have been culturally conditioned to discount or ignore outright these lower-level communications, we do so at our own peril when it comes to possible threats, long-term gastro-intestinal disorders and illness, and—very importantly—even intuitive ways of knowing. Thus, the gut brain is to be thought of principally as a sensing organ, gathering and responding to all manner of information about the changing conditions both inside the body and outside as well; in effect providing us with immediate feedback about both dangers and opportunities in the environment, often referred to or thought of as intuition.

> The gut brain is ... principally a sensing organ, gathering and responding to all manner of information about the changing conditions both inside the body and outside as well; ...providing us with immediate feedback about both dangers and opportunities in the environment.

While we have paid dearly for this split over the last two centuries and more (not only cleaving body from mind, but also mind from heart as it were), the self-correcting nature of the scientific enterprise has come to show that such a split precludes an accurate description of the interface between mind and body. In doing so, this paradigmatic split has seriously interfered with humanity's progress toward achieving its full potential. Resuming that progress requires a worldview that upholds the purposeful pursuit of integrated and holistic development as key to the fulfillment of human development and human destiny.

Having offered something of a historical perspective on the brain-body split, let's look briefly at body intelligence from the perspective afforded by cultures that are fundamentally different from our own, in that they somehow managed to avoid the historic split that we still struggle to overcome.

Eastern Conceptions of the Body-Mind

Many other cultures—especially those less "head-centric" than our own—readily accept the notion of a body brain. They hold perspectives that derive from a long history of observation and practices that appear to have worked well in certain ways. To learn about these ancient perspectives, so different from the Western view in many ways, can be instructive. Take for example the view held in common by a majority of these cultures: that the "belly" is viewed as sacred since it is the home of the soul. Consider that Japanese martial arts, Chinese healing arts, African dances as well as those of Old Europe, the Middle East, India, Polynesia, and Native America have long served as forms of "body prayers, honoring and energizing the belly to awaken the soul-power dwelling within the body's center."[23]

More contemporarily, in Chinese medicine the area centered behind the navel is referred to as *Shen Ch'ue*, or "mind palace," and is thought by some to be the primary center of learning and the experience of truth.[24] The *dantien*, located just below the naval and thought to be the geographic center of the human body, is given great emphasis in Chinese martial arts, as it is in Japanese martial arts where it is referred to as the *tanden*. Moreover, for the Japanese, the abdomen, or specifically the hara or belly (thought also to include the diaphragm and stomach as well as the abdomen), is considered to be an area where one is able to experience the greatest *presence of mind*. Again, Shepherd: "To ask someone in Japan to 'think with his belly' is to ask him to ponder an issue with his whole Being and truth" (p. 68). A "person of hara" is one who approaches life with confidence, courage, creativity, equipoise, endurance, integrity and purpose. The closest word for such a person in the West might be "gutsy,"[25] with its implications of confidence and courage.[26]

---

23 To use a pleasing turn of phrase taken from the writing of Lisa Sarasohn at http://www.honoringyourbelly.com/inspiration/articles/soul-power.html

24 An example of which, again, shows up in the writing of Philip Shepherd, *New Self, New World: Re-covering Our Senses in the Twenty-First Century*, 2010.

25 Again, thanks go to Lisa Sarashon, above.

26 One of us (TB) recalls a high school coach's often used term, "intestinal fortitude," in his attempts to inspire bravery and perseverance on the gridiron.

Charlie Badenhop, a Westerner who, for some 25 years, lived and studied martial arts and other aspects of Japanese culture, developed an astute understanding and keen appreciation of the central role that the hara plays in Japanese society. Translating it into more Western terms, Badenhop refers to the fact that we have both a somatic mind and cognitive mind, respectively supported by the brain in our gut and the brain in our cranium. He goes on to say that each of these minds speaks a different language, one a preverbal, sense-based language that speaks directly to us and to others in a variety of undeniable ways: in "gut reactions," the "full" feeling of satisfaction, the "sick" feeling of nausea, the urge to vomit, and abdominal pain, and so forth, each of which is telegraphed through familiar facial expressions and body movements. The somatic mind, Badenhop claims, because of its association with the enteric nervous system affects our emotions, movements, the "felt-sense" of our environment and our experiences within it. This "felt sense," he suggests, is often associated with intuition.

According to Badenhop, the Japanese use a time-honored method for training the intuition, learning to cultivate nonverbal skills by effective use of the hara, which can with practice be sensitized to process "gut feelings" about another person's unvoiced motivations and moods. Badenhop (2009):

> It is the primary way in which senior level Japanese officials and executives conduct business, and takes precedence over almost all other forms of decision-making. It does not consist of 'winging it' based on generally ill-defined intuition; rather it is a skill and art which sets some people apart from all others in Japanese society and consists of learning and skills which are in some ways closely guarded secrets even today.

This provides an interesting example of a socially sanctioned and valued form of training (we don't think the word "educating" necessarily works here) that gives recognition and puts to good use an important, although little studied and not scientifically well-understood, form of intelligence.

Badenhop maintains that what Gershon calls the second brain is equivalent to what Asian cultures have been calling the hara or tanden. In saying that, "Most if not all Oriental art forms teach the student to focus their attention in the lower abdomen, and to perform with this focus being the primary source of intelligence," he is suggesting that it is possible to train ourselves to tune into "the tender soft spot in the belly" and thereby better enable ourselves "to learn from and synthesize the intelligence of the somatic self with the intelligence of the cognitive self. It is just such a dual perspective that helps us to have a fuller understanding of our total experience."

Finally, speaking to the enrichment factor in our lives as we learn to trust in and develop intuitive intelligence, Badenhop points out that

> The enteric nervous system or hara, organizes information differently than the brain in the skull, and thus the enteric nervous system offers a viable alternative to your intellectual experience of life. If you organize your experience differently, you will definitely have a different perspective, and thus a different reaction to what is taking place. By melding the perspective of our somatic intelligence with the perspective of our cognitive intelligence we tap into a new realm of possible solutions. It is the somatic self's ability to sense what is taking place, along with the cognitive self's ability to negotiate amongst various distinctions, words, strategies, and abstractions that allows for the evolution of a mature self.

Intuitive Intelligence: Head, Heart, and Hara

Intuitive intelligence represents a legitimate and much needed area of study and research. However, since its presence (or absence) can be difficult to detect and measure empirically, scientists aren't always eager to risk their time and careers looking into something that appears so elusive. The irony is that many scientists are among the first to admit that intuition plays a key role in creative breakthroughs and their most significant discoveries. Albert Einstein is widely quoted as having said, "The intuitive mind is a sacred gift and the rational mind is a faithful servant. We have created a society that honors the servant and has forgotten the gift." He is also quoted as saying, "The only really valuable thing is intuition."

William James, one of America's truly great minds and perhaps greatest scientist of the late nineteenth and early twentieth centuries, had this to say about intuition, "Instinct leads, intelligence does but follow" (2007, p. 264). We are reasonably certain that he would have been comfortable substituting the word "intuition" for "instinct," for in this context it amounts to much the same thing. And Jonas Salk, whom we remember for his brilliant work in discovering and developing the polio vaccine, is widely quoted as saying: "We should trust our intuition. I believe that the principles of universal evolution are revealed to us through intuition. And I think that if we combine our intuition and our reason, we can respond in an evolutionary sound way to our problems."

While science has been slow on the uptake, there are those (nonscientist, "citizen scientists," and some lab scientists) who aren't necessarily willing to wait for the imprimatur of mainstream science to validate the "what and how" of intuition. They are enthusiastically pursuing a course of understanding and practical application.

It is interesting that in many cultures, not just the Japanese and Chinese, the center of the body has for millennia been considered to be the seat of intelligence and/or the seat of the soul. Easy to perhaps dismiss as misguided or naive, these notions can come across as vaguely superstitious when viewed through a mindset that has given scant attention to the possibility that there is something to these ancient cultures and their native understanding of how the body operates. That these cultures gave primacy to the brain in the belly has, until fairly recently, met with deep scientific skepticism. However, as the following description states—taken from an on-line course at Massachusetts Institute of Technology—there seems to be an emerging interest in the role of physical intelligence as somehow fundamental and crucial to how cognition operates.

> At MIT, the body is present as an object of study, but is all but unrecognized as an important dimension of our intelligence and experience. Yet the body is the basis of our experience in the world; it is the very foundation on which cognitive intelligence is built.

The fact is we instinctively recognize how important this body center, or hara, experience is to learning and performance. In many sports—diving, gymnastics, ice skating are prime examples—as well as in the martial arts, dance, playing a woodwind instrument, or singing, great emphasis is placed upon training this area of the anatomy. For it is that center—combined with breath—from whence all that performance grace and power emanates. Equally important, by sinking into the center and letting the body intelligence take over, one learns that this may be the surest way to stop the incessant chatter of the cranial brain, an infamous way to ruin an otherwise laudable performance. We have come to understand that the cranial brain must be brought under control at times—set aside to keep it from messing things up but good.

In this globalized, interconnected, information age, it makes sense to use proven Western and well-founded Eastern approaches to integrated brain-mind-body intelligence. We shall return to this topic, taking up in the final chapter such related themes as the role of movement, rhythm, play, imagination, and other pertinent aspects related to the childhood education of the body brain and their all-important effects on the cranial brain.

Important and revealing though it is to realize how neglected has been the body brain and its vast intelligence in our culture, there is yet another unique and powerful brain-based intelligence; one that is receiving widespread attention due to a host of findings that have led to a major reconsideration of its role in health, learning, behavior and human affairs. We are referring to the intelligence of the heart. It is to the heart brain and recent revelations about it that we now turn.

Chapter 12

The Heart Has a Mind of Its Own

"About sixty to sixty-five percent of all the cells in the heart are neural cells which are precisely the same as in the brain, functioning in precisely the same way, monitoring and maintaining control of the entire mind/brain/body physical process as well as direct unmediated connections between the heart and the emotional, cognitive structures of the brain."

    – Joseph Chilton Pearce

"People with high levels of personal mastery…cannot afford to choose between reason and intuition, or head and heart, any more than they would choose to walk on one leg or see with one eye."

    – Peter M. Senge

"Here is my secret. It is very simple. It is only with the heart that one can see rightly; what is essential is invisible to the eye."

    – Antoine de Saint-Exupery

Introduction

Pondering a future fraught with enormous challenges while hopefully affording unforeseen opportunities for humanity, neuropsychologist and clinical professor at the University of Hawaii, and best-selling author of 18 books and over 200 journal articles, Paul Pearsall, PhD, inquires: "There are two questions that the thinking heart might ask about the new millennium. It may wonder if we can survive the world our brain has created for us and the pace at which it is running us and, even if the brain is clever enough to keep us alive in its new millennium world, will we want to live in a world if we only end up feeling more disconnected, hostile, self-protective, afraid, and alone in the universe—brilliant minds lacking loving souls" (1998, p. 16).

Acclaimed writer and author, Charles Siebert (1990), reflects upon two deep ironies that reflect our modern relationship to the heart: that the medical establishment persists in viewing the heart solely as a pump, and that heart disease remains the number one killer of men and women in our society and therefore a source of real concern and anxiety for many. Siebert:

> I think that this increased cardiac paranoia is something more, a subconscious rebellion against the demystification of the heart, the reduction of a once profound source of mystery…to a mere machine. In response to this medical reductionism, we may be suffering a kind of collective heart attack, a modern metaphysical one—pained by the weakening of long-held notions of the heart as the home of the soul and seat of deep emotions. (p. 54)

Thinking heart? More than a mere pump for moving blood? Subconscious rebellion against the demystification of the heart? Collective heart attack? What, you might well be thinking, is going on here?!

These notions might seem utterly fanciful, more like the musings of a poet or mystic, certainly not those of scientists. And it's true, until fairly recently, to talk about the heart as an "organ of intelligence" and not merely a pump for moving blood, would likely have evoked skepticism from many and derision from others, especially those with a background in the life sciences. Beyond considerations of the purely physical or biological facts related to the organ, references to the heart as something more are typically dismissed as matters of mere sentiment, conveyed in such terms as "sweetheart," "listen to your heart," "my heart just isn't in it like it used to be," "my heart breaks for you." Far from scientific by any stretch, such phrases reflect the poetic and metaphoric uses to which the word has been applied over the centuries.

The heart is often referred to in religious or spiritual contexts as a way by which to remind or instruct the faithful about the importance of such attitudes and activities as love, gratitude, forgiveness, generosity and so forth. Meister Eckhart, the great Christian mystic reportedly proclaimed that, "God is born in the Heart and the Heart is born in God." In this sense, it is the deepest and truest aspect of self, in which the union between the divine and the human takes place. The Sufi mystic,

Jalal-al-Din Rumi, poetically proclaimed that, *There is a candle in your heart/ready to be kindled/There is a void in your soul/ready to be filled/You feel it, don't you/You feel the separation/from the Beloved.* The point is, in these and in basically all religious and spiritual traditions, this place, deep in the heart, is the symbolic point of contact with our innermost being, or highest self.

These common ways of referencing the heart imply to their users that an intuitive form of intelligence exists that operates apart from the cranial brain, an intelligence that can serve as guide to issues of a moral, ethical and relational nature. Yet to think of the heart as having an actual brain (and, by implication, a mind) of its own can understandably stretch credulity. It turns out however that this may well reflect a valid scientific description, if what has been discovered over the past few decades turns our to be accurate. We find this emerging view of the heart as an organ of intelligence a compelling one, one that could lead to a very different (and much needed) story of what it means to be fully human: a humane humanity. That said, the research we are about to report is clearly open to a variety of interpretations, the conclusions being drawn not infrequently in contrast to one another. Opinions run the gamut, from outright rejection of the notion of an "intelligent heart," to passionate embrace of the idea. See what you think.

One emerging scientific view portrays the human heart as a highly complex, self-organizing, dynamic and interactive information processing center which, as we have learned, is a rather complete description of mind. For example, when it comes to brain-heart interactions, scientists until fairly recently concerned themselves with the ways in which the brain exerted control over the heart. More recently, in studying the interactive nature of heart-brain communication, cardiac science has discovered that it is very much a two-way process, with the heart (along with the body-brain; see Chapter 11), exerting influence on the brain in ways that can very much affect perception, emotions and performance. This view is supported by evidence suggesting four principal ways by which the heart carries out this influence, thereby qualifying it to be considered an organ of intelligence.

1. **Neurologically.** The heart sends nerve impulses to the brain in the same way that the brain sends them to the heart. The heart, as we

shall see, uses the same kinds of neurons and neurotransmitters as does the brain; in effect the heart has its own brain.

2. **Biophysically.** The heart also communicates biophysically, using pressure waves from the contractive pulsing of this large and powerful muscle.

3. **Hormonally.** Due to recent discoveries of hormones produced by the heart, it is now considered a part of the endocrine system (which was not the case prior to the nineteen-eighties).

4. **Energetically.** Finally, and perhaps most intriguingly, it communicates energetically, using electromagnetic field interactions.

The Brain in the Heart

No mere pump, the heart has other vastly intelligent functions, the most important of which is that of sensory organ and center for encoding, processing and distributing information. As these crucial functions have become better understood, the notion that the heart has its own brain are beginning to take hold. It should be said before proceeding further that claims about the heart as being more than an organ to pump blood are not without controversy. While the implications are exciting to contemplate, it is important to keep in mind that at this point these are matters of interpretation. In short, because the heart-brain-mind connection is a relatively new field of study, it is open to a variety of critical interpretations and, not surprisingly, contrasting opinions.

In any case, considering the evidence that has been steadily accruing in various corners of the cardiac science world for over half a century, one finds it increasingly difficult to dismiss the assertion that the heart (like the body or gut) has a brain of its own. Take, for instance, the work of the neurocardiac spousal team, John and Beatrice Lacey (Lacey and Lacey, 1978), who, in the 1970s and early

> No mere pump, the heart has other vastly intelligent functions, the most important of which is that of sensory organ and center for encoding, processing and distributing information.

1980s, were among the first to establish that the heart sends messages directly to the brain, thereby modulating perceptual and cognitive performance via input from the sensory neurons of the heart, aortic arch, and carotid arteries. That these messages appear to control and direct the brain's response suggests that when the "logic" of the heart and that of the brain differ the heart can hold sway. According to the Laceys, these heart messages are capable of going directly (meaning that they are unmediated) to various regions of the brain—essentially there is no "call interrupt" when it comes to heart-brain communication—especially since the information flowing between the two cannot be turned off.

With connections going directly to such parts of the brain as the amygdala, hippocampus, thalamus, and prefrontal cortex, the heart has a direct and immediate influence on emotional processes, sensory experience, and memory. The heart also appears to influence reasoning, problem solving, and learning. Pearce puts it this way:

> About half of the heart's neural cells are involved in translating information sent to it from all over the body so that it can keep the body working as one harmonious whole. And the other half make up a very large, unmediated neural connection with the emotional brain in our head and carry on a twenty-four-hour-a-day dialogue between the heart and the brain that we are not even aware of. (Quoted in Mercaoliano and Debus, 1999, p. 1)

J.A. Armour, MD, PhD (2003), found that the heart contains a cell type known as intrinsic cardiac adrenergic, which synthesizes and releases neurotransmitters once thought to be produced only by neurons in the brain and nerve ganglia. This discovery, according to Armour, in combination with the known fact that the heart contains some 40,000 neurons of various types comprising a nervous system, qualifies it to be considered the "little brain in the heart," or, "heart brain" (2003. p. 5), a term that he first began using in 1994. Moreover, Armour was among the first to point out that the heart can form memories, stating that, "The local neuronal circuitry of this 'heart brain' displays short-term memory capabilities" (p. 5), a theme to which we will return shortly.

It is estimated that between 60 and 65 percent of the cells within the heart are neural cells (the remainder being muscle cells), identical to the neural cells in the brain. These cells transmit signals through the same connecting links called ganglia, with the same axonal and dendritic connections found in the brain and, as well, utilize the exact same kinds of neurotransmitters found in the brain. They function in the same precise manner as the brain, which is to receive, process, and distribute information pertinent to all areas of the body.

Stephen Buhner (2004) reports that individual neurons in the brain alter their behavior in response to signals received from each heartbeat, with groups of neurons changing their grouping and firing patters in response to cardiac input (p. 83). He points out that information flowing into the body impacts the heart first, flowing to the brain only after it has been perceived by the heart. Buhner:

> What this means is that our experience of the world is routed through our heart, which 'thinks' about the experience and then sends the data to the brain for further processing. When the heart receives information back from the brain about how to respond, the heart analyzes it and decides whether the actions the brain wants to take will be effective. (p. 83-84)

Pearce also found the implications intriguing:

> The heart responds to messages sent to it from the emotional brain, which has been busy monitoring the interior environment of dynamic states such as the emotions and the autoimmune system, guiding behavior, and contributing to our sense of personal identity. The emotional brain makes a qualitative evaluation of our experience of this world and sends that information instant-by-instant down to the heart. In return, the heart exhorts the brain to make the appropriate response. Of course all of this is on the nonverbal level. In other words, the responses that the heart makes affect the entire human system. (Mercaoliano and Debus, 1999, p. 2)

The Feeling and Remembering Heart-Brain

Along with the dynamic head-heart interaction, the neural cells embedded in the heart seem fully capable of creating memories just as they do in the cranial brain. If so, it turns out we don't remember only with our heads. Apparently, the memories most often stored in the heart are those tied to specific emotional experiences and the meaning that accompanies them. That the heart appears to be fully capable of forming memories is a major (if rather astonishing) theme in Pearsall's book, *The Heart's Code*, mentioned earlier. His report on heart transplant recipients taking on the memories of their donors—a provocative claim if ever there was one!—eventually led to the formation of the ground-breaking Cleveland Clinic's, Heart/Mind program.

While there is by no means a scientific consensus on this as a valid phenomenon, there are scientists and physicians that support his contention. Among those included in Pearsall's book, for example, is Gary E. R. Schwartz, PhD, a Harvard educated, Yale University professor, researcher and author of over four hundred scientific papers and eleven edited academic books. Interestingly, Schwartz serves as director for the VERITAS Research Program of the Laboratory for Advances in Consciousness and Health in the Department of Psychology at the University of Arizona, established primarily to test the hypothesis that the consciousness (or personality or identity) of an individual can survive physical death. As such, he has (in our view) rather courageously undertaken research in an area that can be an easy target for derision from the scientific community. In any case, Pearsall has collaborated with Schwartz on a number of thought-provoking publications about the phenomenon of memory transfer via transplantation.

In addition to remembering, the heart-brain's neural circuitry apparently enables it to act independently of the cranial brain to learn, make decisions and even feel and sense, at least according to a team of researchers at Institute for HeartMath, located in Boulder, California. For over three decades the team has studied the neural circuitry of the heart and concludes, like Armour, that it qualifies as a "heart-brain." As stated in one of the research summaries, "The heart-brain, as it is commonly called, or intrinsic cardiac nervous system, is an intricate network of complex ganglia, neurotransmitters, proteins and support cells, the same as of the brain in the head. The heart-brain's neural circuitry enables it to act independently of the cranial brain to learn, remember, make decisions and even feel and sense" (2015, p. 5).

Furthermore, with every beat the heart transmits to the brain and throughout the body complex patterns of neurological, hormonal, pressure and electromagnetic information. Thus, neurological signals from the heart not only affect the autonomic regulatory centers in the brainstem, but also cascade up into higher brain centers involved in emotional and cognitive processing, including the thalamus, amygdala and cortex. In these ways, information originating from the heart operates as a continuous and dominant influence in the processes that ultimately determine our perceptual and emotional experience. Besides the processes described above, it turns out that the heart has even more ways by which it powerfully influences and shapes not only our perceptions and emotions but our thought processes and behaviors as well.

This brain-in-the-heart is unique in processing specific types of information that work to harmonize all the organs of the body (the cranial brain does not play this role). One of its chief functions is to act as harmonizer and not only for the body, for it plays the same role regarding the life of our emotions, as we shall see. In short, the heart appears to "have a mind of its own"—what Pearce calls *intelligence*—when the need exists to temper the survival-oriented, ego-centered proclivities of the intellect in the world of human affairs. But we're getting somewhat ahead of ourselves.

The Intuitive Heart

An aspect of heart intelligence finally getting the recognition that is overdue, at least from a scientific perspective, is intuition. Describing intuition (a topic examined in Chapter 11 as well) as a "process by which information normally outside the range of cognitive processes is directly sensed and perceived by the body's psychophysiological systems as certainty of knowledge or feeling (positive or negative) about a nonlocal object, entity, or event," (McCraty et al, 2004, p.1), researchers at the Institute for HeartMath go on to say that, "intuitions can encompass information about entities in the material world, as well as abstract constructs such as thoughts and ideas." Their contention is that creative and intuitive processes are not limited to the brain alone, but rather are "whole-body functions emerging from complex interactions among the body's psychophysiological systems."

Some heart researchers acknowledge the role of the entire body regarding intuition. Using unique detection and measurement protocols, they argue that the heart and brain can receive and respond to information about a future event before the event actually occurs (McCraty et al, 2004a)—considered to be in the realm of precognition, and largely dismissed by the scientific establishment as impossible. These researchers report that,

> Both the heart and brain appear to receive and respond to information about a future emotional stimulus prior to actually experiencing the stimulus. The fact that the heart is involved in the perception of a future external event is a surprising, even astounding result, especially from the classical perspective that assigns the brain an exclusive role. (McCraty et al, 2004b, p. 334)

The Heart As Endocrine Gland

Along with its functions as sensory organ and center for encoding, processing and distributing information, the heart also produces hormones. This function wasn't known until the 1980s when it was reported in *Scientific American* that a new hormone, atrial natriuretic factor (ANF, also considered a peptide), had been discovered. This discovery subsequently led, in 1983,[27] to a reclassification of the heart as part of the endocrine system.

ANF is released when the powerful upper chambers of the heart contract and appears to be instrumental in acting as a calming and harmonizing agent on every organ of the body, as well as blood vessels, immune system, and hypothalamus (which, among other things, is involved in our emotional states). ANF also influences the thalamus and pituitary gland in the limbic (emotional) area of the brain, thus affecting memory and learning. The Institute for HeartMath research has also shown that ANF exerts a powerful effect on the prefrontal cortex, seat of our highest cognitive functions (McCraty et al, 2006).

---

27 See Cantin and Genest, "*The Heart as an Endocrine Gland*," *Scientific American* Vol. 254, p. 76, 1986. See also Pearsall (1998), p. 68-69.

The Electromagnetic Heart:
An Arc of Great Power and Meaning

Since 1963, when the electromagnetic field (or EMF) of the heart was first detected, the ability to detect and measure this field has significantly improved, which has led to a much better understanding how the heart communicates with the rest of the body including, of course, the brain. A few words about EMF: In addition to being a form of energy, the EMF also serves as a carrier of information. In the case of the brain, the energy being conveyed is in the form of brain waves (see Chapter 10) and the information is related to various states of consciousness. In the case of heart "waves," researchers argue that they convey information that is emotional in nature (as we shall see) and because the EMF of the heart is so much more powerful than that of the brain, the emotional information actually has a much greater effect on our thoughts than the other way around. That evident influence is completely consonant with findings described by the hugely popular neuroscientist and author, Antonio Damasio,[28] showing that emotions play a central role in social cognition and decision-making.

Researchers report that the rhythms of the brain fall into synchronization naturally with the rhythmic activity of the heart. This has to do in part with the EMF of the heart—the body's most powerful electromagnetic source: electrically it pulses at an amplitude approximately 60 times greater than that of brain signals, while the magnetic component of the field generated by the heart is reportedly 5000 times more powerful than that of the brain. Combining the strong EMF signals with the pressure waves the heart sends throughout the circulatory system means that the heart—as the body's most powerful rhythm generator—can either harmonize or overpower (and thereby disrupt) the other working rhythms and electrical currents that govern the brain and other organs. As the various actions

As the various actions of the heart send forth energy and information to virtually every cell of the body, thereby serving as a carrier wave providing information to synchronize all the activities of the body.

---

28 See for example, his early work, *The Feeling of What Happens: Body and Emotion in the Making of Consciousnes*, Mariner Books, 1999. Several more superb books have followed that critically acclaimed best-seller.

of the heart send forth energy and information to virtually every cell of the body, thereby serving as a carrier wave providing information to synchronize all the activities of the body. As goes the heart, so goes the body—and the brain!

Meet Our Toroidal Heart-Field

Just as a magnet placed under a sheet of paper with iron filings on its surface will reflect its field in the way the filings arrange themselves on the surface (try it sometime!), so too can the magnetic field of the heart be revealed by an array of detectors, which can yield a three-dimensional image of the field. Through this measuring process, the heart's magnetic field appears torus shaped, resembling a donut with a hole in the middle—a mathematically perfect version of which appears below (see Figure 42).

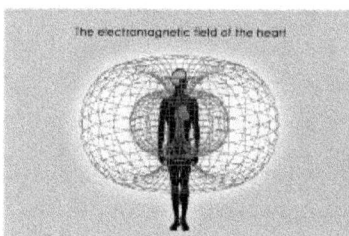

Figure 42. Electromagnetic Field of the Heart.
Image from Wikimedia.

As can be seen in the illustration, the axis of the field extends from the base of the spine to the top of the brain, creating a dipole like any magnet. Interestingly, these toroidal-shaped EM fields also extend from and surround our planet Earth, the sun, and black holes formed by collapsing stars. Some astronomers assume that a toroidal EMF extends from and around our spinning Milky Way galaxy as well, based on the detectable fields emanating from distant spiral galaxies like our own. At the micro-level, living organs and cells also emit comparably shaped EM fields.

Pearce, citing the work of the celebrated British mathematical physicist, Roger Penrose, describes the fact that, at the synaptic connection between dendrites and axons, there exists an EMF as well. And Buhner tells us that blood cells, as they spin through their vessels, form tiny torus-shaped fields that, taken together, create EM fields within the spinning vortex of the bloodstream. EM fields embedded within EM fields! Macro, micro: as above, so below apparently.

As mentioned, the field depicted in Figure 42 is rendered as a mathematically perfect shape. Its actual shape is nowhere near as perfectly symmetrical, and changes with each beat of the heart. Its changeability follows from the fact that the heart responds dynamically to alterations, however minute, in external and internal environments and circumstances—a harmonizing agent amidst a vast sea of energy and information currents. As pointed out by Buhner,

> The heart produces a range, a spectrum, of electromagnetic frequencies. Any frequency in this spectrum can contain a significant amount of information, just as one particular frequency on the radio dial can contain huge amounts of information. And each section of the field, no matter how small, contains all the information encoded within the whole field. (Buhner, 2004, p. 86-87)

This fact—that all information in the field is contained within any section of it no matter how small—has evidently become common knowledge, yet its importance in understanding just how powerful is the heart's influence, possibly even beyond the body, is only just becoming apparent. It entails one of the most intriguing aspects of any toroid EM field: that it is holographic. This means all the information being broadcast is available everywhere, as far as that field may extend. Consistent with the well-known nature of EMF, the field of the heart has unknown limits.

With current technology, the magnetic portion of the field can be detected extending to a distance of at least several feet away from the body, according to HeartMath. Again, in theory there is no known limit how far electromagnetic information can travel—from any source, not just the heart—which holds the possibility that information can interact with the fields of those around us, and beyond. And, if it turns out to be demonstrably true, this is where things get really interesting. Before touching on the implications of that possibility, a necessary detour.

Emotional States and Heart Waves

A comparison was made earlier between various states of consciousness and their brain wave manifestations (as measured by an electroencephalogram, or EEG) on one hand, and heart waves (as measured by a SQUID magnetometer) as carriers of information reflecting emotional states on the other. As the influences of the heart's EM field on the operations of the brain became clearer, new insights about the role of emotions in human learning, autonomic nervous system (especially related to stress), and peak performance states began to emerge. Let's look at some of these insights.

It certainly is not difficult to conjure personal examples of being in a positive emotional state, to feel the sense of ease and wellbeing that accompanies it, with our thoughts perhaps leading us effortlessly towards a solution to a vexing problem or perhaps into an enjoyable free-flow state of creative ideation. On the other hand, a negative emotional or mood state can have quite the opposite effect: making it nearly impossible to feel relaxed, while handily choking off the free flow of ideas. Not unlikely, we can find ourselves ruminating endlessly though a host of negative thoughts and beliefs. Dana Thomasino (2007), reporting on the role of emotions in intuitive intelligence explains:

> Positive emotions appear to broaden the scope of perception, cognition, and behavior and to enhance creative and intuitive capacities. Conversely, negative emotions tend to restrict perception, produce more reactive, rigid, and stereotypic patterns of thought and action, and have been found to be associated with reduced task performance and impaired intuitive judgments. (p. 3)

Both of these distinct emotional states are well known to us all, so it doesn't necessarily arrive as news. What is new, however, are how various emotional states, as reflected in the heart waves, are played out in the brain.

> Positive emotions not only feel better subjectively, but tend to increase synchronization of the body's systems, thereby enhancing energy and enabling us to function with greater efficiency and effectiveness. (McCraty et al, 2001, p. 3)

Taken from a publication by Institute for HeartMath (McCraty et al, 2006) amalgamating numerous studies on topics, the following highlights include the nature and function of heart waves and their connection to positive and negative emotional states; stress and autonomic nervous system imbalance; their various effects on cognition, learning, creativity and personal performance—all topics of interest to educators. Much of what this line of research is based upon is a phenomenon known as heart rate variability (HRV), the beat-to-beat variation and what it reflects about emotions, stress and wellbeing. More specifically, it is the rhythmic pattern of heart activity that most directly associates with all three phenomena. There are two important aspects to this association: heart rhythm and the pattern itself. Let's look more closely at each, in turn.

A Measure of Wellbeing: Heart Rate Variability and Coherence

Rhythmically, *heart rate variability* (HRV), the physiological phenomenon of natural variation in the time interval between heartbeats, is the standard measure of neurocardiac function, since it provides a clear window through which to view the interplay between heart–brain interactions and autonomic nervous system (ANS) dynamics— more specifically, the shifting balance between sympathetic-and parasympathetic-nervous system activity. With different emotional states as the variable under consideration, scientists have more recently been studying the difference in HRV pattern as reflected in positive, versus negative, emotional states. Figure 43 (below), depicts a markedly different HRV *pattern* between the negative emotional state of frustration, for example, and the positive emotional state of appreciation. The degree of harmony versus disharmony is clearly discernible. Note that while variability in heart rate is apparent in both frustration and appreciation, the pattern is very different; appearing irregular and chaotic in the former state, smooth and harmonious in the latter.

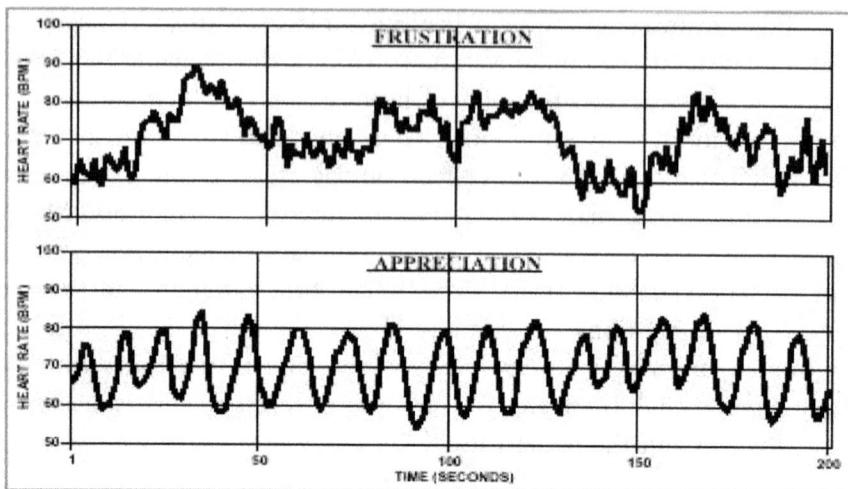

Figure 43. Heart Rate Variability Patterns: Frustration versus Appreciation. Image by Institute of HeartMath.

The term most often used to describe the level or degree of harmony is coherence, defined as a measure of how much order is taking place both in the heart rhythms and the autonomic nervous system (ANS). The greater the coherence the better is organ viability and systemwide health. The level or degree of coherence is reflected in heart rate variability, from high-to low-coherence, to incoherence. In the words of IHM researchers (McCraty et al, 2006),

> Efficient or optimal function is known to result from a harmonious organization of the interaction among the elements of a system. Thus, a harmonious order in the rhythm or pattern of psychophysiological activity signifies a coherent system, whose efficient or optimal function is directly related…to the ease and "fluidity" of life processes. By contrast, an erratic, discordant pattern of activity denotes an incoherent system, whose function reflects the difficulty and 'strain' of life processes. (p. 3)

As might be expected, researchers report that whereas positive emotions foster higher levels of coherence, negative emotions create the opposite condition: incoherence, a disharmony or disorder within and between the heart's rhythms and ANS. A coherent heart rhythm reflects and is causally related to efficiency throughout the entire nervous and organ systems of the body, a state more precisely described as *psychophysiological coherence*. This naturally leads to a lowered stress (or strain) level on the organ systems of the body (including, of course, the heart itself). An incoherent heart rhythm, on the other hand, reflects disorder or disharmony throughout the organ systems and, if it becomes chronic, is causally linked to heart problems as well as to an array of stress related illnesses that can manifest when the ANS is under prolonged strain (for more on stress, strain and illness, see Chapter 8).

Commenting on the differences in rhythmic patterns depicted in the above graphic, the researchers state that, "The heart rate variability pattern shown in the top graph, characterized by its random, jerky form, is typical of feelings of anger or frustration" (McCraty et al, 2006, p. 17). This relates to an increase in the processes related to acute sympathetic nervous system activation—often referred to as fight, flight, or freeze—which, if prolonged, can devolve into the General Adaptation Syndrome (described in Chapter 8), with predictably ill effects on the heart and other organ systems. On the other hand (referencing to the bottom portion of the graphic), "Sincere positive feeling states like appreciation can result in highly ordered and coherent HRV patterns, generally associated with enhanced cardiovascular function" (McCraty et al, p. 18)." This phenomenon is associated with activation of the parasympathetic nervous system, the rest and digest arm of the ANS, related to balance and efficiency throughout the system. Simply stated, when the heart's rhythms are disordered and inharmonious, it's a clear indication that the nervous system, heart and brain are out of sync. In such a state of incoherence, our ability to think clearly and perceive events accurately is compromised. On the other hand, when the heart's rhythms are smooth and even we have a feeling of calm energy, enthusiasm and ease of thought; we feel a sense of flow, leading to the possibility of enhanced creativity and problem solving.

Heart Coherence, Positive Emotional States, and Enhanced Brain Function

Some researchers emphasize the point that consciously eliciting such positive emotional states as appreciation, love, gratitude and forgiveness can evoke a heart waveform pattern that appears ordered or coherent (organized as a pattern of stable, smooth, cyclic waves), as so-called *frequency-locking* occurs between the most powerful oscillator, that of the heart, and all other biological oscillators in the body. In other words, *entrainment* takes place, resulting in harmonization of all body systems. When this occurs one typically has a feeling of relaxed alertness, an overall sense of wellbeing, accompanied by a greater likelihood of creative ideation and effortless problem solving. As mentioned above, the pattern of heart rhythms also has a measurable effect upon those of the brain. Some research shows that, given the power of the heart's EMF, heart coherence *entrains* the brain into what they refer to as heart-brain synchrony, or synchronization. An early study of synchrony (McCraty, Atkinson, 1999) using a simple IHM technique for evoking a positive emotional state describes the result: the electrical activity of the brain apparently entrained into a synchronous alpha waveform. This simple IHM technique, which invites a practitioner to intentionally focus on the heart while eliciting a feeling of sincere gratitude or appreciation, reportedly resulted in "psychophysiological coherence" which, in turn, succeeded in entraining or phase locking the brain into an alpha state.

Recall (from Chapter 10) that when an alpha state (the natural abode or "default setting" for young children) is intentionally evoked in a classroom—several times throughout the day being optimal—learning, creativity, health and wellbeing of the children (and teacher!) is enhanced. With confirmation coming from research such as the above, it makes even more sense to include regularly scheduled "alpha breaks" for students of all ages.

Recall, aslo, that this state of optimal function goes by a variety of names. One, "Flow," is a term popularized after the landmark publication and best-selling book, based upon the research of University of Chicago psychologist, Mihaly Csikszentmihalyi (1990). Another, "The Zone," is a term that shows up most often in athletics, and refers to the state of complete absorption, hallmarked by relaxed but intense concentration, and often experienced as a loss of self-consciousness, a sense of mastery or control, and effortless movement. Other terms include, "Peak Performance" and, less often, "Super Learning." What these popular descriptors have in common is an underlying state of psychophysiological coherence.

Before concluding the chapter on the heart's evident influence on the organ systems of the body—and most especially upon the operations of the brain—there is one more feature that we wish to cover: the connection between HRV and social interaction.

Social Well-being and the Beating of the Human Heart

An intriguing Scientific American article by social psychologist, Andrew Waytz (2010) reports on findings applying heart-rate variability to the quality of human interaction:

> It turns out that the heart is not only critical for survival, but also for how people relate to one another. In particular, heart rate variability (HRV), variation in the heart's beat-to-beat interval, plays a key role in social behaviors ranging from decision-making, regulating one's emotions, coping with stress, and even academic engagement.

Waytz goes on to describe the work of Stephen Porges on previously under-appreciated aspects of how the vagus nerve (the most extensive nerve trunk in the human body and about which we will have much more to say in the following chapter) functions in mammals in the process of social contact, proximity and intimacy. Called Polyvagal Theory, Porges's intriguing research findings on infant-parent bonding emphasizes the role of the variability of the heart rate in the formation and maintenance (or lack thereof) of relationships. Other research cited by Waytz suggests that the capacity to alter HRV is predictive of social skill; that high variability appears to make for greater social adaptivity as well as social sensitivity. Waytz puts a fine point on the promise this new knowledge holds when he says, "The heart has complex interactions with how we treat and evaluate others, how we cope with social stress, and how we manage our emotions, and research has only begun to explore the relationship between cardiovascular processes and social life (2010)." We look forward to learning more from these lines of research in the future. In the meantime, it's worthwhile keeping in mind the strong association between high HRV, positive affect, learning and well-being. It very much affirms the move to routinely incorporate social-emotional activities in our schools.

The Surprisingly Simple Techniques to Evoke Heart Coherence

In the course of their research and experimentation with ways by which heart coherence might be evoked, IHM discovered that intentionally focusing on positive emotions such as love, caring, appreciation, forgiveness and non-judgment is key. It should be noted that a key qualifying word in the previous sentence is sincere. While IHM techniques are trademarked under names such as *Freeze-Frame, Inner Ease, Quick Coherence,*[29] and others, they are actually quite simple and straightforward. They share much in common with the kind of meditation practices used over millennia in contemplative Christianity, Islam, Buddhism, and other religious traditions. What makes their use more compelling for many Westerners is the scientifically-tested efficacy. The essence of these techniques include common elements, described as follows. Since appreciation is reportedly the easiest positive emotion to evoke we'll use that as example.

1. Sit quietly with eyes either closed or nearly so.

2. Place one hand over the heart area and the other on the lower abdomen (an optional but effective step).

3. Focus on the breath, imagining breathing in through the heart and out through the lower abdomen.

4. Bring to mind a person, place, thing, or even pet (the latter has shown itself to be particularly effective) about whom or for which there is a sincere and felt sense of appreciation.

5. Continue to gently hold the feeling of appreciation for 3-5 minutes.

6. If you wish, extend this feeling outwards to others.

This kind of exercise has numerous variations of course. The wonderful thing is that something like the above can be done several times during the day and—so importantly—can easily be taught to students and incorporated into the rhythm of daily classroom activities.

---

29 To learn more about these techniques, visit https://www.heartmath. org/resources/heartmath-tools/

The Heart-Zone: When Fields Interact

If, as some researchers suggest, the electromagnetic field extends well beyond the boundary of the physical body, what happens when these information-rich fields interact with those around us? It's an intriguing question, the implications of which are suggestive. In one attempt to answer this question, a team at Institute for HeartMath designed a protocol to capture any information exchange that might take place between individuals—in effect, experimental subjects who were either touching or simply being within close proximity. Using EEG and ECG, along with a SQUID-based magnetometer (capable of measuring the EMF of the heart at a distance of some eight to twelve feet away), their findings appear to confirm that a mutual effect does occur, and as reported in a quantifiable way. For example, in an early experiment (McCraty et al, 1998), researchers found that the heartbeat signal of one individual actually registers in the brainwaves of the other, suggesting that we are attuned to the emotions of others, much moreso than we are probably aware. Reflecting on the possible meaning of this finding, the report states, in part,

> This study represents one of the first successful attempts to directly measure an energy exchange between people, and provides a solid, testable theory to explain the observed effects of many healing modalities that are based upon the assumption that an energy exchange takes place....One implication is that the effects of therapeutic techniques involving contact or proximity between practitioner and patient could be amplified by practitioners consciously adopting a sincere caring attitude, and thus introducing increased coherence into their cardiac field. (McCraty et al, 1998, p. 1)

Having determined that the electromagnetic field of the heart conveys information reflecting a measurable range of emotional states, and as well that the field is detectable up to several feet beyond the surface of the bodies of research subjects, IHM researchers had sought to determine if a coherent HRV might be key to the quality of information and energy exchange between individuals. In other words, the team was intrigued by the possibility that a consciously generated coherent heart wave—accomplished by eliciting a positive emotional state—in one individual could show up and even alter the EEG and ECG of another.

In their own words,

> The fact that the heart generates the strongest electromagnetic field produced by the body, coupled with our findings that this field becomes measurably more coherent as the individual shifts to a sincerely loving or caring state, prompted us to investigate the possibility that the field generated by the heart may significantly contribute to this energy exchange. (McCraty et al, 1998, p.1)

Their finding and tentative conclusion is intriguing and, if substantiated by others, quite profound. It suggests the possibility that by consciously focusing on an emotional state such as appreciation, caring, forgiveness, or love, a coherent heart rhythm could be evoked, which in turn could lead to an increased synchronization between that individual's heart rhythm and brainwave pattern and that of another. Highlighting this finding, the investigators state that, "the results of these experiments have led us to conclude that the nervous system acts as an antenna, which is tuned to and responds to the magnetic fields produced by the hearts of other individuals" (McCraty, 2015, p. 39).

Speculating on the implications of the study, the researchers suggest that individuals who enter into a coherent state become more sensitized to the EM signals being generated in the hearts of those around them. The report ends on this note:

> In conclusion, this study represents a further step in uncovering the physiological underpinnings of subtle, ongoing energetic forms of communication between people. Results have countless implications, and invite continued scientific exploration of the relationship between emotions, physiology and human interactions. (p. 26)

Heart Coherence and The Great Model Imperative

One implication might be this: Like the harmonious sounds of a well-tuned stringed instrument that, when struck, will enliven through resonance other stringed instruments in the vicinity, one can picture the possibility of something similar occurring in the intertwined heart fields of a classroom. As principal model in the classroom—not unlike a symphony conductor—the teacher sets the tone and calls the tune, so to speak. Thus, by consciously and regularly evoking positive emotional states a teacher can, with confidence, trust that the heart-and brain-waves of students may well be falling into sync. Moreover, by inviting all students to periodically engage in evoking a positive emotional state, the resonant field of the classroom can become an environment that facilitates ease in learning and a felt sense of wellbeing.

> ...by inviting all students to periodically engage in evoking a positive emotional state, the resonant field of the classroom can become an environment that facilitates ease in learning and a felt sense of wellbeing

In the next chapter, we take up the topic of the emergent mind and its near total dependence for healthy integration on the degree of emotional resonance with the principal care providers; resonance, of course, that is a product of heart coherence.

Chapter 13

The Contingent Mind: Nurture, Feedback, Play and the Neurobiology of Human Development

"Human connections shape the neural connections from which the mind emerges."

– Daniel Siegel, MD

"From the standpoint of human evolution no behavior development could have been more fundamental than the brain's potential for play."

– Paul MacLean

Overview of Chapter Thirteen

The emergence of the human mind is an experience-expectant and wholly contingent process, dependent for its proper unfolding on the quality of relationships and opportunities for adaptive learning.

Nearly all the information presented up until now has been directly or indirectly related to the cranial brain; its structure, function, maturation and development, care and maintenance. We initially proposed thinking of the brain more accurately as brain-mind and, even more accurately, brain-body-mind, since it is impossible to effectively separate one from the other. We then spent several chapters devoted solely to the cranial brain, the miraculous and, by widespread agreement, most complex 3-pounds of matter in the known universe. This was followed by coverage of two other aspects of the nervous system, the enteric (body-or gut-) brain and the heart-brain, the further understanding of which we believe holds great promise for deepening our grasp of how best to undertake an authentically whole-child education.

From the outset we have approached the topic of the brain and its myriad functions by examining its mammalian-specific evolutionary origins. If we assume that the mind is what the entirety of the nervous system—cranial-heart-and body-brains—does, we can then explore the evolutionary foundation of the human mind by relating it to the mammalian nervous system. By emphasizing the inseparability of the brain-body-mind, it follows that the conditions working to shape the brain are also those that affect the arising of the mind. Intent on providing a practical understanding, we limit our coverage of what is otherwise a vast subject area to those factors critical to the formation and development of a healthy, fully functioning human brain-mind.

The factors essential to the mind's formation are of course those that determine, to an indeterminate extent, the ability to learn. We consider learning to be a recursive process of acquiring knowledge and skills as a result of experiences that enable adaptive changes, based upon improved performance and enhanced future learning. By *recursive* is meant that learning (as we define it here) leads to greater, more effective learning, while *adaptation* remains the central feature of our definition of intelligence as *the capacity to respond to new situations, adapt to changing conditions, and learn from experience.* This way of thinking about learning is certainly congruent with evolutionary theory, cognitive science and neuroscience.

> We consider learning to be a recursive process of acquiring knowledge and skills as a result of experiences that enable adaptive changes, based upon improved performance and enhanced future learning.

Importantly, the factors essential to the formation of the mind are also those that if conscientiously applied can work as correctives for children whose minds—for a variety of reasons—are off to a less than good start due to issues such as neglect and/or abuse. This is no small thing, for childhood deprivation related to poverty and to violence continue to be haunting and significant impediments to the healthy development of far too many children and young people.

The information presented also serves as a foundation for understanding a phenomenon that has been a source of perennial interest and inspiration over millennia and, more recently, the scientific community and increasingly the general public: *mindfulness meditation.* That so many educators worldwide have been drawn to explore its purported benefits is timely, for personally and professionally it has much to offer as a means by which to enhance the functioning of the body-brain-mind. We will explore this topic fully in the next chapter, *Minding the Mind.*

Towards an Understanding of the Developing Mind

While the word *mind* can mean so many different things as to render it a nearly meaningless term, what we offer here is a way to consider mind meant to answer some basic questions that are, or ought to be, of interest to all. At the same time we relate the concept of mind to some of this book's overarching themes regarding childhood development, learning and well-being. Often missing in teacher preparation and education, the model of the mind that we explore holds the potential to significantly benefit individuals pursuing a teaching vocation and as well to validate, affirm, and inspire new and veteran teachers in the day-to-day challenges and rewards of the profession.

Beyond the difficulty of finding agreement on the use of the word, a central challenge to a scientific understanding of mind is principally one of measurement. That is, how does one utilize the defining tool of science—measurement—when by any definition the mind is an immaterial entity? Many neuroscientists side-step the question altogether by focusing exclusively on what can be measured, i.e., the brain. Some even go so far as to deny the existence of mind altogether. Teachers however cannot be so cavalier, for the entire edifice of education and learning rests on the assumption that students obviously have minds— minds that need to be nurtured and developed!

While long the subject of fascinating philosophical and scientific debates, the question of how the brain relates to the mind and the mind to the brain need not overly concern us. As neuroscientist Jeffrey Schwartz (2002) points out, without a brain there simply is no mind. Concisely parsing the issue he states, "The neural connections that form brain circuits are necessary for the existence of mind as we know it. To check this, simply imagine a skull emptied of its brain; when the brain is gone, so are the contents of the mind" (p. 36). To which he adds, "This is not to say that the puzzle of how mind is interconnected with brain is anywhere close to solution" (p. 48). While we concur, we also believe that the approach we take can help resolve some crucial aspects of how the development of the brain relates to the development of the mind. We will return to the seminal work of Schwartz on how the "attentive mind" influences structural changes in the brain when we take up the topic of mindfulness practice in Chapter 14.

In Chapter 11 we made use of a definition of mind as, *that element or complex of elements in an individual that feels, perceives, thinks, wills, and especially reasons.* In effect, these elements constitute what the mind does. What we wish to offer in this chapter is a description that can usefully account for its formation, developmental origins, critical influences, possible impediments, and immense potential. In approaching this description we need to return to and expand upon our earlier discussion of the autonomic nervous system.

Autonomic Nervous System: New Knowledge, New Insights

In Chapter 8, the autonomic nervous system (ANS) was introduced and its crucial role in regulating the human stress response explicated at some length. In this chapter we build upon that information, placing particular emphasis on the role that the ANS plays in the evolution and consequent development of the human mind. We begin with a review of the ANS then turn to recently acquired knowledge that bears importantly on the formation of the human mind.

To recap what was covered earlier, ANS is that portion of the peripheral nervous system that carries sensory impulses to the brain and motor impulses from the brain to the body. In so doing it serves to monitor and regulate a host of involuntary, automatic (thus the term, autonomic) physiologic actions. Operating largely below our conscious awareness, the ANS functions to maintain the various organ systems of the body via the process known as homeostasis or "steady state—the delicate balance that underpins our physical existence, ensures our survival, and defines our flourishing" as it has been beautifully described.[30] In addition, and

---

30 Maria Popova, newsletter@brainpickings.org.

ubiquitous in all vertebrate species, the ANS serves to automatically and immediately respond to anything that even hints of threat, doing so by activating the stress-mediating hypothalamus-pituitary-adrenal, or HPA, axis, as was explicated in Chapter 8. This "hardwired" response actually reflects an evolutionary advance, as the mammalian nervous system evolved to enable a wider range of strategies to ensure adaptive success. It is both the range and, perhaps more significantly, the order of those reactive strategies that will concern us in this chapter, for they play a crucial role in the quality of mental[31] development.

To continue our review, let's reconsider evolutionary brain function at its most elemental.

The Primacy of the Threat-Response and the Down-Shifted Brain

Recall that a fundamental function of the mammalian brain-mind is to prioritize which information gets attended to first, and that always has been and will be anything perceived as a threat. When this occurs the brain is said to "downshift," the lower, ancient reptilian circuits of the brain taking over in an automatic and reactive manner, meant to enact an immediate, unthinking, threat-eliminating response. Said another way, the default setting of the brain is attuned to safety and survival above all else. Unfettered by concerns of threat the brain "up-shifts," the possibility for high-brain learning—characterized by the pursuit of novelty, challenge and feedback—is enabled. Below (Figure 44) is a simple schema of that prioritization. Note the order in which the functions take place, an important theme to which we shall return.

---

31 Our use of the word *mental* is meant to be synonymous with the word *mind*.

The Triune Brain

FOUR FUNCTIONS

Low brain	1. Focus on threat
High brain	2. Seek novelty
High brain	3. Seek challenge
High brain	4. Seek feedback

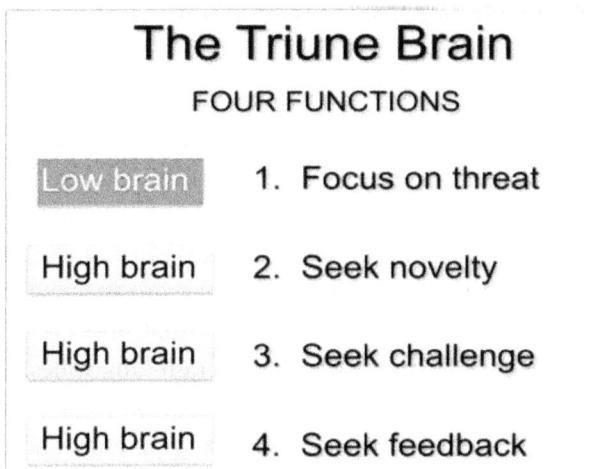

Figure 44. Hierarchy of Brain Functions.
Image by Tim Burns and Jim Brown.

As an abundance of superb research makes clear, a chronically heightened and overwrought stress response in early childhood can have negative effects on the developing brain-mind, possibly for life. In addition to the effects on health and longevity,[32] a heightened threat response during childhood has been shown to significantly affect an individual's perceptions, shading one's outlook in an overly fearful, distrusting, defensive manner. This in turn can have decidedly negative effects on learning and social-emotional development, as well as health.

---

32 From U.S. Centers for Disease Control and Prevention: "Childhood experiences, both positive and negative, have a tremendous impact on future violence victimization and perpetration, and lifelong health and opportunity. As such, early experiences are an important public health issue. Much of the foundational research in this area has been referred to as Adverse Childhood Experiences (ACEs). Adverse Childhood Experiences have been linked to risky health behaviors, chronic health conditions, low life potential, and early death. As the number of ACEs increases, so does the risk for these outcomes. The wide-ranging health and social consequences of ACEs underscore the importance of preventing them before they happen. CDC promotes lifelong health and well-being through Essentials for Childhood – assuring safe, stable, nurturing relationships and environments for all children. Essentials for childhood can have a positive impact on a broad range of health problems and on the development of skills that will help children reach their full potential." Source: https://www.cdc.gov/violenceprevention/acestudy/about_ace.html

In light of the growing number of individuals so afflicted, this has broad and far-reaching implications for the well-being of those individuals and, by extension, the family, community and the planetary home we share.

Thus, the "chronically heightened and overwrought stress response" that was sensitized and primed[33] in infancy and childhood—in addition to being extremely susceptible to manipulation—can end up in a downward spiraling, recursive loop that serves to maintain a chronic low-brain response to an apparently frightful and menacing world. The price exacted is a regrettable loss of individual and collective human potential, as the creative, innovative high-brain languishes. This is a loss of potential we can no longer afford, for the multiplying challenges are too many, the urgent need for creative response and widespread commitment too great.

Homeostasis and the Biology of Balance

Although the ANS has three interrelated, interactive branches—including the enteric nervous system (discussed in Chapter 11)—it is typically thought of as having only two, the sympathetic nervous system (SNS) and the parasympathetic nervous system (PNS). Commonly considered antagonistic to one another, the two branches are actually more complementary in nature. In simplistic terms, we can think of the SNS complex as the accelerator or gas-pedal and the PNS as the brake.

The job of the SNS is to produce a state of arousal and readiness for action, at the extreme of which is the involuntary, automatic "fight or flight" reaction, hard-wired through evolution to prepare us for immediate and unthinking action in the face of threat. In contrast, the

> The job of the SNS is to produce a state of arousal and readiness for action, at the extreme of which is the involuntary, automatic "fight or flight" reaction... In contrast, the role of the PNS complex is recovery and constitutes the "rest and digest" phase of the rebalance cycle present in all species

---

33 The term used for this in the literature on stress is "kindling," which refers to the sensitizing of the so-called HPA axis—the hypothalamus, pituitary and adrenal glands, the main organs responsible for activating the stress response. For a more detailed explication, see Benson, 1975 and 2004 in the reference list.

role of the PNS complex is recovery and constitutes the "rest and digest" phase of the rebalance cycle present in all species. The two branches work in tandem to establish and maintain the viability of the organ systems of the body through the process of homeostasis.

Whereas the SNS largely predominates during the day and in periods of wakeful alertness, the PNS predominates mostly at night and during sleep, a time of restoration for the internal environment. To say that one predominates over the other during the diurnal/ nocturnal cycle isn't to say that they are dormant in the off-cycle. Far from it. Recall from our earlier coverage of the ultradian cycle (Chapter 9)—typically 90-120 minutes in duration—there is a natural rhythmic oscillation between the SNS and the PNS throughout the day as we (ideally) shift between periods of activity and rest.

It is the balance between the two, the homeostatic mechanism, that is important. And therein lies the rub: Too much of one and not enough of the other can, over time, create a range of problems. As changing conditions, unexpected challenges and occasional emergencies call upon the SNS for more "juice," there ought to be subsequent PNS activation in order to facilitate a balanced recovery. This back and forth homeostatic balance, known as *vagal tone*, between the two systems constitutes the functional viability of the ANS. With so much dependent upon balanced ANS function—overall health and wellbeing, mental acuity, ability to learn, and more—we owe it to children to provide every opportunity for them to return to a balanced state.

> This back and forth homeostatic balance, known as vagal tone, between the two systems constitutes the functional viability of the ANS.

An excellent indicator that children are in a balanced ANS state comes in the form of *delight*. This makes sense, since periods of delight optimize brain waves and balance brain chemicals involved in learning and wellbeing, while simultaneously toning the vagus. This is just as true for us adults, of course, but since we can easily grow accustomed to "getting by" without the presence of delight it can be easy to overlook just how essential this state is for the maturing nervous system. Delight is, after all, the state of feeling and sensation that accompanies *flow*, first described by researcher Mihaly Csikszentmihalyi (1990) in his bestselling book of the same title. In it, he described *flow* as the mental state in which one is completed immersed and fully involved in whatever one is doing; a state of energized focus and feeling of success in the process of the activity. The following can serve as important ways to invite states of nearly instantaneous delight in children—and ourselves, if we care to partake—thereby toning the vagal system in the process.

Delight, Flow and the Toned Vagal System

Delight, of course! The word itself says it all, since it is nearly synonymous with play. It probably comes as no surprise that anything related to active involvement in the arts can easily invoke a state of delight, with the added likelihood of entering into a flow state as well. Dance and movement, dramatics, drawing and painting, sculpting, music and rhythm—all invite feelings of pleasurable delight and consequent wellbeing. Speaking directly to the role of music in vagal toning, for example, Stephen Porges (2010), whose paradigm-shifting work will be taken up later, makes the point that music—especially wind instruments or singing—strengthens the vagal system due to the slow out breath and mastery of the facial muscles. "This simple mechanical change in breathing," he states, "increases the calming impact and health benefits of the myelinated vagus on our body…and may promote positive outcomes improving several features related to quality of life" (p. 9).

Listening to or observing artistic endeavors can also be a source of great delight as we all know, so it isn't necessarily the case that we must be actively involved, as the above suggests. In fact, children benefit immensely from environments—such as the classroom, or hallways—where *touches of beauty* enhance the experience. Plants, flowers, artwork, soft music; all these and more add immediacy of delight in small but important ways. Some years ago I, (TB), was, for example, invited to give a talk at an elementary school at which classical music played in lieu of a passing bell, continuing as children moved from one setting to another. Commenting to the principal about how calm things seemed with dozens of children in the hallways—typically a heavily supervised transitional time—she proudly remarked that the incidents of problem behaviors during passing time had dropped significantly upon implementing the change earlier in the school year.

One cannot help but notice how children almost automatically and without exception enter into a trancelike state during story-telling time. No surprise there: our progenitors relied on story-telling as a potent means by which to pass along, in the formative years of early childhood, the most important values, mores and expectations of the tribe. Interestingly enough, in all cultures, past and present, the main protagonists in stories told to children are animals, most often the furry type: foxes, coyotes, and so forth. Of course, stories can be so potent because of the tone and modulation of voice on the part of the storyteller, which serves to remind us once again about MacLean's emphasis on audio-vocal communication as a principal means by which the brain develops.

Two other things to consider: one is pace and transitions. Children have a much different relationship to time than we do as adults. By slowing down the pace of activities and in particularly transitions between activities the nervous system of children can remain for longer periods of time in that relaxed, alert state that facilitates learning and enhances wellbeing. Finally, for those children displaying obvious difficulty and perhaps disturbing behaviors when it comes to self-management during transitions, experienced classroom teachers have been known to provide a sort of "protected space" into which they can temporarily retreat. This can include small enclosures, sometimes with a curtain, into which the child learns to go until the conclusion of the ordinary minor chaos that can accompany a transition settles out.

The Paradox of Adaptive Homeostasis: Allostasis and the Overwhelmed Nervous System

A complex and multifaceted issue, the notion of ANS balance and vagal tone is particularly crucial during childhood. It is therefore important to understand another, somewhat paradoxical, aspect of the ANS: that it is both homeostatic and adaptive: it can and does make dynamic adjustments in accordance with the demands placed upon it over time. The problem is that these adjustments can eventually lead to chronic maladjustment, imbalance and consequent learning and health challenges. This is precisely the case with the most important evolutionary survival function relative to threat: the stress response.

In his delightful and provocatively entitled book, *Why Zebras Don't Get Ulcers (2004)*, best-selling author and professor of biological sciences, neurology, and neurological sciences at Stanford University, Robert Sapolsky, PhD, has spent decades studying the physiological effects of stress on health. What makes Sapolsky's stress studies so unique are his decades-long observations of mammals in their natural habitats. For over 30 years Sapolsky and a small team of graduate students spend part of the year on the Serengeti plains of Africa, where they dutifully record the social behavior of our nearest relatives, the apes and baboons, taking blood samples in order to better understand the neurobiology and neurochemistry of the stress response.

Comparing the human (especially contemporary humans—us) stress response to other animals, Sapolsky (2007, p. 1) observes, "The stress response is incredibly ancient evolutionarily. Fish, birds and reptiles secrete the same stress hormones we do, yet their metabolism doesn't get messed up the way it does in people and other primates." This, he explains, is because in the short-term stress hormones are "brilliantly adapted" to act successfully in the face of unexpected threat. Sapolsky: "You mobilize energy in your thigh muscles, you increase your blood pressure and you turn off everything that's not essential to surviving, such as digestion, growth and reproduction.... You think more clearly, and certain aspects of learning and memory are enhanced. All of that is spectacularly adapted if you're dealing with an acute physical stressor—a real one." But not, he points out, when stressors are more psychosocial and more or less unrelenting—our very real modern dilemma.

Sapolsky emphasizes the point that if the stress response chronically turns on for purely psychological reasons—constant worry about money, a sick spouse, child or parent, world events, for example—it is still triggering the release of adrenalin and other stress hormones, which can and all too frequently does result in severe consequences to health: elevating the risk of adult onset diabetes, high blood pressure, heart disease, which grows greater with each passing year, as epidemiological reports indicate.

Stated at it most succinct and stark, Sapolsky says, "If you plan to get stressed like a normal mammal, you had better turn on the stress response or else you're dead. But if you get chronically, psychosocially stressed, like a Westernized human, then you are more at risk for heart disease and some of the other leading causes of death in Westernized life" (p.2).

In line with our concern for healthy childhood development—and in addition to setting the stage for the kinds of problems that chronic over-stress can result in for adults—Sapolsky points out that the continual release of glucocorticoids can suppress the secretion of normal growth hormones. "There's actually a syndrome called stress dwarfism in kids who are so psychologically stressed that growth is markedly impaired." As revealed by the headline-making and shocking discovery after the fall of communism in the early nineteen-nineties, this was precisely the case for the so-called Romanian orphans who had, by the thousands, languished in cribs with little attention from caregivers. Many of the survivors were found to be far, and sometimes irreversibly, behind in their mental development and physical growth.

As Sapolsky points out (and other researchers emphasize), in a stressful environment, such as the one just described, the body conserves energy for brain development. But even with that conserved energy, the IQs of children can be as much as 40 points lower than average.[34] While alarming and obviously an extremely abnormal circumstance, it nevertheless underscores how critical are nurture, feedback and play for the growth and health of body and brain.

Obviously less extreme but still concerning, when the SNS branch is continually called upon to meet the growing demands of our hectic lives—one typified by little or no recovery time—we end up with what Hans Selye (see Chapter 8) termed carry-over stress, or *distress*. What started off as an evolutionary plus—the ability to adapt to changing circumstances—now becomes a negative as the organ systems of the body, constantly being called upon to adapt, then readapt, re-readapt, and potentially maladapt, succumb to *allostasis*. To a greater or lesser extent, this describes contemporary life for us all.

---

34 NPR radio, "Researchers still learning from Romania's orphans," Sept. 16, 2006.
   https://www.npr.org/templates/story/story.php?storyId=6089477

Contemporary Childhood, Chronic Distress and the Enfeebled Mind

While a certain amount of stress and pressure are important and healthy for children to experience, when those pressures and stresses become excessive, we need to be concerned. This is precisely the situation in which we find ourselves. Given our demanding, increasingly stress-filled lives effecting this crucial balance is getting harder and harder to achieve and sustain, the cumulative effects of which are proving to be corrosive to health and wellbeing. The problem is that in our fast-paced, consumer-obsessed, media-driven and hyped-up world, more and more of us are falling into states of chronic over-stress and consequent imbalance.

The overall elevated level of SNS arousal is concerning enough for us adults—who can be expected to exert at least some degree of control over the stressors affecting our lives—but for children, whose vulnerable nervous system are at risk, a chronically over-charged SNS can result in nervous system disorders such as attention-deficit hyperactivity, developmental delay, stress-related health problems, and worse. This has become a source of increasing concern as a new norm of chronic imbalance now has childhood in its grip, as evidenced by the fact that time devoted to free play, periods of rest and recovery, idle daydreaming and downtime, even sleep—all the components connected to PNS-activated rest and recovery mode—have so noticeably diminished.

In effect, short-circuiting the nervous system can significantly interfere with the natural course of its otherwise healthy development. Even in the best of circumstances, absent trauma and neglect, the all-too-common phenomena of over-stress, in combination with the "hurried child syndrome," (Elkind) seems to be at the root of many childhood problems as the medical and mental health communities have made clear.[35] We are reminded of Marietta Johnson's (1996, p. 29) admonition that, "A lengthening childhood, as society increases in complexity, is absolutely essential to progress." This profound plea—more than a century ago, in 1904!—to allow the slowly maturing

---

35 For example, preview the work voluminous studies undertaken and/or collated by physician and epidemiologist Dr. Bruce Perry, MD, PhD, visit his website, Child Trauma Academy at http://childtrauma.org/cta-library/trauma-ptsd/

human nervous system to unfold and integrate at the speed of life must certainly come as something of a shock to those of us who live our hurried, overly busy, tech-driven lives at seeming warp-speed.

Thanks to new insights about the ANS, we are in an improved position to positively affect the brain-body-mind of children, while offsetting—to an indeterminate extent—potentially far reaching damage to children's nervous systems. In effect we can provide them with the gift of an extended childhood, one that supports a viable nervous system and greater wellbeing. In order to fully appreciate how we can positively affect the viability of the ANS, and thus the development of mind, we need first to revisit basic triune brain functions.

The Developing Mind and Polyvagal Theory

Paul MacLean's triune brain theory (see Chapter 2) emphasizes the evolutionary trajectory of the human brain, as reflected in its bottom-to-top organization and maturation: R-complex or reptilian brain at the base, then limbic cortex or paleo-mammalian brain, the neocortex or neo-mammalian brain crowning both at the top (see Figure 4, Chapter 2). MacLean's seminal evolutionary insights on the development of the mammalian brain-mind is reflected in the contemporary work of a number of scientists, including neuroscientist and former chair of the National Institute of Child Health and Human Development, Maternal and Child Health research committee, Stephen Porges, PhD.[36]

Briefly introduced in Chapter 3, Porges, like MacLean before him, has had a long-standing interest in the evolution of the mammal brain-mind, although, while MacLean's work focused more on the central nervous system, Porges' is centered mostly on the autonomic nervous system. While both concern themselves with the evolutionary developments that have benefitted mammalian adaptive success, Porges' particular area of interest concerns the evolution of the vagal nerve complex and its largely unrecognized role in facilitating the healthy development of the human mind.

---

36 For an up-to-date list of his scientific contributions, go to https://www.ncbi.nlm. nih.gov/pmc/articles/PMC3108032/ or http://stephenporges.com/index.php/ bibliography

A major component of the ANS, the vagal nerve derives its name from the Latin word *vagary*, meaning wandering. Having the longest course of the nerves emanating from the cranium, it is widely distributed throughout the viscera or gut, enabling it to monitor a vast range of crucial functions—most of which relate to the functioning of the PNS. It is estimated that between 80% and 90% of the information flow via the vagus travels to the brain, with only 10% to 20% going the other way around. With such extensive information pathways to provide the brain with vital information about the status of the viscera, the vagus can be thought of as the main nerve trunk uniting body and mind.

Of the many tasks carried out by the vagal complex, two can serve as examples of its importance to physical health and cognitive wellbeing. One is its role in immune system functioning and how that relates to regulation of the inflammatory response, and the other its vital role in the formation of memories (due to its modulation of important neurotransmitters like norepinephrine, a primary function of which is to consolidate learning). Taken together, these two functions have led medical scientists[37] to reconsider possible ways of treating pernicious and seemingly intractable diseases—such as diabetes, Alzheimer's, coronary heart disease and even some forms of cancer—by intervening directly and indirectly into vagal functioning. Direct intervention—known, not surprisingly, as vagal nerve stimulation—has been shown to successfully treat inflammation and epilepsy, for example, a part of a new field of medical study, known as bioelectronics,[38] sometimes touted as "the future of medicine." Using implants that deliver electric impulses to various body parts, scientists and doctors hope to treat illness with fewer medications and fewer side effects.

Indirect intervention refers to the fact that the action of the PNS can be enhanced, for example, by eliciting the so-called relaxation-

---

37 Chapter 14 provides a rather survey of the scientific research and practices that continue to evolve from a new understanding of the ANS, and which can help provide teachers with knowledge and skills to enhance personal and professional wellbeing.

38 See for example, "Bioelectronics could lead to a new class of medicine," ACS News Service Weekly Press: https://www.acs.org/content/acs/en/pressroom/presspacs/2014/acs-presspac-july-2-2014/bioelectronics-could-lead-to-a-new-class-of-medicine.html

response, enhancement that can similarly be achieved by engaging in mindfulness meditation. While this is good news for those who suffer from seemingly intractable illnesses such as those mentioned above, it is equally important to realize that—learned and practiced from an early age—these practices are proving to be a marvelous and unexpected source of enhanced learning and wellbeing in children. We shall have much more to say about this in the next chapter.

For Porges, optimal human development is related to what he calls, state-regulation (think also, self-regulation). His explication of how the vagal complex acts in support of this critical function is highly consonant with MacLean's family triad, a rendering of which appears as Figure 45, below. Simply stated, the principle way by which self-regulation (an essential component of emotional intelligence) develops is via the family triad, nurture, feedback and play. Like MacLean before him, Porges' interest in the evolution of the mammalian nervous system has led to some astonishing insights, to which we now turn.

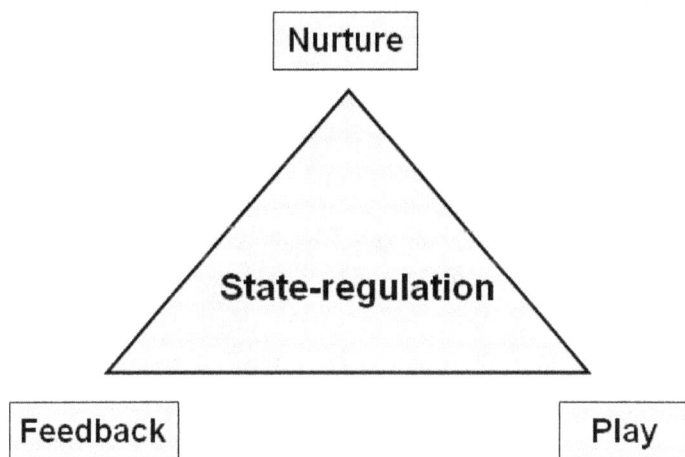

Figure 45. Porges' State-Regulation and MacLean's "Family Triad."
Image by Tim Burns and Jim Brown.

The term, polyvagal, appears to suggest the existence of more than one vagus; however, it is instead meant to draw attention to a variety of significant functions—some of which have gone largely unrecognized and now being widely hailed—that influence the nascent mind. Polyvagal theory is based upon, and significantly adds to, the model of autonomic functioning described above with respect to both its reactive aspects (i.e., fight-or-flight) and its role in affecting balance between the two main branches (sympathetic and parasympathetic). What polyvagal theory adds is a unique insight into an under-appreciated evolutionary dimension of ANS functioning—one that relates significantly to the development of mind.

Porges suggests that the mammalian drive to avoid danger while ensuring safety resulted in a unique and critical adaptation. Like all animal kingdom species, mammals depend for their survival and success on the evolutionary more ancient fight, flight and freeze reactions. But because of the dangers to life and limb that these responses often entail and because of the unique nature of mammalian existence a different survival strategy became necessary—due principally to the fact that almost by definition mammalian species are highly social. As such, evolutionary success depended to an unparalleled extent on social cues and behaviors, termed "social engagement behaviors," that allow for close proximity and near-constant interaction. As an adaptive strategy this of course has proven to be a brilliant success.

In order to avoid or resolve the inevitable conflicts inherent in social proximity, mammals developed a repertoire of social engagement behaviors designed to quickly and effectively allay threat while inviting reciprocal nurture. In so doing, the ANS evolved to enable a range of overt and subtle capabilities previously unseen in nature, chief among which, using MacLean's term (see Chapter 3), vocal-visual communication. What Porges came to recognize is the order in which evolutionary survival strategies get enacted by mammals—what he refers to as a "phylogenetically ordered hierarchy" of responses. According to Porges, a close examination of how mammals mobilize against potential threats from members of their own species reveals that responses occur in the reverse of their evolutionary progression (Porges, 2018, p. 61). That is, social engagement behaviors are enacted first, followed, if necessary, by fight or flight and—only in the most threatening and dire circumstances—a freeze response.

A closer examination of this response hierarchy, to which we now turn, reveals two essential aspects of the nascent human mind: its dependence on social interaction and reliance upon learning in order to facilitate proper development. In other words, as highlighted in the opening sentence of the Chapter Overview, *the emergence of the human mind is an experience-expectant and wholly contingent process, dependent for its proper unfolding on the quality of relationships and opportunities for adaptive learning.*

Fight, Flight, or Freeze and The Mammalian Vagal Complex

That the fundamental priority or basic operation of the brain is reacting to threat seems inarguable, evolution having prepared vertebrates with two well-honed primary and unthinking reactions to imminent danger: *mobilizing* SNS fight-or-flight and PNS-orchestrated *immobilization* (a freeze state).[39] To Porges goes credit for parsing the evolution of two very distinctive and phylogenetically derived operations of the PNS/vagal branch. Of the two operations it is the dorsal, or backside, that is evidently phylogenetically older. Called into play, ancient vertebrates could quickly immobilize, feigning death, thus potentially avoiding danger. Consider what many fish species, reptiles, even mammals such as rabbits and deer do when they sense danger. They freeze and then, if necessary, flee. When absolutely necessary they will even feign death in hopes of escaping with their lives.

Clearly this feigning-death strategy is to be deployed only in life-or-death situations since, as Porges points out, the need for an immediate SNS shutdown reaction can go awry, leading to fainting or collapse and possibly even unintended death, as the heart-and pulse-rate and even body temperature dramatically plummet. This rapid down-regulation in the presence of dangerous circumstances can and does occur in humans of course, beholden as we are to our evolutionary mammalian forebears. Notably in humans, it is often accompanied by psychological dissociation as well, a condition that when repeated and left unrecognized and untreated can lead to significant mental and physical health problems that can seriously impede the course of normal, healthy development.

---

39 Porges avers that this may have had to do in part with basic biology since the SNS reaction demands much more metabolic activity, fueled by the availability of resources (i.e. oxygen and food). The far more ancient invertebrate adaptive defensive maneuver of appearing inanimate (i.e., feigning death) being far less demanding of resources. (2018, p. 50-51)

As evolution proceeds, Porges observes, a second vagal pathway function appears, one that exerts control over *both* forms of defense: SNS mobilization and PNS immobilization. This most recent adaptive control mechanism is found only in mammalian society and is associated with the ventral (frontal) branch of the vagus nerve. Interestingly this part of the vagal complex controls the muscles of the face, heart and diaphragm/lungs, notably those frontal parts of the body that are used (a point given great emphasis by Porges) when interacting or "interfacing" with another. Thus, eye-gaze, facial expression, breathing, tone of voice, body posture came to play an essential role in down-regulating an over-charged SNS, permitting mammals to relax their guard, safely approach and engage one another. Porges: "This emergent social engagement system provided the mechanism for co-regulation of physiological state, as mammals conveyed cues of safety and danger—via vocalizations, head gestures, and facial expressions—to conspecifics"[40] (pp. 51-52).

Co-regulation. This feature of mammalian social behavior is of immense importance to educators and care-providers to understand and appreciate. It appears that modulated co-regulation is the direct, unmediated way by which mammalian physiology is de-stressed, while simultaneously promoting health and optimizing learning ability. In other words, attuned interaction is the state specific trigger that prompts the ANS to rebalance and thereby support growth, health and restoration. This seemingly simple behavioral feature actually undergirds the entire edifice of the human nervous system upon which the emergence of the human mind and fostering of lifelong wellbeing depend. Let's explore this feature further.

The ventral part of the vagal complex appears to play a principle role in dialing down the ancient, reactive components of the autonomic nervous system, while simultaneously prompting what Porges calls the "social engagement system." Freed from the need to be threat-wary and reactive, a sense of safety assured, mammals rest, recover, heal, and in turn seek out opportunities for new learning via the exclusively high-brain triumvirate, novelty, feedback, play. This in turn facilitates integration of the entire nervous system with its various dedicated neural circuits,

---

40 Conspecific refers to members of the same species.

while simultaneously serving to enhance state-or self-regulation—a core component of heightened social-emotional intelligence.

As alluded to above, there are clear health implications as well, for when the ANS is constantly optimized for defense, well-being is sacrificed and health suffers—exactly as depicted in those ACE studies mentioned earlier. Thus, a sense of safety also serves as a foundation for good health. This makes perfectly good sense, for absent threat the calming and restorative ventral vagal state directs the nervous system. This calm, relaxed state of recovery, often accompanied by day-dreaming and reverie, is vitally important to the restoration of healthy wellbeing and creativity, as was detailed in Chapter 9. This state, recall, also correlates with specific brain wave configurations that reflect the so-called default mode, characterized by a mix of highly restorative theta waves and synchronous alpha waves that associate with the relaxed, alert state indicative of enhanced learning and performance.

A final, essential point. Whereas the defensive reactions, fight-flight-freeze, are just that: reactive—hard-wired and instinctual—social engagement behaviors are responsive, meaning that they need to be learned, practiced and thoughtfully applied in situations that might otherwise trigger our powerful low brain into reacting or worse, overreacting. As mediated by the ventral vagus nerve, mammals—including of course us humans—must learn to temper responses to interpersonal challenges and threats. It's important to emphasize that last phrase, must learn to temper responses to interpersonal challenges and threats, because this is decidedly not an automatic, hard-wired, instinctive reaction.

And for mammals, as pointed out back in Chapter 2,[41] learning is almost exclusively and entirely initiated through modeling. The so-called "model imperative," in this as in every other case, requires the presence of individuals capable of modeling a tempered response to interpersonal challenges and threats—the learning of which, as a species,

---

41 Recall the "model imperative:" Pearce (2002): "The family triad includes by default nature's imperative that a model be given for all aspects of development." (p. 100). "Nature's imperative, then, and her over-arching developmental rule, which has enormous consequences, is that no intelligence or ability will unfold until or unless given the appropriate model environment. Mind and environment give rise to each other through the new-born brain only if the environment is there" (1992, p. 20).

we are in dreadfully conspicuous need! In the chapter to follow, we go into considerable depth on the importance of recommended ways to model and teach the skills related to self-modulation and rebalancing the nervous system.

Figure 46, below, captures in summary form the evolutionary and hierarchic nature of the autonomic nervous system. With this we are now prepared to investigate the emergence and development of the human mind.

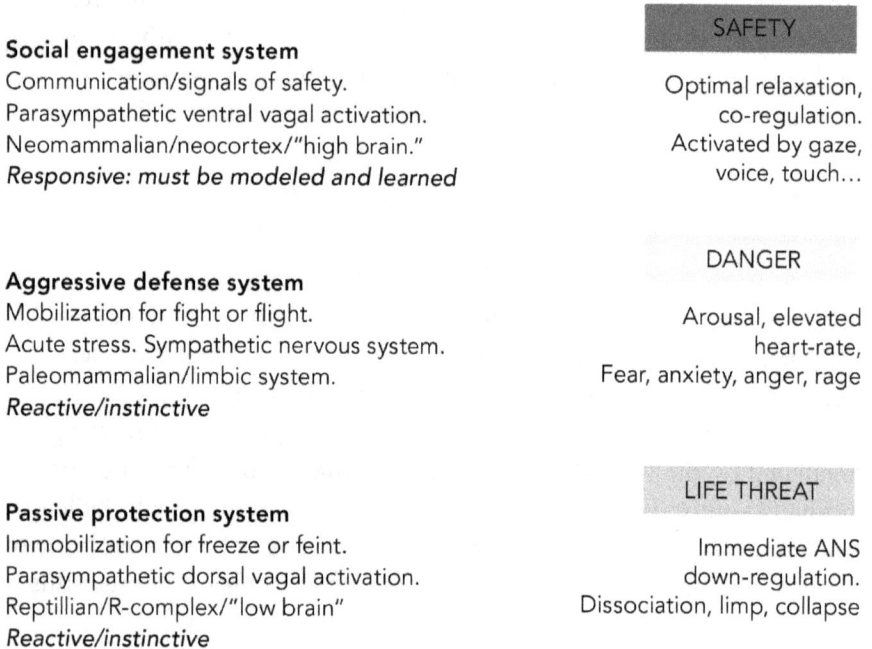

	SAFETY
Social engagement system	Optimal relaxation,
Communication/signals of safety.	co-regulation.
Parasympathetic ventral vagal activation.	Activated by gaze,
Neomammalian/neocortex/"high brain."	voice, touch…
Responsive: must be modeled and learned	

	DANGER
Aggressive defense system	Arousal, elevated
Mobilization for fight or flight.	heart-rate,
Acute stress. Sympathetic nervous system.	Fear, anxiety, anger, rage
Paleomammalian/limbic system.	
Reactive/instinctive	

	LIFE THREAT
Passive protection system	Immediate ANS
Immobilization for freeze or feint.	down-regulation.
Parasympathetic dorsal vagal activation.	Dissociation, limp, collapse
Reptilian/R-complex/"low brain"	
Reactive/instinctive	

Figure 46. Evolution of ANS response-activation, according to Porges. Image by Tim Burns and Jim Brown.

Interpersonal Neurobiology and the Development of Mind

If one wished to find a particularly well thought-out model of the developing mind and its formative influences, it would need to be based on solid scientific theory, peer-reviewed research, and include demonstrably positive outcomes when put into practice. For it to be most helpful to teachers the model would provide a useful understanding of overall student development while illuminating the learning process—in effect, answering the question: will knowing this help my students flourish educationally and developmentally? We believe that one model in particular meets these criteria. It comes from the recently emergent field of human endeavor known as *interpersonal neurobiology* (IPNB). What follows is an explication of the model that, we believe, will provide teachers with a clear understanding of the human mind and its formative process.

Interpersonal Neurobiology and Bio-Psychosocial Integration

Seemingly simple, the IPNB model draws from several well-established disciplines, each of which offers a unique perspective on the course of human development. Included among these are child development, neuroscience, evolutionary biology, cognitive psychology, psychiatry and psychotherapy, as well as complex systems and emotional intelligence (Siegel, 1999, p. 2). By melding these important areas of investigation, IPNB provides an integrative framework that promotes understanding the connections between human relationships and neurophysiological functioning. The fundamental tenet is this: the human brain is directly and powerfully shaped—for better and for worse—through interaction with significant others, which in turn gives rise to the mind.

> The human brain is directly and powerfully shaped—for better and for worse—through interaction with significant others, which in turn gives rise to the mind.

At the forefront of IPNB is a group of loosely affiliated scientific researchers who happen also to be mental health clinicians and educators,[42] the combination of which provides ample opportunities to test and refine the model in real life settings. While their emphasis is on the development of a clinical model dedicated to helping traumatized

---

42 Chief among these scientist-practitioners are Daniel Siegel, MD (1999, 2001, 2007, 2010) Stephen Porges, PhD (2011, 2018) and Alan Schore, PhD (2001, 2003), whose publications and educational endeavors, taken together, continue to broaden and deepen the field.

individuals recover and thrive despite earlier childhood psychic insult, the model can be of great interest to anyone concerned about the course of human growth, development and potential across the lifespan.

From its inception as a ground-breaking way by which to conceptualize the developing mind, to its enthusiastic reception by those with a keen interest in how human development can best be supported across the life span, the ideas and methodologies IPNB has spawned, will be of special interest to educators. By examining its premises, principles and practices we think teachers will gain greater clarity about both the formation of the human mind and the conditions that best support its balanced, healthy unfolding. One of IPNB's principal founders, Daniel Siegel, MD, a well respected researcher, successful clinician and popular educator, states that, "Educators can benefit from insights into how emotion and interpersonal relationships are fundamental motivational aspects of learning and memory" (1999, p. xii)." In our view, educators can also gain a significant working knowledge of how to best help students—of whom there appears to be increasing numbers—to self-right and "bounce forward" despite setbacks from various traumas.[43] The most common traumas are often related to abuse and neglect, and such traumas, left untended, might otherwise hinder students' developing minds

While wholeheartedly supporting the sincere desire of most teachers to provide all the social, emotional and even mental-health support possible, we need to be clear that this is emphatically *not* to say that teachers ought to see or place themselves in the role of professional therapist. Clearly this it is not the job of teachers unless, that is, certified and authorized to do so. That said, anyone who works with children knows first-hand and sometimes to an alarming extent that the academic struggles and social-emotional difficulties experienced by some students are related to the traumatic circumstances in which they live.

Eager to find anything that can help students develop bright, shining minds and, equally motivated to help alleviate the growing levels of neuropsychiatric disorders, we think IPNB has much to offer busy,

---

43 To learn more about fostering resiliency in traumatized children, readers are invited to read Tim's book, *From Risk to Resiliency: A Path With Heart for Our Children, Our Future,* Dallas: Marco Polo Publications, 1994.

dedicated classroom teachers. Consider the alarming prediction, made at the turn of the millennium, that by the year 2020 disorders such as depression are anticipated to reach over 50 percent internationally, becoming one of the five most common causes of morbidity, mortality, and disability among children. Sadly, this seems to have largely come to pass.[44]

Mind: A Process, Not a Thing

We begin our exploration of the IPNB model by considering its most stripped-down definition of mind, to which we shall add other elements as we proceed:

> Mind is a process that regulates the flow of energy and information. (2007, p. 5)

Note that mind—and this is a crucial distinction—is a *process*, not a thing; more a verb than a noun. Distinct from the solid materiality of the brain, the mind is a dynamic non-material entity. Importantly, Siegel (2010, p. 54) describes mind as "embodied," meaning that, "the regulation of energy and information flow happens, in part, in the body. It occurs where we usually imagine our mental life taking place, in the circuits and synapses of the brain, inside the skull. But it also occurs throughout the body, in the distributed nervous system, which monitors and influences energy and information flowing through our heart and our intestines." Not surprisingly perhaps, this view of "the distributed nervous system...flowing through our heart and our intestines," aligns completely with our view that intelligence arises not solely from the cranial brain but from the gut-and heart-brain as well.

IPNB adds another irreducible dimension of the mind; one not found in any other explicit definition or description that we know of: it is profoundly *relational*. The flow of energy and information between and among people alters the flow of information and energy in the brain—and body. Thus, the complete definition:

---

44 World Health Organization (2001). Mental Health: World Health Ministers Call for Action, p. 6. http://www.who.int/mental_health/advocacy/en/Call_for_Action_MoH_Intro.pdf

The mind is an embodied and relational, self-organizing emergent process that regulates the flow of energy and information both within us and between and among us and others. (2018)

Stated somewhat differently, the mind appears as the flow of energy and information both within the interactions taking place neurophysiologically—that is, within an individual brain—as well as interpersonally, the way in which two brains interact with each other. Thus, as an undergirding principle of IPNB, the mind doesn't just come from one brain, rather it is embedded in the relationship and interactions with others. We are, due to the social nature of the evolved brain, hard-wired to be connected to other brains.

The appeal of the IPNB model of the developing mind, we think, is its *insistence* on social interaction—the more empathic and warm the better—as a non-negotiable condition. This factor also makes it completely consonant with MacLean's family triad, nurture, feedback and play (explicated in Chapter 2), what we have been referring to (if not insisting upon) as nature's mandates for normal, healthy development.

Principles of Interpersonal Neurobiology

The IPNB model validates what every teacher already knows: that human relationship is the key to how the human brain develops and the mind unfolds. What the model itself can offer is scientific confirmation of this all-important fact. The three principles upon which the model is based serve to illuminate how, by engaging in what turn out to be surprisingly simple, everyday and common-place behaviors, teachers facilitate and support the emergent mind. The principles are as follows (Siegel, 1999, p. 2):

1. The human mind emerges from patterns in the flow of energy and information within the brain and between brains.

2. The mind is created within the interaction of internal neurophysiological process and interpersonal experiences.

3. The structure and function of the developing brain are determined by how experiences, especially within interpersonal relationships, shape the genetically programmed maturation of the nervous system.

Simply stated, "Human connections shape the neural connections from which the mind emerges" (p. 2). Human relationship and brain development, Siegel is saying, are inextricably bound together, the emergent self-organizing brain-mind the inexorable result—a point made tragically clear by those stories of acute social deprivation recounted earlier, namely the so-called wild boy of Aveyron, as well as the horrifically treated Genie (see Chapter 7). Clearly, as relationships go, so goes brain and mind, the result of the simple fact that the human brain is an evolutionarily derived and profoundly social organ, hard-wired to arise and develop through interaction, as mind and brain give rise to one another.

Reinforcing this fundamental premise, Siegel states (2001, p. 1) that, "The mind develops at the interface between human relationships and the unfolding structure and function of the brain;" and, "It is in this manner that interpersonal experiences directly shape the genetically driven unfolding of the human brain" (Siegel 1999, p.3). Clearly, quality of close relationships plays the most essential role in directing how genes either work together (or fail to do so) to orchestrate the stage-wise symphony of growth and development that is our birthright. Important interpersonal elements of communication help to foster or, when absent, hinder the development of such neural integration. The result of the triadic interplay, *embodied mind, coherent brain, empathic relationships is multifaceted integration,* which is the most significant factor in determining the course of cognitive, emotional and social development in humans, according to IPNB (see Figure 47, next page).

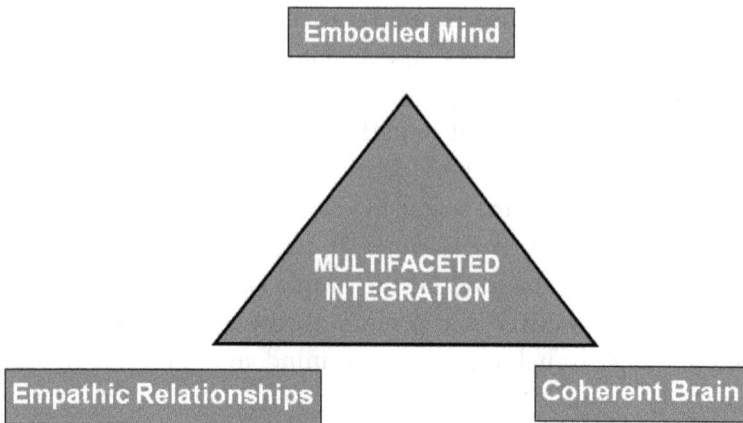

Figure 47. Multifaceted Integration.
Image based on work of D. Siegel.

Importantly, the model places emphasis on the human mind as existing throughout the entirety of the physical body—it is "embodied." This matter-of-fact statement serves to resolve the four-hundred year old dilemma known as *Cartesian dualism*, the notion posed by the 17th-century philosopher and mathematician Rene Descartes, that mind and body are distinct and separate entities. There is no separation; they give rise to and shape one another. Moreover, to repeat for emphasis, the model makes clear that the presence of warm and nurturing relationship is a non-negotiable requirement for proper integration.

Response Flexibility and Mammalian Success

Let's consider one specific outcome (or lack thereof) related to neural integration, and it is a mighty important one for humans: so-called, response *flexibility*. Described by Siegel as, "the capacity of the brain to respond to changes in the internal or external environment with a flexibly adaptive range of behavioral or cognitive responses" (p. 13), this subtle yet crucial capacity appears evolutionarily only in mammals. It represents, in effect, *learning* as a crucial adaptive mechanism and implies something altogether different in terms of cognitive response: the ability to *reflect*. Reptiles, in contrast, wholly reliant on reactive (i.e. instinctive, or at least preprogrammed) behaviors to ensure immediate success, are incapable of this sort of behavioral, let alone cognitive, flexibility. In mammals, this evolved capacity for learning came about due to the social context in which maturation and development takes place. Moreover, it is only in humans that we note the heightened need for state-or self-regulation. This is the point emphasized in Porges' schema as the predicate for success in both social and cognitive realms.

Coincidentally, this ability to reflectively respond to internal emotional states—one's own as well as that of others—is the bedrock foundation of emotional intelligence, or so-called EQ (Goleman, 1995). Lacking these and other subtle and not so subtle social-emotional abilities, an individual may well be plagued by all manner of social and emotional challenges and difficulties and, sadly, without ever really knowing why. And, thanks to rapid advances in the brain sciences, much of which is due to increasingly sophisticated imaging technology, we can actually peer into the neural mechanisms that undergird emotional intelligence, state-regulation, response flexibility and so forth.

The capacity for adaptive response-flexibility, for example, is principally determined by the maturation (i.e., integration) of a specific brain area known to mediate and regulate this and other crucial facets of social-emotional intelligence: the right orbitofrontal region. Located just behind the right eye socket, "This region is uniquely positioned to link the major regions of the brain, including the associational cortex, limbic circuits, and brainstem areas....In this manner, the orbitofrontal region enables the more complex 'higher order' abstract processing of the neocortex to be integrated with the 'lower order' somatic and emotional functions of the deeper structures" (Siegel, 1999, p. 13). Considered a crucial biological control system—the senior executive of the emotional brain, as described by Allan Shore (2000, 2001)— its successful integration facilitates healthy, modulated control over a panoply of behavioral responses, among which are included monitoring, adjusting, and correcting for internal emotional responses—the basis upon which state-regulation and self-reflective awareness develops—and very importantly, inhibitory control (Siegel, p. 34).

Integration Across Domains: A Key to Individual and Species Success

While IPNB emphasizes the role of neural integration in appropriate brain development, it also takes a broad view of the need for integration in other domains as well. These domains include (Siegel, 2007)[45] human consciousness, memory, and narrative integrity (the crucially important way that we extrapolate meaning from our life experiences, thereby forming an autobiographically coherent sense of self). Interpersonal integration is another, of course—our unyielding need for connections to other people in order to feel in balance and to develop well; the nonnegotiable process by which humans come to regulate the body, balance emotional states, and develop self-awareness. Reflecting on the role of integration in a social context, Siegel considers it "a core process essential for mental well-being within the individual and the family, and perhaps fundamental for the healthy functioning of a nurturing community" (Siegel, 1999, p. 2).

Siegel describes one other facet of integration, intriguingly referred to as transpirational and defined as the emergence of enhanced levels of integration across all domains which can lead to transpersonal experiences. This life-invigorating and spirited state is variously described as eliciting a sense of connection to a much larger whole; going beyond one's personal life to form a more all-inclusive sense of self; enjoying a dissolution of the sense of isolation from others and even from oneself. Who among us wouldn't welcome such a state from time to time (a state about which we will have more to say in Chapter 15)!

There is another recent and relevant finding that adds an intriguing dimension to the discussion of those elements deemed essential to how the mind takes form, principally as the need for and result of social interaction: mirror neurons.

---

45 For the reader interested in an in-depth exploration of the nine domains of integration, see Siegel's 2007 book, *The Mindful Brain: Reflection and Attunement in the Cultivation of Well-Being*. W.W. Norton and Co. Inc.

Mirror Neurons and the Self-Reflective Mind

It was Italian scientists who chanced to note an unexpected phenomenon in a laboratory monkey who happened at the time to be harnessed to a neuro-feedback device measuring brain activity. It seems that the pattern of brain activity in the motor cortex of the harnessed monkey—who was at the time passively observing the behavior of another—was so similar to the brain activity in the active monkey as to suggest that the observer monkey's brain was being "primed" to imitate the action observed in the other. In effect, the observing monkey's brain seemed to be mirroring the active monkey's brain activity. This serendipitous laboratory occurrence, and astute recognition by the scientists present, has led to areas of interest and research that continue to refine and expand our understanding of the human mind. This, then, is the story of so-called mirror neurons.

Described as a special class of previously unrecognized cells, a mirror neuron fires both when an animal performs an action and when the same action is performed by another—smiling, for example, or reaching for an object. Directly observed in primate species and perhaps in other mammalian species (the verdict is still out), the neuron is said to "mirror" the behavior of the other, as though the observer were itself acting. Humans also have mirror neurons, thought to be the most complex neurons and found in several areas of the high brain. As such they are thought to be "far smarter, more flexible and more highly evolved than any of those found in monkeys, a fact that scientists say reflects the evolution of humans' sophisticated social abilities," according to science journalist, Sandra Blakeslee (2006, p.1).

"Mirror neurons," in the words of Marco Iacoboni, a neuroscientist at the University of California at Los Angeles dedicated to their becoming better understood,

> are the only brain cells we know of that seem specialized to code the actions of other people and also our own actions. They are obviously essential brain cells for social interactions. Without them, we would likely be blind to the actions, intentions and emotions of other people.

By providing a kind of inner imitation of the actions of another, mirror neurons enable us to understand others as they lead us to 'simulate' the intentions and emotions associated with those actions, according to Iacoboni. They make it possible for us to empathize, arguably the most human and perhaps most important of all emotions. This makes sense since it is well known that children exhibit empathetic response ability very early in life.

Moreover, that the human brain is suffused with mirror neurons provides the perfect neuroscientific explanation for so-called *Theory of Mind*, the concept that humans are adept at inferring a wide range of mental states in each other, states that include not only intentions, but hopes, expectations, imaginings, desires and beliefs (Leslie, 2001).

Resonance, Attunement and Co-regulation

Activating those parts of the brain that subconsciously take note of both the overt behaviors and, as is now thought to be the case, even the intentions of others, mirror neurons in humans enable far more complex and subtle abilities than most mammals have. While primates are skilled at decoding some of the subtleties and nuances of voice, facial expression and eye gaze—skills without which their survival as a member of primate society would likely be imperiled—humans are especially adept. When decoding the subtle expressions of another, the mirror neuron system is thought to actually re-create another's internal state in such a way that a state of *resonance*—defined as a reciprocal change in physiologic, affective, and intentional states within two parties—occurs between them. The establishment of a resonant feedback loop in the human brain is, according to IPNB, facilitated by what is referred to a contingent communication, or attuned interpersonal interaction.

The more resonance in the system, the more efficient and effective the co-regulation—described earlier as the means by which harmonious interaction results in a palpable, felt sense of threat reduction and safety. This serves, in turn, to soothe and rebalance the autonomic nervous system. And a balanced ANS serves to integrate the brain in all dimensions: bottom-to-top, side-to-side, back-to-front, limbic to frontal (the primary social-emotional linkage) and so forth. The result of all this non-negotiable need for social interaction: a coherent brain and an integrated mind, one capable of revealing the promise of the adaptive, actualized self: reflective, regulated, and flexibly responsive.

Mirroring, Modeling, Attunement and the "Love Code"

Adding further support to just how profoundly social is the human brain, the discovery of the mirror neuron system supports Burton White's (Chapter 9) assertion, from half a century earlier, that mammalian learning depends on the presence of a model (what Pearce termed the *great model imperative*). This dedicated neural system also underscores the importance of love as central to the human experience. For, as is made clear by IPNB clinical studies as well as the findings at HeartMath Institute (see Chapter 12), when two heart-brain-minds establish a felt connection—when they enter into resonance with one another—the state of neural firing throughout the body of each individual becomes more coherent, with each matching that of the other.

Sue Carter (who happens to be the wife of Stephen Porges) is an authority on mammalian pair bonding and attachment and the role of oxytocin in forging that bond. Their respective areas of interest have converged in recent years and they have formulated an intriguing concept they term the *love code* which, according to Porges, involves a two-part dance. The order is crucial. Phase one is a core element in social engagement, one that involves negotiation of psychological proximity and distance in support of safety, whereas phase two is physical contact and intimacy. Porges: "To articulate this as a code [means] that if it is done in the proper order, healthy bonding and attachment would occur, and if the order were shifted [reversed] the outcome could be disastrous (Porges, 2018a, p. 20)." By means of explication, in his role as clinician he makes the observation that, paradoxically, it is not uncommon for couples who seek therapy to do so out of a lack of feeling safe in one another's presence—despite the fact that they are bonded. This observation seems obviously true once pointed out and has ramifications well beyond couples therapy, for it argues for the primacy of safety as a social engagement support in any setting, be it a therapy room or a classroom. Porges and Carter suggest that the love code acts as a "preamble to attachment."

Full-Circle: Intelligence, Mind and Nature's Mandates

Clearly the quality of interpersonal experience determines the degree to which the brain becomes integrated. This is a crucial point. Since the brain is a complex set of neural systems that tend to function not so much in isolated or disparate ways as they do together, it is the degree or quality of integration that is critical to the development of the mind. Simply stated, the more integrated is the developing brain, the more integrated is the emergent mind. And it is the quality of the bonding and attachment experience, including its preamble to attachment, that is the determining factor in both.

When certain basic interpersonal elements of communication are present in early childhood the likelihood for successful neural integration is high. Conversely in their absence we can expect to find all manner of problems, from learning disabilities, to mental health problems, to physical health challenges. In consideration of themes or premises central to this book, it seems we have come full-circle. The premise that, *intelligence is the capacity to respond to new situations, adapt to changing conditions, and learn from experience,* reflects perfectly the premise that, *the mind is an embodied and relational, self-organizing emergent process that regulates the flow of energy and information both within and between individuals.* Together they bring us back to the central organizing theme of this book, *nature's mandates*: nurture, feedback and play. This chapter has been devoted to the most recent and applicable findings on how nurture and feedback facilitate the development of the human mind. In concluding the chapter, we turn now to the third element of the *family triad*, play.

The Play Imperative and the Up-Shifted Brain

Mammalian evolution is nothing if not a marvel; an ironic marvel, one so obvious as to be lost sight of, forgotten about. Think about play. It has taken us centuries, if not millennia it seems, to truly appreciate just how ingenious a solution it is to the challenge of tapping into and releasing human intelligence. Consider that nature has yet to devise a better means by which to ensure that the high-brain, so dominant in humans, integrates, develops, grows whole. And if nature were to concoct a perfect recipe for play it would invariably Involve liberal amounts of novelty, feedback and challenge. This triad is inseparable from and undergirds just about any definition or description—of which there are many—of the role of play in human learning and intelligence. Here are just a few that we think reflect the power of play.

Diane Ackerman (2000), in her absorbing reflections on the genesis of human creativity, states that, "Play is an activity enjoyed for its own sake. It is our brain's favorite way of learning" (p. 11). She goes on to point out that the more an animal needs to learn in order to survive, the more it needs to play. While we may consider play as optional, she points out, it is so fundamental to evolution that without play humans and many other mammals would perish! We are reminded here of MacLean's assertion (covered in Chapter 2 and appearing in the epigraph) that, from the standpoint of human evolution no behavior development could have been more fundamental than the brain's potential for play!

Play and human potential authority, Joseph Chilton Pearce, consistently maintained that play is the major way by which the creative intelligences and capacities of the child develops. Play, he insisted, is "the very force of society and civilization," even going so far as to say, "a breakdown in ability to play will reflect in a breakdown of society" (1992, p. 164). And, in a plea to take seriously the absolute need for play to sustain curiosity, creativity and wellbeing across the lifespan, David Elkins, author of the best-selling and highly acclaimed, *The Hurried Child*, states at the conclusion of his more recent, *The Power of Play* (2007, p. 218), "It is only when we integrate play, love, and work that we, as children and adults, can live happy, healthy, and productive lives." Apparently, play is nature's way of dealing with stress for children as well as adults.

If the above sampling isn't convincing enough of the value of play, here is another by heart surgeon Ross Ungerleider, MD, that sums up the "seriousness" of play: "The opposite of play is not work; it is depression. And the consequence of play is creativity, empathy and joy" (Pearce-McCall, 2015, p.61).

Given ample opportunities to engage in various forms of structured and open play—"the work of childhood," as more than one wise person has put it!—children grow, heal as necessary, and thrive naturally.

Teachers can be confident that every moment spent in movement and play is an assurance that students (of any grade-level or age) are following Nature's Plan for holistic, healthy development. As principle models in the lives of our students we of course need to be cognizant of the need for play in our own lives.

To that end, consider the fact that many of us (to paraphrase Julie Cameron)[46] tell ourselves that if only we had more time, we'd have fun; yet most of us fill new free time with new work. Perhaps it would be helpful to ask ourselves how much time we spend each day or week enjoying unfettered fun!

Concluding Thoughts

Throughout this book we have emphasized the point that access to the genetically innate but latent neural fields enabling higher learning, rather strictly requires a felt sense of safety. This is likely not news to attuned teachers, who rather quickly learn that tone of voice, body language, gestures, touch, eye-contact, the timing and intensity of response, along with humor and a playful spirit are keys that unlock the heart and open the mind to learning. What might be new are the myriad other demonstrable benefits—for learning of course but also for enhanced health, therapeutic healing and personal growth across the lifespan—that accrue from these seemingly simple, everyday, pedestrian gestures.

Emphasized throughout this chapter is the fact that integration of the various branches of the human nervous system leads to coherence of mind, which in turn is contingent on the quality of human interaction. It is our hope that the abundance of quality

The same social engagement signaling mechanisms—described in such detail here—that enable learning, wellbeing, growth and creative potential are already present in many of the daily interactions with students. And while they might not seem to be that significant, trust the science, they are.

---

46 Author of over 30 books, Cameron writes eloquently about creativity and the role of playfulness. Check out her breakthrough 1992 book, *The Artist's Way: A Spiritual Path To Higher Creativity* for a real treat.

scientific evidence that underscores these conclusions be appreciated and relished by teachers who understand these things rather instinctively. The same social engagement signaling mechanisms—described in such detail here—that enable learning, wellbeing, growth and creative potential are already present in many of the daily interactions with students. And while they might not seem to be that significant, trust the science, they are. In the oft-quoted words attributed to the late, Dr. Leo Buscaglia, award-winning University of California special education professor and author (known affectionately as "Dr. Love" by his students, as his was the first ever course offered at a major university with the title, Love 101), "Too often we underestimate the power of a touch, a smile, a kind word, a listening ear, an honest compliment, or the smallest act of caring, all of which have the potential to turn a life around."

A final thought. The preceding crucial, life-enhancing forms of social engagement should not be construed as being solely teacher to student, for it goes both ways. Students achieve a sense of calming safety and reassurance through the empathic relationship with teacher, but teachers likewise benefit from appreciative feedback provided by students. Moreover, student to student, or peer, relationships benefit in the same fashion, knowledge about which can be made clear to students whenever possible. Many teachers, in fact, make it a point to teach explicit social-emotional knowledge and skills that include pearls such as this.

With the intention of providing the latest research on the enhancement of the brain-mind, we turn now to one of the more timely, exciting, and important undertakings in the scientific world: the exploration and explication of how the multifaceted human nervous system can benefit from mindfulness meditation practice.

Chapter 14

Minding the Mind: The Benefits of Paying Attention to Attention

"Because behavioral habits (good or bad) can strongly influence the brain's 'wiring-up,' especially in developing brains, meditation offers great potential for positively impacting the neural circuitry of attention and emotion regulation. The earlier one starts, the thinking goes, the more beneficial meditation may be."

– Brenda Patoine

"When the mind is focused, whether through meditation or other repetitive mental activities, the body responds with a dramatic decrease in heart rate, breathing rate, blood pressure (if elevated to begin with) and metabolic rate—the exact opposite of the fight-or-flight response."

– Herbert Benson, MD

"Learning to pay attention to how one pays attention is synonymous with learning to learn."

– Les Fehmi, PhD

Introduction

"We are fortunate to live in a time when the investigation of the mind through meditative science comes face-to-face with the investigation of the brain through material science. The conjunction of these different but complementary approaches provides us with an incredible opportunity" (Yates, 2017). We could not agree more with this assertion by John Yates PhD, neuroscientist and, for over forty years, meditation teacher. In his *Scientific American* article, Yates goes on to say,

> The knowledge of the mind that meditation provides can be of enormous value in guiding the future research of neuroscientists. On the other hand, this continued unfolding

of our knowledge of the physical brain can allow us to understand more clearly the most amazing and powerful experiences of adept meditators, including awakening. This cognitive transformation, characterized by wisdom, compassion, and freedom from most forms of suffering, might ultimately become available to millions, completely transforming human society and helping us solve the enormous threats our species and our planet now face.

Based upon our own personal experiences in and understanding of the practice of meditation, we find ourselves in agreement with Yates' contentions and feel especially aligned with his timely and hopeful vision. While it is beyond the scope of this book to enter into an exploration of his compelling term "awakening," described as a transformation of consciousness and freedom from suffering, there remains a great deal else to understand and appreciate about other known benefits. These include improvements in learning and memory, stress amelioration, and enhanced wellbeing, all of which are demonstrable results of developing a consistent mind-body practice.

Of the various claims about the purported benefits following from a regular meditation practice, the one perhaps most pertinent to educators may well be how meditation has been shown to improve the ability to attend. In much the same way that, in the preceding chapter, we restricted ourselves to those factors shown to give rise to a healthy, fully functioning mind, in this chapter we devote much of it to the key factor in learning: the viability of the brain's attentional networks. That said, and because meditation has become such a popular and to some extent controversial topic, we want to put our emphasis on attention into the broader context of meditation practice: its historical significance, recent scientific interest, purported claims, and relevance to educational practice. We begin with the introduction of meditation to the West.

Back to the Future of Mindfulness Meditation Practice

Nearly a century ago, the intrepid French explorer, author, and Buddhist scholar, Alexandra David-Neel, distinguished herself by becoming the first European woman to cross the Himalayas and reach

Lhasa, Tibet, known then as the Forbidden City, as it was strictly off-limits to foreigners. Described as steely-willed, she was determined to access the city in pursuit of furthering her knowledge of Tibetan Buddhism and, in particular, deepening her understanding of its meditative practices, about which there was little known in the West. Thus, she set out in 1924 with a small entourage, apparently going over 19,000-foot mountain passes in mid-winter without benefit of supplementary oxygen and wearing crude leather boots, whereupon she successfully entered the city and commenced her studies.

During the course of her life, which spanned just over 100 years, David-Neel wrote nearly three dozen books on eastern religions and is still held in high regard for her early writings on Tibetan Buddhism, among the first to reach the West. In her 1932 book, *Magic and Mystery in Tibet*, she describes a scene in which young monks engage in a meditation practice known as *tum-mo*, which translates literally as "inner fire." It's a fascinating portrayal and easy to understand how her readership became enthralled. Entered into during a deep state of relaxation and consisting of breathing and visualization techniques, practitioners are enabled to increase internal body temperature to the point where it becomes possible to comfortably endure extremely cold conditions. She shares her observations of what takes place: "The neophytes sit on the ground, cross-legged and naked. Sheets are dipped in icy water, each man wraps himself in one of them and must dry it on his body." The process is repeated until daybreak, then "he who has dried the largest number of sheets is declared the winner of the competition" (p. 227).

Clearly, the rather astonishing feat of drying icy sheets in winter, and at high elevation no less, requires the ability to significantly raise one's body temperature. Sure enough, when replicated and measured under laboratory conditions some four decades later, the average recorded temperature increase for those individuals versed in the technique was an astonishing 8.3 degrees centigrade, or about 15 degrees Fahrenheit (Benson, 1982)! This finding could only mean one thing: a well-practiced mind could alter the function of the autonomic nervous system, something that was not thought possible at the time. In effect, a new realization was about to take hold, albeit gradually, one that eventually led to a complete reconsideration of both the autonomic nervous system and—much more significantly—the implication that the immaterial mind could alter physical operations of the body as well as change the physical structure of the brain.

Through a series of serendipitous events, recounted in his best-selling 1975 book, *The Relaxation Response*, Herbert Benson, MD, would come to lead a team of researchers from Harvard Medical School in rigorously studying the amazing mind-body capabilities of Tibetan monks.

Prior to undertaking those studies, the team had carried out extensive research on practitioners of Transcendental Meditation, or *TM* as it is often called, and in the process worked out the standards by which Western scientific medicine could demonstrate the efficacy of meditation in altering important autonomic nervous system functions. These scientific methods and standards would come to form the basis of what is today referred to as contemplative science. What initially impressed the investigators was the practitioners' ability to enter into a state of deep relaxation, resulting in a marked reduction in blood pressure—and, most significantly, one that extended well beyond the practice session. Over time the Harvard team was able to document significant improvements in maladies ranging from hypertension, headaches, and cardiac arrhythmia, to premenstrual syndrome, anxiety, and mild to moderate depression (Benson, 2000).

Interested in exploring the further reaches of what might be possible through extensive, intensive mental training and armed with the latest technology to measure physiologic states, the team would travel to Dharmsala, India, home of the exiled Tibetan community.

There they would spend much of the 1980's carrying out studies on monks who had for years been practicing tum-mo meditation, the same practices observed and recorded by an astonished Alexandra David-Neel decades before.

Early Scientific Investigations

Having come to the attention of the scientific community, these and other future discoveries eventually led to even more exacting methods of measuring the effects of meditation, including sophisticated brain wave and heart-rate variability analyses (see Chapters 10 and 12, respectively), as well as immunological, metabolic, hormonal and neurochemical assays. Initially viewed by much of the scientific community as, at best, a questionable undertaking, over the last three decades the Harvard team has succeeded in establishing the field of meditative science as a highly respectable undertaking; and a hugely popular one among the general public in the last decade. Reflecting this attitudinal change in what had been a highly skeptical scientific community, the number of annual professional publications in this field has risen dramatically, from the very first one published in the early 1970s to several hundred each year currently(as a quick glance at the American Meditation Research Association website[47] will attest). Benson underscores the views of most professional colleagues in his reflections on the beginnings of the work: "Three decades ago it was considered scientific heresy for a Harvard physician and researcher to hypothesize that stress contributed to health problems and to publish studies showing that mental focusing techniques were good for the body" (2000, p. x).

The Unexpected Success of the Relaxation Response

Written for, and having assumed that the book would likely have appeal only to, those in the medical profession (or at least those with a scientific background), Benson was evidently surprised by the popular reception of *The Relaxation Response* (1975). Within weeks of its appearance it shot to the top of the *New York Times* bestseller list, with some 40 subsequent printings, translated into more than a dozen languages, and over 4 million copies sold to date!

That *The Relaxation Response* was such a huge success can likely be accounted for by timing, for its publication coincided with the growing interest in what would come to be known as the "self-help" movement. And rightfully so, as the nineteen-seventies saw a notable rise in awareness and growing concern about the limits and possible negative consequences inherent in Western approaches to medicine. Powerful, effective and often necessary as they are, surgery, pharmaceuticals, and

---

47 Founded in 2013, AMRA serves as an aggregator of research devoted to meditation; the mission: "to support empirical and conceptual efforts to: (1) establish an evidence base for the process, practice, and construct of mindfulness; (2) promote best evidence-based standards for the use of mindfulness research and its applications; and (3) facilitate discovery and professional development through grant giving." https://goamra.org/

various forms of radiation and chemotherapies have little if anything to offer by way of illness prevention and health maintenance. It makes sense that individuals would want to play a more active role in maintaining, even enhancing, health while preventing and when necessary recovering from illness; thus, the growing popularity of self-help literature.

Defined as, "an inducible, physiologic state of quietude" (Benson, p. xvii), the evidence from studies on the practice of the Relaxation Response demonstrated that individuals suffering from stress-based illnesses—including hypertension, some forms of diabetes, chronic headaches, gastrointestinal disorders and even some forms of cancers (Benson, 1985, 2000)—were often able to stop the progression of the illness and even reverse it, achieving a return to health. Now, with over three decades of outcome studies on the effectiveness of this simple practice, the positive outcomes no longer seem quite so surprising.

Speaking Personally

I, Tim, can speak directly to how, as a beginning classroom teacher, this book positively affected me in ways both personal and professional. Still struggling through my second year of public-school teaching, I felt constantly overwhelmed by the demands and desperate to find a way to better manage the accumulation of stress I was carrying. While I can no longer recall how I came across the book, I do know that I was very impressed by the scientific evidence undergirding the claims of efficacy. I began immediately to engage in the simple procedure and, with daily practice over a period of weeks, came to notice my stress level was markedly reduced, my mental state more balanced, and the roller-coaster ride of emotions much more even. What a gift!

Impressed with the results, I decided to teach the practice to my students (which, by the way, I never labeled as "meditation," calling it instead by its less-charged name, "Relaxation Response"). Once made familiar with the protocol, most students seemed to genuinely appreciate the few minutes of class period set aside each day for the practice. Over the years I have had the good fortune of occasionally having contact with former students who, almost without fail, mention how much they appreciate my having introduced them to the practice at such a formative time of life. It is especially gratifying to know that, decades later, mind-body practices, such as the Relaxation Response, have been introduced by classroom teachers to students of all ages. While nowhere near as well known or popular as what has come to be known as mindfulness meditation, the Relaxation Response helped pave the way for the acceptance of mindfulness practices.

A Few Words of Caution: Common Misconceptions Abound

Having emphasized the positive outcomes of practices such as the Relaxation Response (or any other form of what is essentially a mindful form of meditation), it is important to keep in mind a few caveats in order to not create unwarranted expectations or false hopes. There are at least three common misconceptions that need to be addressed in order to more accurately convey what mindfulness meditation can offer.[48] We'll highlight the first one here and come back to the other two when we take up the discussion of meditation, per se. The first oversimplification is that *doing these practices will help one to feel better, calmer, and improve health*. If this seems to contradict popular claims it actually doesn't. Easily overlooked, because the results can be so positive, is the amount of time and practice required to realize them. These potentially regenerative practices are decidedly not a quick fix. And, like any other well-learned behavior, it takes time and effort. In fact it isn't uncommon for those starting out to be aware that sitting quietly can apparently make the symptoms of chronic pain, for example, or difficult emotions, seem more intense, almost as if they have worsened—and who in their "right mind" would invite that? However, it isn't necessarily the case that things have actually gotten worse and more likely that because the afflictions were

> Easily overlooked, because the results can be so positive, is the amount of time and practice required to realize them. These potentially regenerative practices are decidedly not a quick fix.

---

48 Credit for the "three most prevalent inaccuracies" goes to Marta Brzosko in a very thorough online article entitled, How to Experience Your First Insight in Mindfulness Meditation: A complete guide and 8-week plan to an effective mindfulness meditation practice. https://betterhumans.coach.me/how-to-experience-your-first-insight-in-mindfulness-meditation-b1b294096881

present all along, they are finally being attended to and experienced more fully. So, temporarily at least, they may cause one to feel worse.

The Relaxation Response: Setting the Stage

Herbert Benson (2000) describes the Relaxation Response as an innate capacity of the body to enter into a special state via mental focus, while simultaneously counteracting the harmful effects and uncomfortable feelings of stress. Succinctly articulated as "an inducible, physiologic state of quietude," (p. xvii), Benson goes on to point out the specific effects of what amounts to mindful quietude:

> When the mind is focused, whether through meditation or other repetitive mental activities, the body responds with a dramatic decrease in heart rate, breathing rate, blood pressure (if elevated to begin with) and metabolic rate—the exact opposite effects of the fight-or-flight response. (2000, p. xvii-xviii)

Note that there are two key elements involved in eliciting the response: mental focus and what he refers to as "repetitive mental activities," both of which play an essential role in the procedure, as described below.

Nearly forty years of refining the technique has led to the following recommendations. Typically, scientific pre- and post-measures employ a 30 to 60 day period of time to determine what, if any, changes have taken place. While many individuals find benefit right away, when starting out it is important to be prepared to devote the recommended 10 to 20 minutes, once or twice daily, for a period of at least 30 days, keeping in mind that the beneficial results may not become apparent during the first week or two. It is worth noting that anything less than 10 minutes has not been shown to produce optimal results; nor has extending the time to more than 20 minutes been shown to be necessary in order to achieve beneficial outcomes.

Practicing the Relaxation Response: The Four P's

Although Benson doesn't use our "Four P's" as a guide, its use as a mnemonic can serve as a reminder of just how simple is the practice—simple, yes, but not always easy! What follows is a description of the four main ingredients that comprise the successful practice of mindfully quieting the nervous system and body using the Four P's.

Place. The first *P, place*, emphasizes the importance of sitting in a quiet, interruption-free space for the daily 10 to 20 minute practice sessions. While not absolutely necessary, it is probably best done at the same time and place each day, perhaps in the early morning and/or the late evening just before retiring for the night.

Posture. No special way of sitting is required, although sitting as opposed to lying down is highly recommended. This is because, in our era of chronic sleep deprivation, lying down might very well induce a sleep state. Not that that wouldn't be a good thing; napping, as we have discussed, is especially great. However, what is required for the crucial readjustments to the nervous system that mindful calm can enact over time is a quiet, peaceful, alertness. So, no special posture necessary—just sitting upright in as relaxed a manner as possible.

Point of Focus. Over the course of the first decade of refining and teaching the Relaxation Response, the Harvard team discovered that a certain subset of practitioners achieved markedly better outcomes in all areas being measured. Upon examination, it turned out to be those who included in the practice sessions prayer, or something akin to prayer, perhaps a kind of personal mantra, or positive affirmation. Initially this came as a surprise to the scientists, as they had been particularly keen on making this a purely secular practice, without any religious undertones whatsoever—this, in order to make the practice appealing and accessible to anyone and everyone regardless of religious belief or affiliation.

The notable distinctions in results between those who included prayer, mantras, or some other form of positive self-suggestion and those who did not eventually led researchers to include what came to be called "the faith factor." Benson reports (1996) that after twenty-five years of refining the practice two essential steps emerged as key to eliciting the innate regenerative capacity of our physiology, the first of which is the repetition of a word, sound, phrase, or concise prayer.

The key is to find the word or phrase tied most closely to one's deepest values or most meaningful beliefs. For example, one might repeat any of the words, Peace, Shalom, Om, or Namaste; repeat the Christian phrase, "The Lord is my shepherd," or "Our Father who art in Heaven;" repeat the Muslim, "Isha'allah;" or the Jewish "Sh'ma Yisreal." It might also be something secular such as, "be still," "just let go," or even, "relax." Thus, the faith factor would emerge as crucial to the success of the practice and is encouraged by those who teach the procedure. "In this way," reports Benson, "we observed that all types of people were able to incorporate their own belief system or values into evoking the Relaxation Response" (2000, p. xx).

One other small but important point before moving on to the fourth particularly essential step in eliciting the Relaxation Response. The word, phrase, sound, etc. should be timed to each out-breath, as this is linked to the activation of the parasympathetic nervous system (the in-breath activates the sympathetic branch of the autonomic nervous system), which has a number of positive implications associated with calming and balancing the nervous system (see Chapter 8 for a complete discussion).

Passive. The fourth P, and an especially essential step in successfully enacting the quieting response, is often found to be the most challenging and not infrequently the cause of individuals new to the practice giving it up entirely (likely long before any benefits are realized): maintaining a passive attitude towards mental chatter and mind wandering. It is important to recognize that the mind is rarely if ever quiet; it constantly churns out a steady stream of thoughts, over which we seem to have little if any control. In many respects we are not to blame for this, although it can be alarming to realize just how relentlessly and restlessly active it can be when we sit still and attempt to quiet it.

Thus, the admonition to maintain as much as possible a passive attitude towards the seemingly uncontrollable machinations of the mind; not worrying about how well one is performing the practice; setting aside any judgements or self-criticism; and simply returning to the point of focus with each out breath. In fact the best way to do this, as the Harvard team was to discover, is exceedingly helpful—when the mind has wandered, as it most certainly will time and time again, simply say, "Oh, well," then return to the out breath and point of focus. Over and over again. Simple? Yes. Easy? Maybe.

From Relaxation Response to Advanced Meditation Practice

Having worked out a simple yet demonstrably successful procedure, one that could be easily taught to and practiced by individuals seeking health-related help for a variety of ailments, the Harvard team began to consider what other, more advanced, forms of meditation might contribute to practitioners wishing to incorporate them. It was at this juncture, during the nineteen-eighties, that the Harvard team made those repeated trips to northern India where they observed, measured, and recorded the same astonishing feats first reported by Alexandra David-Neel some 60 years prior.

Benson reports that, "our team witnessed incredible mind/body feats. Monks, in little clothing, remained alive and well, practicing an advanced form of meditation in temperatures of zero degrees Fahrenheit, at altitudes over fifteen thousand feet in the Himalayan mountains" (2000, p. xxxix). They also watched the same mind-boggling feat David-Neel had earlier witnessed: monks capable of raising their body temperature high enough to dry within minutes wet sheets draped over their bodies in near-freezing temperatures.

East Meets West: An Early Beginning and Auspicious Encounter

The Harvard team was not the only group of scientists interested in the purported benefits of meditation, although they were certainly among the first. As such, they had to weather a fair amount of derision from colleagues who looked askance at anything—like meditation—seemingly "New Age." Fortunately, for the tens of thousands of patients as well as those seeking the means by which to initiate effective self-care, the East-meets-West collaboration between pioneering, persistent scientists and the willing and ever-patient Tibetan monks, perhaps nothing could have been more timely and important to improved health, sustained well-being and even spiritual development.

From the first scientific study published in 1971 (cited earlier) to the hundreds now carried out annually, interest in mindfulness meditation has grown nearly exponentially. Interestingly, along with growing popularity something of a backlash has recently developed, undoubtedly related to some misrepresentations and unfounded, at times exaggerated and over-zealous, claims. Coupled with the carnival-like commodification and monetization of mindfulness meditation lately, it seems prudent to undertake an exploration of both well-established (i.e., the accumulated knowledge about the autonomic and central nervous systems) and contemporary (i.e., meditative or contemplative science) findings, as a means by which to best understand the purported benefits of what has come to be known as mindfulness meditation or mindfulness practice. Fortunately, there are a number of resources available that serve to provide accurate, reliable information. One such excellent resource, for example, is the Mind and Life Institute.[49]

Founded in 1987 by Tenzin Gyatso, the 14th Dalai Lama, spiritual leader of the Tibetan people, along with lawyer and entrepreneur, Adam Engle and Francisco Varela, a world-renowned neuroscientist, the Institute is dedicated to bridging the divide between the world-views offered by venerable contemplative practices and wisdom traditions, and those of Western scientific methodologies. It has played a leading role in sponsoring contemplative science dialogues, research and publications over the past three decades.

Another reliable source of information is the American Mindfulness Research Association (AMRA),[50] founded in 2013 as a clearinghouse for research.

Its stated mission, in part, is "to support empirical and conceptual efforts to: 1) establish an evidence base for the process, practice, and construct of mindfulness; 2) promote best evidence-based standards for the use of mindfulness research and its applications." Although access is based upon an annual subscription, the fee isn't exorbitant and could be well worth it in terms of the voluminous amount of research in their archives.

---

49 https://www.mindandlife.org

50 https://goamra.org.

Minding the Mind: Mindfulness Meditation Comes of Age

As we move from the discussion of the Relaxation Response to the more popular, more familiar mindfulness meditation it is worth noting just how similar they are. Indeed, aside from its well-known origins in Buddhism,[51] as a secular practice mindfulness meditation shares a great deal in common with not only the wholly secular Relaxation Response but also with Transcendental Meditation and other forms of meditation practice. For example, contemplative Christianity, a two-millennia old tradition, continues to play an important role (as Benson and colleagues make clear) in harmonizing the mind and enhancing the spirit of dedicated practitioners.

Over the past two decades, *Mindfulness-Based Stress Reduction*, or MBSR, has emerged as the most popular from of mind-body practice. It was developed in the 1970s by Jon Kabat-Zinn, PhD while he was a professor of medicine at the University of Massachusetts Medical Center. While MBSR and Relaxation Response are far more similar than different, "the scientific philosophies and meditative traditions upon which each is founded are somewhat different, differences that reflect in the exercises taught to patients and interested others."[52]

Highlighting the difference in emphases, the authors suggest, for instance, that whereas the Relaxation Response focuses on eliciting directly a physiologic state of deep rest (the opposite of the "fight or flight" stress response), MBSR emphasizes mindful, non-judgmental self-observation as the means, albeit indirectly, by which to elicit innate healing capacities. Both programs have been shown to successfully decrease stress and increase mindfulness in participants, although some nuanced differences in brain function became clear in that study, which we leave to the interested reader to pursue.

---

51 Well beyond the scope of this book, it is important to note that Buddhism, while clearly one of the world's great religions, is considered by many adherents as, first and foremost, a venerable twenty-five centuries old science of mind.

52 As reported on Eurek Alert: The Global Source for Science News. https://www. eurekalert.org/pub_releases/2018-06/ mgh-mma061318.php. We leave it to the interested reader to learn about the specific differences in brain function.

The discussion offered below pertains to the impact of practicing mindfulness or meditation upon learning and development, an issue pertinent to the primary purpose of this book. Since the notion of mindfulness can suggest many things and be interpreted in many ways, it seems best to begin with an operational definition of mindfulness. Following that, we review and build on the basics of the stress response (covered in Chapter 8). This sets the stage for an examination of the positive physiological effects that have been shown to occur as a result of regular meditation practice.

To conclude the discussion, we briefly highlight the varieties of mindfulness meditation along with their intended purpose, with special emphasis on the promise it can hold for classroom learning, both individually and collectively.

Toward a Definition and Description of Mindfulness Meditation

Currently there exists no universally accepted definition of mindfulness, as a result of which some investigators (Bishop et al, 2004) have called for one, arguing that it will bring needed precision to the field, in order that "testable theoretical predictions for the purpose of validation and refinement" (p. 231) be made possible. In the meantime, what is perhaps the most widely accepted, popular definition of mindfulness is suggested by Kabat-Zinn (2012, 2013), who was introduced two pages ago: "Mindfulness is the awareness that emerges through paying attention, on purpose, in the present moment, and non-judgmentally to the unfolding of experience moment by moment" (2011, p. 291).

As for the term meditation, we think Kabat-Zinn's broadly conceptualized definition, offered in his classic 1988 book (with the great title), *Full Catastrophe Living: Using the Wisdom of Your Body and Mind to Face Stress, Pain and Illness*, is also well formulated. Meditation, he states, is "...the process of observing body and mind intentionally, of letting your experiences unfold from moment to moment and accepting them as they are" (2013, p. 10).

Succinctly stated, mindfulness is a practice cultivated through periods of meditation during which a form of mind-body training takes place through the process of focusing attention on thoughts, feelings, or sensations as they arise within the broad field of awareness. In other words, rather than leaving these phenomena in the background of our awareness, we use attention to observe them, but without becoming overly identified with or overly reactive to them. Instead, we practice merely observing then letting them go.

The result is a more disciplined mind, one that can be freer of negative thoughts and emotions. The essence of the entire endeavor comes down to how one pays attention—a seeming simple and natural act which, as we shall see, actually has myriad facets and important implications for body, brain and mind well-being. Attention, as we shall see, is key.

Toward Conceptual Clarity: Essential Elements of Mindfulness

As a means by which greater rigor might be brought to its study, a group of mindfulness investigators, led by University of Toronto psychologist, Scott R. Bishop (2004), suggest a way to satisfy the scientific requirement for definitional and procedural clarity. They begin this task by proposing that mindfulness meditation consists of two components. The first component involves the self-regulation of attention so that it is maintained on immediate experience, thereby allowing for increased recognition of mental events in the present moment. The second component involves adopting a particular orientation toward one's experiences in the present moment, an orientation that is characterized by curiosity, openness, and acceptance. (Bishop et al, 2004, p. 232)

Sounding similar to the definition provided by Kabat-Zinn, their proposal does provide somewhat greater precision, as was the intent of the authors. Other researchers, similarly intent on achieving agreement on what is meant by the term mindfulness, have succeeded in pushing the field towards even greater conceptual clarity. Using Kabat-Zinn's definition as a starting point, for example, Shapiro et al (2005), have further developed those core components, from which they derive a simple yet intriguing conceptual model. Importantly, the model they propose also addresses, at least in part, the second query posed by contemplative science, "How do mindfulness-based interventions actually work?" Referring to the core components as axioms—defined as "fundamental building blocks out of which other things emerge" (Shapiro et al, 2005 p. 3)—the authors' model proposes three essential elements, as follows:

1. "Paying attention" or, simply, attention,

2. "On purpose" or intention,

3. "In a particular way" or attitude.

What follows in the article is a simple triangular model of the axioms, meant to illustrate their interactive nature. "Intention, attention, and attitude are not separate processes or stages," they write, "they are interwoven aspects of a single cyclic process and occur simultaneously. Mindfulness is this moment-to-moment process" (p. 4).

We appreciate this approach to the construct of mindfulness, as it satisfies what we think of as whole-brain learning, or the way in which the brain processes information and learns: the *what, why and how* of experience. That is, *what* constitutes the actual practice (paying *attention* to experience), *why* is one practicing (to facilitate *intention*), and *how* does one actually proceed (by cultivating a particular *attitude*—that is, without judgement)?

Using their formulation, let's look at the three building blocks in the following order: *intention, attitude, and attention*. We leave attention for last because it plays a central role in themes addressed throughout this book, and requires the most discussion. Let us recall MacKinnon's admonition earlier, that "Understanding provides the prologue to our actions … The true value of mindfulness practice is realized when we understand the mechanism as well as the method." Since attention is the mechanism of both mindfulness and learning, better understanding can lead to more informed and effective classroom practice.

Elements Two and Three: Appropriate Intent and Correct Attitude

Shapiro and his co-authors suggest that intention be thought of as akin to a personal vision; it is the motivating reason one takes up mindfulness practice in the first place—although it can and perhaps will be one that evolves over time. Referencing an intriguing earlier study (Shapiro, 1992), they describe the dynamic, shifting nature of intention for many long-term meditators, along a continuum from achieving greater physiologic self-regulation, to self-exploration, and finally to self-liberation. Intriguingly, and perhaps not surprisingly, the earlier study determined that outcomes were clearly related to intentions: "Those whose goal was self-regulation and stress management attained self-regulation, those whose goal was self-exploration attained self-exploration, and those whose goal was self-liberation moved toward self-liberation and compassionate service" (Shapiro, 1992, p. 4). Such is the evident power of intention.

As one of the three legs of the stable stool of mindfulness practice, *the quality of attitude* also bears significantly on the state of mind that develops from the practice. This component is perhaps the most subtle of the three in that without such consciously invited qualities of mind and heart as acceptance, curiosity, compassion, non-striving and equanimity, practice can devolve into an unwitting cultivation of more hard-edged and "heartless" states of self-judgement and self-condemnation. Given our level of knowledge about the heart-field and the effects of both positive and negative emotions on the operations of the brain-mind (covered in Chapter 12), this view of attitudinal orientation is worth a closer examination.

Mindfulness and Compassion: A Multiplier-Effect

Highly regarded Buddhist scholar, teacher, and author Jack Kornfield (1993, 2009) reminds us that tools for training the heart have been around for millennia, forming part of our human heritage every bit as much as the hard-wiring of the fight-flight-freeze response. And while those "tools" are not automatic by any stretch—and may well require the presence of a model who has learned and embodied the results— they nevertheless continue to exist as part of that heritage for one very good reason: they promote both individual and collective survival and thrival. What's more, as Kornfield points out, those tools have been well researched, and their benefits replicated in thousands of scientific studies over the course of three decades (and 1500 years of empirical research by Buddhist practitioners) describing the beneficial outcomes of mindfulness and compassion when practiced together. Kornfield cites the work of Richard Davidson, professor of psychology at the University of Wisconsin–Madison and founder of the world-class research institute there, Center for Healthy Minds, reporting the discovery by Davidson and his associates that when mindfulness and compassion are practiced together, the measurable changes to the nervous system occur on the order of ten times faster than they do with mindfulness practice alone.

> When mindfulness and compassion are practiced together, the measurable changes to the nervous system occur on the order of ten times faster than they do with mindfulness practice alone.

Thus, the practice of mindfulness is viewed as a mind-body exercise entailing self-observation, essential elements of which are the willingness to acknowledge and accept as worthy of our attention all thoughts, feelings and sensations as they arise within the mind. This self-observant process is optimally carried out free of over-identification with the content of what arises. In the words of the authors, "Through intentionally bringing the attitudes of patience, compassion and non-striving to the attentional practice, one develops the capacity not to continually strive for pleasant experiences, or to push aversive experiences away" (p. 5). This is no small thing. Central to regular mindfulness practice is the nonjudgmental attention one can bring to the machinations and habits of the grasping and the avoidant mind and its predictable and recurring bouts

Back to the Primary Element: Attention

Distilled to its most essential feature, meditation trains the faculty of attention by refining it. Since any form of explicit learning[53] requires the ability to pay attention, it seems obvious that incorporating the means by which attentional capacity in students can be cultivated and refined will have a positive effect on learning outcomes. Therefore, by making available opportunities to practice focused attention a priority and routine element in education, we give to students a key to successful learning and the means by which they can facilitate and enhance their innate intelligence.

---

53 As a reminder, there are two fundamental forms of learning: implicit and explicit. The former, sometimes said to comprise over 90% of what we learn over the course of a lifetime, is largely unconsciously acquired, while the latter must be consciously attended to, examples of which are early childhood language acquisition and learning another language in adulthood.`

The science of attention is extremely robust and quite fascinating. Taking the time to survey it can prove both highly informative and serve as a means by which to better understand and incorporate those findings into daily classroom practice.

Using Attention for a Change of Mind

Jeffery Schwartz, MD, research psychiatrist at the School of Medicine, University of California at Los Angeles, is credited with making some of the initial discoveries about neuroplasticity and the specific mechanisms by which it operates. His celebrated success in apparently helping individuals suffering from Obsessive-Compulsive Disorder, or OCD, to successfully alter their own neural networks led him to the conclusion that, "Sustained focused attention [attention density] is the key to stabilizing and strengthening brain circuits" (2011. p. 67). That discovery also served to underscore the scientifically supported mechanism, discovered some 70 years earlier, by which learning is encoded into the neuronal structure of the brain. As Schwartz writes, "Focused attention holds together and stabilizes brain circuits so that they can wire together by Hebb's law" (p. 66). Recall that Hebb's law (see Chapter 4) states, in rather pithy fashion, "Neurons that fire together, wire together," a latter-day corollary for which is, "Neurons that fire apart, wire apart."

While making it clear that, "Experience coupled with attention leads to physical changes in the structure and future functioning of the nervous system" (2002, p. 339), Schwartz emphasizes the state of attention brought to experience as being the critical ingredient in systematic alteration of neural circuits. Schwartz: "Attention is the key to brain plasticity....the attentional state of the brain produces physical change in its structure and function" (p.18). In other words, it is the quality of attention brought to experience that initiates the change process. Indeed, "The way an individual willfully focuses attention has systematic effects on brain function, amplifying activity in particular brain circuits" (p. 334). Summing up an enormous amount of information on brain plasticity and learning, Schwartz ends his book by stating very simply, "Attention must be paid" (p. 323).

While Schwartz was busy working out the role of attention training in hopes of assisting individuals suffering from OCD (and coincidentally linking attention to brain plasticity) other lines of research by contemplative scientists were well underway in pursuit of a clearer understanding of how mindfulness meditation practice appeared to alter brain circuits as well. A parallel line of investigation involved an attempt to clarify the mechanism by which both depression and anxiety seemed to respond so well to mindfulness training. The story of what was uncovered perfectly illustrates the point made by Schwartz that, "The way an individual willfully focuses attention has systematic effects on brain function, amplifying activity in particular brain circuits." Let's pursue that story line, one that takes us to the heart of how mindfulness practice can effectively change the brain—and the promise it holds for introducing it to children at an early age.

Default Mode and Task Positive Networks and Mindfulness Practice

In an earlier discussion on the importance to the nervous system of balanced time spent between focused concentration and defocused mental refreshment (see Chapter 10), part of that discussion centered on the role of the Task Positive Network (TPN) and Default Mode Network (DMN). To recap, the TPN was described as being active during periods of attention consciously directed upon a particular feature within awareness, be it a task, an object, a person, and so forth—the attentional mode that typically involves a narrowed focus. In contrast, the DMN (coincidently operating at all times in the background and thus, "by default") takes over when focused attention is no longer required, resulting in defocused and more diffuse awareness.

Importantly, when one mode is operating the other is automatically deactivated since they work in opposition to one another. In other words, they function in a reciprocal yet mutually exclusive manner, not unlike the sympathetic and parasympathetic branches of the autonomic nervous system. Both modes of attending are important of course as, in the normal course of events, we move between periods of outer-directed goal seeking and inwardly directed self-reflection, a balanced approach to learning and performance which also ensures nervous system viability and overall health.

That problems can develop when too much time is spent in one mode and too little in the other comes as no surprise (a main theme in Chapter 10). In Task Positive network overload, for example, we risk overburdening the sympathetic nervous system and inviting mental exhaustion at the least; whereas, in default mode we risk being not only spacey and overly dreamy but possibly becoming directionless and under-productive—or worse. New research in fact points to a direct relationship between excessive DMN activity and a much greater likelihood of experiencing depression and/or anxiety.

Providing a more nuanced understanding of the two attentional modes, current research characterizes the DMN as trending towards awareness of the past and future, but largely inactive in the here-and-now present. In a very nice summary article on the latest research, Matthew MacKinnon points out that "a well-balanced DMN helps us plan tasks, review past actions to improve future behavior, and remember pertinent life details" (MacKinnon, 2014). While the DMN can be used appropriately to plan, organize, and review, he goes on to say that "we must always be wary of its runaway force" for, if left unchecked, the network can turn overly inward-directed and self-referential—in effect, becoming a ruminative network. Moreover, according to MacKinnon, the DMN is highly correlated with negative mood states and certain mental illnesses such as depression and anxiety—a "runaway force," indeed, for individuals suffering from the disorders.

The TPN, on the other hand, as the task-action network, engages whenever we attend in the here and now. As such, it is the direct line to being mindful and grounded in the present moment. In this state, worry and sadness tend not to exist, depression and anxiety are not present. Because the DMN and TPN are mutually exclusive, *intentionally activating the TPN will deactivate the DMN*, and herein lies the crux of what happens during periods of mindfulness practice: re-minding ourselves to simply pay attention to thoughts, feelings, sensations, we *intentionally activate* the TPN. As MacKinnon puts it:

The next time you feel helplessly lost in worry or self-recrimination remind yourself of the power of the TPN. Go for a walk, practice yoga, sense your breath, or engage fully in a conversation with a friend. You need not overpower your DMN to escape negative thoughts. You need only to intentionally engage your TPN and allow your natural physiology to disengage your DMN.

These are excellent suggestions, and we wish to emphasize that this is precisely what occurs during mindfulness meditation practice. By following the breath while merely observing thoughts, emotions and sensations as they arise—and likely carry us away until we use our awareness to non-judgmentally witness, then return to the breath—we engage the TPN time after time, strengthening those neural circuits while simultaneously short-circuiting the DM network and its tendency towards rumination, sadness and worry.

Schwartz' work with OCD individuals demonstrated that, with practice over time, they were able to alter their own neural circuits, resulting in reduced obsessive-compulsive behavior. In the same way, mindfulness practice, by altering the Default Mode and Task Positive networks has been shown to reduce negative rumination, while improving mood, and a more realistic self-appraisal. Again, as Schwartz put it, "The way an individual willfully focuses attention has systematic effects on brain function, amplifying activity in particular brain circuits" (Schwartz, 2002, p. 334).

To get a sense of the way in which mindfulness practice can positively alter the neural circuits, we invite you to try this brief activity. After reading the following simple directions, sit quietly, let your eyes soften and defocus, then follow the breath: either the rise and fall of the lower abdomen or the gentle passage of air through the nostril tips. As your mind begins to wander (which it undoubtedly will), simply say either, "oh, well," or label it as, "thinking," and bring attention back to the breath. Do this for at least a few minutes, noting that when the mind wanders for very long it very likely does so in the direction of the past memory or future plans and preoccupations—a normal tendency of the DMN. Each time you catch and bring the mind back to breath, or the present moment, you have succeeded in activating the TPN.

Such a practice carried forward and done with regularity accomplishes several things at once: neural circuits that help us live more in the present and less in the past or future are strengthened; positive mood states are more easily attained and maintained; and greater power of concentration, essential to in-depth learning, is cultivated.

To sum up findings on the two reciprocal, mutually exclusive attentional networks, consider this. When the mind wanders, which it invariably will (hundreds of times a day would not be particularly surprising, nor would it be necessarily abnormal!), what mindfulness meditation provides is a conceptually powerful and, over time, a highly practical way to literally switch modes.

When the mind (in DMN-mode) begins to wander from potentially positive and creative ideation to negative rumination, regular meditation practice can develop the ability to recognize the shift and, by intentionally directing attention to the breath, a sound, a sensation, the TPN is switched on and the DMN off.

If, as Schwartz and other scientists make clear, paying attention is key to modifying neural circuits what else might we need to understand about this lynchpin element in brain plasticity and, therefore, in how learning and intelligence might be enhanced? First, as we just found, we can benefit from basic knowledge about so-called attentional networks of the brain.

Interestingly, for more than half a century psychologists have been pursuing this area of investigation as something of a "holy-grail" for achieving a unified-field theory of human psychology. A second and related area of importance, one very close in nature to the theme of mindfulness meditation, are investigations being carried out on attentional styles and their role in learning, knowledge about which can lead to more informed classroom practice.

Further Findings on Attentional Networks

In a journal monograph entitled, "Research on Attention Networks as a Model for the Integration of Psychological Science" (2007), scientists Michael Posner and Mary Rothbart revisit the seminal research and theories of McGill University neuropsychologist, Donald O. Hebb (he of, "Neurons that fire together, wire together," fame). According to the authors, the larger purpose of Hebb's decades-long career had been to unify all major themes in the scientific study of human psychology— "social, cultural, differential, experimental, and physiological areas" (p. 1). To that end Hebb evidently believed (as do the authors of the paper under consideration) that understanding the attentional networks of the brain can provide the access key to this unification. While that pursuit may or may not result in a unified theory, it does underscore the fundamental importance of the work being undertaken to better understand the complexities of attentional networks.

As stated by the authors, "We believe that the connection between neural networks, genes, and socialization provides a common approach to all aspects of human cognition and emotion" (p. 1). In other words, standing between nature (genes) and nurture (socialization) are the neural networks dedicated to attention; networks that undergird all psychological processes. They contend that

> Attention serves as a basic set of mechanisms that underlie our awareness of the world and the voluntary regulation of our thoughts and feelings. The methods used to understand attentional networks in terms of anatomy, individual differences, development, and plasticity can be applied readily to explore networks related to other aspects of human behavior. (p. 6)

Studies undertaken on attentional networks are many and varied, reflecting the highly complex nature of the brain circuits in question. As such, there are a variety of approaches and several ways these systems can be described, one of which featured the DMN and TPN. In the case of Posner and Rothbart, three networks are conceptualized, each related to different aspects of attention: alerting, orienting and executive, defined as follows. "Alerting is defined as achieving and maintaining a state of high sensitivity to incoming stimuli; orienting is the selection of information from sensory input; and executive attention involves mechanisms for monitoring and resolving conflict among thoughts, feelings, and responses" (p. 7). While the three networks operate interactively, they also follow a temporal sequence, alerting to orienting to executing, during a given perceptual event. What might be thought of as attentional success obviously requires the proper development and integration of all three networks, the ultimate success of which is dependent upon the appropriate stimulation of the networks when first awakened and made active (i.e., early childhood). Routine over-stimulation and/or under-stimulation of the nervous system during this crucial period can result in destabilization of the entire system, often showing up as learning and behavioral problems when a child enters school.

Notably, the executive network is located almost exclusively in the frontal lobes and pre-frontal cortex and in that respect seems to share commonalities with the Default Mode Network. That the three networks operate sequentially (alerting to orienting to executing) provides insight into childhood and adolescent disorders of attention such as ADD and ADHD; disorders which appear to be trending upwards at a rather worrying rate.[54] While these maladies have been proven to be the result of a malfunctioning alerting network, ultimately these disorders manifest as, and are diagnosable by, the inability to execute certain functions, included among which are inhibitory control, consequential thinking, future planning, emotional management, empathy and, over time, self-reflection—all of which is to say executive function is languishing.

The good news, as reported in studies such as the one under consideration by Posner and Rothbart, is that due to neuroplasticity it is entirely possible for the brain to rewire itself through practice—the practice of paying attention. While any number of things can help this process, from behavioral-cognitive therapy, modifications to diet, sufficient exercise, time outdoors, limits placed on screen time, and neurofeedback, to medication (when maladies such as ADD and ADHD are accurately diagnosed and the medication closely monitored by an attending physician), learning to meditate can be added, as more and more studies point to promising results accruing to regular practice. Addressing this promise, the authors state:

> We believe that the evidence we have obtained for the development of specific brain networks during early childhood provides a strong rationale for sustained efforts to see if we can improve the attentional abilities of children. In addition, it will be possible to determine how well such methods might generalize to the learning of the wide variety of skills that must be acquired during school. (p.17)

Fortunately for educators and students, a great deal of work has already gone into the development and implementation of programs and

---

54 For example, in a survey of nearly two hundred thousand children and teens aged 4 to 17 reported in Psychiatry Advisor, the estimated prevalence of diagnosed ADHD increased over a 20-year period, from 6.1 percent in 1997 to 1998 to 10.2 percent in 2015 to 2016. See https://www.psychiatryadvisor.com/home/topics/adhd/last-20-years-saw-increase-in-prevalence-of-adhd-in-children/

techniques devoted to the enhancement of awareness, flexible attentional skills, and positive, learning-ready mind states. That this successful effort pertains at all levels of education, from pre-kindergarten through secondary and tertiary, is a most auspicious and quite welcome and growing trend. Of the many programs now available to introduce and integrate mindfulness practice into school settings, two that we believe are particularly credible are Mindful Schools and Calm Classroom.[55] Like most resources available today, both include aspects of Social-Emotional Learning (or SEL) that, along with learning mindfulness practice, affords at an early age the unparalleled opportunity for integrated and holistic development.

Improved Attentional Flexibility and Enhanced Creativity and Problem-Solving

In a *Scientific American* article entitled, "The Real Neuroscience of Creativity," (2013) Columbia University psychologist, Scott Barry Kaufman reports on the dual role of the executive attention network in the creative process. He points out that a major element in the creative process involves the ability to focus attention like a laser beam, an ability called into play when concentrating on a challenging task, attempting to reason something out, or engaging in complex problem solving that puts heavy demands on working memory. Think: an engaged TPN. While an essential component of the overall creative process, Kaufman points out, the executive network also needs to deactivate in order to allow for another crucial element to emerge: the so-called imagination network (really, the beneficial element of the DMN given a different name), the "off-line," defocused state of reverie so friendly towards creative ideation, alternative perspectives, when past experiences and remembrances and future possibilities are co-mingled in new combinations; in general, what Einstein called "recombinant play."

A third, so-called salience network, described by Kaufman as involved in monitoring both the executive and imagination networks, provides the switching mechanism between the two, as needed for the

---

55 Mindful Schools (https://www.mindfulschools.org/resources/explore-mindful-resources/) and Calm Classroom[1] (https://calmclassroom.com/?gclid=EAIaIQobChMI-ujfmdTY5AIVg9dkCh1PyQelEAAYAyAAEgKdi_D_BwE)

task at hand—moving back and forth between intense focus and relaxed defocus. Because the salience network constantly monitors both external events and the internal stream of consciousness it is undoubtedly the network particularly improved upon by the practice of meditation. This, because meditation involves active monitoring of thoughts, feelings and sensations, and strengthens the innate ability to switch modalities.

At this point it will be helpful to explore of what, exactly, paying attention comprises. Not to do so might leave the unfortunate impression, and reinforce the mistaken notion, that paying attention (as in, "Are you paying attention!?") is the only means by which learning and memory formation can occur. Fortunately, this is not at all the case. In fact, chronic overly narrow-focused attention can be quite stressful and cause for concern. In part, because of the widespread societal belief in the outdated and discredited notion that only by narrowly focusing attention is learning possible, it has to a large extent become the default mode of attention for nearly all of us—to our detriment.

Paying Attention to Attention

"To realize fully our human potential is to learn to be aware of, to choose flexibly, and to implement effortlessly an expanding, dynamic range of attentional styles for the optimum allocation of our resources." (Fehmi, 2003, p. 1)

So says Les Fehmi, PhD, neuropsychologist, pioneering expert in the development of clinical neurofeedback technologies and protocols; whose decades-long research in and contributions to brain wave theory and practical application we visited in Chapters 9 and 10. Fehmi's groundbreaking investigations into body-mind interaction can serve to round out our inquiry into the role of attention, while offering a more complete answer to the question, "How do mindfulness-based interventions actually work?" Fehmi's insights also provide an informed response to our fourth query, "What is the impact of practicing mindfulness or meditation upon learning and development?" Commenting on just such a question, Fehmi reflects on the possibility and promise of introducing attentional practice to all age groups:

Attention training deserves the highest priority in the child rearing process and on into and throughout adulthood and, therefore, deserves a prominent place in our public and private school systems at every level. Learning to pay attention to how one pays attention is synonymous with learning to learn. (Fehmi, 2003, p. 33-34)

Let's look more closely at how "learning to pay attention to how we pay attention" can in turn enhance learning ability itself, for herein lies the crux of the argument for teaching students mindfulness meditation and other forms of body-mind practice—and why so many schools are currently introducing them as a mainstay of the curriculum.

Dimensions of Attention

In the same manner that "Styles of attention and the timing of their occurrence are obviously factors for all learning" (p. 11), Fehmi points out that, "Attention to attention, the implementation of attention skills and the integration and balancing of attention styles, can significantly enhance the quality of life" (p. 33).

Femhi's initial interest, going back half a century, began with research into the relationship between attentional styles and brain wave activity; studies which revealed just how precisely they reflect one another. As one might expect, when the style of attending alters so does the dominant pattern of brain wave activity (see Chapter 10). His contribution has in part been to measure and quantify this relationship. Using neurofeedback (see also, Chapter 10) as his primary research and clinical tool, he parsed in detail the nature of attention, showing its precise effects not only on brain waves but on physiology as well.

While Fehmi's seminal work is quite elaborate, with invaluable insights into learning and wellbeing, here we wish only to underscore the importance of *attentional flexibility*—his term for which is "Open-Focus Attention." He describes four types or aspects of attention that can be used to enhance that learning and wellbeing. Cautioning that in a given society one style will invariably be favored over another, Fehmi emphasizes the fact that we are in a sense meant to employ different modes in different circumstances. He states that,

> We possess the potential to attend to any given content of attention in a variety of styles, individually, in combination, and by degrees. However, with socialization training and by habit, we usually attend to familiar and similar situations

in essentially the same way, that is, habitually. There is little doubt that all successful learning and optimal performance involves directing appropriate styles of attention. (p. 11)

Scope of Attention: From Narrow to Broad, Objective to Absorbed

What Fehmi describes as the scope of attention extends from narrowly focused to broadly diffused. In this sense, he is describing the Task-Positive and Default-Mode networks. What he adds is a distinctive and more nuanced second bi-pole dimension, described as a kind of proximity to experience: distant or close, "extending from objective or separate from the contents of attention...to absorbed or immersed" (Fehmi, 2003, p. 9). By way of example, consider that reading and comprehending these words necessarily requires the ability to call upon narrow, pointed attention, characterized by the ability to block from awareness unwanted sensory stimulation. The ability to concentrate and comprehend would be seriously compromised if we were incapable to bringing into play this form of attention.

Carried to an extreme of chronic overuse, however, this style of attention can rather easily turn against us, possibly resulting in attentional rigidity, which has been shown to be a source of allostatic stress (see Chapter 8) for most of us and, increasingly, for children as well. Fehmi puts it this way:

> While rapid and complete attentional narrowing and objective focus is at times necessary for optimal behavior, there is, in our day, an unfortunate tendency toward overuse and consequent chronic rigidity of narrow-objective attentional processing (p. 10).... The ongoing effort associated with the maintenance of narrow focus...becomes a stress producing habit. (p. 12)

To remedy this and regain greater attentional flexibility, he recommends a frequent shift of attention in the opposite direction, to something more relaxed and diffuse. This makes allowance for all available internal and external stimuli, in effect "all-around, three dimensional, simultaneous" (p. 9). Similar to the earlier experimental practice that we offered, this can be accomplished starting with softening and perhaps closing the eyes (recall that closing the eyes immediately elevates the production of synchronous alpha brain waves). Diffusion of attention can then deepen by inviting in sounds and sensations that may have been present when focused narrowly but were screened from awareness by the need to maintain narrow focus.

This shift could also entail bringing attention to where the body makes physical contact with the act of sitting or the way the breath moves in and out as the chest rises and falls—as a consequence of this intentional shift of attention accumulated stress is resolved and released.

As we have emphasized throughout this book, for learning and wellbeing the maturing nervous system requires regular visits to calming and restorative alpha and theta waves—the state experienced as diffuse, relaxed, and absorbed. This attentional mode and brainwave state is, of course, evoked during periods of free-play, reverie, downtime, meditation and other mindfulness practices, as well as artistic and musical involvement.

Moreover, recall the brain states associated with the blood-flow research mentioned in Chapter 9. Conducted by Swedish researchers in the 1980s, with the newly introduced Positron Emission Tomography (PET-scan), the findings showed distinct differences in blood-flow between high-load and low-load sensory input. When sensory stimulation remains high, a greater concentration of blood appears in the posterior, sensory processing areas of the cortex. In contrast, when sensory stimulation is dampened, as much as 25 percent more blood perfuses into the frontal lobes—associated with enhanced executive function. Paradoxically, by shifting attention from narrow focus, which requires effortful screening of unwanted sensations, to purposeful attention on those same sensations it is typically experienced as a pleasurable sense of relaxed calm that, in turn, renews the capacity for subsequent narrow task-focus.

Fehmi's decades-long involvement in research, writing and clinical practice on attentional styles is highly consonant with more recent discoveries in allied fields of neuroscience and contemplative science (including, as we pointed out, the "discovery" of TPN and DPN). His seminal findings are timely, as popular interest in the benefits of mind-body practices continues to grow, included among which are greater nervous system ease and balance, less carry-over stress from daily activities (that seem to ever-multiply), enhanced learning and performance, and optimized health. Before highlighting further the evidence in support of these contentions, we wish to add one other piece that, as promised earlier, may both surprise and delight.

The Role of the Arts in Strengthening the Attentional Networks

Earlier in this chapter we discussed the contributions made by Michael Posner and Mary Rothbart towards an understanding of how attentional networks can be improved, and neuroplasticity enhanced, using meditative practice. In an apparent attempt to show how similar positive neural changes might be induced by indirect means other than meditation, Posner teamed up with science writer, Brenda Patoine to explore how active involvement in the arts might accomplish the same ends.

In their fascinating 2009 DANA Foundation paper, "How Arts Training Improves Attention and Cognition," they make a compelling case for routine childhood involvement in the arts (music, dance, drama, painting, creative writing, poetry, etc.) as a means by which the attentional networks of the brain, and therefore human intelligence, can develop and flourish. They make the bold claim, supported by other researches which they site, that education in the arts can transfer to seemingly unrelated cognitive abilities. In other words, they argue, a child's involvement in an art form that sustains their interest can lead to subsequent strengthening of their brains' attention networks—and in the process improve cognition and intelligence more broadly.

They offer evidence that it does in fact transfer. This assertion, if substantiated in further research, would completely undermine the specious rationale for reducing or eliminating the arts in childhood education; the argument, with no apparent credibility, that the arts are somehow frivolous rather than being foundational to the development of human intelligence. They write:

> We know that the brain has a system of neural pathways dedicated to attention. We know that training these attention networks improves general measures of intelligence. And we can be fairly sure that focusing our attention on learning

and performing an art—if we practice frequently and are truly engaged—activates these same attention networks. We therefore would expect focused training in the arts to improve cognition generally. (Posner and Patoine, 2009)

For the unconvinced, they argue that,

Some may construe this argument as a bold associative leap, but it's grounded in solid science. The linchpin in this equation is the attention system. Attention plays a crucial role in learning and memory, and its importance in cognitive performance is undisputed. If you really want to learn something, pay attention! We all know this intuitively, and plenty of strong scientific data back it up.

We encourage the reader interested in pursuing that "strong scientific data" to read the article in its entirely, as it is richly informative. For now, what we wish emphatically to point out is that the preservation of training in the arts during childhood, adolescence and even adulthood ought to be considered a top educational priority, rather than being considered a "frill"—or worse, eliminated from our schools entirely. Direct involvement in one or more of the arts appears to afford a parallel and important means by which to reap many of the same benefits that routine participation in mindfulness meditation practice affords, not the least of which is strengthening the attentional networks.

Direct involvement in one or more art forms appears to afford a parallel and important means by which to reap many of the same benefits of routine participation in mindfulness meditation practice, not the least of which is strengthening the attentional networks.

We turn now to the third and fourth questions that have guided our discussion of mind-body practice: Are mindfulness-based interventions effective? What is the impact of practicing mindfulness or meditation upon learning and development?

Mindfulness-Based Interventions: Scientific Scrutiny Makes Its Case

In an article describing the positive effects of mindfulness meditation practice, the above-mentioned science writer Brenda Patoine (2016) reports that,

> Mindfulness-based meditation is now firmly established as a valid stress-reduction tool and is backed by a growing body of solid science illuminating its effects on the brain and health. It is being applied to an ever-growing list of conditions and life situations, including keeping kindergarteners calm, boosting job satisfaction, overcoming addiction, and beating back pain. (p. 1)

Addressing the benefits that stand up to scientific scrutiny, Patoine reflects on the growing concern that some purported claims aren't necessarily in line with the science. Indeed, since mindfulness meditation practice has become an estimated 1.5 billion-dollar business, according to at least one estimate (2019, p.1), it isn't surprising that some degree of hype might be present, as a result of which a healthy and necessary skepticism seems appropriate.

It should also be mentioned that as the research on mindfulness-based interventions continues to experience exponential growth, the body of scientific evidence supporting these treatments has come under criticism for being of questionable methodological quality. Responding proactively to the accusation on lack of rigor, a group of researchers (Goldberg, et al, 2017) undertook a systematic review that, after carefully vetting thousands of references spanning the previous sixteen years, used 142 qualifying studies to examine the issue of rigor in detail. While addressing those areas still in need of improvement, their findings suggest overall modest qualitative improvements in the areas under scrutiny, and a strongly worded conclusion to continue on the path to improved rigor. So, with these two cautions in mind—possible over-hyped claims and methodological concerns—let's proceed to examine what otherwise appear to be demonstrable benefits.

In general, it is possible to sort the available research into two broad categories. One has to do with investigations taking place in areas where a mental or physical health challenge exists—challenges such as pain management, addiction, physical ailments like fibromyalgia and migraine, post-traumatic stress disorder, depression and other forms of emotional distress, and even serious psychiatric conditions such as psychosis and bipolar disorder.[56] The other category deals not so much with health challenges, per se, as it does with the quest for enhanced or improved memory, cognition, job or life satisfaction, relationships, spirituality, even longevity.

Many of the benefits ascribed to mindfulness meditation seem particularly related to its known influence on two major brain systems: attention and emotion. Since both of these interactive systems are critical to self-regulation, the possibility for enhancement is no small thing.

Greater self-regulation facilitates the ability to focus attention without distraction and enhances the ability to exert control over emotional impulses. Keeping in mind that the field of contemplative science is relatively young and still in the process of working out effective protocols, the studies that have been undertaken generally point toward positive alterations in those brain systems as a result of consistent, long-term meditation.

As an important tool of investigation, the use of sophisticated imaging technology has made it possible to determine pre-post changes in brain structure and function. That is, when followed longitudinally over, say, a two-month period of time, accurate measures of brain gray matter increase or decrease can be obtained. One such eight-week study, for example, by a team at Massachusetts General Hospital was reported in the peer reviewed journal, *Psychiatry Research* (Holzel et al, 2011). The results showed gray matter increases in several areas of the brain, most notably the hippocampus, seat of memory consolidation and a part of the greater emotional regulation system. This is obviously a very positive outcome. The same study also found that "participant-reported reductions in stress also were correlated with decreased grey-matter density in the amygdala, which is known to play an important role in anxiety and stress."[57]

---

56 In addition to the Patoine reference, another excellent resource that summarizes recent findings can be found at https://endpoints.elysiumhealth. com/the-science-of-meditation-1442df86a5fb For a more thorough description of benefits see also Goleman and Davidson (2017), found in the reference list for this chapter.

57 As summarized on Science Daily: https://www.sciencedaily.com/releases/ 2011/01/110121144007.htm.

The 8-week timeframe is notable, both as regards the earlier caveat about the need for long-term practice, and the fact that it takes approximately that duration of time for neurogenesis to affect discernible alterations in brain structure.

Patoine (2019), reporting on the work of Michael Posner (whose important research we described earlier) and others on the attentional and emotion-regulating areas of the brain, describes the use of a recently developed brain-imaging technology known as Diffusion Tensor Imagingto study specific changes in the brains of experienced meditators. She relates the consistent findings that neural pathways linking the prefrontal cortex to emotional regions in the brain appear to be strengthened by meditation. These are beneficial brain changes, positively impacting the neural circuitry of attention and emotion regulation.

Yet another line of research points to a specific aspect of brain physiology as the potential mechanism underlying beneficial meditation-induced change. It involves the ongoing health and reproducibility of brain tissue, related to a recently discovered feature of cells — including neurons and glial cells in the brain – called telomeres. These are described as protective caps on chromosomes, and they tend to degrade naturally as we age. This process is sped up when higher than usual levels of stress are chronically present.

As telomeres wear down—get shorter—chromosomes can no longer be properly protected, resulting in cells that are unable to replenish and which consequently malfunction or cease functioning altogether. But an enzyme called telomerase, can actually add DNA to the ends of chromosomes, and slow, prevent and partially reverse the shortening of telomeres.

When it is used as an outcome measure for participants engaged in mindfulness practice, studies show improved telomere length as a function of increased levels of telomerase. For example, one such study appearing in the journal, *Brain, Behavior and Immunity* (Conklin et al, 2018), showed a measurably enhanced quantity of telomerase over the course of a three-week insight meditation retreat. Another study reported in the *Annals of New York Academy of Science* entitled, "Can meditation slow rate of cellular aging? Cognitive stress, mindfulness, and telomeres" (Epel et al, 2009) reported similar results. Furthermore, a recent meta-analysis appearing in the journal, *Psychoneuroimmunology* (Malouff, 2014), focussing on the results of four randomized control trials (a total of 190 individuals), concluded that mindfulness meditation appeared to lead to increased telomerase activity. These and dozens of other similar studies report that mindfulness practice can be a means by which telomere health and longevity can be extended. This is promising news that we are eager to follow.

Mindfulness-Based Interventions in the Schools

Given our extensive coverage of how mindfulness practice can improve brain function, learning and wellbeing, it must come as no surprise that we are enthusiastic advocates of making it available to students as an integral part of daily classroom activities. The growing interest in introducing mindfulness-based interventions into educational settings stems mainly from findings related to ways by which brain function and structure appear to alter over time. With the evidence showing the appearance of greater activity in brain areas associated with emotional regulation and high-level cognitive functions (abstract thinking, reasoning and decision-making), it seems reasonable to assume that the same phenomena occurs in young people who practice meditation as well. The same goes for evidence showing down-regulation of activity in areas of the brain related to stress and anxiety.

Given our extensive coverage of how mindfulness practice can improve brain function, learning and wellbeing, it must come as no surprise that we are enthusiastic advocates of making it available to students as an integral part of daily classroom activities.

When undertaken as a routine school-based activity, anecdotal and observational reports of positive changes in student behavior are very encouraging. Beginning with a view towards overall findings, we will then discuss a poignant example of what can happen when a school district beset by a multiplicity of urgent social, demographic, political and financial challenges commits to a well-organized and broad-based effort to bring mindfulness interventions to the school community.

Because the overall effectiveness of mindfulness interventions with youth had yet to be assessed through a comprehensive meta-analysis, a research group endeavored to close that (Zoogman et al, 2014) a few years ago. After carefully vetting all journal articles between 2004 and 2011 on the subject of incorporating mindfulness practice in settings for youth (mainly schools, but also treatment facilities and youth-oriented social programs), 20 such studies were selected. In general, the analysis determined that, "mindfulness interventions with youth overall were found to be helpful and not to carry iatrogenic harm" (p. 1). Based on their findings, the authors conclude with a number of recommendations, among which are, "mindfulness can safely be used with youth to address a broad range of social and emotional targets" and, "mindfulness can be integrated into a broad range of settings for youth, to include community, youth programs, and schools" (p. 11).

With respect to how a particular school system might benefit from introducing mindfulness-based interventions to both students and faculty, we offer the story of a large school district neighboring the one where one of us (TB) spent his earliest school years and the other (JB) attended graduate school, worked and lived nearby for several years: Oakland Unified School District, California. The main player in the success story is Mindful Schools,[58] established in 2007 and recently the subject of a fair amount of media attention due to the positive results they appear to have achieved in offering mindfulness-based interventions to students and teachers in one of the nation's largest and, arguably, most challenged school districts.

In preparation for the Mindful Schools Research Study (using their own curriculum and undertaken in collaboration with the University of California, Davis) during the 2010-2011 school year, a literature review was conducted that included findings on the benefits youth might gain from mindfulness-based interventions. The reported benefits fell into three main categories: improved cognitive outcomes, social-emotional skills, and overall well-being. More specifically, the studies referenced[59] reported gains in such areas as attention and focus, grades, emotional regulation, behavior in school, empathy and perspective-taking, social

---

58 Details available at https://www.mindfulschools.org/

59 See: https://www.mindfulschools.org/about-mindfulness/research/#reference-20

skills, test anxiety, stress, relief from post traumatic symptoms and depression.

In addition, the teachers whose students took part, were also provided the opportunity to learn the practice, perhaps encouraged by research showing when teachers undertake a mindfulness practice they often report greater efficacy in doing their jobs, more emotionally supportive classrooms (Jennings, 2013), and better classroom organization (Flook, 2013).

The Mindful Schools Research Study, involved 937 children and 47 teachers in 3 Oakland public elementary schools and stands as one of the largest randomized-controlled studies on mindfulness and children to date. The study, in sum,[60] showed the kind of positive results that have attracted worldwide interest, with the participant group far exceeding the control group in areas including paying attention, classroom participation, ability to self-calm and self-control, self-care and demonstrating care for others. Needless to say, it is studies like this that have prompted interest by other educators, parents, the general public and, more recently perhaps, the scientific community with its needed critical eye and occasional skepticism.

While acknowledging the aforementioned criticisms of contemplative science research, Oren J. Sofer, senior program manager at Mindful Schools, disagrees with those who maintain that, because of shortcomings in many studies, it's too soon to bring mindfulness meditation into schools. Sofer: "You can overstate the research and make claims that haven't been validated, but saying that it's 'experimental' I believe is understating the research." To which he adds: "I think it's important to research this stuff, but at the same time, I think it's important to have common sense. Do we as adults and educators in society have a responsibility to teach children to be self-aware? You don't need a research study to answer that question."[61]

---

60 A detailed explication of study-design, intervention descriptions, methodology, measure choices and so forth can be obtained at https://www.mindfulschools. org/pdf/Mindful-Schools-Study-Highlights.pdf

61 As quoted in a very good summary of the challenges and opportunities related to introducing mindfulness meditation to youth. https://www.vox.com/science-and-health/2017/5/22/13768406/mindfulness-meditation-good-for-kids-evidence

Like many others who advocate for adoption of mindfulness interventions and other forms of body-mind practices in the school setting, we await with interest studies now underway that are meant, in part, to address criticisms and concerns which have been leveled. One such very large-scale undertaking, focused on teen mental health and mindfulness-intervention, was launched in the United Kingdom in 2015. The seven-year, three-part undertaking, carried out by teams at the University of Oxford and the MRC Cognition and Brain Sciences Unit, in collaboration with the University of Exeter, includes the first large, randomized-control trial of mindfulness training. It includes 76 schools and will have involved nearly six thousand students aged 11 to 14 by the time of completion. According to a University of Oxford press release,[62] the study includes research meant to establish, among other things, whether and how mindfulness improves the mental resilience of teenagers, as well as an evaluation of the most effective way to train teachers to deliver mindfulness classes to students.

We end this chapter by echoing the comments of researchers who conducted their own systematic review of youth-oriented mindfulness-based interventions (Zenner, 2014), and raise a hearty cheer for the enthusiasm with which they commend the introduction of mindfulness practices into the school setting. School appears to be an appropriate setting for such interventions, since children spend a lot of time there and interventions can be brought directly to groups of children in areas of need as part of a preventive approach at little cost.

Mindfulness can be understood as the foundation and basic pre-condition for education. Children need to learn to stop their mind wandering and regulate attention and emotions, to deal with feelings of frustration, and to self-motivate. Mindfulness practice enhances the very qualities and goals of education in the 21st century. These qualities include not only attentional and emotional self-regulation, but also prosocial dispositions such as empathy and compassion, self-representations, ethical sensitivity, creativity, and problem-solving skills. They enable children to deal with future challenges of the rapidly changing world, ideally becoming smart, caring, and committed citizens.

---

62 http://www.ox.ac.uk/news/2015-07-16-large-scale-trial-will-assess-effectiveness-teaching-mindfulness-uk-schools

Chapter 15

The Anatomy of Embodied Education: Mindful Integration of Brain, Body and Heart Intelligences

"If we develop the higher structure of our brain/mind, it automatically integrates the lower ones into its service."

— Joseph Chilton Pearce

"If we were to design a tool from scratch to improve learning, health, and overall wellbeing, it would look like the arts."

— Susan Magsamen

"Educators are healers. Educators and healers both trust in the wholeness of life and in the wholeness of people. Both have come to serve this wholeness."

— Rachel Naomi Remen, MD

From Theory and Research to Impact

Introduction

The prime motivation for and central focus of this book has been to offer a vision of human possibility based upon current scientific knowledge, reflected in ancient wisdom traditions, and grounded in plain common sense. In support of this vision, and over the course of the preceding fourteen chapters, we have carried out a wide and far-ranging conversation. Perhaps more accurately we have engaged in an open argument: arguing on behalf of children, their concerned parents and dedicated teachers. Our sense is that many, perhaps most, know instinctively the accuracy and aptness of this book's premises. And, while parents and teachers don't necessarily need to know the neuroscience behind the practices routinely undertaken in support of whole-child development and learning, we believe this knowledge can serve as a boost in confidence and competence needed to stay the course. This is no small thing for teachers. In the face of well-meaning but often thoroughly misguided educational policies and the discouraging social and politicized trends undermining support of public education, many if not most classroom teachers continue to cope with unprecedented levels of stress and, by all reports, demoralization. There is far too much at stake to allow our collective potential to remain stalled, for broad-based access to, and maximum development of, innate intelligences and creative capacity is central to successfully engaging the myriad challenges of accelerating social, technological and unprecedented planetary changes.

Touching upon dozens of topics, our goal has been to articulate that which we believe undergirds human potential at a time of daunting challenges—and how that potential can be realized. The critical word here is potential, referring to those latent qualities or abilities that may be developed and lead to future success (implying that they may or may not be developed). As reflected in the book's title, we concern ourselves with the reality that throughout the past, much of humanity's innate, inherent potential has remained latent and largely unfulfilled. In accordance with our use of the term *anatomy* in the book's title, we have endeavored to examine in detail this untapped potential through a careful "dissection" of the evolutionary, biological and neurological underpinnings of the embodied human brain and mind.

Emphasizing the critical need to foster an integrative intelligence—brain, body, heart, and spirit working together—we mean to encourage those who press for a holistic, whole-child, integral approach to education. This most worthwhile of goals is best accomplished *mindfully*, both in the sense of actions thoughtfully considered and skillfully carried out, and in the more specialized sense of *mindfulness*. Referred to as a kind of discipline or formal training, mindfulness practice (to which Chapter 14 is devoted) specifically entails various forms of body-based meditation.

Tying together the myriad topics is the book's overarching theme: *the quest to best understand and make imminent the human birthright of the* **significant** *developmental wholeness, healthy well-being and integrated intelligence.*

Albert Einstein is credited with having said that, "the significant **problems** we have cannot be solved at the same level of thinking with which created them," thereby framing the central conundrum of our age: how to foster, in a critical mass of individuals, the intellect, guided by *intelligence*, that will give rise to new ways of thinking, feeling, and engaging the pressing challenges and unique opportunities before us now and most definitely into the foreseeable future. Responding to the challenge implied by Einstein's assertion, our goal is to make clear the nature of innate human intelligence as revealed through neuroscience, wisdom traditions, and basic common sense.

The pursuit of our goal is organized around themes related to maximizing human potential: developmental wholeness, integrated intelligence, well-being, and enhanced learning. Frankly, in light of the myriad daunting challenges and threats to our collective well-being, we can see no other alternative than to mindfully and vigorously pursue such a hopeful and realizable vision of human possibility. A bright and shining future for this and all subsequent generations is a vision whose time has come.

In this, the final chapter, sub-divided into four sections, we summarize and bind together the book's themes and topics as follows.

In Section I we establish a **Context**: a discussion of critical distinctions between intelligence and intellect, and their relevance to the pressing challenges humanity faces. We also make clear our use of the term, *Nature's Plan*, alluded to at various times throughout the book.

This is followed by **Section II, Meta and Core Concepts**, the essential ideas that inform an effective approach to learning, teaching and human development.

The third section, **Aligning Theory and Research With Practice and Impact**, features a presentation of our unique framework for achieving optimal human learning and development.

The final **Section IV, Guiding Strategies in Fulfilment of Optimal Learning and Development**, describes ideal classroom practices that align most closely with and serve as prompts to optimal whole-child development.

Section I. Context

Intelligence and Intellect: A Critical Distinction

Human intelligence concerns itself with the answer to the question, *Is this appropriate?* Intellect, in contrast, is driven by the question, *Is it possible?* This, according to Joseph Chilton Pearce (1992, pp. xix and 187), whose influence on our own understanding of human potential occurs in several places throughout this book, his spirit present on every page (see for example, Chapters, 2, 4, and 12). Until his recent passing at age 90, Pearce was preoccupied with *the nurture, care and optimal education of our children and young people.*

The legacy of his decades-long attempt to define and insightfully articulate the human predicament, along with the potentially dire consequences of not fully grasping the distinctions between *intelligence* versus *intellect*, is very much bound up in the pages of this book.

Pearce's intriguing distinction between intellect and intelligence is, we think, a compelling response to Einstein's provocative assertion that, "we cannot solve our problems with the same level of thinking we used when we created them." *Intelligence*, says Pearce, moves us to act in accordance with individual and collective wellbeing. The ability to pursue beneficial outcomes while avoiding harmful ones, is evident in all forms of life, down to one-celled organisms. He asserts that the critical feature of intelligence is its unrelenting urge towards what is *appropriate* to the fulfillment of life, as reflected in an overall sense of wellbeing. In effect, intelligence is forever guided by that question: Is this appropriate?

Is it appropriate (to use an example posed by Pearce) to develop and mass-produce toxic chemicals, of which there are now some 10,000 violently toxic and carcinogenic types, that eventually find their way into our environment at the alarming rate of over 100 million tons per year? The answer to this, and similar questions about often self-defeating and therefore deeply baffling human behaviors, is of course a resounding, *No, of course not!* How, then, did this and all other essentially life-threatening forms of human behavior come about? Through the misuse of *intellect*, Pearce asserts.

Intellect, a component of intelligence, can and does function without apparent regard for what is appropriate to wellbeing and the continuity of life. This is because intellect, as conceived by Pearce, is beholden to a fundamentally different orientation, function, and even neurological basis—the quest for novelty. Whereas, intelligence is driven above all else by the quest for appropriateness, intellect is propelled by a singular quest: *Is it possible?* Is it possible to: develop a more effective weapon of mass destruction? ...develop artificial intelligence that could out-smart its creators? ...extend a human life indefinitely? Frightening enough possibilities, but ones that we read about almost daily. This is intellect untethered from intelligence.

Intelligent possibilities alternative to the litany just above include:

- the pursuit of a more sustainable, renewable, energy economy;
- access to affordable, quality healthcare and lifelong educational opportunities.

These are quests guided by something quite distinctive: conscience, moral judgment—in a word, intelligence.

Obviously, intellect can be used either in service to humanity's lowest and darkest urges or as a means by which our highest aspirations can be fulfilled. The deciding factor: whether intellect is guided by innate intelligence or willful ignorance.

It is here that Pearce makes a thrilling, if controversial, interpretive leap. Intelligence and intellect, he argues, are totally different processes, designed by evolution for very different purposes, the latter meant to be subservient to the former. Our intelligence, he asserts, is "heart-centered," connected with the deepest intuitive roots of life and ultimately in synchrony with what he refers to as Nature's Plan, an intentionally provocative term (our use of which we address shortly). In contrast, intellect, in hot pursuit of possibility, is "brain-centered," mainly concerned with controlling outcomes and largely unconcerned with, oblivious to, or willfully ignorant of the hidden costs or unintended consequences—not infrequently thoroughly unwise and often antithetic to planetary wellbeing.

Both words—intelligence and intellect—can, of course, connote many meanings; it very much depends on which of their many facets are under consideration. Our interest is in casting the widest possible net, one that can hopefully capture the essence while remaining clear, straightforward and practical in application. To those ends, and with our previous discussion of Pearce's distinctions in mind, we define intelligence as

> *the capacity to respond to new situations, adapt to changing conditions, and learn from experience in a manner that is fully supportive of wellbeing and the continuity of life.*

This way of thinking about intelligence is consonant with that of the great Swiss developmental psychologist, Jean Piaget. Trained as a biologist, Piaget was keenly interested in how an organism adapts to its environment (the capacity he termed—as we do—*intelligence*)[63]. To Piaget, behavioral adaptation to the environment is guided by mental organizations called schemata—the mental maps an individual uses to represent the world and prompt action. This adaptation is driven by the survival need to obtain balance between existing schemata and the ever-changing environment. As for intellect—*functioning in pursuit of novel possibilities*—it is neither inherently good nor bad, positive or negative. Its ultimate use, like the development of the human mind, is fully contingent on developmental influences.

Nature's Plan for Human Development

So, what, exactly, is meant by the term, Nature's Plan—or at least our use of it as an idea central to the themes of this book? First of all, our use of the term is definitely not meant to assert a particular dogma; rather, we use it to suggest an organizing principle that can serve to make sense of the troubling and dangerous predicaments we humans have caused, as well as a possible way forward to a more promising future.

Yet another concept introduced to us by Joseph Chilton Pearce (who also used the interchangeable terms, *Nature's Agenda* and *Nature's Mandates*), Nature's Plan posits a discernible, describable and predictable progression in the way intelligence emerges

Nature's Plan posits a discernible, describable and predictable progression in the way intelligence emerges developmentally, through interactions within the human brain-mind, and between a child and caregivers.

---

63 Huitt & Hummel (2003). Piaget's theory of cognitive development. Educational Psychology Interactive. Valdosta, GA: Valdosta State University. http://www.edpsycinteractive.org/topics/cognition/piaget.html.

developmentally, through interactions within the human brain-mind, and between a child and caregivers. These interaction are of course also influenced and shaped, if more subtly and less tangibly, though influences specific to a given culture and, more broadly, the natural world.

Viewed through the lens of evolution, the Plan exists in the human genome as influenced by the epigenome—those biological mechanisms that work to switch genes on and off, and to amplify or diminish their effects (see Chapter 6 for a complete discussion). These interactions are dynamic and reciprocal, which is to say that any emergent trait or behavior leading to successful adaptation is selected, genetically encoded, and thereby preserved and passed along to future generations as innate potential.

Admittedly somewhat provocative, the terms Plan or Agenda are meant to serve as something of a middle-ground to our usual ways of thinking about how things come into existence in the universe, either as completely random, chance occurrences, or by preordained supernatural design. Pearce, was by no means alone in his desire to discern generalizable principles undergirding nature and the operations of the universe—the province of the branch of science known as cosmology. Albert Einstein, for example, was quite keen on elucidating principles that might serve to join together knowledge derived from the scientific facts of material existence with essential values meant to inspire our attitudes about and actions in relationship to the material universe.

The mission of authentic education then is to maintain alignment with those elements of *Nature's Plan* working to assure the proper unfolding of the predictable stage-wise, developmental progression of human intelligence. By attending well to that core mission, whole-child development and overall well-being is largely assured. As well, another outcome inherent in authentic education entails the distinct possibility for healing all manner of possible childhood traumas—a topic of utmost importance to which we shall later return.

Education for the 21st Century

The distinction between intelligence and intellect seems particularly important to understand at this time because in humankind's unrelenting quest to master the environment, it has until now been able to conveniently ignore unintended consequences. This is no longer possible—the bill, as most now realize, has come due. Far too much is at stake to continue along the path of seemingly benign ignorance and willful denial. From the mounting evidence of unraveling in our over-exploited natural world, to the alarming consequences of an ever-warming planet, we are clearly in need of a fundamentally different approach to how we live together on our imperiled planet. Warning signs are everywhere. From the rapidly melting Polar regions and Greenland ice sheet to the shocking decline in birdlife and the so-called "insect apocalypse," there is no longer doubt that our life-supporting ecosystems are in the process of collapse. Moreover, as climate change accelerates, and the predicted future pandemics arrive, societal chaos is likely to increase, following centuries of exploitation, oppression, enslavement, and genocide of peoples and cultures. Both the recent, overwhelming drought-and war-driven "climate refugee" crisis, and the worldwide economic shutdown in the face of COVID-19 serve as dramatic examples.

In addition, the young have for decades been showing clear and disturbing symptoms of familial and societal disorientation and strain. From the 25% school dropout rate in the U.S. (amounting to over 1.2 million students annually—that's 7,000 students a day),[64] to the alarming rise in homelessness, incarceration, depression and suicide among the young, it seems undeniably evident that our system of education and social safety nets are no longer functioning adequately to meet their pressing needs. In short, the evidence of compounding crises can no longer be ignored if we are to survive and thrive into the future.

Paradoxically, while the need for a fundamental change in direction in how we relate to the planet and one another has perhaps never been greater, the knowledge of how that change might come about has never been more fully realized or accessible. Other than the political will to alter the perilous course that humanity (and therefore much of the living world) is on, we believe the necessary change in "our level of thinking" will come about principally through commitment to making authentic education the birthright of all.

---

64 According to the Organization for Economic Co-operation and Development (OECD). See https://all4ed.org/articles/education-at-a-glance-international-comparison-places-the-united-states-near-the-bottom-in-high-school-graduation-rates-and-college-graduates/

Authentic Education versus Contemporary Schooling

It is edifying to reflect on the origin of the word, "education." Derived from Latin, the word has two distinct meanings: *educere*, "to draw forth," and *educare*, "to train or mold." Once we become aware of the difference between the two, the ongoing debates about the purpose of education in contemporary society can be more readily discerned—the outcomes of which chart the course for the structure of both schooling and education (the distinctions between the latter two to be made clear as we proceed). As pointed out by Bass and Good (2004),

> There is an etymological basis for many of the vociferous debates about education today. The opposing sides often use the same word to denote two very different concepts. One side uses education to mean the preservation and passing down of knowledge and the shaping of youths in the image of their parents. The other side sees education as preparing a new generation for the changes that are to come—readying them to create solutions to problems yet unknown. One calls for rote memorization and becoming good workers. The other requires questioning, thinking, and creating. To further complicate matters, some groups expect schooling to fulfill both functions, but allow only those activities promoting educare to be used. (p. 162)

Herein lies the rub: "To further complicate matters, some groups expect schooling to fulfill both functions, *but allow* only those activities *promoting educare to be used.*" The authors further describe the dilemma: "In the overall scheme of things, *educare* and *educere* are of equal importance. Education that ignores educare dooms its students to starting over each generation. Omitting *educere* produces citizens who are incapable of solving new problems. Thus, any system of education that supplies its students with only one of these has failed miserably" (p. 164). Clearly, a balance is desirable. The problem is that educational systems, for all kinds of reasons, including their essentially conservative nature, nearly all default to those activities promoting *educare*, almost exclusively. "A culture has been established," as Bass and Good point out, "that is remarkably resistant to change" (p. 164).

The magnitude of challenges now before us requires that we come to terms with the nature of cultural resistance to which Bass and Good refer. Otherwise, *educere*, with its potential to free human intelligence to respond appropriately, will continue to languish as we unwittingly continue to enact that strangely familiar "definition" of insanity as, "doing the same thing over and over while expecting different results." As they pointed out, of all societal institutions, education has long been recognized as the most conservative and slowest to change—witness the prevailing industrial-style model still based on an agrarian calendar. This is largely due to the fact that, unlike other societal institutions with which they may or may not have gained some familiarity, parents have all attended school and, for better and for worse, received some kind of education. In the normal course of events few, if any, busy parents (let alone policy-makers) take the time to seriously consider how an increase in *educere* might serve to benefit their own children while at the same time enhance sustainability and thrival for generations yet to come. While understandable, it would be very lamentable were we to continue with "business as usual" at this most pivotal time.

Educere connotes a profound trust in the human condition, assuming that intelligence is innate and will, with appropriate stimulation, be drawn forth. An approach to education that flows naturally from such an assumption—that timing is everything and over-stimulation is as unwelcome to childhood development as under-stimulation—places it in rather stark contrast to the enterprise of modern schooling. The paradigm prevailing now takes quite the opposite approach, largely viewing children as empty vessels in need of filling with facts and figures. And from a developmental perspective this approach can, and often does, create harmful results—most especially when rushing children into levels of mental activity well before the nervous system has matured, which can be catastrophic to healthy development. It is illustrative to revisit the critical observation by educator Marietta Johnson (see also Chapter 13), originator of a movement to address early childhood development in America, called *Organic Education*.

> A child who uses symbols too early cannot be as clear a thinker as one whose thought is stimulated by doing.... Little children are not ready for the analysis of symbols which learning to read entails. It is a great strain on the teacher also

to try to teach children symbols when they should be using things. The many methods of teaching reading testify to the difficulty of such work. (Johnson, 1996, p. 22)

When considering Johnson's educational philosophy and practice, it is sobering to realize that her concerns were expressed a century ago. Vigilant as to how education ought to proceed, that is according to the dictates of natural development, she goes on to say, "Schooling is inadvertently but primarily planned by national textbook and educational materials companies" (p. ix).

Harvard University professor and author, Howard Gardner, famous for his work in formulating the paradigmatic Multiple Intelligence framework, has been unflinching in his criticism of the direction taken by contemporary schooling. He is credited with saying that,

> Human development in general, and each child's development in particular, has a kind of organic rhythm to it, and its disturbance can be very damaging. The whole trend now to thrust high school curricula and testing into kindergarten is anti-developmental thinking gone mad. (Beem, 2020)

The "organic rhythm" to which Gardner refers is, of course, the predictable, stage-wise trajectory of self-development that is consistent with Nature's Plan, the broad outlines of which appear to be as follows (see Figure 48):

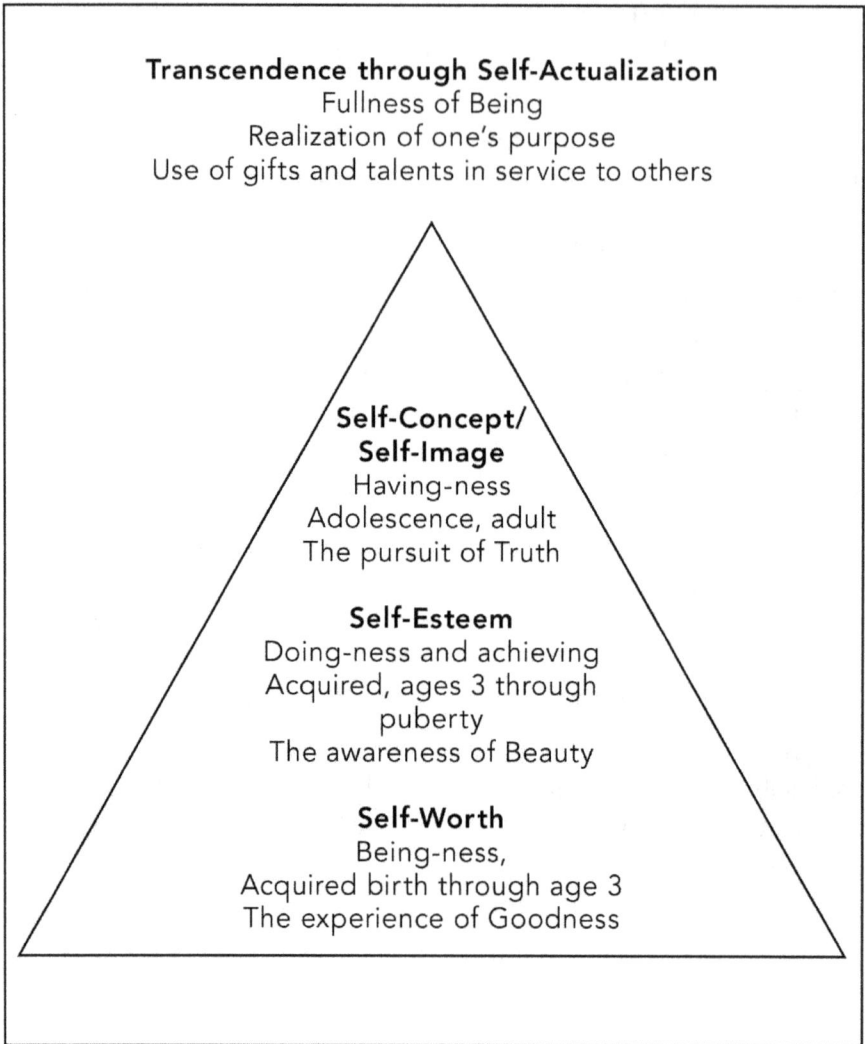

Figure 48. The Pyramid of Self-Development in Fulfillment of Nature's Plan (read from bottom to top). Image by Tim Burns and Jim Brown.

The stage-wise process of self-development portrayed in the graphic can be said to take place basically as follows: *from* **self-worth**, *to* **self-esteem**, *to* **self-concept** *or* **-image**, *to* **self-actualization** *and, critically,* **self-transcendence**.

As reflected in the vast literature of developmental psychology, each stage in the formation of a fully functioning and mature self can be characterized as a dynamic impulse, moving from: *a fullness of* **being**, *to* engaged **doing**, *to satisfied* **having**, *and finally to the ultimate fulfillment of* **giving**, **sharing** *and* **serving**.

There is one other element, as reflected in the graphic, to be considered in any serious examination of the purpose and process of authentic education. Although seldom if ever discussed in contemporary educational circles, the fact that it has fallen so far out of favor seems to be reflected in virtually every problematic aspect of contemporary human affairs. We're referring to those core values, *Goodness, Beauty* and *Truth*, thought by early Greek philosophers to be the foundation for human happiness and spiritual fulfillment. An important legacy of Western thought, these essential values continue to illuminate what is essential and what is not for a life well-lived. Fortunately, these values do play a central role in certain contemporary educational philosophies, an example of which is Waldorf education, which stems from the ideas of the Rudolf Steiner a century ago. Such a value orientation is, as pointed out earlier, also central to an understanding of what is meant by the terms, *Nature's Plan and Cosmological Principle*. Recall Einstein's passion for elucidating principles that might serve to join together knowledge derived from the scientific facts of material existence with essential values meant to inspire appropriate attitudes about and actions in relationship to the material universe.

The fulfillment of stage-wise, emergent properties culminates in a fully realized sense of self-actualized purpose, the mature expression of which is serving and being of benefit to others. Arriving at this stage of psychological and spiritual maturity, we suggest, is the fulfillment of Nature's Plan—viable as the way to ensure our collective survival and thrival into a fraught future, but only insofar as greater numbers of individuals are able to access and realize it.

Section II. Meta and Core Concepts

—concepts that together undergird an effective and authentic approach to learning, teaching and human development

At the outset of the book we suggested going straightaway to this final chapter, essentially using the first fourteen chapters as deep background information in pursuit of a fine-grained understanding of the great variety of topics offered to support the book's broad theme. To that end, we begin with our undergirding core concepts as they pertain to the main theme of optimal human development, integrated intelligence and enhanced learning.

This chapter can also serve as a thorough summative review for those who began with the first chapter and continued up to this point. In addition, we include an important "meta-concept"—living in the background of the entire book, hinted at but never fully explicated—that puts to full use one of science's most powerful and useful concepts, one that has found its way into numerous domains of enquiry: emergent-causal properties of the brain-mind. Keeping the following core concepts in mind, while becoming familiar with the upcoming schemas, will serve to ensure a clear understanding and appreciation for the role teaching is meant to play in lifelong learning, integrated intelligence and optimal human development.

The table below outlines the singular Meta-Concept and five supporting Core Concepts that undergird Nature's Plan for optimal learning and development.

META-CONCEPT: Self-Organizing Emergence	
Core Concept 1	All Learning Depends on Models, Practice and Application
Core Concept 2	Mind and Intelligence Emerge Through Social Interaction
Core Concept 3	Learning and Development is an Experience-Dependent Process
Core Concept 4	Environmental Enrichment is Key to Brain Plasticity
Core Concept 5	Attention Must Be Paid!

Figure 49. Meta-Concept and Core Concepts of Nature's Plan.
Image by Tim Burns.

Meta-Concept: Self-Organizing Emergence

We begin our exploration with the Meta-Concept, *Self-Organizing Emergence*. We use the term meta-concept because it is present in and fundamental to all of the Core Concepts we describe. Recognized as a major organizing principle in the natural world by ancient philosophers and contemporary scientists alike, the concept, *emergent causal properties of self-organizing, complex systems*, may sound overly esoteric and abstract; however, its importance in helping us to understand both the developing brain-mind and the process of authentic education is without equal. In short, it is essential and priceless knowledge, the essence of which really isn't at all difficult to grasp.

Found throughout the animate and inanimate worlds and recognized for their centrality as organizing principles in fields as diverse as physics, chemistry, biology, medicine, economics, technology, and neuroscience, the related concepts of *self-organization in complex systems* and *emergent-causal properties* have important pedigrees in both philosophy and science. Understanding how these interrelated processes operate in support of learning and intelligence builds an unassailably sound scientific and philosophical foundation for considering the practices of authentic education that promote Nature's Plan for fulfilling human potential. Let's explore how this is so, beginning with *self-organization in complex systems*, after which we discuss *emergent properties of the brain-mind*. This will be followed by a discussion of the Core Concepts. We conclude this section by returning to the Meta-Concept, emergent-causal properties, clarifying what is meant by *causal*—and the very hopeful implications it holds for whole-child development in the face of early childhood trauma and setback.

Self-Organization in Complex Systems

Sometimes referred to as spontaneous order, self-organization is the process by which highly complex systems spontaneously acquire and maintain their structure or function in a seemingly purposeful manner. *Seemingly* purposeful because, remarkably, nothing is in charge; there is no single agent of change at work within the system to make it happen. Instead, each element or part is capable of responding to signals from every other element or part across the entire system in ways both known and mysterious to science. In so doing, these systems are capable of adapting to changing conditions, both internally and externally. In effect, the system "learns" how to respond adaptively and effectively to changing circumstances (keeping in mind a core distinction in our earlier definition of *intelligence* as the ability to adapt to changing conditions). This complex, dynamical process is hallmarked by periods of fluctuation from disorder, to reorganization, to reorder, over and over again as it adapts to changing conditions. This process can be observed in aspects of life as varied as the formation of snowflakes, clouds and planetary systems, to the growth of plants, functions of every bodily organ, and—of most interest to us here—the development of the human brain.

Considered to be the most complex matter in the known universe, with its 80-to-100-billion neurons, each of which connects with some 10,000 other neurons leading to a thousand trillion possible neural processes, the degree of complexity in this two-fist-sized mass of gray matter is absolutely staggering to contemplate! Functionally, neurobiologists make the point that the highly distributed nature of the near-infinite, extraordinarily complex neural systems, ceaselessly operating in parallel and simultaneous fashion, do so without need of a central convergence center to do the organizing. In effect, the brain perfectly illustrates the phenomena of self-organization. Importantly, the mechanism by which self-organization is maintained is feedback[65] from the internal and external environment.

In sum, the self-organizing nature of the human brain means that it builds itself—and its "product," the mind. Evolutionarily designed to adapt to virtually any circumstance—natural, social, cultural—the developing brain can be thought of as an individually unique, self-organizing, emergent entity, the expression of which constitutes intelligence and the outcome of which is wholly contingent upon the nature of the model environment, the quality of relationships, and the type and timing of feedback. Going to the very heart of how education is meant to proceed, the notion of emergent process is the most powerful conceptual tool yet discovered working in support of a proper understanding of both the brain-mind and human development.

---

65 Strictly speaking the term feedback in the context of complexity theory has a more nuanced meaning, a fascinating subject although beyond the scope of this book. As used here, it is meant to be colloquial.

Emergent-Causal Properties of the Human Brain-Mind, Part One

Recall our definition of mind, taken from Interpersonal Neurobiology (see Chapter 13), as *an embodied, relational, self-organizing emergent process that regulates the flow of energy and information both between and among us and others.*

Used several times throughout the course of this book, the term emergent process, or emergence, is the conceptual piece perhaps most necessary to an understanding of teaching's essential role as catalyst for releasing the mind's innate, latent potential. The concept also provides the context for best understanding the developmental frameworks, and subsequent suggestions, provided below.

Related to self-organization, the concept of emergent process has a distinguished philosophical and scientific legacy, currently accepted as a fundamental principle of Complexity Theory. As pointed out above, these principles are usefully applied in fields ranging from biology, chemistry and physics, as well as economics, sociology and psychology. Simply stated, emergent process describes the way elements comprising a self-organizing system interact and combine—be they particles, elements of language, neural networks, natural systems, or even ideas. As they interact, new combinations are created that in turn give rise to novel and—here's the real point—increasingly complex creations.

A simple illustration can serve to make clear the notion of emergence. In the graphic below (Figure 50, Emergence in the Natural World) are shown building blocks encompassed by the biosphere (life) and noosphere (mind). Read from bottom to top, the graphic conveys, at a glance, emergent process at work, as increasingly greater complexity, novelty and diversity—in a word, creation—become manifest.

EMERGENCE

BIOSPHERE	NOOSPHERE
Organisms	Narrative, Discourse, Exposition
↑	↑
Organs	Story
↑	↑
Cells	Paragraph
↑	↑
Molecules	Sentence
↑	↑
Atoms	Words
↑	↑
Subatomic particles	Phonemes

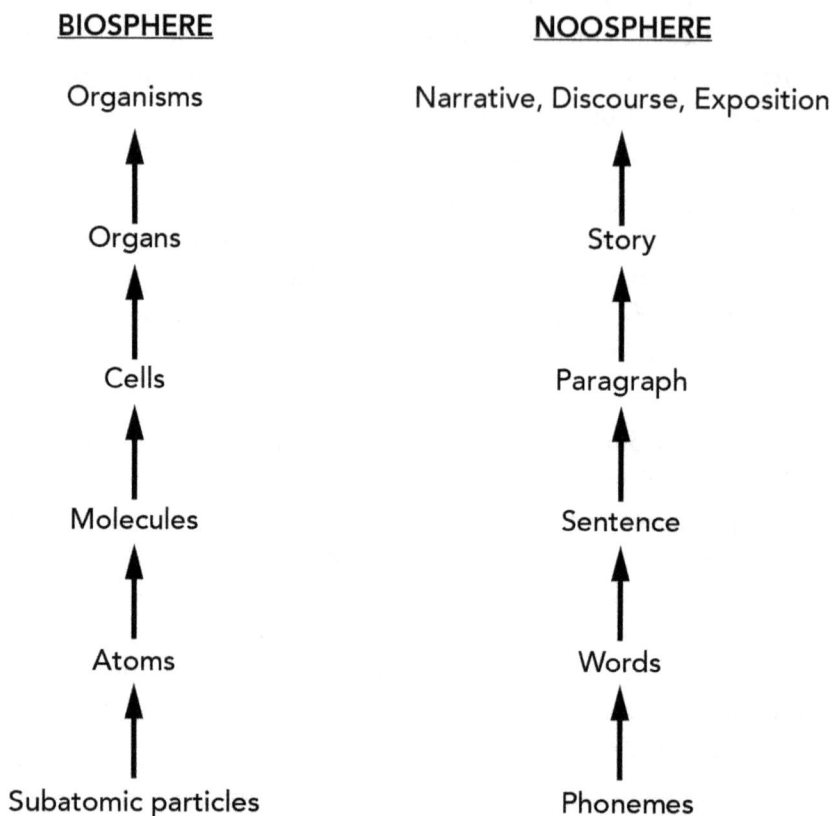

Figure 50. Emergence in the Natural World.
Image by Tim Burns and Jim Brown.

This seemingly simple, yet powerful scientific conceptual tool is, as we have indicated, fundamental to a proper understanding of how education is meant to function. Emergent process, and many other topics related to complex systems thinking applied to education, are developed more fully in Jim's companion book *Mindleap: A Fresh View of Education Empowered by Neuroscience and Systems Thinking* (Brown, 2021).

To reiterate, self-organizing, emergent process constitutes the basic dynamic at work in each of the following five Core Concepts.

Core Concept 1: All Learning Depends on Models, Practice and Application

Half a century ago Burton White (see also, Chapters 9, 11, 13), founding director of the Child Development Center at Harvard University, formulated one of the most cogent and elegant descriptions of mammalian learning that we've encountered. Here it is:

1. **Stimulus of the model.**

2. **Practice, repetition, variation.**

3. **Application or generalization.**

That's it. Simple. Straightforward. While numerous books have been, and will undoubtedly continue to be, written in great detail about various aspects of each step in the progression, this three-part model absolutely captures it. Here's a summation.

Unlike reptiles, or other, "lower" forms of life, whose learning is limited to and proscribed by instinctual, reflexive patterns of behavior, mammalian learning provides for open-ended, flexible, adaptive learning. This higher-level learning is limited only by nature's requirement that a model (as person, thing or environment) be present to stimulate the latent neural fields that will then translate and transform the stimulus into learning via steps two and three, above. This of course has to do with the fact that unlike reptiles, mammalian learning derives from wholly distinct areas of the evolved brain. The cerebral cortex (of which reptiles have none), enormous in humans while diminished in size in "lesser" mammals, is principally devoted to adaptive success—success that can be derived only from continual learning. The model stimulus requirement noted by White is especially keen in humans because of the very highly evolved, yet very slow-to-mature, brain.

Critically important to understand, is what White and others, including Harvard's Howard Gardner, refer to as the model imperative. According to this mandate, in the absence of an appropriate model at the appropriate time, learning and development cannot unfold, regardless of intelligence capacity. Especially in the earliest, most formative stages of brain development, up to the first year or so of life and continuing to some extent into early childhood, the system is incapable of creating its own model; therefore, no model, no development. Reflecting on this imperative, Pearce proclaims that the character and nature of the model in a system is the major determinant of the character and nature of that particular kind of system—adding that, thanks to the power of the model imperative, one can rise above the early models, given better ones later on (Pearce, 1994).

Access to models at each step of the long developmental progression brings with it a quickening of latent neural fields. Unknown to either White or MacLean, the recently discovered so-called mirror neurons resonate to the observed behaviors (i.e., stimulus) of others; the dormant fields are thereby brought "online" in preparation for each new level in the stage-wise developmental learning process. Certainly in the earliest days, weeks, and months of life, the most important model is the warm, loving and attentive care provider. As described in Chapter 13, early human development is inordinately contingent upon a wide range of verbal and non-verbal communication, including touch, eye gaze, and those naturally soothing and pleasing vocalizations—from cooing, and laughter, to the sing-song voicing of the mother or mothering person. While warm, close interpersonal relationships will remain key to healthy mental, social, and emotional development and well-being throughout life, the world itself increasingly provides the model environment. From the type of toys selected for the growing child, to the timing and kind of media content made available; from routine access to the wonders of nature, to the exciting involvement with authentic education—all serve to stimulate those latent neural fields, so long as the child enjoys the requisite feelings of safety and secure attachment to available care providers. Further on in the chapter we provide specific suggestions for each stage of the developmentally appropriate model environment.

Serving to stabilize, ensure and secure the learning are **practice, repetition**, and **variation**, assured by the marvel of neuroplasticity (see Chapters 4 and 6 for detailed explications). After modeling, this constitutes White's second step in the mammalian learning progression. To a very large, although not exclusive extent, human-specific learning is distinguished from mammalian learning by the third step, **application** and **generalization**, the latter indicative of the unique ability we enjoy to transfer a learning experience in one setting or context to another.

For example, a young student given the guidance and opportunity to care for a school garden, or for small animals such as gerbils, learns the importance of care and attentiveness to the life needs of others with whom we share the world. Or a teen, provided the opportunity to engage in community service is more likely to similarly engage as an adult. An adult, returning to school to earn a degree in nursing, does so with full faith that every concept and skill learned will apply and generalize to the work setting. Significantly, this last step, so simply and elegantly proffered by White, constitutes the very reason or rationale for the enterprise of education. Everything taught in our schools is meant—or ought to be meant—to adequately prepare the young to apply and generalize learning in a variety of circumstances well beyond the immediacy of the lessons.

Common as well to all mammalian species, learning, intelligence, and mind arise together interactively within the context of social relationships. This is intensely true for us humans. The context within which this optimally takes place, according to the celebrated evolutionary neurobiologist, Dr. Paul Maclean (see Chapters 2 and 13), is invariably the triadic interaction found in all mammals, and referred to by him as the Family Triad: nurture, feedback and play.

Core Concept 2: Mind and Intelligence Emerge Through Social Interaction

In our attempt to provide the best, most practical, working definition of mind, we have found that the emerging field of Interpersonal Neurobiology, or IPNB (see Chapter 13 for a complete explication), afforded us an incomparable choice. As formulated by Daniel Siegel, MD, one of principal founders of IPNB, *mind is an embodied and relational, self-organizing emergent process that regulates the flow of energy and information both within and between oneself and others* (Siegel, 2014). The fundamental tenet undergirding this definition is this: the human brain is directly and powerfully shaped—for better and for worse— through interaction with significant others, which in turn gives rise to the mind.

The organizing principles of IPNB are as follows:

1. The human mind emerges from patterns in the flow of energy and information within the brain and between brains.

2. The mind is created within the interaction of internal neurophysiological process and interpersonal experiences.

3. The structure and function of the developing brain are determined by how experiences, especially within interpersonal relationships, shape the genetically programmed maturation of the nervous system.

Our attraction to this conception of mind stems from its straightforward and seemingly inarguable emphasis on **social interaction as the essential component for robust development.** This way of looking at how mind arises is both scientifically supported and fundamentally sensible—a doubly appealing prospect. As relationships go, so goes brain and mind—what could be more obvious?

> As relationships go, so goes brain and mind

Thus, the human brain, as an evolutionarily derived and profoundly social organ, appears hard-wired to emerge and develop through human interaction, mind and brain dynamically giving rise to one another, the principal outcome of which is the emergence of increasingly more complex and powerful levels of intelligence—as will become clear when the vast and venerable field of developmental psychology is overviewed later in the chapter. This brings us to our third core concept: How environmental enrichment, always present where authentic education is practiced, enhances the brain.

Core Concept 3: Learning and Development is an Experience-Dependent Process.

The fact that some seventy-five percent of the human brain is comprised of gray matter, essentially cortical neurons the primary function of which is apprehension and learning, helps to make clear our highly adaptive nature as a species—adaptations which, in turn, serve our ability to continually learn from experience and apply it in a broadly generalized manner. We can say that *learning*, then, *is a recursive process of acquiring knowledge, skills and/or characteristics as a result of experiences that enable adaptive changes, based upon improved performance and resulting in enhanced future learning and adaptation.*

The now-common recognition that the human brain is fully capable of self-modification and self-organization in response to learning stems from one of science's most protracted debates: whether or not the central nervous system was even capable of modification. That debate is over, the profound fact of brain plasticity having become a basic tenet of neuroscience. There is, however, a glaring caveat: the emergent qualities of the brain-mind are fully contingent upon the character of the model environment.

To say it another way, the emergence of the human brain-mind is an experience-expectant and wholly contingent process, dependent for its proper unfolding on the quality of relationships and opportunities for adaptive learning. Based on what we covered earlier, the contingency factor no doubt makes sense—for all mammals, including us, it's about relationship. What exactly, then, is meant by the term, experience-expectant, and of what importance is it?

The term *experience-expectant process*, also referred to as *activity-dependent process*, stands in contrast to its counterpart, *experience-dependent process*, or *plasticity* (see Chapter 7 for complete treatment of this fascinating topic). While both depend upon and are outcomes of neuroplasticity, the ability of the brain to continually change and modify itself, experience-dependent process is far more beholden to plasticity than is experience-expectant. This is an important distinction that, while somewhat nuanced, helps explain how authentic education invariably reshapes the brain for the better.

Experience-expectant refers to the genetically driven requirement that certain specific experiences take place in the course of the earliest stage of development, the absence of which can and likely will thwart their genetic expression which, in turn, greatly increases the likelihood of developmental delay and possible deficit. Notably, these processes are found in the organ systems of the brain and body, an example of which is vision. In the earliest moments, hours and days after birth, the absence of light finding its way into and thereby "awakening" the latent neural fields of the visual cortex, the visual system will likely fail to come "online," resulting in visual impairment and even blindness for life. Such common and universal species-wide "expectations" take place within the context of what is normally provided (i.e, exposure to light in the case of vision). This includes, in addition to visual stimulation, sound (in particular the sound of the human voice) as it relates to the development of hearing and bodily movement. In experience-expectant process, genes trump environment. Said in another way, nature is paramount over nurture.

Over time, genetically driven experience-expectancy is superseded by experience-dependent process, described as the ongoing process related to the creation, organization, and reorganization of neural connections occurring as a result of individually unique life experiences. Differing life situations and circumstance influence how certain areas of the brain develop and continue to grow, change and modify. Research has shown that animals raised in a complex and engaging environment have more dendrite development and more overall synapses than do animals who are raised in an environment with no stimulating or engaging features (see Chapter 7 for complete coverage). This has been shown in human brains as well with, for example, violinists and Braille readers having an increased cortical development in the section of the brain that corresponded to the fingers of the left hand (which is used predominantly when playing the violin or reading Braille); as well as New York City taxi drivers, whose hippocampi are significantly different from non-drivers due to the amount of time spent learning traffic routes.

Here, environment trumps genes; nurture is paramount over nature. In short, experience-dependent process determines which genes get expressed and which do not. During the first few years of life, when neural connections are formed at an intensely rapid rate, both of these processes are hard at work establishing the neural foundation for learning, intelligence and well-being—or lack thereof. It is during this critical period that exposure to basic social experiences and appropriate multi-sensory stimulation are needed, without which the likelihood of acquiring necessary social-emotional skills and cognitive abilities throughout life can be compromised, forming barriers to success in every aspect of life.

A final point: whereas experience-expectant process refers to genetically predetermined quite specified outcomes (with the model environment serving as trigger or initiator), experience-dependent process relies almost exclusively on open-ended, generalized, culturally determined experiences as the mechanism for releasing innate genetic potential. In short, healthy brain-mind development in infancy and beyond depends upon a wide range of quality experiences—by definition, those occurring within that family triad of mammalian needs: nurture, feedback and play.

Classroom teachers will want to take note that while much of experience-expectant process has taken place before even the youngest students arrive, providing a setting in which plentiful human warmth and nurture is present, with abundant opportunities for both feedback and play, can and very often does ensure that development will proceed according to Nature's agenda; and not just for learning but for healing from earlier trauma (the latter being a topic to which we return at the end of this chapter).

> Providing a setting in which plentiful human warmth and nurture is present, with abundant opportunities for both feedback and play, can and very often does ensure that development will proceed according to Nature's agenda.

This brings us to the fourth core concept, one that ties together experience-dependent process with environmental enrichment and brain plasticity, thus providing a reasonably precise formula for how authentic education functions to maximize human possibility: Environmental-enrichment.

Core Concept 4: Environmental-Enrichment is Key to Brain Plasticity

The scientific verification of the brain's innate plasticity, well-founded by as early as the nineteen-sixties, initiated the overthrow of a long-standing, completely erroneous, belief: that differences in human intelligence from one individual (or, more egregiously, race) to another is a function solely of genetics; that environment had little if anything to do with it. In fact, environment has everything to do with it, as is now recognized by one of science's most recent and revolutionary fields of research, *epigenetics* (an offshoot of genomics, both topics addressed in Chapter 6) attests. The verification of plasticity's existence led naturally to an interest in two related questions. First, what are the mechanisms by which plasticity occurs; exactly how does it take place? Second, since environment plays an obvious role, what are the key elements or constituents within the environment that optimize plasticity? This is precisely the kind of scientific finding that will be of interest to parents and educators, alike.

Leaving the answer to the question of how plasticity takes place (a more recent discovery) to the next Core Concept, we go back further in time to those milestone mid-sixties studies whose intent was to show that the kind of environment in which a mammal is raised will have a demonstrable impact on brain structure and function—down to the level of differences in neural organization (a topic fully addressed in Chapter 7). Over the course of a decade or so, using carefully controlled conditions and exacting measures, the picture would became clear. Using rats, whose cerebral cortices although obviously much smaller, are identical to ours in terms of structure and basic function (see Chapter 4), the impact of varying environments on neural networks gradually became clear. Rats raised in a variety of purpose-built laboratory environments, from those considered "impoverished" (that is, essentially, lacking in playmates and playthings), to "standard," to "enriched," exhibited markedly different neural organization.

Using microscopic brain dissections and measurements, researchers have been able to able to discern differences down to the level of the spines on dendritic neurons (see Chapter 7 images), and it became immediately apparent that the differences were profound. Rats raised in enriched environments had significantly more dendritic branches, larger cell bodies, increased quantity of synapses, multiple contact sites (the spines) and increased neurogenesis (new brain cells) at multiple sites (see image, Chapter 7, p. 110). Her undertaking, similar to others at various university research centers that produced similar results, would soon challenge and eventually overthrow the prevailing belief that the organization and development brain was solely a product of genetics. Her popular books, aimed at the general public, helped broadcast the good news about enrichment studies and the implications for raising and educating children.

So what exactly constitutes environmental enrichment? It's pretty straightforward and sensible, and because of its known impact on plasticity, the conditions and factors are obviously of interest to educators. First, foremost and common to brain-mind function in all mammals, *brain enrichment can only occur in threat-free environments*. At the very first sign of threat, the mammalian brain "down-shifts" from high-to low-brain circuits in order to ensure survival through ancient pathways devoted to automatic fight-flee-freeze behaviors (see Chapters 8 and 13).

Here a distinction needs to be made between stress and threat. While a threat is certainly stressful, this is decidedly not to say that all stress must be eliminated in order to support learning, for it is by now well established that a certain degree of stress is actually necessary and helpful to elevate the neurotransmitters associated with learning and memory.

Following from a threat-free environment, and in no particular order, are some by now quite familiar allies in brain-mind development and well-being: namely, *novelty, challenge and feedback*—the nature-made prescription for which is (as you may have guessed) the *family triad, nurture, feedback and play.* We'll return to and address these discoveries with greater specificity in the upcoming section of the chapter devoted to strategies and classroom practice.

Core Concept 5: Attention Must Be Paid!

Of the revolutionary scientific discoveries affecting our view of human potential, the recent notion of attention as a prime mover in brain plasticity continues to reverberate throughout the allied fields still emanating from the discoveries of neuroscience. These fields, just to provide a flavor, include so-called *trans-differentiation* (the latest iteration of stem-cell manipulation used to treat a variety of diseases and based on new procedures to stimulate neurogenesis in targeted areas of the brain), *optogenetics* (the merging of optics and genetics to allow control of precisely defined events within a particular cell and from which we all stand to benefit due to its noninvasive ability to enact positive changes in brain function), *social neuroscience* (the study of the neural, hormonal, cellular, and genetic processes that define social species, and stemming from the now-mainstream notion that the brain does not work in isolation and neither do humans), and *contemplative neuroscience*, to name a few.

Contemplative neuroscience, formally established some twenty-five years ago, is the branch of neuroscience devoted to understanding the mechanisms by which mindfulness practice alters the structure and function of the human nervous system (see Chapter 14 for complete coverage). With each year, more evidence accumulates pointing to the myriad benefits accruing to long-term, consistent practice. From decreased stress and greater ability to recover from trauma, to enhanced self-modulation of emotions; from decreased depressive and anxious-depressive symptoms, to improved academic success, enhanced resilience and greater overall well-being—all are particularly relevant to student health and success. This goes far to explain why mindfulness practices are being introduced and incorporated into the daily classroom activities of thousands of schools, worldwide.

Emergent-Causal Properties of the Human Brain-Mind, Part Two

By way of introducing the concluding topic for this section of the chapter, consider the following. Therapy, in the sense of a treatment designed to bring about relief or healing from a psychological disorder, is the time-honored intervention for mending an ailing mind or broken spirit. A specific definition of course depends on the type of therapy, the particular therapist, and the length or duration of the therapeutic process. Generally speaking however, when properly carried out, it can offer relief from psychic insult and injury, no small thing for the millions of children living with the lingering effects of issues related to abuse and/or pernicious neglect. A haunting statistic to this effect appeared in a millennial World Health Organization (2001) report stating that by the year 2020 neuropsychiatric disorders would rise by over 50 percent internationally, to become one of the five most common causes of morbidity, mortality, and disability among children. Sadly, that prediction has turned out to be accurate. This is cause for serious concern, and not just for the afflicted children but as well for societies around the world that must deal with the consequence of half its members being functionally depressed. That said, there is reason for hope—not surprisingly perhaps, hope that stems from another expression of Nature's Plan for human development. Here is the story.

A construct derived from complex systems theory, *emergent properties of the human brain-mind*, explicates the mechanism underlying the stage-wise progression of intelligence as it unfolds—or is meant to unfold. As made clear in Chapter 13, the development of the human brain-mind is contingent upon the availability of favorable social conditions, in particular the so-called *Family Triad*: nurture, feedback and play (see Chapter 2). The natural course that emerging intelligence follows under favorable conditions can, of course, be thrown off course or even completely thwarted when conditions are less than favorable—that is, absent nurture, feedback and play. Worse, when early childhood conditions in which neglect and/or abuse (either through malicious intent or mindless ignorance) are sufficiently prevalent, hindered, or distorted, failure to develop can be the result.

Fortunately, as a vast amount of research in behavioral science and the growing body of literature on resilience attest, overcoming adversity and living, learning and loving well in spite of traumatic setback, while not inevitable, is distinctly possible. Statistically speaking, the majority of individuals who suffer childhood trauma recover and "bounce back," managing to live meaningfully and well despite their earlier painful circumstances and, equally important, do not necessarily pass along the consequences of earlier harm to their progeny.[66] Nature's Plan, as it turns out, includes a corrective mechanism, one that lies at the heart of how traumatized individuals can and do recover—and is therefore just as important as *emergence* to the development of the brain-mind. In fact, it is inextricably tied to it.

The corrective mechanism to which we refer is known as *causal process* or, intriguingly, *downward causation*, a dynamic that acts as a complement to *emergent process*, found in all *complex systems*.

As such, it greatly adds to our understanding of how intelligence emerges or unfolds and, equally, how that emergent intelligence can then serve as a corrective or healing (i.e., to make whole) mechanism. Before we elucidate more specifically how this process works to benefit traumatized children, some background information.

The notion of a theory linking emergent and causal properties was introduced by scientist and philosopher, Donald Campbell some 50 years ago (Campbell, 1974). As a companion concept to the theory of emergence, the notion of downward causation (according to Campbell and others) arose as a means by which to clarify how natural selection functions in evolution: whereas emergent process is responsible for the vast number of possible combinations that may arise though interaction of parts or elements within and between levels of organization, downward causation is the mechanism by which natural selection (the end result of

---

66 See for example, *From Risk to Resiliency: A Path With Heart for Our Children, Our Future*, by Tim Burns, a book that summarizes protective factor research.

evolutionary pressures) determines which of those possibilities actually come to exist.

A good summation of how the two processes combine conceptually comes from scientist and author, Bernd Olaf Kuppers (in Beckermann et al, 1992, p. 243): the whole is more than the total of its parts (emergence) and the whole determines how the parts behave (downward causation). Described in this way the ideas appear to be quite simple—and in a way they are. However, they are still being worked out and debated by scientists and philosophers alike, featuring occasional heated, esoteric discussions, for example, about the difference between so-called strong, medium, and weak downward causation (see for example, Anderson et al, 2000). Despite the half-century of ongoing debate on the details, the dual concept of emergent-causal properties in complex systems is well established, with important implications for the role of education in fostering both learning and wellbeing in children.

As previously described, *emergent* process is the driving evolutionary force in both the species-wide and individual developmental progression of human intelligence. What we learn from understanding *causal process* is how each stage of emergent intelligence can, in turn, be used to correct insults and injuries to the developing psyche of a child. In effect, causal process is the therapeutic complement to the corrective healing of a traumatized nervous system that *emergent process* is to the healthy development of the nervous system. To understand how causal process acts as a corrective, consider those best practices undergirding successful outcomes in psychotherapy—and how similar they are to best practices evident in the authentic education classroom.

First and foremost, consider that the basis for success common to both classroom learning and successful psychotherapeutic outcome is the quality of relationship established between teacher and student, therapist and client/patient. In both cases, a sense of warm connectedness (nurture by any other name) is key to enabling the central nervous system to upshift from fight-flight-freeze, threat-detection (the default mode in many situations where childhood abuse and/or neglect has predominated), to learning-mode and all that that entails. In the same way that a healing therapeutic relationship starts with the felt-sense of personal safety and security, a threat-free, nurturing classroom environment can immediately, if gradually, prompt the nervous system to reset itself. Depending of course on the severity of the chronic, high-stress or even threat-filled situation, children in a nurturing classroom often show improved learning and behavior. This is, in fact, the most significant finding in the vast literature on resiliency and protective factor science, going back more than 50 years: that the presence of a caring and supportive adult or (absent a healthy adult presence) even peer can initiate a resiliency response which, if not "hard-wired" like the fight-flight-freeze response, is certainly innate.

Accepted as scientific theory, causal process is also the ultimate philosophical and scientific rationale undergirding those practices thought to account for how the central nervous system can adaptively and correctively alter in both clinical and classroom settings. This view draws empirical support primarily from the new field of epigenetics (see Chapter 6), which demonstrates how differing environments causally affect genomic change; change that in turn can lead to altered functioning of the nervous system. This is where *downward causation*, a variant of causal process, also comes into play.

Described above by Kuppers as "the whole determines how the parts behave," *downward causation* suggests, in the case of the human nervous system, that as each level of holistic intelligence unfolds through emergent process, it has the capacity, in turn, to act correctively by modifying the nervous system in such fashion as to enable it to function in accordance with Nature's Plan. With nurture serving as the prime epigenetic "force field" prompting the emergence of each stage-wise intelligence level, downward causation can then act as a corrective. In light of this, consider the various commonly used forms of therapeutic practice known to facilitate recovery from psychic insult and injury.

First and foremost, as pointed out above, establishing a caring and supportive relationship creates the necessary condition for altering the architecture of the nervous system. The sufficient conditions then become, most especially with children, interventions such as play therapy, movement/dance therapy, art therapy, and even speech therapy, while psychodrama, cognitive-behavioral therapy, and existential therapy are often the modalities of choice with adolescents and adults. As will be made clear below, this particular order is not necessarily coincidental, for it is also consonant with and reflects those activities and processes known to prompt the stage-wise development of human intelligence beginning in infancy and childhood: bonding and attachment, movement, play, the arts (including music, drama and others) and so forth.

In sum, whereas emergent process serves as proactive prompt for the stage-wise development of adaptive intelligence, causal process is necessarily reactive—reactive, that is, to childhood insults and injuries. Put another way, while education is meant to enact innate stage-wise intelligence and whole-child development, education can and frequently does play a critical role in healing traumatic childhood insults through downward causation. Together, emergent-causal process constitutes a formidable combination working to facilitate Nature's Plan for holistic human development and integrated intelligence. Quoted earlier, Rachel Naomi Remen, MD, expresses it perfectly:

> There is a place where 'to educate' and 'to heal' mean the same thing. Educators are healers. Educators and healers both trust in the wholeness of life and in the wholeness of people. Both have come to serve this wholeness. (Glazer, 1995, p. 35)

Interestingly, the etymology of both words, whole and healing, are the same. They come from the Old English word *hal*, from which are derived as well the words holistic, hallowed, and holy. In the same way that reflecting upon the origin of the word *education* might lead to a very different approach, reflecting on the deep meaning of *whole*-child development might ignite a wide-spread recognition of authentic education as the means by which to foster such development. This would include recognizing teachers as principal agents promoting whole-child development as they provide the context, content and contact that enable wounded children to experience health and wholeness as the foundation of genuine intelligence. In the next section we share our frameworks for bringing greater awareness to these processes.

Section III. Aligning Theory and Research with Practice and Impact

Our unique frameworks for achieving optimal human learning and development.

Stages of Brain Maturation and Emergent Intelligence

In the two tables below (Figures 51 and 52) we present our unique frameworks for achieving optimal human learning and development in line with Nature's Agenda. Figure 52 (read from bottom to top, beginning on the left side) provides an encapsulated view of key stages of human development, as described by various developmental experts, including for example the well-known and widely recognized stages of cognitive and moral development by Jean Piaget and Lawrence Kohlberg, respectively.

Piaget made it clear that some children may pass through the stages at different ages other than the average, and that some children may show characteristics of more than one stage at a given time, yet he was insistent that cognitive development always follows this sequence, that stages cannot be skipped, and that each stage is marked by new intellectual capacities and a more complex understanding of the world.

Developmental psychologists, including Kohlberg, Maslow, Erikson, Vygotsky and others were in agreement with this general principle. Not surprisingly perhaps, each of the developmental stages (along with the approximate age range for each, at farthest left) matches with fair precision the major milestone stages of brain maturation, birth through adolescence and beyond. Displayed between the stages of brain development on the graph are the emergent domains of intelligence that correlate with each of those stages. And therein lies the meaning and entire point of the graphic: to highlight intelligence as it is meant to emerge in a stage-wise progression, according to Nature's Plan.

Developmental Stages and the Brain

Brain Stage	Intelligence Domain	Piaget Cognitive	Erikson Virtues	Maslow Needs	Kohlberg Moral	Steiner Spiritual
Brain-Heart Integration	Heart: Wisdom and Compassion	Post-formal operations	Care/Wisdom: Generativity vs. Stagnation/ Integrity vs. despair	Self-actualization: morality, creativity, acceptance	Post-conventional: principled conscience universal ethic	Spiritual orientation
Neo-mammalian: Frontal cortex Teen to Adult	Thought: Abstraction & Meaning-making	Formal operations	Fidelity: Identity vs. Role confusion Love: Intimacy vs. Isolation	Esteem orientation: confidence, achievement, respect for & by others	Conventional: social-contract to Post-conventional	Soul orientation
Neo-mammalian: Posterior cortex Ages 6- 11/12	Thought: Concrete & Problem-solving	Concrete operations	Purpose: Initiative vs. Guilt Competence: Industry vs. Inferiority	Belonging orientation -------------- Esteem orientation	Conventional: conformity authority social-order maintenance	Truth orientation
Paleo-mammalian: Limbic system Ages 2 - 6	Social-Emotional: Relationship	Pre-operational "The dreaming child"	Will: Autonomy vs. Shame & Doubt	Love and affection orientation	Pre-conventional: punishment & obedience	Beauty orientation
Reptilian: Brain stem/ Cerebellum Birth - 2	Body: Self-preservation	Sensory-motor	Hope: Trust vs. Mistrust	Survival and Safety orientation	N.A.	Goodness orientation

Birth - Age 2   Ages 2 - 6/7   Ages 6/7 - Puberty   Teen - Adult   Mature Adult

Figure 51. Stage-wise Progression of Brain Maturation and Intelligence.
Image by Tim Burns and Jim Brown.

Framework for Optimal Human Learning and Development

Having established the core principle of intelligence as an emergent phenomenon of self-organizing brain-mind, we'll now pull together into an overarching framework the ideas, main themes and myriad topics of this book—the ultimate aim of which is to tie the big picture of human learning, development and potential to the practical, day-to-day loving exertions of classroom teachers. Figure 52 (also read from bottom to top, beginning on the left side) provides, at a glance, a broad overview of the crucial role authentic education is meant to play in facilitating Nature's Plan for the emergence of human intelligence. The framework does so by moving from a more abstract conceptualization of emergent human intelligence[67] (the far left column) to increasingly specific actions and activities that facilitate that emergence. The reader will note that the framework omits the stages of brain development, a point that is central to the previous graphic.

The Framework is an integrative synthesis of the book's overarching theme, innumerable topics, and several core concepts, all backed by a compelling body of rather detailed research findings in the preceding fourteen chapters—and affirmed by our combined eighty-some years of professional experience in a variety of both educational and clinical settings. Our intent has been to create a body of exciting ideas and compelling information as a way by which to affirm teachers who, perhaps knowing it, perhaps not, by putting forth their best efforts are working to advance Nature's Agenda for optimal learning and intelligence.

---

67 Credit goes to Ken Wilber, for the names we ascribe to the top two tiers, Global-Systemic and Transpersonal-Transrational intelligences.

FRAMEWORK FOR OPTIMAL HUMAN LEARNING AND DEVELOPMENT

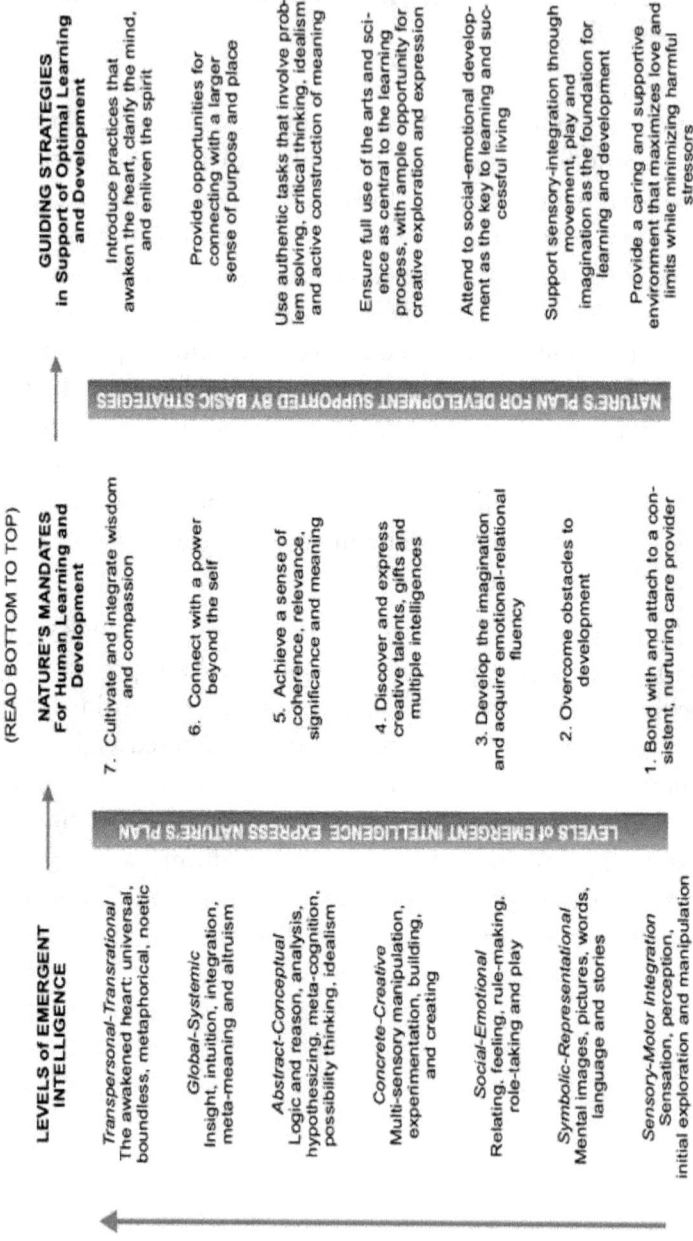

(READ BOTTOM TO TOP)

LEVELS of EMERGENT INTELLIGENCE

Transpersonal-Transrational
The awakened heart: universal, boundless, metaphorical, noetic

Global-Systemic
Insight, intuition, integration, meta-meaning and altruism

Abstract-Conceptual
Logic and reason, analysis, hypothesizing, meta-cognition, possibility thinking, idealism

Concrete-Creative
Multi-sensory manipulation, experimentation, building, and creating

Social-Emotional
Relating, feeling, rule-making, role-taking and play

Symbolic-Representational
Mental images, pictures, words, language and stories

Sensory-Motor Integration
Sensation, perception, initial exploration and manipulation

LEVELS of EMERGENT INTELLIGENCE EXPRESS NATURE'S PLAN

NATURE'S MANDATES For Human Learning and Development

7. Cultivate and integrate wisdom and compassion

6. Connect with a power beyond the self

5. Achieve a sense of coherence, relevance, significance and meaning

4. Discover and express creative talents, gifts and multiple intelligences

3. Develop the imagination and acquire emotional-relational fluency

2. Overcome obstacles to development

1. Bond with and attach to a consistent, nurturing care provider

NATURE'S PLAN FOR DEVELOPMENT SUPPORTED BY BASIC STRATEGIES

GUIDING STRATEGIES in Support of Optimal Learning and Development

Introduce practices that awaken the heart, clarify the mind, and enliven the spirit

Provide opportunities for connecting with a larger sense of purpose and place

Use authentic tasks that involve problem solving, critical thinking, idealism and active construction of meaning

Ensure full use of the arts and science as central to the learning process, with ample opportunity for creative exploration and expression

Attend to social-emotional development as the key to learning and successful living

Support sensory-integration through movement, play and imagination as the foundation for learning and development

Provide a caring and supportive environment that maximizes love and limits while minimizing harmful stressors

Figure 52. Framework for Optimal Learning and Development (read from bottom to top). Image by Tim Burns and Jim Brown.

We suggest viewing and using the Framework as a dynamic guide to those core elements of human development that work in fidelity to Nature's Plan. From the expression of that Plan as emergent levels of intelligence (the far left column) to the innate and powerful urgings or impulses (the middle column) that act as both cause and effect for the emergence of each intelligence—the fulfillment of which instills a strong sense of confidence, efficacy and agency in the world—to the broad strategies (the far right column) that have, for millennia, been instinctively deployed by human beings to prompt, guide, and direct those impulses, what remains to accomplish are a number of specific classroom practices, suggested by us as a means by which teachers can more easily discern the connection between the Framework and the activities offered to students on a daily basis.

While we think that the **human intelligence** contents of the Framework are fairly **unfolds in a predictable** straightforward and self-explanatory, **and known sequence** a few points might need clarification. Again, read from bottom to top beginning at the far left column, Levels of Emergent intelligence, this column is a summation of what developmental psychology (referencing also the previous graphic), and cognitive development in particular, has elucidated though careful observational science spanning nearly a century—the unifying theme of which is that human intelligence unfolds in a predictable and known sequence. Of various possible ways to label the successive steps we've chosen those that, as word-pairs and keyword descriptors, convey the essence of each step in the progression.

The approximate age ranges for each step, while not displayed in the Framework, are similar to the previous graphic. Using general age-related descriptors rather than years, they are as follows: Sensori-Motor, infancy; Symbolic-Representational, toddlerhood through early childhood; Social-Emotional, early through middle childhood; Concrete-Creative, middle childhood through late childhood; Abstract-Conceptual, adolescence. Each stage relates to a change both in thought process and a significant alteration in worldview—what Piaget called a schema, or mental representation of the world. The final two, Global-Systemic and Transpersonal-Transrational, represent stages exclusive to fully mature adult functioning; neither of which, like all stages of intelligence, can emerge in the absence of appropriate model stimulation and opportunities to practice and apply the attitudes and behaviors that accompany each. We will return to a full discussion of each stage in the final section of the chapter.

Section IV. Guiding Strategies in Support of Optimal Learning and Development

Alignment with Nature's Plan

That we face one of the most fraught periods in our long, challenging and fruitful evolutionary journey is no surprise—at least to those who are willing to acknowledge it. As the accelerating and alarming effects of climate warming continue to exert pressure on every societal institution in ways at which we can only guess, we must be prepared to successfully engage them. We have argued in this book that doing so depends on how well, through nurture and education, we prepare the coming generations; that successful preparation is ultimately contingent upon how closely we hew to Nature's Plan; and, that this Plan, encoded in our DNA, derives from our ability to flexibly learn and intelligently adapt. The good news is that the elements of this Plan are not hidden, nor are they mysterious. In fact, they are rather obvious and in truth not all that complicated to understand and enact. Unfortunately, blessed as we are with such large and powerful brains, we humans exhibit a tendency to overthink and complicate matters that might otherwise be successfully engaged by a simpler, more straightforward approach. We call this straightforward approach, *Guiding Strategies in Support of Optimal Learning and Development* (see Figure 53), the enactment of which can ensure what we all desire for the coming generation: wellbeing, confidence, courage, and capability.

Meant to illustrate two broad impulses that together enact Nature's Plan, the upward-pointing arrow is indicative of Guiding Strategies that serve to prompt the stage-wise emergent properties of the brain-mind; the downward-pointing arrow indicative of those same properties that, once activated and stabilized, can serve as causal agents for self-healing and attaining wholeness despite earlier setbacks and trauma—a crucial point addressed at the close of the preceding section.

GUIDING STRATEGIES
in Support of Optimal Learning
and Development

Introduce practices that
awaken the heart, clarify the mind,
and enliven the spirit

Provide opportunities for
connecting with a larger
sense of purpose and place

Use authentic tasks that involve problem
solving, critical thinking, idealism and
active construction of meaning

Ensure full use of the arts and science
as central to learning process, with
ample opportunity for creative
exploration and expression

Attend to social-emotional
development as the key to learning
and successful living

Support sensory-integration through
movement, play and imagination
as the foundation for learning and
development

Provide a caring and supportive
environment that maximizes love
and limits while minimizing harmful
stressors

Figure 53. Guiding Strategies in Support of Optimal Learning and Development
(read from bottom to top). Image by Tim Burns and Jim Brown.

Provide Nurturing Care In
A Supportive Environment

In one of the largest-ever brain studies, beginning in the nineteen-fifties and peaking in the nineteen-eighties, a team of National Institutes of Mental Health scientists, led by Paul MacLean, MD, posited the human brain as three interconnected "biological computers," each with its own unique intelligence, memory, default behaviors, and sense of space and time. Popularly referred to as the reptilian, paleo-mammalian, and neo-mammalian brains, it became known as the Triune Brain theory. While criticized for making unwarranted interpretive leaps considered to be misleading, the theory is still widely credited with introducing an evolutionary view of how our nervous system has developed and is meant to function.

Less well known and of far greater importance was the team's articulation of those elements considered essential for both mammalian evolutionary success and for healthy brain maturation and development in humans—the so-called Family Triad, nurture, feedback and play (see Chapter 2). This triad of essential elements provides the basis for secure parent-infant attachment bond, nature's strictest requirement for healthy brain-mind development in all mammalian species, while providing the matrix within which the myriad sensory and motor neural fields achieve proper development and integration.

Moreover, as indicated in our earlier, Pyramid of Self-Development in Fulfillment of Nature's Plan (see Figure 48), a secure attachment bond suffuses our infant at the cellular, preconscious level with the priceless gifts of genuine self-worth, and Goodness. Recall that Goodness, along with the values, Beauty and Truth are, according to the ancient Greek philosophers, foundational values of spiritual maturity and fulfillment.[68]

When, for whatever reasons, these neural fields fail to properly develop and integrate, a variety of problems are more likely to develop. In addition to the well recognized conditions that stem from sensory dysfunction (autism, Aspergers, and attention deficit hyperactive disorders), recent research suggests that Sensory Processing Disorders,

---

68 For an explication of this theme in the context of contemporary philosophy, see Steve McIntosh, The Natural Theology of Beauty, Truth and Goodness. http://www.integralworld.net/mcintosh4.html

or SPD (also known as Sensory Dysfunction Disorder), affect far more children than has been previously acknowledged.[69]

Hallmarked by difficulties in processing sensory stimulation, SPD can result in a wide range of symptoms, including hypersensitivity to sound, sight and touch, along with poor fine-motor skills and easy distractibility. This, in turn, often results in both learning and social-emotional difficulties, the result of which can be chronic frustration for the children, parents and teachers, alike.

Not surprisingly perhaps, and underscoring just how fundamental is the family triad to proper neural integration, the treatment protocol for SPD typically involves an intervention such as that developed by Stanley Greenspan, MD, and Serena Wieder, PhD,[70] featuring multiple, structured and facilitated "floor-time" sessions which involve nurturing play between parent and child. Over time, the "out-of-sync" child learns to respond appropriately and function more normally, reflecting a greater degree of sensory integration, according to the researchers.

With the addition of one other crucial element, Nature's Agenda for learning, adaptation and well-being will have been successfully initiated. That elemental is Nature itself, and our direct, unmediated, daily interactions with it. As strange as it may be to consider in our tech-saturated and therefore highly mediated lives, as a species our minds and our intelligence arose in the context of constant interactions with "wild" nature. All of our senses, our minds, our intelligences are still beholden to the natural world, and we always struggle and languish in the absence of that intimate connection. The growing disconnect from the natural world comes at an enormous cost, from depression, obesity, Attention Deficit Disorder (ADD) and even Sensory Processing Disorders (SPD), while the most alarming consequence may well be our apparent disregard for the fact that so little is being done to prevent our life-supportive environments from continuing to unravel before our very eyes. Unfortunately, this ignorance is fairly understandable given how

---

69 Some current estimates indicate 5 to 16 percent of school-aged children are affected by SPD. See for example, University of California research entitled, "Breakthrough Study Reveals Biological Basis for Sensory Processing Disorders in Kids." https://www.ucsf.edu/news/2013/07/107316/ breakthrough-study-reveals-biological-basis-sensory-processing-disorders-kids

70 See https://www.webmd.com/children/sensory-processing-disorder#2

little time we spend outdoors bonding with the natural world—less than one hour out of each day for both children and adults in Western societies. Fortunately, this is changing, as awareness of the myriad benefits of time spent out-of-doors in close contact with the natural world appears to be growing.

Perhaps without fully realizing it, classroom teachers routinely provide the model environment for whole-child learning and development when nurture, feedback and (largely outdoor) play feature prominently. By affording a safe and secure place, suffused with love, appropriate limits, and a playful presence, teachers ensure that healthy brain-mind development and the stage-wise unfolding of intelligence will proceed, or even self-correct, in accord with nature's requirements. A major factor at play in such an environment is vagal system activation. Recall from Chapter 13 that key to engaging the high brain for ease in learning is a dampened-down sympathetic nervous system (activated during situations of fight-or-flight). The means for doing so is basically the same in all mammalian species: interactions featuring warm and inviting eye-gaze, soothing tone of voice, and gentle touch.

Considering how seemingly small gestures can have such an outsized positive affect upon brain development is to appreciate both Nature's Plan and a teacher's role in enacting it. To restate what the late professor of education and author, Leo Buscaglia, said with respect to the power of seemingly small gestures: "Too often we underestimate the power of a touch, a smile, a kind word, a listening ear, an honest compliment, or the smallest act of caring, all of which have the potential to turn a life around." Considering the power of downward causation to rectify brain-mind dis-regulation (so often occurring in situations of childhood abuse and/or neglect), the family triad—nurture, feedback and play—whether in a therapeutic setting or, far more likely, in a classroom setting, is key to healing and recovery.

Following from the critical in-arms period, during which infant development is optimized by that secure attachment bond, nature's second mandate is truly a force to be reckoned with: overcome obstacles to development. Everything serving as an irresistible source of curiosity to be engaged with all the senses, our toddler is driven to explore and learn by the non-volitional power of will—all caregiver efforts to restrain or curtail mightily resisted. As our toddler enters early childhood, all the tireless exploration, fueled by the power of imagination and need for play, is accompanied by an explosive growth in language development. Each force combines with and reinforces the other as the next stage-wise emergence unfolds: symbolic-representational intelligence. Coinciding with the preschool period of learning and development, the classroom environment is marvelously aligned with Nature's Agenda when the emphasis is on the three primary elements: imagination, movement, and play. Just make sure to engage in these activities as much as possible out-of-doors, where the world of nature can add its full measure!

Support and Encourage Sensory Integration Through Movement, Play and Imagination

Isn't it fascinating how early childhood story-telling so often features furry mammals with humanlike characteristics and behaviors? This ancient tradition is of course the means by which important norms, mores and customs are transmitted to the young. Interestingly, and perhaps not coincidentally, this hallowed method by which cultural expectations are transmitted takes place during the limbic stage of childhood brain development (see Figure 51). MacLean (see Chapter 3) termed this the paleo-mammalian stage and how fitting that childhood stories are replete with animal characters such as the Three Little Paleo-Mammalians (be they Pigs or Bears!), for they serve perfectly to convey those expectations in a manner that completely captivates those young and highly impressionable listeners.

Further emphasizing the essential role of stories in fostering the highest reaches of human intelligence, Albert Einstein is reported to have responded to a query about how one might become a great scientist by saying, "If you want your children to be intelligent, read them fairy tales. If you want them to be very intelligent, read them more fairy tales."

Stories prompt and help to develop the power of imagination, one of evolution's great achievements. Apparently this fact was not lost on our forebears since without doubt story-telling and language arose together. What has been lost, unfortunately, is the intimate human interaction that accompanied story-telling for millennia. Story-telling, now almost entirely taken over by powerful screen technologies, has mostly become an imagination-free undertaking. This is because the images are conveyed into the brain by radiant light, something that the human brain has not evolved to process effectively. Rather, we have evolved to obtain visual information about our world from reflected, not radiant, light. A powerful radiant light source, the medium of screen technology effectively drives images into the brain in ways for which evolution has not made provisions. At least two major concerns have arisen as a result.

One concern relates to how overpowering is the medium to the imaginal capacity of the growing brain. Rather than imagination being activated by stories told in the context of intimate human contact, the relentless flow of screen images actually impedes and takes the place of imagination, while the immature mind is held captive, passively absorbing all manner of images.[71] Referring to a growing body of evidence that describes a range of disturbing outcomes thought to be related to captive screen use, some critics argue that we are now engaged in what amounts to an evolutionary experiment: raising generations of children whose primary relationship to others and the world is mostly in the realm of a highly mediated, virtual facsimile.

A second factor, or set of factors, raising serious concern has to do with accumulating evidence suggesting the possibility of serious brain disorganization in children. A recent study, for example, reported in the *Journal of American Medical Association, Pediatrics*, describes an alarming result of early screen exposure: namely, "lower microstructural integrity of brain white matter tracts supporting language and emergent literacy skills in prekindergarten children." White matter, myelin (see Chapter 4), is the insulating tissue through which messages pass between different areas of gray matter (consisting of neurons), the function of which is to ensure a highly integrated brain-mind. Obviously, anything that can impede that integrity is of real concern.

If hearing and assimilating stories is the input end of the cycle of time-honored, evolutionary-based learning and development, and imagination the means by which those stories are personalized and transformed into creative possibility, play is the output end of the cycle. There is a profoundly simple reason that play is found in every species of mammals: it is evolution's most important strategy for ensuring success

---

71 This effect was thoroughly explicated in the 1978 book, *Four Arguments for the Elimination of Television*, by Jerry Mander. See Reference List.

in actively learning about and adapting to the social environment and cultural milieu into which a growing child must find a place. Recall from Chapters 2 and 13 that a distinguishing feature of mammalian adaptive success has been the emergence of social intelligence, the "rules" for which are practiced and learned through play.

Children learn primarily through absorption, not instruction, the chief feature of play—what Maria Montessori referred to as the absorbent mind of the child. As mandated by nature, absorbed play is the means by which mind, heart and body, or thought, feeling and action, flawlessly combine to form an integrated sense of self and, as such, is the most serious undertaking in a child's life. Most serious because children are literally building their construction of knowledge of the world, themselves, and the relationship between the two—and in the process, laying down the foundations for later forms of intelligence. Whoever came up with the phrase, "play is the work of childhood," couldn't have put it more succinctly or accurately. Synonymous with real learning, play (both structured and, in particular, unstructured) is the essence of authentic education during childhood.

Attend to Social-Emotional Intelligence

Long regarded as unworthy of consideration for its possible role human reason and rational decision-making—in short, human intellect—a revolutionary reconsideration occurred following the mid-nineteen nineties publication of two best-selling books: Daniel Goleman's, *Emotional Intelligence: Why It Can Matter More than I.Q.*, and Joseph LeDoux's, *The Emotional Brain: The Mysterious Underpinnings of Emotional Life*. Goleman followed a decade later with another groundbreaking and popular book, *Social Intelligence: The New Science of Human Relationships*. In it, he synthesizes and connects findings from evolutionary biology and brain science, emphasizing just how wired to connect we are while also addressing the surprisingly deep impact of our relationships upon every aspect our lives. Fast-forward twenty-five years and what is now generally referred to as social-emotional intelligence has emerged as an area of broad scientific inquiry and widespread practical application. From education and child development to success in our most important intimate relationships, as well as in business and industry, there is a growing recognition of the critical role played by our inner, emotional life, and outer, social skills.

While student emotional well-being and social skill acquisition has always been a concern of educators, recent research showing the connection between social-emotional learning and academic performance has resulted in a growing and welcome focus on SEL (as it is known to practitioners) in the classroom. This is an encouraging trend. Everyone desires academic success for children; the perennial question is, how best to achieve it? The answer, at least in large part, appears to be: by making social-emotional learning a priority. Those who promote social-emotional proficiency as an educational priority point out other apparent outcomes as well: children and adults come to better understand and manage emotions, learn to set and achieve positive goals, feel and show empathy for others, establish and maintain positive relationships, and make responsible decisions—this, from the Collaborative for Academic, Social, and Emotional Learning (CASEL).[72] Together these outcomes have also been shown to result in improved classroom and school climate, one of the most important factors related to school success.[73]

In addition to these important outcomes, ongoing longitudinal studies have been in place to track outcomes related to future success. Indicative of many such studies, one designed to follow kindergarteners into their 20s showed very favorable outcomes both socially and occupationally when comparing those children exposed to a pro-social skills program with a control group that was not.[74] Among their findings, researchers report that "students demonstrating better prosocial behavior were more likely to have graduated college, to be gainfully employed, and to not have been arrested than students with lesser prosocial skills."

---

72 In existence for over 25 years, CASEL remains at the forefront of efforts to provide expert assistance, research and resources for school districts intent on supporting student and teacher emotional and social wellbeing. For more information and a free guide to establishing a school SEL program, visit https://casel.org/

73 Numerous examples exists showing the relationship between SEL and improved school and classroom climate. One such example: https://www.educationdive.com/news/sel-a-critical-component-in-improving-school-climate/542999/

74 See https://psychcentral.com/news/2015/07/30/kindergarteners-socialemotional-skills-good-predictor-of-adult-success/87780.html?li_source=LI&li_medium=popular17

In sum, providing students with routine opportunities for social-emotional learning and practice has been shown to improve academic achievement while also leading to success in other areas of life. This isn't particularly surprising when viewed in light of Nature's Plan, which apparently places a premium on social intelligence as key to mammalian evolutionary success. Since social intelligence depends on emotional intelligence the two are inextricably linked.

Assuming Nature's Plan for development has proceeded reasonably well—that is if infant and early childhood attachment-bonds have been sufficiently well established; a robust imagination has developed through supportive fantasy and play; fitness and coordination are proceeding apace through daily, outdoor engagement in exercise and various forms of fine and gross motor activities; and, the acquisition of basic social-emotional fluency is proceeding—then a pivotal stage will have been reached.

Ensure Full Use Of The Arts and Science As Central To Development of Human Intelligence

In a book intriguingly entitled, *The Scientist in the Crib: What Early Learning Tells Us About the Mind* (2001), three early childhood cognitive neuroscientists make the point that even very young children use some of the same methods that allow scientists to successfully explore and learn about the world. That from the very outset babies, like scientists, use their curiosity, innate knowledge and learning ability to form ideas about the world, then conduct experiments to either support or rectify their findings. That this innate and invaluable scientific mindset, the most elegant expression of maturing intellect, should somehow diminish and even get lost as children grow older is a puzzlement and profound loss.

Equally innate in earliest childhood is love of the arts. Whether provided with an opportunity to engage in music, dance, painting, writing or any other art form, the same curiosity and involvement that drives a scientific mindset is being exercised to the fullest. In fact, both endeavors share many thought processes and, indeed, outcomes in common.

In Chapter 14, an entire section was devoted to recent neuroscience research describing the role of the arts in the proper development of so-called attentional networks, as a result of which brain plasticity is greatly enhanced. In addition, the research describes other significant features of the emerging mind that stand to benefit from involvement in the arts, not the least of which are executive function, cognitive flexibility and overall intelligence. While contemporary research continues to reveal myriad brain-mind benefits accruing to early involvement in the arts and science, these benefits were certainly not unknown to our progenitors.

"To develop a complete mind, study the science of art; study the art of science." Attributed to one of humankind's towering geniuses in both science and the arts, this quotation by Leonardo da Vinci suggests something quite intriguing about our quest to best understand the process by which Nature's Plan for emergent mind is furthered. His assertion that the human mind is apparently incomplete without engagement in the arts and sciences underscores the discoveries being made in contemporary neuroscience. While it isn't clear what exactly da Vinci meant by a "complete mind," it suggests something deeply insightful: that processes involved in both pursuits are the very means by which the mind is refined and elevated—indeed transformed—from the merely mammalian to uniquely human.

To be sure, the processes of careful observation, analysis, problem-identification, problem-solving and synthesis typical of both science and the arts are quintessential expressions of human intelligence—processes that have clearly been part of the human experience for millennia. Consider the recently discovered cave paintings that go back in time more than thirty thousand years, with ongoing discoveries of all manner of tools going back much, much further. Both endeavors, cave painting and tool making, require those processes which serve as both cause and effect in the development and evolution of the frontal lobes of the brain, according to authorities on the subject.

Pondering further the implications of da Vinci's assertion, we find ourselves wondering about the nature of the fully humanized mind: what else might be considered in regard to the cultivation of scientific and artistic sensibility that serves to elevate and refine it? To satisfy that curiosity we must go back in time from da Vinci, some five centuries ago, to the very roots of Western thought in Greece about twenty-five centuries ago.

How best to develop and refine the human mind was, of course, a central preoccupation of our Western forebears, the ancient Greek philosophers, artists, and scientists. Universally admired for their stunning artistic and scientific achievements, the Greeks were also instrumental in producing lasting philosophical insights into the nature and workings of the human mind. Recall the earlier discussion about how their passion for understanding material reality arose in tandem with a compelling desire to find a suitable structure through which this knowledge might also best evoke a corresponding admiration for physical reality—thus combining apperception with appreciation, since one without the other was considered to be an incomplete way of knowing. The result of this unitary pursuit led to what has come to be known variously as the three fundamental discernments or three primary transcendent properties; or, more simply, the three value categories: *The Good, The True,* and *The Beautiful.* Each of these properties contains its own means of discerning and verifying knowledge. In addition to being the proper means by which to pursue both understanding and affectionate appreciation of physical reality, active involvement in these essential value spheres was also considered by the ancients to be the means by which life fulfillment and spiritual maturity might best be attained.

While greatly overshadowed and marginalized by contemporary surrogate values of consumerism and material acquisition, any serious consideration of how best to find authentic, lasting happiness and strong sense of meaning seems inextricably connected to the core values, *Goodness, Truth,* and *Beauty.* As pointed out by McIntosh (2007), these three value spheres have been emphasized by a continuous line of Western thinkers beginning with Plato and Aristotle, that includes Immanuel Kant, Sigmund Freud, Albert Einstein, Rudolph Steiner, Alfred North Whitehead, and, most recently, Ken Wilber—a list that also includes Eastern political leaders, spiritual teachers and poets, such as Mohandas Gandhi, Sri Aurobindo, Thich Nhat Hanh and Rabindranath Tagore. That the human brain, mind and intelligence have together emerged in accordance with natural law and the dynamics of evolution is emphasized by McIntosh: "There are some very good reasons for the remarkable agreement about this specific triad of values....Beauty, truth, and goodness have received continuous veneration because they correspond to some very deep intuitions about the way the universe works....[these]

primary values are essential descriptions of the primordial influences at the heart of all evolutionary development" (p. 3).

Grounding these lofty ideals and supporting their development during childhood are urgently needed priorities and are, or ought to be, central to the very purpose of humanistic education. Earlier we discussed how a strong attachment bond suffuses our infant with goodness and worth at a cellular, preconscious level while providing a safe, secure sense of being that serves to propel balanced, healthy self-development. Interestingly, and not at all unrelated, near the end of his life Albert Einstein is reported to have said, "The only question worth asking is, is the universe a friendly place?" Whether or not (like other quotes attributed to him) he actually said it, the question is a potent one, the answer to which might well be highly correlated with the emergence of personality traits characterized by fearlessness versus fearfulness, curiosity versus complacency, kindness versus meanness, selflessness versus selfishness, and so forth. In short, an internalized sense of *The Good* can be viewed as the foundational experience out of which inner security, good faith, a sense of morality, and ethical behaviors—or lack thereof—will be ultimately based. What, then, of *The Beautiful?*

Early and middle childhood, the life stages during which *Concrete-Creative* intelligence is meant to emerge and flourish, are hallmarked by a growing awareness of the larger world that blends seamlessly with the impulse to find and explore avenues for expansive discovery and creative expression. According to Piaget, this stage of cognitive development is best pursued through learning derived from the hands, the head, and the heart—precisely what involvement in the arts and a hands-on approach to science afford. This time period marks the stages, according to Erikson (see Figure 51) of initiative and industry, versus guilt and inferiority; it is a uniquely formative time, as gifts and talents are discovered and cultivated, self-confidence builds. That children derive great joy in unfettered discovery, experimentation, building, creating, and accomplishing, especially when done so out-of-doors, comes as no surprise. What began in earliest childhood as an innate, irresistible attraction to the natural world and all its beauty will, with support and guidance, continue throughout the middle childhood years and beyond as a natural desire to bond with and to protect nature's creations.

The point is this. if we deem it important that all features of intelligence in children develop in an integral and holistic manner, which is to say morally, ethically and aesthetically as well as emotionally and intellectually, the pivotal window of opportunity during which this comes together is the *Concrete-Creative stage*. The means by which this holistic, balanced development is promoted appears to be routine involvement in the arts and science, the basis whereby the mind we share in common with the mammalian kingdom is transformed into something altogether and uniquely human—a mind that operates in synchrony with *The Good and The Beautiful*. The remaining value sphere, *The True*, is developmentally a central preoccupation, and at times an under-appreciated feature of healthy adolescence.

Use Authentic Tasks Involving Problem Solving, Critical Thinking, Idealism and Active Construction of Meaning

If the previous stage, *Concrete-Creative*, is pivotal to harnessing the power of imagination to a self-directed and fulfilling sense creativity, and the confidence that arises with it, the *Abstract-Conceptual* stage is equally pivotal to the fusion of *intellect with intelligence* (according to our earlier distinction between the two). Always alert to otherwise unexplored aspects of human development and its inherent potential, the pioneering thinker, Joseph Chilton Pearce, offers intriguing insights into the dynamics undergirding this fusion in his monumental work, *Evolution's End: Claiming the Potential of Our Intelligence*. Not found in any other source material of which we are aware, Pearce describes three characteristics of the adolescent period that drive this fusion of *intellect* with the *intelligence of the heart*. They are, to use his own descriptors, felt-states, emotional pressures with no specific content, and a burning sense that "a secret, unique greatness exists within …that seeks expression" (Pearce, 1992, p. 190).

Pearce reminds us that starting around age eleven, and growing in intensity throughout the middle teens, an idealistic image of life arises and takes hold of the imagination, adding that this "noble idealism" impels teens to search for some model or expression of it—"a need pushing them like the will that appears in a toddler" (p. 191). This idealistic image represents, to us, the archetype of *The True* which combines, at around age fourteen or fifteen, with a sense of "great expectation that something tremendous is supposed to happen" (p. 190). This highly charged felt-state, however, very often cannot find suitable expression, for the appropriate cultural models have gone missing in contemporary society. Whereas, Pearce argues, in previous eras the mythic heroes of the Old Testament, Norse gods, Knights of the Round Table, and Homeric legends served to convey messages to the young that "the highest reaches of humanity arose from people depicting every human failing, failings so magnified as to be unmistakable, yet finally overcome" (p. 191), contemporary teens come of age imprinted on one-dimensional cartoon super-hero characters and/ or outright anti-heroes, proffered by commercially driven media culture intent upon taking advantage of the very human need to identify with a power greater than self. That no suitable model symbolic of the greatness being sought appears in contemporary culture can and does turn many teens against society, something that would have been unthinkable to our progenitors. Such is the unrequited longing of the heart. So, what can be done to meet the deepest urges and desires of teens?

Recall that the two and one-half decades-long spiral of brain maturation reaches its culmination in the frontal lobes and prefrontal cortex, the areas of the brain most responsible for a range of executive functions (see Chapter 3) having largely to do with *intellect*. These highly evolved functions make up what can be termed the *Abstract-Conceptual* level of intelligence, so integral to fully realized adult maturity. They include, but are by no means limited to functions such as analysis, planning, hypothesizing, problem-solving, consequential thinking, emotional regulation and, critically, empathy, among a host of others. From an evolutionary perspective these are hard-earned capacities, with clear adaptive advantages in complex, rapidly changing societies.

That these innate capabilities exist only as a possibility, or potential outcome, is as always wholly reliant on the stimulating presence of a model and opportunities to practice and attain mastery of them; meaning, of course, that development is far from assured. The most significant personal and societal outcome for the latter—lack of development—may well be failure to acquire a sense of coherence, relevance, significance and meaning; a failure that by general consensus is a principal cause associated with the epidemic of youth depression, anxiety and even suicide.[75]

Recall H. Stephen Glenn's definition of spirituality as, *an active sense of identification with a power greater than self that provides a sense of meaning, significance and purpose*—a definition that arguably accounts for the very best and worst of aspects human behavior. The quest for meaning and purpose, so persistent in and important to our species, lies very much at the heart of the second value sphere, *The True*. To describe the very human desire to find *Truth* as a restlessness of the heart is not far from the mark for, as was pointed out in Chapter 12, the heart has been shown to have a mind of its own. And while the heart's *intelligence* can be denied or ignored it is always there, admonishing us humans to act in accordance with the harmonious wellbeing of all concerned.

In light of the above, what best-practice strategies can be relied upon to support healthy, balanced and integrated cognitive, social-emotional and spiritual development during the adolescent period, while also spurring them along in their search for *The True*? Several practices emerge from the literature that serve to ensure authentic and meaningful involvement with others and the world-at-large, while also greatly enhancing resiliency and academic success (see Benard, 1991)[76]. These include mentorships, peer-to-peer teaching/ coaching, service learning, cooperative learning, and adventure learning, each of which make use of authentic, real-world tasks that involve and foster problem solving, critical thinking, active construction of meaning, all in service to youthful idealism. Given the vast amount of protective factor research that continues to validate such practices, it is no wonder that schools and youth-serving organizations worldwide have adopted these proven strategies to great advantage—which coincidently also serve to ensure

---

75 See for example, Harris and Udry. National Longitudinal Study of Adolescent to Adult Health, 1994-2008. Carolina Population Center, University of North Carolina-Chapel Hill, Inter-university Consortium for Political and Social Research, 2018-08-06. https://doi.org/10.3886/ICPSR21600.v21

76 The highly influential 1991 Benard publication, Fostering resiliency in kids: Protective factors in the family, school, and community launched what became a worldwide revisioning of how best to support the healthy development of young people in our families, schools and communities. See also Burns, From Risk to Resiliency (1994), with foreword by Benard, as well as Milstein and Henry (2000).

that the all-important idealistic drive to discover one's own truth emerges in a grounded, useful, and enlivening manner.

Provide Opportunities to Connect With an Enlarged Sense of Purpose and Place

Meant to be synonymous with mature adulthood, *Global-Systemic* and *Transpersonal-Transrational* are descriptors used by Wilber and others to distinguish between two possible, "higher" domains of human intelligence, together comprising a stage more commonly referred to as Post-formal Operations (also called, Post-Piagetian or Neo-Piagetian thinking). While only hinted at by Piaget, this culminating stage of intelligence was added to his influential stage-wise cognitive progression by latter-day students and disciples.

We wish to be clear that the terms, "higher" or "highest" intelligences are not meant to convey a sense of hierarchy—at least insofar as that might connote something grander, more noble, more special. Rather, one can consider it hierarchical to the extent that each step or stage in the developmental progression is a more expansive and inclusive way of attaining knowledge. Each emergent form of intelligence represents a new and more powerful way to structure knowledge about the world and ourselves; more powerful because intellect is able to come up with new and novel ways of acting upon ones experiences. In addition, as each level of intelligence unfolds it reinforces, enfolds and transforms that which came before. A classic example of this transformation: children who (as part of the observational studies carried out by Piaget and others), when invited to view and comment on recordings made of them working through problems at the previous stage of development, would often proclaim shock and disbelief at their earlier mode of thought—sometimes commenting on how "stupid" they had been and occasionally going so far as to accuse the adult researchers of doctoring the videos!

In short, each emergent intelligence deserves recognition and respect for what it is: a profound expression of Nature's Agenda for human development as it is meant to unfold. Each stage of development is a whole, complete, and we might even say perfect, expression of a particular kind of intelligence, one that needs to be fully exercised and integrated through stage-appropriate activities. Moreover, humans are marvelously adept at seeking and, if available, finding the appropriate model environment to prompt it—finding opportunities for using and practicing its particularities, and applying it in and generalizing it to other settings. Unless, that is, the Agenda is disrupted or worse, thwarted. Forcing, pushing, cajoling or even "rewarding" children through each stage, while perhaps well-intended, is questionable at best and inappropriate at worst. As Pearce frequently admonished, the best way to maximize human potential is to take our cues from the child. Children are keenly adept, if only we are paying attention, at making their developmental needs clearly known.

The designation *Global-Systemic*, sometimes called *Planetary Thinking*, denotes a profound shift in perception of the world and one's place in it. Concisely describing this shift, Leonardo da Vinci is reported to have spurred us to, "Realize that everything connects with everything else." Awakened to this intelligence level, one is enabled to perceive "the big picture," the patterns of connectedness binding together all levels of existence; creation, not as separate, disparate, and isolated pieces, serving only to baffle and confuse, but nature as it actually exists. Thus awakened, *intellect*, no longer captivated solely by novelty and possibility, may yet yield to a heartfelt appreciation for the intricate web of life. The heart aroused, *intellect* can finally "wise up" and assume its proper relationship to *intelligence*—Nature's Agenda achieving fulfillment at last.

When activated and awakened, this new way of perceiving can evoke a fervent desire to protect the web of life at all costs, not infrequently prompting one to take action. We saw this recently, as millions of young people "took to the streets," in protest of the persistent and toxic denial and political paralysis that continue to stand in the way of a sane and vigorous response to climate change—a shining example of whom is the Swedish teen, Greta Thunberg, designated "Person of the Year" by *Time Magazine*. This collective awakening affords us a possible silver-lining in the all-too-abundant alarming news about the accelerating and potentially calamitous effects of global warming. Once *Global-Systemic Intelligence* is aroused, what appears almost certain is this: having perceived a fundamental design in what were previously experienced as highly disconnected and therefore confusing perceptions and experiences of the world, individuals rarely revert back. Supported by authentic education, the number of individuals reaching this level of intelligence will only continue to grow—and press for responsive leadership and responsible governance.

Introduce Practices That Awaken The Heart, Clarify the Mind, And Enliven The Spirit

Historically, what we are calling *Transpersonal-Transrational Intelligence*, has been the province of philosophy (from the Greek, *philosophia, love of wisdom*) and, later, psychology (Greek, *study of soul or spirit*). Studied and extensively described in the late nineteenth century by William James (widely recognized as the "father of American psychology"), the ground he broke is being tilled to this day by scientists and scholars intent on understanding the highest realms of human consciousness. More recently, interdisciplinary research involving such diverse fields as psychology, cognitive and contemplative science, anthropology, neuropsychology, neuroscience and ethnobiology (especially the subfield dedicated to the study of such powerful psychedelic botanicals as peyote, psilocybin and ayahuasca) has established a body of knowledge that significantly contributes to our understanding of these further reaches of possible human experience. Noting the importance of art and science in making this realm of consciousness accessible, Albert Einstein expressed it this way: "The most beautiful experience we can have is the mysterious. It is the fundamental emotion which stands at the cradle of true art and true science. Whoever does not know it and can no longer wonder, no longer marvel, is as good as dead, and his eyes are dimmed."

One example of a fascinating, multifaceted, examination of this realm of human experience is contained in the anthology, *The Highest State of Consciousness*, by John White (1972). One of a dozen or so publications on the subject of consciousness by White, this early volume brings together papers written by some three dozen leading experts in answer to the question, What is the highest state of consciousness and how might it be attained? Introducing this broad inquiry, White addresses a central conundrum found in nearly all attempts to describe this realm: its characteristic noetic, ineffable nature—to use two words frequently appearing in the literature. A sample of his musing:

> What is the highest state of consciousness? St. Paul called
> it 'the peace that passeth understanding' and R. M. Bucke

named it 'cosmic consciousness.' In Zen Buddhism, the term for it is satori or kensho, while in yoga it is samadhi or moksha, and in Taoism, 'the absolute Tao.' Thomas Merton used the phrase 'transcendental unconscious' to describe it; Abraham Maslow coined the term 'peak experience'; Sufis speak of fana. Gurdjieff labeled it 'objective consciousness' while the Quakers call it 'the Inner Light.' Jung referred to individuation, and Buber spoke of the I-Thou relationship. (White, 1972, p. v)

Whatever words or metaphors used to describe it and by whatever means one might gain entry into it, connecting with this transformational realm of experience can result in what is often described as a spiritual awakening—signature qualities of which (setting aside accounts of miraculous undertakings) can include an enhanced sense of peace and wellbeing, gratitude and appreciation, kindness and compassion, humility, tolerance, wisdom, equanimity. While the precise mechanisms by which such a transformation might take place are by no means clearly understood, White speculated that prayer, meditation, acts of service, great faith, or even grace likely play a role in setting the stage for such an experience by altering the neural networks of the brain.

Interestingly, White's contention is supported by recent scientific evidence (extensively reviewed in Chapters 12 and 14) suggesting that any long-term heart-centered and/or mindfulness practice can reconfigure the neural fields of the heart and brain resulting in a transformed mind. This is also consonant with the view that *Transpersonal-Transrational intelligence* reflects a balanced and forged relationship between mind-driven *intellect* and heart-centered *intelligence*. Perhaps that is why those who, through one means or another, enter into a transcendent state often describe it as resulting in a state of quiet mind and open heart, the outcome of which is more likely to be actions carried out with greater wisdom and compassion—indeed, actions motivated by *The Good, The True,* and *The Beautiful.*

Fortunately, it needn't require a religious or psychedelic experience to attain to this immensely satisfying realm of consciousness—a realm that, should sufficient numbers of individuals connect with it, might well alter the course of human destiny. Indeed, the most appropriate way to introduce practices that awaken the heart, clarify the mind, and enliven the spirit—in other words, stimulate *Transpersonal-Transrational intelligence*—in a classroom setting is by providing routine opportunities for students to be in a *flow-state*.

Characterized by a sense of focused absorption, freedom from negative rumination, a sense of timelessness, and complete enjoyment in the process of whatever the activity (Csikszentmihaly, 1990), *flow-state* experiences can occur more frequently and in more circumstances than is commonly recognized, especially when those activities reflect one's guiding purpose. For children, driven by the need to move, exercise, explore, imagine, play, spend time in nature, socialize, and create, these activities are their purpose. Not surprisingly, when feeling safe, secure, and supported, children quite naturally enter into a flow state—a point brought home by the discovery that the default brainwave frequencies of early childhood are nearly identical to those that adults experience during a flow state (see Chapter 10).

Not coincidentally the descriptors used for the flow state—timeless present-moment experience, focused absorption and so forth—are the same as those shown to accrue over time with mindfulness meditation practice. As described extensively in Chapter 14 these practices have been shown to alter and improve mechanisms within the neural networks of the brain that, among many other positive outcomes, can serve as an entryway into *Transpersonal-Transrational intelligence*. Not infrequently, individuals who commit to a sustained mind-body practice report experiences that suggest transcendence and transformation, resulting in self-reports of enhanced gratitude and appreciation, less self-induced suffering and greater equanimity.

Combined with the educationally sound flow-state activities mentioned two paragraphs above, providing children and teens with routine opportunities to engage in mind-body practice can serve as two of the most potent factors undergirding lifelong learning, success in virtually all areas, wellbeing and spirited living—and, not coincidentally, fulfilling and culminating Nature's Agenda for the integration of *intellect* and *intelligence*.

Conclusion

In Pursuit of Human Possibility

The human brain-mind has a profoundly paradoxical aspect. On one hand it is capable of producing the most astonishing visions of what might be possible to manifest or create. Literally every human-made tangible and intangible that we encounter—from bridges to buildings, highways and cars, space stations and satellites, the internet and cell phones—all began with a vision, followed by a plan and the wherewithal to realize it. All fulfilled a human need; all were creative solutions to a perceived problem or opportunity, no doubt about it. On the other hand, and unanticipated consequences aside, even when the consequences of our activities and creations are likely or clearly anticipated, somehow we seem to lack the ability and/or motivation to take the steps necessary to appropriately address them, defaulting instead to predictable yet self-defeating strategies of denial and wishful, even outright delusional, thinking. Given the scope of known consequences related to human-induced climate change now well underway and accelerating, these seemingly very human strategies are, equally clearly, no longer tenable—our species and all others are presently at serious risk.

To be clear, not all cultures have exhibited this maladaptive tendency and therein lies hope—models for sustainability thinking and acting do exist. Many North American native cultures, for example, recognized the importance of what can be termed mature consequential thinking as the means by which to ensure a sustainable future. Known as the *Seventh Generation* principle, and thought to have originated with the ancient Iroquois nation, it holds that major tribal decisions must be considered in light of possible effects upon coming generations. Meant to ensure a viable world seven generations and more into the future (approximately 140 years), this ancestral Iroquois wisdom, still followed and practiced, exemplifies the fusion between *intellect*—with its narrowly focused pursuit of possibility to the seeming exclusion of all else—and *intelligence*, which prompts us to consider the wellbeing of any and all concerned in terms of the appropriateness of our actions. In light of current socio-political trends that so often feature media-hungry politicians and their endlessly self-serving decision-making, one has to seriously consider if we are any longer capable of thinking ahead to the wellbeing of the next generation, let alone the next seven. It is well past the time that we honor and re-engage in the kind of thinking that served to sustain and advance our forebears for millennia.

As revealed through neuroscience, wisdom traditions, and basic common sense, the book's overarching theme, *how best to understand and make imminent the human birthright of developmental wholeness, healthy well-being and integrated intelligence*, has afforded us the opportunity to share our understanding and vision of how best to realize innate human potential. Visualizing a bright and shining future for this and all subsequent generations is not just a vision whose time has come, it is one that is profoundly overdue.

Albert Einstein, both a towering scientific genius and one of the great sages of the modern era, still serves as an inspiring model of human possibility. In addition to his obvious pursuit of *Truth* in the realm of the physical universe, he was also particularly devoted to humanistic values, foremost among which were ethics and aesthetics—*Goodness* and *Beauty*. It is a quote near the beginning of this chapter to which we return at the end, giving Einstein the final say: "The significant problems we have cannot be solved at the same level of thinking with which we created them." This book represents, in large part, our own studied response to his provocative assertion—in which we closely examine distinctive levels of thinking and offer guidance in how best to access and engage the highest possible levels. In essence, our response to the conundrum that Einstein posed is: create a culture of *authentic* education in which classroom teachers play the crucial role.

Reference List

Chapter 2

Box, G. E. P. & Draper, N. R. (1987). *Empirical Model-Building and Response Surfaces*. Wiley.

Cory, G. & Gardner, R. (Eds.). (2002). *The Evolutionary Neuroethology of Paul MacLean: Convergences and Frontiers*. Praeger.

Condon, W. S. & Sander, L. W. (1974). Neonate Movement Is Synchronized with Adult Speech: Interactional Participation and Language Acquisition. *Science*, 183(4120), 99-101.

Louv, R. (1991). *Childhood's Future*. Houghton Mifflin.

Louv, R. (2008). *Last Child in the Woods: Saving Our Children from Nature-Deficit Disorder*. Algonquin Books.

MacLean, P. D. (1985). Brain Evolution Relating to Family, Play and the Separation Call. *Archive of General Psychiatry*, 45 (2), 405-417.

MacLean, P. D. (1990). *The Triune Brain in Evolution: Role in Paleocerebral Functions*. Plenum Press.

Pearce, J. C. (1992). *Evolution's End: Claiming the Potential of Our Intelligence*. Harper Collins.

Pearce, J. C. (2002). *The Biology of Transcendence: A Blueprint of the Human Spirit*. Park Street Press.

Chapter 3

Barnes, M. *Ernst Haeckel's Biogenetic Law (1866)*. Embryo Project Encyclopedia(2014-05-03). ISSN: 1940-5030, http://embryo.asu.edu/handle/10776/7825. Arizona State University, School of Life Sciences, Center for Biology and Society.

Dahl, R. E. & Forbes, E. E. (2010). Pubertal Development and Behavior: Hormonal Activation of Social and Motivational Tendencies. *Brain and Cognition*, 72(1), 66–72: http://doi.org/10.1016/j.bandc.2009.10.007

Kalinka, A. T. & Tomancak, P. (2012). The Evolution of Early Animal Embryos: Conservation or Divergence? *Trends in Ecology & Evolution.* 27: 385–393. https://www.sciencedirect.com/science/article/abs/pii/S0169534712000729

Ornstein, R. (1997). *The Right Mind: Making Sense of the Hemispheres.* Harcourt Brace & Company.

Porges, S. (2011). *The Polyvagal Theory: Neurophysiological Foundations of Emotions, Attachment, Communication, and Self-regulation.* W.W. Norton and Co.

Schore, A. (2001). Effects of a secure attachment relationship on right brain development, affect regulations, and infant mental health. *Infant Mental Health Journal,* Vol. 22(1-2), 7-66.

Schore, A. (2003). *Affect Regulation and the Repair of Self.* W.W. Norton and Co.

Siegel, D. (1999). *The Developing Mind: How Relationships and the Brain Interact to Shape Who We Are.* Guilford Press.

Siegel, D. & Bryson, T. (2011). *The Whole-Brain Child: 12 Revolutionary Strategies to Nurture Your Child's Developing Mind.* Bantam Books.

Chapter 4

Begley, S. (2007). *Train Your Mind, Change Your Brain.* Ballantine Books.

Diamond, M. (1999). *Magic Trees of the Mind: How to Nurture Your Child's Intelligence, Creativity, and Healthy Emotions.* Plume Books.

Doidge, N. (2007). *The Brain That Changes Itself.* Penguin Press.

Eliot, L. (2000). *What's Going on in There? How the Brain and Mind Develop in The First Five years of Life.* Bantam.

Giedd, J., Blumenthal, J., Jeffries, N., Castellanos, F., Hong Liu, H.…. Zijdenbos, A. (1999). Brain Development During Childhood and Adolescence: A Longitudinal MRI Study. *Nature Neuroscience,* 2(10). 861-3.

Gould E., Reeves A., Graziano. M. & Gross, C. (1999). Neurogenesis in the Neocortex of Adult Primates. *Science,* 286. 548–552.

Haier, R. (1992). Think of the Brainy as Fuel-Efficient. *New York Times.* https://www.nytimes.com/1992/08/26/news/campus-journal-think-of-the-brainy-as-fuel-efficient.html

Lowrey, L. (1998). *Biological Basis of Learning.* Monograph. University of California.

Maletic-Savatic, M., Manganas, L., Louis, N., Zhang, X., Li, Y. … Enikolopov, G. (2007). SBUMC Researchers First to Image Biomarker of Neurogenesis Science. Brookhaven National Laboratory. https://www.bnl.gov/newsroom/news.php?a=110706

Pearce, J. C. (1992). *Evolution's End: Claiming the Potential of Our Intelligence.* HarperCollins.

Perry, B. D. (2002). Childhood Experience and the Expression of Genetic Potential: What Childhood Neglect Tells Us About Nature and Nurture. *Brain and Mind.* 3. 79–100.

Ramón y Cajal, S. (1959). *Degeneration and Regeneration in the Nervous System, Vol. 2.* Hafner Publishing Co.

Scharfman, H. E. & Hen, R. (2007). Is More Neurogenesis Always Better? *Science.* 315(5810), 336-338. https://www.ncbi.nlm.nih.gov/pmc/articles/PMC2041961/

ScienceDaily (2018). Birth of New Neurons in the Human Hippocampus Ends in Childhood. University of California, San Francisco. www.sciencedaily.com/releases/2018/03/180307141356.htm

Schwartz, Jeffrey M. & Begley, S. (2002). *The Mind and The Brain: Neuroplasticity and The Power of Mental Force.* Harper Collins.

Shatz, C. (1992). The Developing Brain. *Scientific American.* 26. 60–67.

Susuki, K. (2010). Myelin: A Specialized Membrane for Cell Communication. *Nature Education.* 3(9). 59. http://www.nature.com/scitable/topicpage/myelin-a-specialized-membrane-for-cell-communication-14367205

Chapter 5

Cotman, C.S. & Berchtold, N.C. (2002). Exercise: A Behavioral Intervention to Enhance Brain Health and Plasticity. *Trends in Neuroscience.* 6. 295-301.

Diekelmann, S., Büchel, C., Born, J. & Rasch, B. (2011). Labile or Stable: Opposing Consequences for Memory When Reactivated During Waking and Sleep. *Nature Neuroscience.*14, 381-386. https://www.nature.com/articles/nn.2744

Mednick, S. & Ehrman, M. (2006) *Take a Nap! The Scientific Plan to Make You Smarter, Healthier, More Productive.* Workman Publishing.

U.S. Department of Health and Human Services. (2008). Physical Activity Guidelines for Americans. http://www.health.gov/paguidelines/guidelines/default.aspx

Walker, M. (2017). Catastrophic Lack of Sleep in Modern Society Is Killing Us, Warns Leading Sleep Scientist. http://www.independent.co.uk/news/sleep-deprivation-epidemic-health-effects-tired-heart-disease-stroke-dementia-cancer-a7964156.html

World Health Organization. (2015). Physical activity strategy for the WHO European Region 2016–2025. http:// www.euro.who.int/data/assets/pdf_file/0010/282961/65wd09e_ PhysicalActivityStrategy_150474.pdf

Xie L, Kang H, Xu Q, Chen MJ, Liao Y, Thiyagarajan M, O'Donnell J, Christensen DJ, Nicholson C, Iliff JJ, Takano T, Deane R, NedergaardM. (2013). Sleep Drives Metabolite Clearance From the Adult Brain. Science, 342. 373-377. https://www.ncbi.nlm.nih.gov/pubmed/24136970

Yasmin, A. (2011). As We Sleep, Speedy Brain Waves Boost Our Ability to Learn, UC Berkeley News Center, March 8, 2011, Brain in the News, 18(4). 7-8.

Chapter 6

Barry, P. (2007). Genome 2.0: Mountains of New Data Are Challenging Old Views. *Science News.* 172(10).

Harris, L. (2005). New Arrays Open 'Junk DNA' to Exploration. *The Scientist.* 19(19).

Lipton, B. (2005). *The Biology of Belief: Unleashing the Power of Consciousness, Matter and Miracles.* Elite Books.

Louv, R. (1991). *Childhood's Future,* Houghton Mifflin.

Mansuy, I. M. & Mohanna, S. (2011). Epigenetics and the Human Brain: Where Nurture Meets Nature. Electronic version, Cerebrum. The Dana Foundation. https://www.dana.org/article/epigenetics-and-the-human-brain/

Rossi, E. (2002). *The Psychobiology of Gene Expression.* WW Horton and Co.

Rossi, E. (2003). Gene Expression, Neurogenesis and Healing. *American Journal of Clinical Hypnosis.* 45(3).

Schwartz, J. M. & Begley, S. (2002). *The Mind and the Brain: Neuroplasticity and the Power of Mental Force.* HarperCollins.

Smith, G. (2005). *The Genomics Age: How DNA Technology is Transforming the Way We Live and Who We Are.* AMACOM.

Chapter 7

Begley, S. (2007). *Train Your Mind, Change Your Brain: How a New Science Reveals Our Extraordinary Potential to Transform Ourselves.* Ballantine.

Diamond, M. C. (2001). Response of the Brain to Enrichment. *Anais da Academia Brasileira de Ciências (Annals of the Brazilian Academy of Sciences).* 2001 73(2) 211-20.

Diamond, M. & Hopson, J. (1999). *Magic Trees of the Mind: How to Nurture Your Child's Intelligence, Creativity, and Healthy Emotions from Birth Through Adolescence.* Penguin Putnam.

Hirsh-Pasek, K. & Golinkoff, R. M. (2003). *Einstein Never Used Flash Cards: How Our Children REALLY learn —and Why They Need to Play More and Memorize Less.* Rodale Press.

Johnson, M. (1996). *Organic Education: Teaching Without Failure.* Marietta Johnson Museum of Organic Education, Publ.

Lane, H. (1976). *The Wild Boy of Aveyron.* Harvard Univ. Press.

Persell, C. H. (1990) Becoming a Member of Society Through Socialization, Chapter 5, in *Understanding Society: An Introduction to Sociology.* 3rd ed. Harper & Row Publishers, Inc.

Spitzer, M. (2012). *Digital Dementia: What We and Our Children are Doing to our Minds.* Digitale Demenz, Droemer.

Chapter 8

Cain, S. (2012). The Power of Introverts. Ted Talk. https://www.ted.com/talks/susan_cain_the_power_of_introverts#t-1123520

Goddard, G. V. & Douglas R. M. (1976). Does the Engram of Kindling Model the Engram of Normal Long Term Memory? In: Wada JA (ed) *Kindling*. Raven.

Sandi, C. & Pinelo-Nava, M. T. (2007). Stress and Memory: Behavioral Effects and Neurobiological Mechanisms. *PubMed Central*, published online April 15, 2007. ncbi.nlm.nih.gov

Selye, H. (1956). *The Stress of Life*. McGraw-Hill.

Thompson, R. F. (2000). *The Brain: A Neuroscience Primer*. Worth Publishers.

Chapter 9

Austin, J. H., MD. (1998). *Zen and the Brain: Toward an Understanding of Meditation and Consciousness*. MIT Press.

Frackowiak, R., Jones, T., Lenzi, G. & Heather, J. (1980). Regional cerebral oxygen utilization and blood flow in normal man using oxygen-15 and positron emission tomography. *Acta Neurol Scand.* 62(6), 336-44, Dec.

Jensen, E. (2000). *Brain-Based Learning* (Revised). Turning Point Publications.

Jue Mo, Yuelu Liu, Haiqing Huang, Mingzhou Ding. (2013). Coupling between visual alpha oscillations and default mode activity, *NeuroImage* 68, p. 112–118.

Klein, R., Pilon, D., Prosser, S. & Shannahoff-Khalsa, D. (1986). Nasal airflow asymmetries and human performance. *Biological Psychology* vol. 23.

Kreitzman, L. & Foster, R. G. (2004). *Rhythms of Life: The Biological Clocks That Control the Daily Lives of Every Living Thing*. Yale University Press.

Markova, D. (1996). *An Unused Intelligence: Physical Thinking for 21st Century Leadership*. Conrari Press,

Monk, T. H. (1994). When School Schedules Collide with Biological Clocks, *School Administrator* Vol. 51. No. 3. March.

Paul, D. (2006). High Schools, Wake Up! in *USA Today*, 23 Jan.

Reiter, R. J. & Richardson, B. A. (1992). Some perturbations that disturb the circadian melatonin rhythm. *Chronobiol Int.* Aug 9(4) p. 314-21.

Ronnberg, J., Soderfeld, B. & Risberg, J. (1998). Regional cerebral blood flow during signed and heard episodic and semantic memory tasks, *Journal of Applied Neuropsychology.* Vol. 5, No. 3.

Rossi, E. (1991) *The Twenty-Minute Break: Using the New Science of Ultradian Rhythms.* Zeig, Tucker and Co.

Shannahoff-Khalsa, S., Boyle, M., Buebel, M. (1991). The effects of unilateral forced nostril breathing on cognition, *Int J. Neurosci,*1991, 57(3), p. 239-249.

Shannahoff-Khalsa, D. (1993). The ultradian rhythm of alternating cerebral hemispheric activity, *Int J Neurosci.* Jun, 70(3-4), p.285-98.

Shannahof-Khalsa, D. (2001) Unilateral forced nostril breathing: Basic science, clinical trials, and selected advanced techniques. *Subtle Energies & Energy Medicine* 12(2), p. 79.

Skloot, R. (2015). *The Best American Science and Nature Writing.* Houghton, Mifflin, Harcourt.

Sousa, D. (2001). *How the Brain Learns*, 2nd Edition. Corwin Press.

Vitaterna, M. H.,Takahashi, J. S. & Turek, F. W. (2001). Overview of circadian rhythms, *Alcohol Research & Health*, Vol. 25, No. 2.

Wahlstrom, K. (2002). Changing times: Findings from the first longitudinal study of later high school start times, *NASSP Bulletin*, Vol. 86 No. 633 December.

White, B. L. (1995). *The First Three Years of Life*, Revised Edition. Fireside Books, Simon and Schuster.

Willis, J. L. (1990). Keeping time to circadian rhythms, *FDA Consumer*, Vol.24, No. 6.

Chapter 10

Barringo-Paulino, C. I. Barriga-Paulino, C. I., Flores, A. B. & Gómez, C. M. (2011). Developmental changes in the EEG rhythms of children and young adults analyzed by means of correlational, brain topography and principal component analysis. *Journal of Psychophysiology,* 25(3) January. 143-158.

Fehmi, L. G. (2003). Attention to attention. In: Applied neurophysiology and EEG biofeedback, J. Kamiya. (Ed.). *Future Health*. https://pdfs. semanticscholar.org/7e89/ b4c4f99897 93e273257f9f288cd497c7423e. pdf

Fehmi, L. & Robbins, J. (2008). The Open-Focus Brain: Harnessing the Power of Attention to Heal the Mind and Body. *Trumpeter*, 32-33.

Goleman, D. & Davidson, R. (2017). *Altered States: Science Reveals How Meditation Changes Your Mind, Brain and Body*. Avery Books.

Lipton, B. (2005). *The Biology of Belief*. Elite Books.

Lutz, A., Greischar, L., Rawlings, N. B., Ricard, M., & Davidson, R.J. (2004). Long-term meditators self-induce high-amplitude synchrony during mental practice. *Proceedings of the National Academy of Sciences*, 101, 16369-16373. PMCID: PMC526201

Peper, E., Ancolia, S. & Quinn, M., editors (1979). *Mind/Body Integration*, Plenum Press.

Robbins, J. (2000). *A Symphony in the Brain: The Evolution of the New Brainwave Biofeedback*. Atlantic Monthly Press.

Chapter 11

Armour, J. A. (2003). Neurocardiology: Anatomical and Functional Principles. HeartMath Research Center, Institute of HeartMath, Publication No. 03-011. 2003. Available as an electronic monograph at: http://www.heartmath.org/research/scientific-

Badenhop. C. (2009). Learning and adapting with a dual perspective. *Pure Heart, Simple Mind (Shi-endo) Newsletter*. http://www.seishindo. org/2009/03/18/learning-and-adapting-with-a-dual-perspective-2/

Bateson, G. (1972). *Steps to an Ecology of Mind: a Revolutionary Approach to Man's Understanding of Himself*. Ballantine Books.

Bryner, A. & Markova, D. (1996). *An Unused Intelligence: Physical Thinking for 21st Century Leadership*. Conari Press.

Buchbinder, A. (2013). Out of Our Heads: Philip Shepherd on the Brain in Our Belly. *The Sun*, April 2013, p. 6-14.

Gershon, M. (1998). *The Second Brain: Your Gut Has a Mind of Its Own*. HarperCollins.

Hadhazy, A. (2010). Think Twice: How the Gut's "Second Brain" Influences Mood and Well-being. *Scientific American*, Feb 12, 2010. http://www.scientificamerican.com/article.cfm?id=gut-second-brain.

Hannaford, C. (1995). *Smart Moves: Why Learning is Not all in Your Head.* Great Ocean Publishers Inc.

Merriam-Webster.com. http://www.merriam-webster.com/dictionary/

Pearsall, P. (1998). *The Heart's Code: The New Findings About Cellular Memories and Their Role in the Mind/Body/Spirit Connection.* Broadway Books.

Ratey, R. (2008). *SPARK: The Revolutionary New Science of Exercise and the Brain.* Little, Brown and Co.

Robison, T. (2013). Gut Bacteria May Exacerbate Depression: Microbes that Escape the Digestive Tract May Alter Mood. *Scientific American.* October 23, 2013. http://www.scientificamerican.com/article. cfm?id=gut-bacteria-may-exacerbate-depression

Siebert, C. (1990, February). Cover story essay: The Rehumanization of the Heart. *Harper's Magazine.* 53-60.

Swanson, L. W. (1995). Trends in Mapping the Brain: Past, Present and Future. *Trends in Neurosciences,* 18:471-474, 1995, p. 473.

White, B. L. (1985). *The First Three Years of Life.* Fireside.

White, B. L. (1995). *Raising a Happy, Unspoiled Child.* Fireside.

Young, E. (2012). The Gut brain: The Secret of Your Second Brain, *New Scientist,* December 17, 2012. http://www.newscientist.com/ article/mg21628951.900-gut-instincts-the-secrets-of-your-second-brain.html?full=true

Chapter 12

Armour, J. A. (2003). Neurocardiology: Anatomical and Functional Principles. Boulder Creek, CA: HeartMath Research Center, Institute of HeartMath, Publication No. 03-011. Available as an electronic monograph at: http://neuroimaginalinstitute.com/wp-content/uploads/2013/03/ Neurocardiology.pdf. (not secure)

Buhner, S. H. (2004). *The Secret Life of Plants: The Intelligence of the Heart in the Direct Perception of Nature.* Bear and Co.

Goleman, D. (1995). *Emotional Intelligence: Why It Can Matter More Than IQ*. Bantam Books.

Lacey, J. I. & Lacey, B. C. (1978). Two-way communication between the heart and the brain: Significance of time within the cardiac cycle. *American Psychologist, 33* (2), 99-113.

Ledoux, J. (1998). *The Emotional Brain: The Mysterious Underpinnings of Emotional Life*. Touchstone.

Macy, J. (2013). The Greening of the Self. *Spiritual Ecology: The Cry of the Earth*. Llewellyn Vaughan-Lee, ed. The Golden Sufi Center.

McCraty, R., Atkinson, M., Tomasino, D., Tiller, W.A. (1998). The electricity of touch: detection and measurement of cardiac energy exchange between people. HeartMath Research. https://www.heartmath. org/research/research-library/energetics/electricity-of-touch/

McCraty, R. & Atkinson, M. (1999). Cardiac coherence increases heart-brain synchronization. Proceedings of the Annual Meeting of the Pavlovian Society.

McCraty, R., Atkinson, M. & Tomasino, D. (2001). *Science of The Heart: Exploring the Role of the Heart in Human Performance: An Overview of Research Conducted by the Institute of HeartMath*. https://www.heartmath. org/research/science-of-the-heart/

McCraty, R., Atkinson, M. & Bradley, R. T. (2004a). Electrophysiological evidence of intuition: Part 1. The surprising role of the heart. *Journal of Alternative and Complementary Medicine*, 10(1), 133-143. Archived at Heartmath Institute: https://www.heartmath.org/research/research-library/intuition/

McCraty, R., Atkinson, M. & Bradley, R. T. (2004b). Electrophysiological evidence of intuition: Part 2. A system-wide process? *Journal of Alternative and Complementary Medicine*, 10(2), 325-336. Archived at Heartmath Institute: https://www.heartmath.org/research/research-library/intuition/

McCraty, R., Atkinson, M., Tomasino, D. & Bradley, R. T. (2006). *The Coherent Heart: Heart–Brain Interactions, Psychophysiological Coherence, and the Emergence of System-Wide Order*. https://www.heartmath.org/assets/uploads/2016/04/coherent-heart-integral-review-2009.pdf

McCraty, R. (2015). *Science of the Heart: Exploring the Role of the Heart in Human Performance*, Volume 2. https://www.heartmath.org/research/science-of-the-heart/

Mercaoliano, C. & Debus, K. (1999). An interview with Joseph Chilton Pearce. *Journal of Family Life*, 5(1), p. 1.

Pearce, J. (2012). *The Heart-Mind Matrix: How the Heart Can Teach the Mind New Ways to Think*. Park Street Press.

Pearsall, P. (1998). *The Heart's Code: The New Findings About Cellular Memories and Their Role in the Mind/Body/Spirit Connection*. Broadway Books.

Siebert, C. (1990). The rehumanization of the heart. *Harper's*, February.

Waytz, A. (2010). Psychology beyond the brain: What scientists are discovering about the beating of the human heart. *Scientific American Mind*, October 5. https://www.scientificamerican.com/article/the-neuroscience-of-heart/

Chapter 13

Ackerman, D. (2000). *Deep Play*. Vintage Books/Random House. Beras, E. Traces of genetic trauma can be tweaked, *Scientific American*, April 15, 2017. https://www. scientificamerican. com/podcast/episode/traces-of-genetic-trauma-can-be-tweaked/

Benson, H. (1975). *The Relaxation Response*. Avon Books.

Benson, H. (2004). *The Breakout Principle*. Scribbner.

Blakeslee, S. (2006). Cells that read minds. *The New York Times*, January 10, 2006.

Burns, E. T. (1994). *From Risk to Resiliency: A Journey with Heart for Our Children, Our Future*. Marco Polo Publications.

Buscaglia, L. (1972). *Love: What Life is All About*. Random House Publishing Group.

Cameron, J. (1992). *The Artist's Way: A Spiritual Path To Higher Creativity*. TarcherPerigee.

Csikszentmihalyi, M. (1990). *Flow: The Psychology of Optimal Experience*. Harper and Row.

Elkind, D. (2007). *The Power of Play. How Spontaneous, Imaginative, Activities Lead to Happier, Healthier Children*. De Capo Press.

Elkind, D. (2006) *The Hurried Child: Growing Up Too Fast, Too Soon*, 25th anniversary edition. Da Capo/Perseus Books.

Goleman, D. (1995). *Emotional Intelligence*. Bantam Books.

Iacoboni, M. (2008). The Mirror Neuron Revolution: Explaining What Makes Humans Social. *Scientific American*. https://www. scientificamerican.com/article/the-mirror-neuron-revolut/

Johnson, M. (1996). *Organic Education: Teaching Without Failure*. Marietta Johnson Museum of Organic Education.

MacLean, P. D. (1990). *The Triune Brain in Evolution: Role in Paleocerebral Functions*. Plenum Press.

Pearce-McCall, D. ed. (2015). GAINS: The seriousness of play for mind-brain health. https://mindgains.org/ bonus/GAINS-The-Power-of-Play-for-Mind-Brain-Health.pdf

Porges, S. (2010). Music therapy and trauma: Insights from the polyvagal theory. https://pdfs.semanticscholar. org/ae81/423342b0b7e2eb2f0d97e b09b5b19c60de54.pdf

Porges, S. (2011). *The Polyvagal Theory: Neurophysiological Foundations of Emotions, Attachment, Communication, and Self-regulation*. W.W. Norton and Co.

Porges, S. (2018a). The polyvagal theory for treating trauma. Webinar interview: The National Institute for the Clinical Application of Behavioral Medicine, NICABM. http:// stephenporges.com/index.php/ component/content/article/5-popular-articles/25-nicabm-the-polyvagal-theory-for-treating-trauma

Porges, S. & D. Dana. (2018b). *Clinical Applications of the Polyvagal Theory: The Emergence of Polyvagal-Informed Therapies*. W.W. Norton.

Sapolsky, R. (2004). *Why Zebras Don't Get Ulcers*, Third Edition. Henry Holt and Company.

Schore, A. (2000). Attachment and the regulation of the right brain. *Attachment & Human Development*, 2 (1), 23–47.

Schore, A. (2001). Effects of a secure attachment relationship on right brain development, affect regulations, and infant mental health. *Infant Mental Health Journal*, 22(1-2), 7-66.

Schore, A. (2003). *Affect Regulation and the Repair of Self.* W.W. Norton and Co.

Schwartz, J. M. & Begley, S. (2002). *The Mind and the Brain: Neuroplasticity and the Power of Mental Force.* HarperCollins.

Siegel, D. (1999). *The Developing Mind: How Relationships and the Brain Interact to Shape Who We Are.* Guilford Press.

Siegel, D. (2001). Toward an interpersonal neurobiology of the developing mind: Attachment relationships, mind-sight, and neural integration. *Infant Mental Health Journal.* Vol. 22(1–2), 67–94 (2001).

Siegel, D. (2007). *The Mindful Brain: Reflection and Attunement in the Cultivation of Well-Being.* W.W. Norton and Co. Inc.

Siegel, D. (2010) *Mindsight: The New Science of Personal Transformation.* Random House, Inc.

Siegel, D. (2014). The self Is not defined by the boundaries of our skin: The mind is not only embodied but shaped by our relationships as well. *Psychology Today*, online version, Feb. 28, 2014.

Stanford Report, March 7, 2007, Robert Sapolsky discusses physiological effects of stress.

White, B. L. (1995). *The First Three Years of Life*, Revised Edition. Fireside Books, Simon and Schuster.

Chapter 14

Benson, H. (1975). *The Relaxation Response.* HarperCollins Publishers.

Benson, H. (1985). *Beyond the Relaxation Response: How to Harness the Healing Power of Your Personal Beliefs.* Berkley Books.

Benson, H. (1996). *Timeless Healing: The Power and Biology of Belief.* Fireside/Simon and Schuster.

Benson, H. (2000). *The Relaxation Response*, 25th Anniversary Updated Edition. Quill/HarperCollins Publishers.

Benson, H., Lehmann, V. M., Malhotra, S., Goldman, R. F., Hopkins, J. & Epstein, M. D. (1982) Body temperature changes during the practice of tum-mo yoga. *Nature* 298, 402. https://doi.org/10.1038/298402c0

Bishop, S. R., Lau, M., Shapiro, S., Carlson, L., Anderson, N. D., Carmody, J., Segal, Z. V., Abbey, S., Speca, M., Velting, D. & Devins, G. (2004). Mindfulness: A Proposed Operational Definition.*Clinical Psychology: Science and Practice*, 11(3).

Brown, R. & Gerbarg, P. (2012). *The Healing Power of the Breath: Simple Techniques to Reduce Stress and Anxiety, Enhance Concentration, and Balance Your Emotions.* Shambala Publications.

Brown, R., Gerbarg, P. & Muench, F. (2013). Breathing practices for treatment of psychiatric and stress-related medical conditions. *Psychiatric Clinics of North America*, 36(1), 121-140.

Conklin, Q. A., King, B. G., Zanesco, A. P., Lin, J., Hamidi, A. B., Pokorny, J. J....Saron, C. D. (2018). Insight meditation and telomere biology: The effects of intensive retreat and the moderating role of personality, *Brain, Behavior, and Immunity*, 70, 233-245. https://pubmed.ncbi.nlm.nih.gov/29518528/

David-Neel, A. (1932). *Magic and Mystery in Tibet.* Dover.

Epel, E., Daubenmier, J., Moskowitz, J.T., Folkman, S. & Blackburn, E. (2009). Can meditation slow rate of cellular aging? Cognitive stress, mindfulness, and telomeres. *Annals of New York Academy of Science*, August; 1172: 34-53.

Fehmi, L. G. (2003). Attention to attention. In: Applied neurophysiology and EEG biofeedback, J. Kamiya. (Ed.). *Future Health, Inc.* https://www.scribd.com/document/239202594/Attention-to-Attention-Les-Fehmi

Fehmi, L. G. & Robbins, J. (2008). *The Open-Focus Brain: Harnessing the Power of Attention to Heal the Mind and Body.* Trumpeter.

Flook, L., Goldberg, S. B., Pinger, L., Bonus, K. & Davidson, R. J. (2013). Mindfulness for teachers: A pilot study to assess effects on stress, burnout, and teaching efficacy. *Mind, Brain, and Education*, 7(3), 182–195.

Gladwell, M. (2008). *Outliers: The Story of Success.* Little, Brown and Co.

Goldberg, S. B., Tucker, R. P., Greene, P. A., Simpson, T. L., Kearney, D. J. & Davidson, R. J. (2017) Is mindfulness research methodology improving over time? A systematic review. PLoS ONE 12(10): e0187298. https:// doi. org/10.1371/ journal. pone.0187298

Goleman, D. & Davidson, R. (2017). *Altered Traits: Science Reveals How Meditation Changes Your Mind, Brain and Body*. Penguin Random House.

Hölzel, B. K., Carmody, J., Vangel, M., Congleton, C., Yerramsetti, S. M., Gard, T. & Lazar, S. (2011). Mindfulness practice leads to increases in regional brain gray matter density. *Psychiatry Research*, 191(1), 36-43.

Hunter, M. (1982). *Mastery Teaching: Increasing Instructional Effectiveness in Elementary and Secondary Schools, Colleges and Universities*. Corwin Press.

Jennings, P. A., Frank, J. L., Snowberg, K. E., Coccia, M. A. & Greenberg, M. T. (2013). Improving classroom learning environments by Cultivating Awareness and Resilience in Education (CARE): Results of a Randomized Controlled Trial. *School Psychology Quarterly*, 28(4), 374–390.

Kabat-Zinn, J. (2011). Some Reflections on the origins of MBSR, skillful means, and the trouble with maps. *Contemporary Buddhism*, 12, No. 1, May. https://www.umassmed. edu/contentassets/abf4d773534442238acf 329476591dde/ jkz_paper_ contemporary_buddhism_2011.pdf

Kabat-Zinn, J. (2012). *Mindfulness for Beginners: Reclaiming the Present Moment and Your Life*. Sounds True, Inc.

Kabat-Zinn, J. (2013). *Full-Catastrophe Living: Using the Wisdom of Your Body and Mind to Face Stress, Pain, and Living*, (Revised ed.). Random House.

Kaufman, S. B. (2013). *Scientific American* online, The real neuroscience of creativity, August 19. https://scientificamerican.com/beautiful-minds/ the-real-neuroscience-of-creativity/

Kornfield, J. (1993). *A Path With Heart: A Guide Through the Perils and Promise of the Spiritual Life*. Bantam Books.

Kornfield, J. (2009). *The Wise Heart: A Guide to the Universal Teachings of Buddhist Psychology*. Bantam Books.

Patoine, B. (2016). The mindful brain: White-matter changes may explain behavioral effects of mindfulness meditation practices. The DANA Foundation, May 31.

Patoine, B. (2019). The mindful brain: Clinical applications and mechanistic clues of mindfulness meditation progress. The DANA Foundation, July 31.

Posner, M. I. & Rothbart, M. K. (2007). Research on Attention Networks as a Model for the Integration of Psychological Science, *Annual Review of Psychology* 58: pp. 1–23.

Posner, M. I. & Patoine, B. (2009). How arts training improves attention and cognition. The Dana Foundation, September 14, 2009. https://www.dana.org/article/how-arts-training-improves-attention-and-cognition/

Schwartz, J. & Begley, S. (2002). *The Mind and the Brain: Neuroplasticity and the Power of Mental Force.* HarperCollins Publishers.

Schwartz, J. & Gladding, R. (2011). *You Are Not Your Brain.* Penguin Group.

Shapiro, D. H. (1992). A preliminary study of long term meditators: Goals, effects, religious orientation, cognitions. *Journal of Transpersonal Psychology*, 24(1), 23–39.

Shapiro, S. L., Carlson, L. E., Astin, J. A. & Freedman, B. (2005). Mechanisms of mindfulness, Wiley Periodicals, Inc. https://doi.org/10.1002/jclp.20237

Wallace, R. K. (1971). A wakeful hypometabolic physiologic state, *American Journal of Physiology*, 21(3), Sept. 1971. https://doi.org/10.1152/ajplegacy.1971.221.3.795

Wallace, R. K., Benson, H. & Wilson, A. F. (1971). A wakeful hypometabolic physiologic state. American Journal of Physiology, 21 (3).

Yates, J. (2017). Your brain as laboratory: The science of meditation. Scientific American, February 24, 2017. https://blogs.scientificamerican.com/guest-blog/your-brain-as-laboratory-the-science-of-meditation/

Zenner, C., Herrnleben-Kurz, S. & Walach, H. (2014). Mindfulness-based interventions in schools-a systematic review and meta-analysis. *Frontiers in Psychology*, 5, 603. doi:10.3389/fpsyg.2014.00603

Zoogman, S., Goldberg, S. B., Hoyt, W. T. & Miller, L. (2014). Mindfulness interventions with youth: A meta-analysis. *Springer Science and Business Media*, 15 Jan 2014. https://citeseerx.ist.psu.edu/viewdoc/download?doi=10.1.1.1041.6691&rep=rep1&type=pdf

Chapter 15

Alexander, C. N. & Langer, E.J. (1988). *Higher Stages of Human Development: Adult Growth Beyond Formal Operations.* Oxford University Press.

Anderson, P. B., Emmeche, C., Køppe, S. & Stjernfelt, F. (2000). Levels, emergence, and three versions of downward causation. In: *Downward Causation: Minds, Bodies and Matter.* Aarhus University Press. https://www.nbi.dk/~emmeche/coPubl/2000d.le3DC.v4b.html

Bass, R. V. & Good, J. W. (Winter, 2004). Educare and educere: Is a balance possible in the educational system? *The Educational Forum,* (68), 162.

Beckermann, A., Flohr, H. & Kim, J. eds. (1992). *Emergence or Reduction? Essays on the Prospects of Nonreductive Physicalism.* William de Gruyter.

Beem, E. A. (2020). The Waldorf way. http://www.greenlivingjournal.com/page.php?p=1000232

Benard. B. (1991). Fostering resiliency in kids: Protective factors in the family, school, and community. Western Regional Center for Drug-Free Schools and Communities.

Brown, J. (2021). *Mindleap: A Fresh View of Education Empowered by Neuroscience and Systems Thinking.* Psychosynthesis Press.

Burns, E. T. (1994). *From Risk to Resiliency: A Path With Heart for Our Children, Our Future.* Marco Polo Publications.

Csikszentmihali, M. (1990). *Flow: The Psychology of Optimal Experience.* Harper and Row.

Campbell, D. T. (1974). Downward causation in hierarchically organized biological systems, in *Studies in the Philosophy of Biology,* Ayala, F.J. & Dobzhansky, T. (ed.). Macmillan Press. http://dx.doi.org/10.1007/978-1-349-01892-5_11

Course description, Physical Intelligence, PE.910, Massachusetts Institute of Technology, found online at http://ocw.mit.edu/courses/athletics-physical-education-and-recreation/pe-910-physical-intelligence-january-iap-2002/

Gardner, H. (1983). *Frames of Mind: The Theory of Multiple Intelligence.* Basic Books.

Gardner, H. (1985). *The Mind's New Science.* Basic Books.

Glazer, S., ed. (1995), *The Heart of Learning: Spirituality in Education*. Jeremy P. Tarcher/Putnam Books.

Goleman, D. (1995). *Emotional Intelligence: Why It Can Matter More than I.Q.* Bantam Books.

Goleman, D. (2006). *Social Intelligence: The New Science of Human Relationships*. Bantam Books.

Gopnik, A., Meltzoff, A. N. & Kuhl, P. K. (2001). *The Scientist in the Crib: What Early Learning Tells Us About the Mind*. HarperPerennial.

Huitt, W. & Hummel, J. (2003). Piaget's theory of cognitive development. *Educational Psychology Interactive*. Valdosta State University. http://www.edpsycinteractive.org/topics/cognition/ piaget. html.

Journal of American Medical Association, Pediatrics. https://jamanetwork.com/journals/jamapediatrics/article-abstract/2754101

Johnson, M. (1996). *Organic Education: Teaching Without Failure*. Marietta Johnson Museum of Organic Education, Publ. http://www.edpsycinteractive.org/topics/ cognition/piaget.html

Kuhn, D., Langer, J., Kohlberg, L. & Haan, N. S. (1977). The development of formal operations in logical and moral judgment. *Genetic Psychology Monographs*, (95), 97-188.

Kuppers, B. O. (1992). *Emergence or Reduction? Essays on the Prospects of Nonreductive Physicalism*, edited by Ansgar Beckermann, Hans Flohr, Jaegwon Kim. William de Gruyter.

LeDoux, J. (1996). *The Emotional Brain: The Mysterious Underpinnings of Emotional Life*. Touchstone/Simon and Schuster, Inc.

Mander, J. (1978). *Four Arguments for the Elimination of Television*. HarperCollins Publishers.

McIntosh, S. (2007). The natural theology of beauty, truth, and goodness. http://www.integralworld.net/ mcintosh4.html.

Magsamen, S. (2019). Your Brain on Art: The Case for Neuroaesthetics. *Cerebrum*. 2019 Jul-Aug; https://www.ncbi.nlm.nih.gov/pmc/articles/PMC7075503/

Milstein, M. & Henry, A. (2000). *Spreading Resiliency: Making It Happen for Schools and Communities*. Corwin Press.

Pearce, J. C. (1992). *Evolution's End: Claiming the Potential of Our Intelligence.*HarperCollins Publishers.

Pearce, J. C. (1994). "The Awakening of Intelligence" (video series). Touch the Future. https://ttfuture.org/files/2/ members/sym_jcp_awakening.pdf

Pearce, J. C. (2002). *Biology of Transcendence: A Blueprint of the Human Spirit.* Park Street Press.

Renner, J. W. (1976). Significant physics content and intellectual development: Cognitive development as a result of interacting with physics content. *American Journal of Physics*, (3), 218-222. http://lib. dr.iastate.edu/cgi/viewcontent. cgi?article=7917&context=rtd

Renner, J. W., Stafford, D., Lawson, A., McKinnon, J., Friot, E., and Kellogg, D. (1976). *Research, teaching, and learning with the Piaget model.* University of Oklahoma Press.

Siegel, D. (2014). The self Is not defined by the boundaries of our skin: The mind is not only embodied but shaped by our relationships as well. *Psychology Today*, online version, Feb. 28, 2014. https://www. psychologytoday.com/us/blog/inspire-rewire/201402/the-self-is-not-defined-the-boundaries-our-skin

Swimme, B. & Berry, T. (1992). *The Universe Story: From the Primordial Flaring Forth to the Ecozoic Era.* HarperSanFrancisco.

United Nations General Assembly. (2019). Resolution adopted on 20 December 2018: Harmony with nature. https://www. un.org/pga/73/ wp-content/uploads/sites/53/2019/04/A.RES_.73.235.pdf

White, J. (1972). *The Highest State of Consciousness.* Doubleday.

Wilber, K. (1995). *Sex, Ecology, Spirituality: The Spirit of Evolution.* Shambala Publications.

Wilber, K. (2001). *A Brief History of Everything* (Revised Ed.). Shambala Publications.

World Health Organization (2001). Mental health: A call for action by world health ministers. https://www.who.int/mental_health/advocacy/en/Call_ for_Action_MoH_Intro.pdf

Figure Credits

Note: Several images are licensed via Wikimedia Commons or Creative Commons. (See https://creativecommons.org/about/cclicenses/ for information on different CC licenses.)

Fig 1. Hemispheres of the Brain, "Facies dorsalis cerebri." Maksymilian Rose, https://commons.wikimedia.org/wiki/File:02_1_facies_dorsalis_cerebri.jpg. [Public Domain]

Fig 2. Lobes of the Brain, "Lateral View of the Brain." Bruce Blaus, https://commons.wikimedia.org/wiki/Lobe_of_the_brain#/media/File:LobesCaptsLateral.png. [CC BY 3.0]

Fig 3. Beneath The Cerebral Cortex. Maja Petrović/Inspired By Learning.

Fig 4, The Triune Brain. Tim Burns.

Fig 5. Brainstem and Cerebellum, "Gehirn, medial–Lobi en." NEUROtiker, https://commons.wikimedia.org/wiki/File:Gehirn,_medial_-_Lobi_en.svg. [CC BY-SA 3.0]

Fig 6. The Limbic System, "Blausen 0614 LimbicSystem." By BruceBlaus found at Blausen.com staff (2014). "Medical gallery of Blausen Medical 2014". WikiJournal of Medicine 1 (2). DOI:10.15347/wjm/2014.010. ISSN 2002-4436, https://commons.wikimedia.org/wiki/File:Blausen_0614_LimbicSystem.png. [CC BY 3.0]

Fig 7. Comparable Cerebral Cortices, "Comparative Brain size of different mammals." Miguelferig, https://commons.wikimedia.org/wiki/File:ComparitiveBrainSizeGalego.png#-filelinks. Used under license [Public Domain]. English titles added by Maja Petrovic/Inspired by Learning.

Table 1. Intelligence and the Three Brains. Tim Burns and Jim Brown.

Fig 8. Foundation for Mammalian Intelligence. Tim Burns and Jim Brown.

Fig 9. A Universe of Spirals: (a) Nautilus image. "NautilusCutawayLogarithmic Spiral" by Chris 73, https://commons.wikimedia.org/wiki/File:NautilusCut awayLogarithmicSpiral.jpg [CC BY-SA 3.0]; (b) "Low pressure system over Iceland" by NASA's Aqua/MODIS satellite, via Wikimedia Commons https:// commons.wikimedia. org/wiki/File:Low_pressure_system_over_Iceland. jpg [Public Domain]; (c) "A rose made of Galaxies Highlights Hubble's 21st Anniversary jpg" by NASA-hubble, https://commons.wikimedia.org/wiki/File:A_Rose_Made_ of_Galaxies_Highlights_Hubble's_21st_Anniversary_jpg. jpg, via Wikimedia Commons [Public Domain]; (d) "Camargue fg11," Fritz Geller-Grimm via Wikimedia Commons, https://commons.wikimedia. org/wiki/File:Camargue_fg11.jpg [CC BY-SA 2.5]; (e) "A spiral snowflake"

ESA/Hubble via Hubble Space Telescope (http:// spacetelescope.org/ images/potw1619a/) [CC BY 4.0]; (f) "Succulent spiral" By Duff Axsom via (Flickr: Succulent spiral) (https:// www.flickr.com/photos/36515777@ N00/504975350) [CC BY 2.0]; (g) "Droste Daisy" By Alexandre Duret-Lutz from Paris, France (Recursive Daisy), https://www.flickr.com/ photos/24183489@N00/253426762/ [CC BY-SA 2.0]; (h) "Romanesque cauliflower," ChrisSampson87 via Wikimedia Commons https://commons. wikimedia.org/wiki/File:Romanesque_ cauliflower.JPG [CC BY-SA 4.0]

Fig 10. Human Brain Cross-Section, "Human Brain–Midsagittal cut." By John A Beal, PhD Dep't. of Cellular Biology & Anatomy, Louisiana State University Health Sciences Center Shreveport, http://www.healcentral.org/ healapp/ showMetadata?metadataId=40566. [CC BY 2.5] Labels have been added.

Fig 11. Hemispheric Functions of the Brain, "Cerebral Lobes." Derivative work of a picture from the Gutenberg Encyclopedia, https:// commons.wikimedia.org/ wiki/File:Cerebral_lobes.png. [CC BY – SA 3.0] Labels have been added.

Table 2. Functions of the Mature Frontal Lobes. Tim Burns and Jim Brown.

Fig 12. Human Brain. "Human Brain 308," by _DJ_, http://www.flickr.com/ photos/flamephoenix1991/8376271918. [CC BY-SA 2.0]

Fig 13. Neuron. "Pyramidal Hippocampal neuron 40x," MethoxyRoxy, https:// commons.wikimedia.org/wiki/File:Pyramidal_hippocampal_neuron_40x.jpg. [CC BY-SA 2.5]

Fig 14. Gray and White Matter. "Human brain right dissected lateral view description," by John A Beal, PhD, Dep't. of Cellular Biology & Anatomy, Louisiana State University Health Sciences Center Shreveport, http://www. healcentral.org/healapp/showMetadata?metadataId=40566. [CC BY-SA 2.5]

Fig 15. Stages of Neural Organization. Tim Burns and Jim Brown.

Fig 16. Cortex: Six Cell-Layers Thick. "Cajal Cortex drawings," file by Looie496, Santiago Ramon y Cajal created artwork, https://commons.wikimedia.org/ wiki/File:Cajal_cortex_drawings.png. [Public Domain]

Fig 17. Anatomy of a Neuron. Maja Petrović/Inspired By Learning.

Fig 18. Neuron Types. Maja Petrović/Inspired By Learning.

Fig 19. Glial Types. Maja Petrović/Inspired By Learning.

Fig 20. Dendritic Growth and Pruning. Maja Petrović/Inspired By Learning (after M. Diamond, 1999).

Fig 21. Neurogenesis: Stained Newly Created Neurons. "Vertical dendrites-red green" by Jason Snyder, https://www.flickr.com/photos/functionalneurogenes is/5599133523. [CC BY 2.0]

Fig 22. Gray Matter Thinning Age 5-20. Giedd, J. N., et al, "Brain development during childhood and adolescence: a longitudinal MRI study." *Nature Neuroscience*, 2, 1999, pp. 861-863.

Fig 23. Neuron with Myelin Sheath. Maja Petrović/Inspired By Learning.

Fig 24. Glial Cells Surround the Larger Neuron. Thomas Deerinck and Mark Ellisman, NCMIR, UCSD. Used with permission.

Fig 25. Glial Cell forming Myelin Sheath. Maja Petrović/Inspired By Learning.

Fig 26/26b. Cross-sections, Axon and Myelin Sheath. Maja Petrović/Inspired By Learning.

Fig 27. Cardiovascular Fitness Recommendations. Tim Burns and Jim Brown.

Fig 28. Stages of Sleep. By I, RazerM, https://commons.wikimedia.org/w/index.php?curid=17745252. [CC BY-SA 3.0]

Fig 29. Electrical Signatures and Stages of Sleep. Maja Petrović/Inspired By Learning.

Fig 30. Sleep Requirements By Student Grade Level. Po Bronson & Ashley Merryman. Used with permission.

Fig 31. Human Cell. Maja Petrović/Inspired By Learning.

Fig 32. DNA, or deoxyribonucleic acid. Maja Petrović/Inspired By Learning.

Table 3. Domains of Gene Expression. Taken from *The Psychobiology of Gene Expression* by Rossi, W.W. Norton & Co., 2002, page 8. Used with permission.

Fig 33. Hippocampal Neurogenesis: Three Environments. U.S. National Library of Medicine (NLM) Webpages (2003), https://www.ncbi.nlm.nih.gov/pubmcd/12786970. [Public Domain].

Fig 34. Dendritic Branching. Maja Petrović / Inspired By Learning, drawing upon Diamond & Hopson, 1999.

Fig 35. Standard Versus Enriched Dendritic Spines. Maja Petrović / Inspired By Learning, drawing upon Diamond & Hopson, 1999. Used with the permission of the late Marion Diamond.

Fig 36. Homeostasis. Tim Burns.

Fig 37. Allostasis. Tim Burns.

Fig 38. Mind-Body Activities Modulated by Ultradian Rhythms. From *The 20 Minute Break: Using the New Science of Ultradian Rhythms*, by Rossi E, 1991, page 23. Used with permission.

Fig 39. Biorhythmic Variation in the Circadian Cycle. From *Zen and the Brain: Toward an Understanding of Meditation and Consciousness*, Cambridge, by James Austin, MIT Press, 1998, page 340. Used with permission.

Fig 40. Ultradian Performance. From *The 20 Minute Break: Using the New Science of Ultradian Rhythms*, by Rossi E, 1991, page 12. Used with permission.

Fig 41. Brainwave Activity as Shown by EEG. Tim Burns and Jim Brown.

Fig 42. Electromagnetic Field of the Heart. Source: https://commons.wikimedia. org/wiki/File:Heart-field.jpg.

Fig 43. Heart Rate Variability Patterns: Frustration versus Appreciation. Used with permission, Institute of HeartMath.

Fig 44. Hierarchy of Brain Functions. Tim Burns and Jim Brown.

Fig 45. Porges' State-Regulation and MacLean's "Family Triad." Tim Burns and Jim Brown.

Fig 46. Evolution of ANS response-activation, according to Porges. Tim Burns and Jim Brown.

Fig 47. Multifaceted Integration: Key to Learning, Growth and Well-being Across the Lifespan. Based on the work of D. Siegel (1999, 2001, 2007, 2010).

Fig 48. The Pyramid of Self-Development in Fulfillment of Nature's Plan. Tim Burns and Jim Brown.

Fig 49. Meta-Concept and Core Concepts of Nature's Plan. Tim Burns.

Fig 50. Emergence in the Natural World. Tim Burns and Jim Brown.

Fig 51. Stage-wise Progression of Brain Maturation and Intelligence. Tim Burns and Jim Brown.

Fig 52. Framework for Optimal Learning and Development. Tim Burns and Jim Brown.

Fig 53. Guiding Strategies in Support of Optimal Learning and Development. Tim Burns and Jim Brown.

Index

electromagnetic field/EMF, 199, 205-207, 212, 215-216

Elkins, David, 251

Elnitski, Laura, 93

embodiment/embodied, 3, 175, 241-244, 250, 309, 313,

    embodied brain, 3-5, 8-9, 26, 68, 294

    embodied education, 293

    embodied learning, 185-186

    embodied mind, 175, 243, 293

    See also intelligence, somatic

emergent-causal properties, 306-307, 309, 320, 322

emotional intelligence/EQ, 233, 239, 245, 337, 339

emotions, 8, 12, 20-21, 59, 83, 91, 173, 192, 197-198, 201, 203, 205, 208-210, 213-216, 247-248, 259-260, 268, 270, 275, 292, 320, 338

    emotional states, 128, 204, 208-209, 211, 215, 217, 245-246

enteric nervous system, 176, 188-189, 192-193, 224

environmental enrichment, 4, 93, 97-98, 103, 314, 317-318

epigenetics, 4, 94-95, 124, 317, 323

Erikson, Erik, 325, 342

exercise, 69-73

experience-dependent process, 104, 106, 108, 112, 314-317

experience-expectant process, 105-106, 108-109, 113, 218, 235, 315-317

family triad, 24, 27, 181, 233, 237, 242, 250, 313, 316, 319-320, 332-334

feedback, 21, 24-26, 34, 99, 108, 115-116, 119-120, 126, 146, 155, 158, 160, 169, 181, 190, 218, 222, 229, 233, 236, 242, 247-248, 250-251, 253, 308, 313, 316-317, 319-323, 332, 334

    See also biofeedback, neurofeedback

Fehmi, Les, 154, 158-159, 165, 254, 280-283

fight-flight-freeze, 237, 270, 322-323

flow states, 127, 226, 250

forebrain, 17, 21, 114, 118

formal operations, 38

Gage, Fred, 104

gamma brainwave, 156, 166-168

Gardner, Howard, 303, 311

gene expression, 83-84, 86, 89-92, 95-97, 107, 124, 130

general adaptation syndrome/GAS, 118, 120-122, 124, 126, 211

Giedd, Jay, 55, 61-62

Glenn, H. Stephen, 345

glia/glial cells, 40, 42-43, 49-51, 56, 58, 61, 64-65, 68, 107, 288

global-systemic thinking, 327, 329, 346-347

Goleman, Daniel, 168, 245, 287, 337

Golinkoff, Roberta, 99, 103, 107, 112-114

goodness, ix, 305, 332, 341-342, 352

Greenough, William, 99, 106

guiding strategies, 295, 330-331

Haeckel, Ernst, 30

Haier, Richard, 53

Hannaford, Carla, 69, 186

Acknowledgments

Jim's Acknowledgements

Primary appreciation goes to Molly Brown, who held our home and my morale together while this book crept toward fruition, and who spent countless hours consulting and proofreading with me.

To those teachers and advisors who helped me along at crucial stages of my development, contributing mightily to the knowledge and thought that I was able to bring to this project, I offer profound respect and gratitude. They include Drs. Roberto Assagioli, Archie Bahm, Arthur Deikman, James Fadiman, Lester Fehmi, Stanley Krippner, Robert Ornstein, Erik Peper, Marcia Salner, and Susan S. Scott.

And to my long-time friend, colleague, originator and primary author of this book, who had enough trust and regard for me to summon me into the project, I say: Thank you Tim. This has been a long, difficult, and keenly fulfilling ride!

Tim's Acknowledgements

My great, good fortune is to have been an educator, a profession I would not have traded for any other. Three of teaching's greatest inducements are its rewards for curiosity, ongoing learning, and routine opportunities to interact with others around knowledge and ideas. To that end, I wish to thank my colleagues along the way and, most especially, students who were so often my teachers as well. Much of what is written about in this book had the benefit of refinement through interactions with students of all ages, over a long and enjoyable career.

That Jim accepted the invitation to join in this undertaking has made all the difference to the outcome. Without his engagement it is certain that the book would never have been completed. Moreover, his masterful writing and depth of knowledge in all the topics covered vastly improved the original manuscript.

My deepest gratitude and appreciation goes to my wife, Linda, for her ongoing support and love.

The authors wish to thank Maja Petrović who formatted the book for its initial publication as a pdf. Kiri Miller contributed her time and expertise in locating attributions for the dozens of images that enrich the pages of our book. Finally, through his commitment to the shared vision of what this book has to offer, thanks go to Inspired By Learning publisher, David McMurtry, for the book's initial publication.

About the Authors

Tim Burns, MA, is an educator and author whose background includes over forty years of experience as teacher, counselor, adolescent and family drug-treatment program director, and university instructor. He began his career as a high school teacher and has been a course instructor for the Alcohol and Drug Abuse Studies Institute, University of New Mexico; the Division of Extended Studies, Adams State College, Alamosa, Colorado; and presently teaches part-time at Southwestern College, Santa Fe, New Mexico. He also served as program director, St. Vincent Hospital Family Recovery Center in Santa Fe, New Mexico. Over the years, Tim has provided professional development workshops and given presentations to over 2000 schools, agencies, organizations and conferences throughout the United States, as well as in over thirty countries, world-wide. Tim is the author of three previous books and several popular resource manuals and curricula.

As an award-winning artist, Tim provided the illustrations for the book, *WorldWords*, by Victor La Cerva, MD. He holds a black-belt in Aikido, a modern Japanese martial art devoted to neutralizing aggression and redirecting conflict. He is the father of three talented, creative daughters, and the proud grandfather of five. He and his wife, Linda, make their home in beautiful Santa Fe, New Mexico, U.S.A.

Jim Brown, PhD, has spent his entire professional life quietly patrolling the frontiers of discovering and applying knowledge that involves consciousness and neuroscience. He recognized and seized the opportunities to become an early adopter in burgeoning fields such as biofeedback, then neurofeedback, plus theory and practices stemming from humanistic and transpersonal psychology, plus steeping himself in systems theory as a context for all his other fields of focus.

When approached by long-time friend and colleague Tim Burns to collaborate on *Anatomy of Possibility*, he welcomed the opportunity to put into writing much of what he had learned alongside the pioneers in those fields. The work of many such pioneers is integrated and cited within the subject matter of this book*, which details our joint knowledge and understanding of how humans learn and grow, and explores how that knowledge can be applied to refining the vital project of educating/ guiding humans toward intelligent adaptation to a world in crisis.

* Brown has developed and integrated further discussion of topics that did not fit within its scope (such as in-depth exploration of systems theory) into a companion volume, *Mindleap: A Fresh View of Education Empowered by Neuroscience and Systems Thinking*, published by Psychosynthesis Press, 2021.

www.ingramcontent.com/pod-product-compliance
Lightning Source LLC
Chambersburg PA
CBHW060305030426
42336CB00011B/945